A FIELD GUIDE TO
WILDFLOWERS OF THE
SANDHILLS REGION

A FIELD GUIDE TO

Wildflowers of the Sandhills Region

North Carolina | South Carolina | Georgia

To Leah –

Bruce A Sorrie

BRUCE A. SORRIE

The University of North Carolina Press Chapel Hill

A SOUTHERN GATEWAYS GUIDE
This book was published with the assistance of the Sandhills Area Land Trust.

©2011 The University of North Carolina Press. All rights reserved. Designed by Courtney Leigh Baker and set in Minion Pro and Myriad Pro by Rebecca Evans. Manufactured in Singapore. The paper in this book meets the guidelines for permanence and durability of the Committee on Production Guidelines for Book Longevity of the Council on Library Resources. The University of North Carolina Press has been a member of the Green Press Initiative since 2003.

Library of Congress Cataloging-in-Publication Data
Sorrie, Bruce A.
A field guide to wildflowers of the Sandhills region : North Carolina, South Carolina, and Georgia / by Bruce A. Sorrie.—1st ed.
p. cm.—(A southern gateways guide)
ISBN 978-0-8078-3466-4 (cloth : alk. paper)—ISBN 978-0-8078-7186-7
(pbk. : alk. paper)
1. Wild flowers—Sandhills (Ga.–N.C.)—Identification. 2. Wild flowers—North Carolina—Identification. 3. Wild flowers—South Carolina—Identification. 4. Wild flowers—Georgia—Identification. I. Title. II. Series: Southern gateways guide.
QK178.S67 2011   582.130975—dc22   2010043604

cloth   15 14 13 12 11   5 4 3 2 1
paper   15 14 13 12 11   5 4 3 2 1

This book is dedicated to those who came before. Through their exploration, research, publication, and above all, teaching, they built the foundations of botany, plant ecology, and plant geography.

Contents

Acknowledgments

No publication of this magnitude is without the contributions of many people that share in the passion of conserving the natural landscape of the Sandhills region. It is with great appreciation that I begin by thanking the Sandhills Area Land Trust for their tireless efforts in preserving the flora and fauna of the Sandhills and being instrumental in seeking funding for this publication. For their financial support, I am grateful to Cumberland Community Foundation of Fayetteville, N.C., for their belief in this project and its major contribution to naturalists of today and tomorrow, and the Lilly Legacy Fund, established by the grandchildren of Ashton Wilson Lilly for the purpose of supporting the causes and community she loved.

A very special debt of gratitude is due my dear friend and colleague Candace Williams, executive director of the Sandhills Area Land Trust. Without her vision of the book, her insistence that I share my knowledge and expertise for the benefit of future generations, and her persistence in pursuing the funding, this publication would have remained only a dream rather than the reality that it has become.

Additional thanks are due my botanical colleagues who have worked with me through the years: Linda Chafin of the State Botanical Garden of Georgia for providing insightful comments on the text and providing a network of people who know Georgia plants and their locales; John Nelson of the University of South Carolina herbarium for providing insightful comments on the text and its organization and for suggesting important wildflower sites in South Carolina; and Alan Weakley, Carol Ann McCormick, and Steve Seiberling of the North Carolina Botanical Garden and the University of North Carolina herbarium for taxonomic insights, access to specimens, use of photographs, and answers to a host of questions.

Special thanks go to the many people who contributed in a myriad of ways to this publication by means of assistance in the field and knowledge of plant locations in the region: Brady Beck, Finley Bryan, Misty Buchanan, Phil Crutchfield, Matt Elliott, Michele Elmore, Rob Evans, Janet Gray, Scott Hartley, John Jenson, Wes Knapp, Richard LeBlond, Cathy and Paul Linskins, Patrick McMillan, Gil Nelson, Hugh and Carol Nourse, Bill Parsons, Doug Rayner, Ruth and Bob Stolting, and Andy Walker.

Photography is a major component of this guide and critical to connecting the naturalist visually to each species. I am indebted to the many people who spent time afield obtaining images and to their generosity in sharing them for this publication. These photographers are listed in the Photo Credits. Special mention must go to Brady Beck for organizing and improving digital images and in printing working proofs.

Last but not least, thanks to Mark Simpson-Vos of the University of North Carolina Press for supporting the project and seeing the guide through all stages of editing and production to the finished product.

A FIELD GUIDE TO
WILDFLOWERS OF THE
SANDHILLS REGION

The Sandhills Region

NORTH CAROLINA

• Fayetteville

SOUTH CAROLINA

Columbia

GEORGIA

Augusta •

•Macon

•Columbus

Introduction

This book is the first field guide to treat the plants of the fascinating and biodiverse area in the southeastern United States known as the Sandhills region. This guide describes most of the native wildflowers, shrubs, and vines that occur in each of nine distinct natural communities or habitats in this area. While the emphasis is clearly on native plants, many non-native plants are included as well, since they are familiar roadside species we commonly think of as weeds. Because of its broad scope and coverage, the guide will be useful to a wide audience, from beginning naturalists to professional biologists, foresters, and land managers. It is my sincere hope that the guide will instill in people a deep interest in and appreciation for the plants that grace this region and, perhaps more importantly, spark a desire to protect some of the natural areas in which they grow.

Among the significant features that set the Sandhills region apart are its rolling hills, generally poor sandy soil, and abundance of creeks and small rivers. These are obvious to people who live here, visit as tourists, or pass through on a journey elsewhere. Also notable is the region's longleaf pine ecosystem. Longleaf Pine (*Pinus palustris*) was historically the most valuable timber tree of this region (see below) and continues to produce significant wood products and pinestraw. Beneath the Longleaf grow various oaks and a ground cover of Wiregrass (*Aristida stricta*), augmented by a great diversity of plants and animals that make their home in the longleaf pine ecosystem. The Sandhills populations of the federally endangered Red-cockaded Woodpecker (*Picoides borealis*) are among the largest in the nation; there are more populations of the federally endangered Michaux's Sumac (*Rhus michauxii*) in this region than anywhere else. While some plants are well-known, such as Wild Azalea (*Rhododendron periclyme-noides*), Swamp Azalea (*R. viscosum*) with its highly fragrant flowers, and Sweetbay Magnolia (*Magnolia virginiana*), others are not, such as the spectacular blue flowers of Autumn Gentian (*Gentiana autumnalis*). These and hundreds of other wildflowers are included in this guide.

The Sandhills Region

This field guide covers a geologic and physiographic region known as the Sandhills, the innermost portion of the Atlantic Coastal Plain. The Sandhills region extends unbroken from central North Carolina through South Carolina to east-central Georgia, then as scattered pieces to west-central Georgia. Notable Sandhills cities include Fayetteville, N.C.; Columbia, S.C.; and Augusta, Macon, and Columbus, Ga. But if you live in or visit many of the largest metropolitan areas of the southeastern Piedmont or coast—Atlanta, Ga.; Charleston, S.C.; or Charlotte or Raleigh-Durham, N.C.—you are a just a short distance from the Sandhills. The region is characterized by rolling hilly terrain dissected by abundant blackwater streams. A number of major rivers cross through the Sandhills from their origins in the Piedmont or Mountain regions: the Cape Fear and Pee Dee in North Carolina; the Pee Dee, Wateree, Congaree, and Edisto in South Carolina; the Savannah in South Carolina and Georgia; and the Ogeechee, Oconee, Ocmulgee, Flint, and Chattahoochee in Georgia. The juncture between the Sandhills and the Piedmont is called the Fall Line, due to the rocky rapids and low falls, thus giving our region an alternate name: the Fall Line Sandhills. Note, however, that the falls and rocky rapids occur in the lower Piedmont, not in the Sandhills proper; this is a major distinction between the Piedmont and the Coastal Plain, which generally lacks surface rocks. Early settlers, like the indigenous peoples before them, were quick to understand the importance of the falls, first for fisheries and to create settlements at the heads of navigable rivers, later to power mills and to produce electricity.

The rolling hills contrast sharply with the flat terrain of the rest of the Coastal Plain. As one drives into the Sandhills from the outer Coastal Plain, roads suddenly begin to undulate, until 30- to 100-foot drops are the norm. Elevation within the Sandhills region ranges from about 70 feet on larger rivers to about 650 feet on the highest hilltops.

Despite its name, the Sandhills region is not composed simply of sand. To be sure, the name derives from the uppermost layer of sandy soil—grayish white to yellowish white in color and seemingly everywhere—that characterizes the area. In fact, the sand we see is just window dressing, for beneath it lie very deep deposits of clay-gravel and clay-sand laid down over millions of years during the middle Cretaceous geologic period. In the Carolinas, geologists have named these deposits the Middendorf Formation; in Georgia the equivalent is the Tuscaloosa Formation. These rich clay deposits give structure to the landscape and help to slow down erosion of the Sandhills. The clay layers slow rainwater as it percolates through the soil, often deflecting it sideways to form seepages and streamheads. This process is critical to the formation and maintenance of a number of natural communities that require permanent sources of water (and for the plants that do best in wet sandy soil, such as pitcher-plants). Roadcuts and streamside slopes are good places to see Sandhills soil profiles. Underneath the thick layers of clay and sand is bedrock—the same bedrock that is in the Piedmont; it simply has been covered over by aeons of ocean deposits combined with material brought down from eroding mountains. Scattered about the landscape are knolls and hills of hard sandstone. They originated as marine deposits at the bottom of ancient oceans and have resisted erosion better than clays and sands. Perhaps the easiest place to see one of these outcrops is at Sugarloaf Mountain in Carolina Sandhills National Wildlife Refuge in South Carolina.

Soils of the Sandhills region are generally sandy, acidic, low in nutrients, and droughty. One does not expect to see large areas of agricultural crops or extensive cattle or dairy operations here; the poor soils simply do not permit it. The better soils (loamy sands) do allow for peaches, cotton, soybeans, and some corn, but such crops grow only in relatively few places.

The well-drained sandy soils have serious implications for flora and fauna. Rain is absorbed extremely quickly, and puddles last only a matter of hours. Animals must drink quickly and be efficient in how their bodies process water, much like desert species. Amphibians must seek out the deepest pools in which to lay their eggs; otherwise young won't have enough time to morph into adults before all the water evaporates. Such pools are naturally found where there is high clay content in the soil, or a claypan beneath the sandy top layer. Other animals, including mammals and birds, simply must live within easy reach of a reliable water source.

Plants also are constrained by the droughty soils. Most have evolved in one of two different lifestyles. Perennial plants send down deep roots to capture water throughout the soil profile, or they produce storage organs— thick rhizomes or bulbs—that hold water (and are fire resistant) through hard times. Annual plants live only a single growing season; they must produce large quantities of seeds to overcome the challenges of limited water and frequent fire.

FIRE ECOLOGY

Fire is absolutely essential to most Sandhills plant communities. Historically, fires burned every two to four years on average throughout the longleaf pine communities of the region. Lightning initiated the majority of these fires (the highest incidence of lightning strikes in the United States is in the southeastern Coastal Plain), but indigenous people started many fires to improve forage for game and to reduce shrub density for easier travel. In addition, fires reduced the numbers of ticks and chiggers—no small concern for people living off the land. Early European settlers were quick to learn of the benefits of periodic fires, and many landowners practiced this management technique. Today we continue the practice, albeit on a more limited scale, due to the close proximity of residences and towns. Most notably, we practice fire management on nature preserves, wildlife management areas, state and national forests, and military bases.

But the benefits of fire go well beyond those for people and in fact extend throughout the longleaf pine ecosystem to a host of plants and animals. Longleaf Pine itself depends on recurring fires to reduce ground cover and to expose bare mineral soil—the conditions needed for successful seed germination. Wiregrass is a keystone species in longleaf communities, for this plant, more than any other, carries fire across the land. Wiregrass is so dependent on fire that it will not flower or fruit without first being burned. Many other Sandhills plant species are fire dependent, and virtually all are fire tolerant; otherwise they would not last long. As discussed above, the adaptations that plants have developed to deal with limited water also have allowed them to persist in an environment driven by fire.

Animals of all sorts have adapted as well. Fox Squirrels specialize in feeding on Longleaf Pine nuts, living mostly in the canopy where flames don't reach. Pine Snakes use old stump holes to seek refuge from heat and enemies. Bachman's Sparrows nest and feed on the ground but are forced to move on when unburned grass and shrubs become too dense. Pine Barrens Treefrogs often forage on insects that are attracted to the trumpetlike leaves of Yellow Pitcher-plants, which become more vigorous and numerous following fire. (However, during fire events it is critical that there be wetlands nearby where frogs can seek temporary refuge.) The lives of Red-cockaded Woodpeckers are completely enmeshed with the pines and the fire, since they are the only woodpecker to dig nesting cavities in *living* trees and require a relatively open understory in which to forage. The woodpeckers became endangered because of widespread fire suppression and habitat loss.

TREE OF MANY USES

Of all the southern pines, Longleaf Pine produces the best-quality and most-durable wood for most uses, especially construction and flooring. Vast areas of pines were felled to supply wood for building early America's houses. And back in the days of wooden ships, Longleaf Pines produced pitch, turpentine, and tar for use as naval stores. As a result, of the original 90 million acres of Longleaf from Virginia to Texas, only 3 million remain today. Unfortunately, much of the original 90 million acres has been planted in Slash Pine or Loblolly Pine. Because of these planting practices and fire exclusion, the entire community of Longleaf associates has disappeared from those forests.

Today, because of improved methods of producing and planting seedlings, Longleaf Pine is just as competitive as other pines in commercial forestry, and over the long term it will produce a higher grade of lumber. A more recent Longleaf Pine product is pinestraw. The fallen needles are raked and gathered into bales for use as landscaping material and mulch in residential and urban settings. Longleaf Pine needles possess highly desirable color and exceptional durability, and an industry has grown up around pinestraw raking, which has placed added pressure on the remaining forests of Longleaf Pine. In gathering pine needles, workers use hand rakes or machines that often disturb sensitive plants that rely on the mulching effect of pine needles for moisture and protection. One serious side effect of raking is the decline in species diversity. And finally, landowners must now be vigilant against poachers. For a fascinating account of the longleaf pine industry and an overview of the fire ecology of the longleaf pine ecosystem, see *Looking for Longleaf*, by Larry Earley (2004).

PLANT GEOGRAPHY

The Sandhills region stands between two major ecological and geographical regions, the Piedmont and the Coastal Plain, each with different soils, different natural communities, and different ecological processes. I do not mean to imply that the adjacent regions are completely different—there is considerable overlap—but their differences make each region instantly recognizable. Since the Sandhills is technically a part of the Coastal Plain, the great majority of its plants originated there and are adapted to Coastal Plain soils and processes. But a good number of Piedmont, and even Mountain, species also call the Sandhills region home. Mountain Laurel (*Kalmia latifolia*) is a good example: On steep creekside slopes one can find dense thickets of it, sometimes growing above other Piedmont/Mountain plants, such as Galax (*Galax urceolata*) (the same plant that mountain folks gather for decorative and medicinal greens) and Catesby's Trillium (*Trillium catesbaei*). Although they seem to be out of place here in the hot and steamy Sandhills, these plants have thrived in narrow micro-habitats, such as cool north-facing slopes, where growing conditions resemble those of higher elevations. Other Piedmont/Mountain species are more common and help form the fabric of many Sandhills communities: Sourwood (*Oxydendrum arboreum*), Nestronia (*Nestronia umbellula*), Yellowroot (*Xanthorhiza simplicissima*), Silky Dogwood (*Cornus amomum*), Rattlesnake Hawkweed (*Hieracium venosum*), and Plantain-leaved Pussytoes (*Antennaria plantaginifolia*), among others.

The reverse is also true. Many plants that originated and are widespread on the Coastal Plain now also occur in the Piedmont. Since most Coastal Plain plants have adapted to highly acidic soils, you must look for them in similar soils in the Piedmont, especially soils derived from sandstone or granitic rocks. Dry oak-hickory forests, pine-oak slopes and ridges, and margins of impoundments are good places to find them. Examples are Dangleberry (*Gaylussacia frondosa*), Tread-softly (*Cnidoscolus stimulosus*), Bayvine or Bamboo-vine (*Smilax laurifolia*), Squareheads (*Tetragonotheca helianthoides*), Whorled Pennywort (*Hydrocotyle verticillata*), Nuttall's Tick-trefoil (*Desmodium nuttallii*), St. Peter's-cross (*Hypericum crux-andreae*), and Swamp Sweetbells (*Eubotrys racemosa*).

A small number of plants occupy a narrow zone that is centered in the lower Piedmont and the Sandhills. The reasons for this unusual distribution are unclear, but it appears that most of these plants originated in the Piedmont and later adapted to the fire regime and certain soils (notably loamy sand) of the Sandhills region. Examples are Piedmont St. John's-wort (*Hypericum lloydii*), Graceful Goldenrod (*Solidago austrina*), Michaux's Sumac (*Rhus michauxii*), and Earle's Blazing-star (*Liatris squarrulosa*).

Finally, for some species the Sandhills is not only their home, but their *only* home. These plants are found exclusively in the Sandhills region and nowhere else in the world. Botanists call such range-restricted species "endemics"; that is, they are endemic or restricted to a particular, well-defined region. At last count, there were nine species of plants endemic to the Sandhills: Sandhills Blazing-star (*Liatris cokeri*), Sandhills Lily (*Lilium pyrophilum*), Sandhills Lobelia (not yet formally described), Streamhead Bugleweed (*Lycopus cokeri*), Sandhills Ground-cherry (*Physalis lanceolata*), Sandhills Pyxie-moss (*Pyxidanthera brevifolia*), Sandhills Arrowhead (*Sagittaria macrocarpa*), Rayner's Blueberry (*Vaccinium sempervirens*), and Sandhills heartleaf (not yet formally described). And while some of these endemic plants are rare and may need our active help if they are to survive, others are quite common and only need suitable places to grow.

The fate of such species is entirely within our hands, for these plants are so finely tuned to the Sandhills plant communities, weather, soils, and fire regime that they do not grow naturally elsewhere. As stewards of the land, we must ensure that these unique members of our forests and fields are given adequate opportunities to perpetuate themselves, therefore ensuring that future generations will be able to enjoy the richness of these Sandhills region rarities as we know them today.

Rare Species and Conservation

As in any other region of the country, the Sandhills has its share of rare species, both animal and plant. We hear much about the Red-cockaded Woodpecker, a federally endangered bird that is intimately tied to remaining areas of longleaf pine woodland and savanna. However, there are many other rare species that call our region home. A small number are threatened with extinction throughout their ranges, and these have been given protection under the U.S. Endangered Species Act. Such species are designated as federally endangered or federally threatened. Four Sandhills region plants are on the federal rare species list as endangered: Roughleaf Loosestrife (*Lysimachia asperulifolia*), Michaux's Sumac (*Rhus michauxii*), Chaffseed (*Schwalbea americana*), and Fringed Campion (*Silene catesbaei*).

Through the Natural Heritage Program in each state, a large number of species—hundreds of plants and animals—are tracked that biologists believe to be rare within state borders, and many of these occur within the Sandhills region. In North Carolina, 84 state-rare plants can be found in the Sandhills; in South Carolina, 87; and in Georgia, 70. These state-rare species are considered rare for a number of reasons: (1) They may be rare everywhere, such as Carolina Birds-in-a-Nest (*Macbridea caroliniana*) and Georgia Indigo-bush (*Amorpha georgiana*). (2) They may occur barely within the state's borders but are commoner elsewhere, such as Creeping Blueberry (*Vaccinium crassifolium*) in Georgia and Azure Sage (*Salvia azurea* var. *azurea*) in North Carolina. (3) They may once have been numerous but have seriously declined due to loss of habitat or other reasons, such as Sandhills Milkvetch (*Astragalus michauxii*) in all three states. In most states, rare species are split into three or four categories—endangered, threatened, special concern, or significantly rare—based on the number of existing populations and on an estimate of the threats to each species. This book is not the place for defining these categories—readers can contact their own state Natural Heritage Program for detailed lists of rare species—and so we will simply refer to rare species as "rare."

States also have enacted various laws to protect rare species. However, an important point needs to be made regarding plant protection laws. In virtually all cases, such laws are less restrictive than laws protecting animals. At the state level they typically prohibit taking plants from someone else's land *without written permission from the landowner*. On your own land, you can do as you please. Even at the federal level there is a marked difference between animals and plants. If you as a landowner shoot a bald eagle within the bounds of your own property, you are liable to a fine and possible jail time; but if you uproot a federally endangered species of plant from your property, there is no penalty. You will be penalized if you are caught transporting the plant across state lines but not for taking a rare plant from your own land, even if it is the very last of its kind. The reason for this dichotomy goes back to old English law, where all animals belonged to the Crown and plants belonged to the landowner. Animals (especially game species) were deemed more important to people than plants, and so the law of the day reflected that opinion. Perhaps in the future we may see a balance in rare species laws, but for now we must be aware that this discrepancy exists. We must therefore devote a great deal of time to monitoring rare plants and to protecting the most threatened of them by whatever means are at our disposal.

Many options exist for protecting natural areas and endangered species, ranging from private landowner initiatives to acquisition by private or public conservation agencies. In all cases, conservation works best when citizens are well-informed about the value of natural habitat and take an active role in its protection. Because land-use decisions usually cross property and political boundaries, planning and land-use regulations can play an important protection role if supported by local citizens. Ideally, conservation efforts should focus on areas that are the most ecologically significant—areas that have intact, natural habitats. Also important are areas that may have been logged (or even clearcut) or pastured in the past but have grown back up into relatively natural plant communities. Another focus of conservation is on areas that connect existing preserves and can provide valuable corridors for wildlife. And finally, securing broad buffer zones around existing preserves is vital to ensure that the natural communities and the flora and fauna remain viable into the future. The places listed in Places to Visit represent a wide diversity of natural areas and are testament to far-sighted landowners and land managers. We hope that vision continues into the future.

Format and Style Conventions

Organization of the Book

This guide is organized by habitat, or natural community. A natural community is defined as an assemblage of plants and animals that occurs repeatedly on the landscape, recognizably distinct from other such assemblages. Some are easy to distinguish, such as a beaver pond, while others are less obviously distinct, such as an oak-hickory forest versus a mesic (or moist) mixed hardwood forest, and may appear to grade into one another. Important factors that shape communities and help to create differences between them are soil type, soil nutrients and minerals, soil pH (acidity), moisture regime, orientation (such as a north-facing steep slope or a flat floodplain), elevation, and fire history. The science of ecology involves the study of natural communities, how they are organized, and their distribution on the landscape. And while ecologists continue to fine-tune the classification of habitats, the major types are well established and accepted. With a little practice virtually anyone can recognize major habitats, and one of the goals of this guide is to educate people about the environment around them and to help them understand its variety.

This guide addresses nine habitats within the Sandhills region: Dry Longleaf Pineland, Turkey Oak Scrub, Oak-Hickory Forest, Streamheads and Seepage Slopes, Moist Pine Flatwoods and River Terraces, Blackwater Rivers and Cypress-Gum Swamps, Beaver Ponds and Impoundments, Depression Ponds and Vernal Pools, and Roadsides and Disturbed Ground. As the names of several of these communities suggest, they are in fact a combination of two habitats; though professional ecologists may separate them, joining closely related communities makes sense in a field guide intended to help nature enthusiasts and naturalists identify plants. One habitat, Roadsides and Disturbed Ground, is not a natural community as ecologists would define it; but it is the one we see every day, and it contains many native plants, not simply weeds from foreign regions. Moreover, roadsides, utility company rights-of-way, and their like often provide people with their first glimpses of native wildflowers.

In this guide, each natural community is highlighted by colored page tops, so a reader can quickly find the wildflowers associated with that community. Once a reader determines the appropriate habitat, he or she should be able to find a plant by paging through the section with the corresponding color. With only nine major habitat types, a reader can quickly memorize the color for each. Each natural community is described and pictured, a list of the wildflowers found in that community follows, then each species is described and pictured on the subsequent pages. The list of species at the beginning of each community section includes plants that also occur in other habitats (nature is seldom simple!); these are indicated by a swatch of the appropriate habitat color. Species marked with a "T" are mentioned within the text of a closely related plant in the same genus.

Within each natural community, the species are arranged by flower color in this sequence: white, yellow, orange, red, purple, violet, green, brown. For convenience, grasses and sedges are placed in the last two sections, even though many have bright yellow anthers or other colorful flower parts.

This guide is meant to be more inclusive than most wildflower books; that is, it includes a higher percentage of species found in the area covered. Even though the Sandhills region is fairly small geographically, it harbors a large diversity of plant life due to its central position on the landscape: roughly half of the native plants of North Carolina, South Carolina, and Georgia are found here. Included in this guide are herbaceous plants, semiwoody plants, shrubs, and vines—the plant groups that are usually included in a wildflower guide. Trees, treelike shrubs, ferns and fern allies, and many aquatic plants whose flowers are very inconspicuous are excluded, as are the vast majority of grasses, sedges, and rushes. Also excluded are wildflowers primarily associated with brownwater river systems that pass through our region—rivers such as the Cape Fear, Chattahoochee, Congaree, Pee Dee, Savannah, and Wateree. Even so, this field guide cannot include all native wildflowers, so great is the biodiversity of the southeastern United States. The emphasis is on species that are characteristic of the Sandhills region, but the guide also includes widespread species and many that are rarely (or never) portrayed in other wildflower guides. This guide will be useful to users well beyond the area of coverage, particularly in the Coastal Plain.

All plants are native unless stated otherwise. It is my intention to emphasize native plants; therefore, many alien plants from overseas or from other parts of North America are excluded. Only a small number of these nonnatives are included. Readers wishing to learn about alien wildflowers should refer to other guidebooks or technical manuals.

Format of the Text

Each wildflower is described in a brief text that emphasizes important features. It is important to note that these descriptions are *not* complete. A number of features may be omitted because they are not critical to identification or are difficult to see without a dissecting scope. A 10x hand lens is an indispensable tool for the field botanist to observe plant parts. Arrangement of species text is as follows: family name; common name; scientific name; synonym (given in cases where a name long in use has recently been changed); description (measurements are in both decimal and metric systems); interesting facts (names, people, history, cultivation, medicinal use, etc.); identification tips and comparison with closely related plants (if needed); rarity; habitat; overall range; and flowering period.

CONVENTIONS USED IN SPECIES TEXTS

- In common names, first letters are capitalized.
- Measurements, whenever possible, are for plants of the Sandhills region; they may differ in the same species found elsewhere.
- Vegetative parts are "green" unless otherwise specified.
- Leaves are alternate unless otherwise specified.
- Leaves are deciduous unless otherwise specified.
- Stems are erect unless otherwise specified.
- Stems are single unless otherwise specified.
- "Sandhills" with a capital "S" and plural refers to the Sandhills region, the area covered by this guide. Lower-cased "sandhill" or "sandhills" refers to a landform: low hills or mounds or old dunes of sandy soil. "Sandhills" (plural) in a common name refers to a plant more or less restricted to the area covered by this guide; "Sandhill" (singular) refers simply to the plant's preference for dry, sandy soil.

Abbreviations

State names are abbreviated to postal codes: NC, SC, GA, etc. Canadian Provinces are abbreviated thus: N.S., Newf., Que., Ont., Man., Sask., Alb., B.C., etc.

Range statements are given as "from e MD to se MO south to nw FL and e TX." That is, "a line running from eastern Maryland to southeastern Missouri, south to a line running from northwest Florida to east Texas."

Compass points are abbreviated to n, se, w, etc.

Measurements are given in both decimal and metric systems: inches = ″; feet = ′; millimeters = mm; centimeters = cm; meters = m. Measurements less than 2 mm are given only in mm, since conversion to inches is a very small decimal and awkward to read.

Color

In this guide, "purple" refers to a red-magenta or deep red hue. This is the artist's purple, which differs from "violet" by lacking strong blue tones. Thus, the main color in Dwarf Iris is violet, not purple.

Within each natural community, the species are arranged by flower color in this sequence: white, yellow, orange, red, purple, violet, green, brown.

TECHNICAL TERMS

Because so many potential readers are not formally trained in the biological sciences, I have kept technical terms to a minimum. In many cases, when a technical term is necessary, I have given a brief definition in parentheses. In other cases, readers should refer to the Glossary.

Inflorescence types—umbel, corymb, spike, raceme, cyme, and so forth—are not often mentioned in species texts. For many plants, knowledge of inflorescence type is not important to field identification and merely adds technical jargon, especially when the photograph clearly shows the inflorescence. However, for reference purposes, inflorescence types are illustrated in the Flower and Leaf Structure section and defined in the Glossary.

SCIENTIFIC AND COMMON NAMES

In this guide, nomenclature follows that of Weakley (2010) for scientific and common names. In instances where a plant may be known by more than one name, I have employed alternative or additional common names. Scientific names may change over time, as botanists continue to determine who was first to provide a valid Latin name. Names also change when a species is moved from one genus to another; this occurs with increasing frequency as scientists use DNA to determine true relationships among families, genera, and species. For example, users of this guide will note that the once-familiar genus *Aster* has been replaced by *Eurybia*, *Symphyotrichum*, *Doellingeria*, *Sericocarpus*, and *Ionactis*. It has been conclusively shown that true *Aster* is an Old World group and that our species are not very closely related to *Aster*. However, we continue to use the common name "aster" for our species. I have provided synonyms for the wildflowers that have undergone recent name changes.

A scientific name is composed of three items: genus name, species name or epithet, and author's name. For example, *Solidago odora* Aiton is commonly known as Fragrant Goldenrod. The genus name is *Solidago*, which is a group name that includes about 100 species globally. The species name or epithet is *odora* (Latin for "fragrant"). "Aiton" stands for William Aiton (1731–93), the English botanist who named this plant; Aiton's writings clearly describe this plant, and since he was the first to make a valid description in Latin, his name will always be associated with *Solidago odora*. A second example is *Eurybia paludosa* (Aiton) Nesom, the Savanna Grass-leaved Aster. The same William Aiton originally named it *Aster paludosus* (note that Latin endings must agree with gender), but recently Nesom transferred this species to *Eurybia*, a genus related to *Aster*, based on differences in morphology and genetics. Thus, both Aiton and Nesom are credited with proper disposition of the scientific name. A third example is *Commelina erecta* L. var. *angustifolia* (Michaux) Fernald, the Pineland Dayflower. Carl Linnaeus first described the species *Commelina erecta*. About the same time, Michaux described *Commelina angustifolia* as a separate species. As time passed, botanists saw that the differences between the two species were less than originally thought; therefore Fernald reduced *angustifolia* to a variety within *C. erecta*. Note that Michaux is still credited with providing the original name *angustifolia*, by the use of parentheses.

NOTE: The term "variety" in botanical nomenclature is not the same as that generally used in horticulture. It is a category that is meant to show that certain wild populations of a species have distinct physical and geographic differences, yet these differences are not great enough to warrant recognition of these populations as a full species. In horticulture, the term "variety" is often loosely used in place of the word "species," but it is used most often in reference to genetically altered plants (or hybrids) that are created for the horticultural trade.

Flowers and Leaves FUNCTION AND STRUCTURE

Flowers and leaves have very different functions: Flowers carry on reproduction, while leaves conduct photosynthesis. Leaves do other things as
well, but photosynthesis is of paramount importance. In this process, carbon dioxide from the air and water from leaf tissues is combined, in the
presence of sunlight, to form sugar molecules. The sugar molecules store
energy for use by the plant; along with nutrients and minerals taken up by
the plant's roots, this energy is used to grow new leaves and branches and
to enlarge stems. A by-product of photosynthesis is the release of oxygen
into the air—the very oxygen that nearly all life on earth requires. Thus,
the seemingly simple act of absorbing carbon dioxide and releasing oxygen
by green plants has set the stage for, and continues to support, all life on
our planet.

Leaves also have another vital function. Transpiration is the release of
water into the air by leaves. Although each leaf releases tiny amounts, the
amount released by a whole plant or a tree is significant. For example, a
corn plant releases about eight gallons per week. Imagine how much water
vapor is released by an entire forest every day! The loss of transpiration
due to excessive deforestation is a major factor in desertification in many
parts of the globe. That is, across large areas that formerly were forested,
the atmosphere and soil are now drier and the chances of rain are lessened.

When we think of a leaf, we usually picture a flat *blade* with a *leafstalk*
that is attached to a twig, as on a red maple or an azalea. While many leaves
are indeed typical, this guide will introduce you to other leaf forms, from
the nearly nonexistent nubs of Wire-plant (*Stipulicida setacea*) to the for-
midably spiny leaves of thistles (*Cirsium* spp.), and from the needlelike
leaves of Rosemary (*Ceratiola ericoides*) to the bizarre leaves of floating
bladderworts (*Utricularia inflata* and *U. radiata*). See fig. 1 to learn the
major leaf shapes and arrangements.

FIGURE 1 **Leaf Characteristics**

LEAF ARRANGEMENT

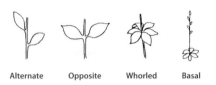

Alternate   Opposite   Whorled   Basal

LEAF TYPE

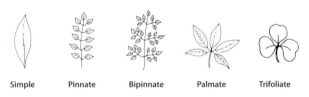

Simple   Pinnate   Bipinnate   Palmate   Trifoliate

LEAF SHAPE

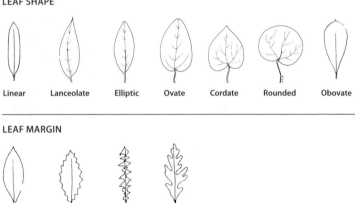

Linear   Lanceolate   Elliptic   Ovate   Cordate   Rounded   Obovate

LEAF MARGIN

Entire   Toothed   Cut   Lobed

Leaves have also evolved over the millennia to perform functions other than photosynthesis and transpiration. I have just mentioned the floating leaves of bladderworts; these are inflated and act as a support to hold the flower stem out of the water. Other leaves of bladderworts are modified into tiny traps in which they catch and digest tiny invertebrates. Sundews are also carnivorous; they use sticky, gland-tipped hairs on their leaves to catch insects. Climbing vines have tendrils that enable them to cling to bark, twigs, and branches; tendrils are in fact modified leaves that perform a very specific duty. Still other leaves have become bright and showy, like flower petals; Dogwood (*Cornus florida*) is a familiar example. The white "petals" actually are modified leaves that grow around the cluster of nondescript flowers. And finally, leaves can protect the plant by producing poisonous chemicals or stinging hairs.

Flowers exist to perform the task of reproduction, and whether large or small, showy or dull, all flowers carry on this process. This guide will introduce you to what may seem to be a bewildering array of wildflower shapes, sizes, and colors, but when examined closely, nearly all flowers show a similar pattern. That is, they are composed of the same basic components. A typical flower (see fig. 2) has *sepals*, *petals*, an *ovary*, and a *style* (female parts), and *stamens* (male parts). *Sepals* occur at the base of the flower. In most wildflowers the sepals are somewhat thicker and stronger than the petals. They enclose the developing flower while in bud and act as a protective layer. Sepals are usually green but can be the same color as the petals (as in lilies and blue-eyed-grasses, for example). Sepals can assume various shapes, they can be hairy or not, and they can have resin dots or gland-tipped hairs on the surface. Like leaves, they can be highly modified.

Petals, of course, are what we see in our mind when we think of the word "wildflower." They often are colorful, have attractive or intricate patterns, exude pleasing or unpleasant scents, and may be produced in masses. The number of petals usually is the same as the number of sepals,

FIGURE 2 **Flower Characteristics**

FLOWER ARRANGEMENT

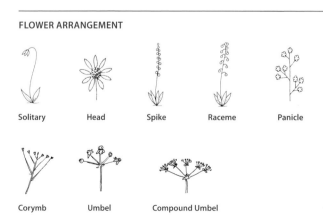

| Solitary | Head | Spike | Raceme | Panicle |

| Corymb | Umbel | Compound Umbel |

TYPICAL FLOWER

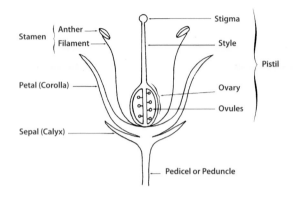

Stamen { Anther, Filament }

Petal (Corolla)

Sepal (Calyx)

Stigma

Style

Pistil

Ovary

Ovules

Pedicel or Peduncle

SPECIAL FLOWER TYPES

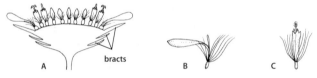

A

bracts

B

C

ASTER FAMILY (Asteraceae)

(a) Diagrammatic section through a sunflower head or inflorescence showing the two different kinds of flowers: ray flowers (b) are the outer flowers or "petals" of the daisy, and disc flowers (c) are the inner flowers that form the center of the inflorescence. In (a) the disc flowers are shown in different stages of development; note the bracts shown just below the flowers.

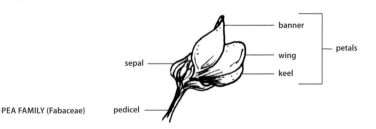

banner

wing

petals

keel

sepal

PEA FAMILY (Fabaceae)   pedicel

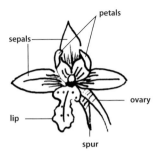

ORCHID FAMILY (Orchidaeceae)

petals

sepals

ovary

lip

spur

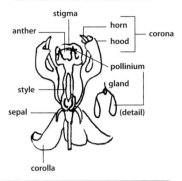

MILKWEED FAMILY IN CROSS SECTION

stigma

anther

horn

hood

corona

pollinium

style

gland

sepal

(detail)

corolla

but it may be half as many, twice as many, or a multiple. In some flowers, two or more petals have become fused together so that what looks like four petals is actually five. In other species there are no petals; in these instances the sepals are usually large and/or colorful. An example is Leatherflower (*Clematis crispa*). The plants of the Sandhills region demonstrate that there are a great many ways that flowers have changed and adapted to fit the conditions in their environments.

In addition to sepals and petals, typical flowers have female parts or male parts or both in the same flower. In some species, individual plants produce flowers with only female parts, while other individuals produce only male flowers; such plants are termed *dioecious*. Species in which the flowers contain both female and male parts are termed *monoecious*. Female parts of a flower include the *ovary*, which is a sac or enclosure in which fertilization takes place. After fertilization, the ovary expands as the seeds grow in size and ultimately becomes the fruit. At the top of the ovary is a slender extension called a *style*; at its tip is a *stigma*. These structures project well beyond the petals of many wildflowers, where they are easily seen, but in other species they may be short and hidden among the petal bases. The stigma is often knoblike but may be split into two or three short segments. Surfaces of the stigma are somewhat sticky so that pollen adheres to them. The style then carries material from the pollen grains down to the ovary for fertilization. Male parts of a flower include the *stamen*, composed of a slender filament capped by a small sac called an *anther*. The anther produces pollen, which is released into the air (wind pollination) or gathered by insects, hummingbirds, or other animals and transported to the stigma of another flower.

Flowers have been modified profoundly via their interactions with pollinators. The importance and intricacies of these interactions are such that whole books have been written about this subject. Suffice it to say that these interactions have changed life on earth and have led to the amazing diversity of plants and animals that we see today. Pollinators range from tiny ants and thrips to beetles, bees, birds (most notably hummingbirds), bats, and tree-dwelling mammals. Because of their small size, mobility, and great diversity, insects have become the primary pollinators worldwide. Plants attract pollinators by scent or by visual clues such as showy flowers. But there is often a reward involved. For example, bees sip flower nectar for their own nourishment while also gathering pollen to feed their larvae. Hummingbirds sip nectar (their reward), but in doing so they get a dusting of pollen on their foreheads that may be deposited on the stigma of another flower. In this way, the plant is assured that cross-pollination takes place. The day-to-day interactions between plants and pollinators has, over millions of years, led to changes in both the plants and the animals, each becoming closely adapted to the other.

Over evolutionary time, the petals of some flowers have changed so much that they are worth describing in detail. See the accompanying drawings of the aster and sunflower family, pea and bean family, orchid family, and milkweed family in fig. 2.

Aster family (Asteraceae). Flowers of this family are usually numerous and grow crowded together in a headlike structure. The head is surrounded with scalelike or leaflike *bracts*, together forming an *involucre*. The involucre provides support and protection for the flowers within. Flowers project from the involucre and are of two kinds. *Disc flowers* are tubular, with five lobes or points at the summit. *Ray flowers* are short-tubular, then have a single strap-shaped lobe projecting outward. This composite head with two flower types gives rise to an alternate family name, Compositae. When disc and ray flowers occur in the same head, the disc flowers are crowded in the center of the head and the rays occur around the margin and look more or less like "petals." Asters, goldenrods, and sunflowers are examples. However, disc flowers and ray flowers do not always occur in the same head. Thistles and eupatoriums, for example, have heads composed solely of disc flowers. Dandelions and hawkweeds have heads composed solely of ray flowers.

Pea family (Fabaceae). The basic pattern in this family is like that of many other families—five sepals and five petals—but here the petals are modified and look very much unlike flowers of other families. One petal (or part of it) stands erect and is called the *standard* (also called the *banner*); it is often oriented at 90 degrees from the rest of the flower. Two fused petals form a *keel* that juts out horizontally; they hold within them the ovary, style, and stamens. Finally, two petals are called *wings*; they may spread outward or lie appressed to the keel. The fruit or bean pod has given this family its alternate name, Leguminosae.

Orchid family (Orchidaceae). Orchids have complex flowers that have evolved to attract specific pollinators. In all orchids there are three sepals and three petals; any and all of these may be modified into interesting, even bizarre, shapes. This is especially true of the lowest petal, which is termed the *lip* and is often highly colored and has a frilled surface or fringed margins. The other two petals often form a tube with the lip, to guide pollinators into the flower. The three sepals usually spread outward; they may have the same or similar color and shape as the petals but more often are different, sometimes strikingly so.

Milkweed family (Asclepiadaceae). Here the five petals are lowermost and form a downward-angled "skirt." The five sepals are small and hidden beneath. Standing above the petals is a *corona*, each of the five parts forming a hoodlike structure. In some milkweeds there is a pointed *horn* projecting a bit beyond each *hood*. In the center of the ring of hoods is a thick stalk with a somewhat circular structure on top; this is actually the conjoined style, stigma, and anthers.

Glossary

Acuminate A long and gradual taper; a more extreme expression of *acute* (see below). Grass and sedge leaves almost always have acuminate tips.

Acute Short-tapered to a point or to a narrow tip.

Appressed Lying flat against a surface.

Ascending Usually referring to stems or branches that stand at an angle, not vertical, not horizontal.

Aster family flowers Flowers in this family are usually numerous and occur bunched together in a headlike structure. The head is surrounded with scalelike or leaflike bracts, together forming an involucre. Flowers project from the involucre and are of two kinds. Disc flowers are tubular, with five lobes or points at the summit. Ray flowers are short-tubular and with a single strap-shaped lobe projecting outward from the summit. This composite head with two flower types gives rise to an alternate family name, Compositae. When disc and ray flowers occur in the same head, the disc flowers are crowded in the center of the head and the rays occur around the margin and look more or less like "petals." Asters, goldenrods, and sunflowers are examples. Thistles and eupatoriums have heads composed solely of disc flowers. Dandelions and hawkweeds have heads composed solely of ray flowers. See fig. 2.

Awn A short to long, usually needlelike extension. An awned leaf has a sharp projection from the leaf tip. Awns can occur on many plant parts, such as bracts, sepals, petals, grass fruits, grass scales, and sedge scales.

Axil Junction of a leaf and stem. In many plants, flower stalks originate from the junctions of leaves and stem.

Bean family flowers For a description of a typical flower, see *Pea-shaped*.

Bipinnate Twice pinnate; referring to a pinnate leaf that is again pinnately divided. There may or may not be terminal leaflets.

Bract A small leaf or leaflike structure at the base of a flower or at the base of an inflorescence.

Calyx The sepals; one of the main divisions of a flower. The calyx occurs at the base of a flower and normally has the same number of parts as the corolla (i.e., 5 sepals, 5 petals). An unopened calyx protects the other flower structures when in bud.

Catkin An inflorescence of unisexual flowers without petals, arranged in a dense, elongate spike or spikelike raceme. Typical of members of the birch and alder family (Betulaceae) and the willow family (Salicaceae).

Clasping Usually refers to leaves whose bases are enlarged and extend around part of the stem.

Cordate Having the shape of a heart. Cordate leaves are oval in outline with a notch at the base.

Corm An underground base of a stem, short and vertically oriented; it may have a thin, papery covering.

Corolla The petals of a flower; not including the calyx.

Crenate With small rounded teeth; usually referring to leaf margins. "Crenate" is a useful term to distinguish from sharply pointed teeth (serrate).

Deciduous Leaves that drop during the fall–winter season. Sometimes also used to describe petals that drop quickly after flowers have been fertilized.

Dioecious Having male and female flowers on separate plants.

Driptip An abrupt narrowing at the tip of a leaf to form a small triangle. Raindrops that strike the leaf tend to collect along the midrib and then run off the driptip.

Ecotone A narrow zone between two different natural communities or habitats, in which some plants of each habitat grow mixed together. In the Sandhills region, the ecotone between dry longleaf pinelands and streamheads takes on special importance as a zone that also supports plant species found nowhere else in the region. Plants that grow here are finely adapted to perennially moist soils (vs. dry pinelands and wet streamheads).

Endemic Restricted to a particular region; occurring nowhere else.

Entire Refers to margins of leaves, calyx, petals, etc., in which there are no teeth, glands, hairs, or other structures.

Equitant Leaves whose bases overlap to form two ranks, as in *Iris* and many *Xyris*. Such leaves normally arise from the base of the plant.

Erect Upright, essentially vertical.

Evergreen Leaves that remain for more than one growing season.

Filiform Extremely slender; threadlike.

Glabrate Essentially hairless. There may be small amounts of hair locally, or scattered wispy hairs, but they are insignificant.

Glabrous Hairless.

Gland-tipped hairs or glandular hairy Hairs with a tiny drop at the tip. The droplets usually glisten and may be sticky, as in *Drosera*, where they function to trap insects, but the function of glandular hairs is not known for most plants.

Gland-tipped teeth Teeth of leaves, bracts, or other parts that have a tiny drop at the tip. The droplet may be soft or hard; the function is unknown for most plants.

Glandular dots Flat, rounded spots on leaves, twigs, or flower parts. They are often yellowish or golden but may be reddish or black in some species. The function of glandular dots is not known for most plants.

Glaucous Covered with a white or whitish or bluish white coating. Honeycups (*Zenobia pulverulenta*) has the most strikingly glaucous leaves of any of our plants. "Glaucescent" means less strongly whitened, or "somewhat whitened."

Glutinous Having a gluey or sticky coating. This coating can in some cases be slippery as well.

Hastate With two lobes pointing outward and somewhat backward; thus shaped like an arrowhead with broad lobes.

Helicoid cyme Coiled into a spiral. This term is used for the coiled inflorescences of many members of the Boraginaceae (borage and forget-me-not family).

Hispid Refers to hairs that are stiff and therefore rough to the touch.

Inflorescence The portion of a plant that bears flowers; a flower cluster.

Involucre A series (or several series) of scales or bracts around the base of a flower or a flower head (such as in the aster family).

Lanceolate Lance shaped. In leaves, tapering from a not very broad base to a narrow tip.

Lenticel A slightly raised area on a surface. Lenticels are usually slender and short, appearing like a shallow cut. This term usually applies to twigs and young bark of the trunks of trees, and bark of any age of shrubs.

Mycotrophic Plants that derive nutrients from decaying plant material via an association with soil fungi. Most such plants lack chlorophyll and therefore the ability to produce their own nourishment from sunlight. Compare with *Saprophytic*.

Obovate, oblanceolate In the botanical sense, "ob-" is a prefix that means "widest towards the tip"; usually it is applied to leaves, sepals, and petals.

Ocrea In the smartweed family (Polygonaceae), the collar around the stem at each leaf node.

Orchid family flowers Orchids have complex flowers that have evolved to attract specific pollinators. In all orchids there are three sepals and three petals; any and all of these may be modified into interesting, even strange, shapes. This is especially true of the lowest petal, which is termed the lip and is often highly colored and has a frilled surface or fringed margins. The other two petals often form a tube with the lip, to guide pollinators into the flower; the three sepals usually spread outward. See fig. 2.

Papillose With small, rounded bumps or projections.

Pea-shaped Refers to typical flowers of the pea or bean family (Fabaceae), in which the five petals are modified into an erect standard (also called a banner), a keel (two fused petals) that juts out about 90 degrees from the standard, and two wings that may lie appressed to the keel or spread outward. See fig. 2.

Pedicel The stalk of a flower. The term is rarely used in this book; I simply use "flower stalk."

Peltate A leaf in which the leafstalk or petiole is attached to the middle of the lower surface, thus resembling an umbrella.

Perfoliate A leaf blade that grows around the stem; thus the stem appears to have pierced through the leaf.

Perigynium The outer covering of a female flower in the sedge family (Cyperaceae), from which the stigmas protrude. In many species the perigynium is distinctly shaped or textured. It remains as the seed matures.

Petiole A leafstalk.

Pilose With long hairs that stick straight out from the surface.

Pinna (plural is "pinnae") A primary division or leaflet of a pinnate leaf. In bipinnate leaves, each primary division is called a pinna and the divisions of each pinna are called pinnules.

Pinnate Referring to a compound leaf that is divided such that the leaflets occur on opposite sides of the stalk. There may be a terminal leaflet (odd-pinnate) or not (evenly pinnate).

Pinnule The ultimate divisions of a bipinnate or multipinnate leaf. See *Pinna*.

Pseudo-whorl With the appearance of a whorl, but the leaves are alternate and have a very small length of stem between them.

Pubescent With short hairs. Technically, it refers to hairs that also stick more or less straight out from a surface, but in this book it covers hairs of various orientation. "Pubescent" implies that the hairs are short, versus "hairy" or "pilose," which implies long hairs.

Punctate With tiny depressions.

Purple This book uses purple in the artist's sense a color somewhere between red and violet. In recent decades people have often used "purple" when they really mean "violet," as when referring to grape juice or iris flowers, but it is inaccurate to do so.

Rachis In a compound leaf, the rachis is the extension of the leafstalk and bears the leaflets.

Radiate With parts spreading from a central point.

Ranks or Ranked Leaves that grow one atop another up the stem, in one vertical row. If all leaves on *each side* of the stem are in the same vertical row, then the leaves are 2-ranked. If leaves are opposite and each pair is oriented 90 degrees from the pair above and below, then the leaves are 4-ranked. Ranks are often easiest to see from directly above a plant.

Recurved Curved outward and often also downward. Used mostly to describe leaves but may also describe bracts of floral heads or the orientation of petals.

Reflexed Abruptly turned downward or backward. Reflexed leaves are bent so that the tips point toward the ground. Reflexed flower bracts (Asteraceae) have outwardly bent tips.

Resin dots Tiny, rounded, golden-yellow dots that usually glisten in strong light. They may be flat on a surface, in slight depressions, or slightly raised. The "resin" may or may not be sticky or fragrant. In some species, resin dots may be some other color and dull.

Rhizome A thick, elongate, underground structure at the base of a stem. It may be horizontal or vertical. Perennial species often have enlarged rhizomes in which are stored starches and sugars to be used during periods of stress.

Rhombic Diamond shaped or spindle shaped, with a distinct angle about midway.

Rugose Having a wrinkled and irregular surface. It also implies that the structure is thick in cross section.

Sagittate Shaped like a narrow arrowhead, with two lateral lobes pointed backward.

Saprophytic plants that derive nutrients directly from living or decaying plants. Many (but by no means all) such plants lack chlorophyll and therefore the ability to produce their own nourishment from sunlight. Compare with *Mycotrophic*.

Scabrous With minute and sharp teeth, prickles, or hairs. The term usually applies to leaf surfaces and margins. Scabrous projections are usually oriented in one direction, so they may cut the skin if one runs one's fingers "against the grain."

Septate Refers to a leaf or a leafstalk in which there are internal, *crosswise* partitions. From the outside of a leaf, septae often show as a pale band (in *Sagittaria*) or a raised band around the leaf or stem (in *Juncus*). In fruits, septate usually means divided *lengthwise* by partitions.

Serrate Sharply pointed in a row, or sawlike; usually refers to teeth on leaf margins.

Sessile Without a stalk. For example, a sessile leaf has no leafstalk, or petiole; a sessile flower has no stalk, or pedicel.

Sinuate With a wavy or undulating margin or surface.

Spadix A dense spike of flowers produced by members of the arum family (Araceae).

Spathe A bract (or pair of bracts) that encloses or surrounds a flower or group of flowers. Spathes are prominent features of the arum family (Araceae), the dayflower family (Commelinaceae), and the blue-eyed-grasses (Iridaceae).

Stellate Starlike or star-shaped; usually referring to hairs that have several spreading branches from a central point.

Stipule A small, leaflike appendage, usually paired, at the base of a leafstalk. Often prominent in roses (*Rosa*) and various legumes (*Desmodium*, *Crotalaria*).

Succulent Fleshy textured, thick in cross section. In leaves this is normally due to high water content.

Tomentose With very dense hairs that are closely matted or tangled.

Translucent More or less transparent; light is visible through it.

Tubercle or tuberculate A small bump or projection sticking above the surface. Tuberculate surfaces have many bumps, which may be blunt or pointed.

Umbel A type of inflorescence in which flowers grow on stalks (usually of similar length) that originate from a single point, like the spokes of an umbrella. In many species of the family Apiaceae (also called Umbelliferae), each main stalk of the umbel supports at its tip a tiny umbel of its own (called an umbellule) that has flowers at its tip.

Whorl Leaves that grow in multiples of three or more at a point on a stem.

Natural Communities

DRY LONGLEAF PINELAND

Dry Longleaf Pineland is the typical longleaf pine woodland of the Sandhills region. It used to be the most widespread and abundant community within the region, occurring on dry slopes and flats throughout, but development, fire suppression, and conversion to pine plantations have reduced most of it to small patches. Fortunately, a number of large and highly significant examples remain within protected areas. Dominants are Longleaf Pine (*Pinus palustris*), Turkey Oak (*Quercus laevis*), Dwarf Post Oak (*Q. margarettae*), and Wiregrass (*Aristida stricta*, two varieties), with a moderate to dense herb layer. Wiregrass is usually dense and carries relatively cool-burning fires through the community. As with Turkey Oak Scrub, many of the member plants are highly adapted to fire; some such as Wiregrass will not flower or fruit without it. Within just a few weeks after a winter or spring fire, there is a burst of plant growth from dormant seeds and rhizomes, soon followed by flowering, which continues through fall. Next season's display is less spectacular, and each subsequent year produces fewer flowering plants until fire occurs again. When particularly well-burned, the oak subcanopy is markedly reduced, and the community then appears savannalike. Further reduction in the density of pines results in a pine savanna.

Three components form the typical community of dry soils: an open canopy of Longleaf Pine, an understory of up to four species of oaks, and a dense layer of wiregrass.

Common associates include Mockernut Hickory (*Carya alba*), Sassafras (*Sassafras albidum*), Dwarf Huckleberry (*Gaylussacia dumosa*), Narrowleaf Blueberry (*Vaccinium tenellum*), Poison Oak (*Toxicodendron pubescens*), Carolina Wild-indigo (*Baptisia cinerea*), Southern Floweringspurge (*Euphorbia pubentissima*), Downy Beardtongue (*Penstemon australis*), Goat's-rue (*Tephrosia virginiana*), Little Bluestem (*Schizachyrium scoparium*), and witchgrasses (*Dichanthelium* spp.).

Dry Longleaf Pinelands are quite variable in structure and composition, depending on soil type, moisture, depth to underlying clay layer, and fire regime. We cannot describe them all, but one variant is particularly interesting botanically. In this variant the soils are markedly loamy and more fertile than the average droughty Sandhills region soils, producing a very diverse herb layer notable for high numbers of legumes, grasses, and composites (aster family). The community is best developed in shallow dry swales (called pea swales or bean dips), on mesic flats, and at bases of relatively steep slopes. Blackjack Oak (*Q. marilandica*) and Bluejack Oak (*Q. incana*) are often the commonest understory trees. Within our region, a number of species are virtually restricted to this community: Small-leaved White Snakeroot (*Ageratina aromatica*), Woolly Three-awn (*Aristida lanosa*), Panicled Tick-trefoil (*Desmodium paniculatum*), Soft Milkpea (*Galactia mollis*), Virginia Marbleseed (*Onosmodium virginia-*

TOP In the loamy-soil variant, finer-textured soils retain more nutrients and support communities with an exceptional diversity of grasses, legumes, and composites (aster family). BOTTOM At well-burned sites, members of the aster family are prominent in the late summer and autumn. Here we see asters, goldenrods, eupatoriums, and blazing-asters.

num), Pitchfork Crowngrass (*Paspalum bifidum*), and Nodding Indiangrass (*Sorghastrum elliottii*). The federally endangered Michaux's Sumac (*Rhus michauxii*) occurs most often in this variant.

Species List
The color after a name indicates the primary natural community or habitat.
T = mentioned in text of another species; not pictured.

Agalinis setacea ❁
 Threadleaf Gerardia
Ageratina aromatica
 Small-leaved White
 Snakeroot
Aletris farinosa T ❁
 White Colicroot
Amorpha herbacea
 Dwarf Indigo-bush
Amsonia ciliata ❁
 Fringed Bluestar
Andropogon gerardii
 Big Bluestem; Turkeyfoot
Andropogon ternarius
 Silvery Bluestem;
 Splitbeard Bluestem
Andropogon virginicus T
 Oldfield Bluestem
Angelica venenosa
 Downy Angelica
Apocynum cannabinum ❁
 Indian Hemp
Aristida stricta
 Wiregrass
Arnica acaulis ❁
 Leopard's-bane
Asclepias amplexicaulis
 Wavy-leaved Milkweed
Asclepias humistrata ❁
 Fleshy Milkweed
Asclepias tomentosa ❁
 Hairy Milkweed
Asclepias tuberosa ssp. *rolfsii*
 Sandhill Orange Milkweed
Astragalus michauxii
 Sandhills Milkvetch
Aureolaria pectinata ❁
 Sticky False-foxglove
Baptisia cinerea
 Carolina Wild-indigo

Baptisia lanceolata T
 Lanceleaf Wild-indigo
Baptisia tinctoria
 Northern Wild-indigo
Berlandiera pumila
 Eastern Greeneyes
Brickellia eupatorioides
 Eastern False-boneset;
 Eastern False-eupatorium
Buchnera floridana ❁
 Florida Bluehearts
Carphephorus bellidifolius ❁
 Sandhill Chaffhead
Ceanothus americanus ❁
 New Jersey Tea
Centrosema virginiana
 Spurred Butterfly-pea
Chamaecrista nictitans
 Sensitive Partridge-pea;
 Wild Sensitive-plant
Chrysopsis mariana
 Maryland Golden-aster
Cirsium repandum
 Sandhill Thistle
Clitoria mariana
 Butterfly-pea
Cnidoscolus stimulosus ❁
 Tread-softly
Commelina erecta var. *angustifolia*
 Pineland Dayflower;
 Sand Dayflower
Coreopsis major var. *rigida*
 Whorled Tickseed;
 Whorled Coreopsis
Coreopsis verticillata ❁
 Cutleaf Tickseed
Crocanthemum canadense ❁
 Canada Frostweed
Croptilon divaricatum ❁
 Slender Scratch-daisy

Crotalaria purshii
Pursh's Rattlebox
Crotalaria rotundifolia
Rabbitbells;
Low Rattlebox
Cuthbertia graminea ❁
Slender Roseling
Cyperus plukenetii
Starburst Flatsedge;
Plukenet's Flatsedge
Dalea pinnata var. *pinnata*
Summer Farewell
Danthonia sericea
Silky Oatgrass
Desmodium ciliare
Littleleaf Tick-trefoil
Desmodium laevigatum
Smooth Tick-trefoil
Desmodium nuttallii
Nuttall's Tick-trefoil
Desmodium strictum
Upland Slender Tick-trefoil;
Pineland Tick-trefoil
Desmodium viridiflorum T
Velvet Tick-trefoil
Elephantopus nudatus
Savanna Elephant's-foot;
Pineland Elephant's-foot
Elephantopus tomentosus T
Upland Elephant's-foot
Epigaea repens
Trailing Arbutus
Eragrostis spectabilis ❁
Purple Lovegrass
Erigeron strigosus var. *strigosus*
Slender Daisy-fleabane
Eryngium yuccifolium
Rattlesnake Master;
Button Snakeroot
Eupatorium album
White Eupatorium
Eupatorium capillifolium T ❁
Slender Dog-fennel
Eupatorium compositifolium ❁
Coastal Plain Dog-fennel
Eupatorium hyssopifolium ❁
Hyssopleaf Eupatorium
Eupatorium leucolepis ❁
Savanna Eupatorium
Eupatorium linearifolium T ❁
Narrowleaf Eupatorium

Eupatorium rotundifolium
Roundleaf Eupatorium
Euphorbia curtissii
White Sandhill-spurge
Euphorbia exserta T
Purple Sandhill-spurge
Euphorbia ipecacuanhae ❁
Carolina Ipecac
Euphorbia pubentissima
Southern Flowering-spurge
Euthamia caroliniana
Slender Flat-topped
Goldenrod
Gaillardia aestivalis
Rayless Blanket-flower;
Sandhills Gaillardia
Galactia erecta
Erect Milkpea
Galactia mollis
Soft Milkpea
Galactia regularis
Smooth Milkpea;
Common Milkpea
Galactia volubilis T
Twining Milkpea
Gaura filipes ❁
Threadstalk Gaura
Gaylussacia dumosa ❁
Dwarf Huckleberry
Gentiana autumnalis
Autumn Gentian
Gentiana villosa T ❁
Striped Gentian
Helianthus atrorubens
Purpledisc Sunflower
Helianthus divaricatus ❁
Woodland Sunflower
Hieracium gronovii T
Beaked Hawkweed
Hieracium marianum
Maryland Hawkweed
Houstonia purpurea ❁
Summer Bluet
Hypericum hypericoides
St. Andrew's Cross
Hypericum setosum ❁
Downy St. John's-wort
Hypoxis hirsuta ❁
Upland Stargrass
Hypoxis wrightii
Pineland Stargrass

Ionactis linariifolius
Stiff Aster; Spruce Aster
Iris verna var. *verna*
Dwarf Iris
Lactuca graminifolia
Slender Wild-lettuce
Lespedeza angustifolia
Narrowleaf Bush-clover
Lespedeza bicolor ✳
Bicolor Bush-clover
Lespedeza capitata
Silvery Bush-clover
Lespedeza cuneata ✳
Chinese Bush-clover
Lespedeza hirta T
Roundleaf Bush-clover
Lespedeza procumbens T
Trailing Bush-clover
Lespedeza repens
Creeping Bush-clover
Lespedeza stuevei T ✳
Stueve's Bush-clover
Lespedeza virginica ✳
Slender Bush-clover
Liatris cokeri ✳
Sandhills Blazing-star
Liatris secunda T ✳
One-sided Blazing-star
Liatris squarrosa
Long-bracted Blazing-star
Liatris squarrulosa
Earle's Blazing-star
Linum floridanum
Savanna Flax
Lithospermum caroliniense ✳
Sandhill Puccoon
Lobelia nuttallii ✳
Nuttall's Lobelia
Ludwigia hirtella T
Rafinesque's Seedbox
Ludwigia virgata
Savanna Seedbox
Lupinus diffusus ✳
Sandhill Lupine
Lupinus perennis T ✳
Sundial Lupine
Marshallia obovata var. *scaposa*
Savanna Barbara's-buttons
Mimosa microphylla
Eastern Sensitive-brier

Minuartia caroliniana ✳
Carolina Sandwort
Monarda punctata
Spotted Beebalm
Morella pumila
Dwarf Wax-myrtle
Muhlenbergia capillaris
Upland Muhly
Oenothera fruticosa
Southern Sundrops
Onosmodium virginianum
Virginia Marbleseed
Orbexilum lupinellum
Sandhill Scurfpea;
Lupine Scurfpea
Orbexilum pedunculatum var.
psoralioides ✳
Sampson's Snakeroot
Parthenium integrifolium var.
mabryanum
Mabry's Wild-quinine
Pediomelum canescens
Buckroot
Penstemon australis
Downy Beardtongue
Penstemon laevigatus T
Smooth Beardtongue
Phaseolus sinuatus
Trailing Wild Bean;
Sandhill Bean
Phlox nivalis var. *nivalis*
Pineland Phlox
Physalis lanceolata
Sandhills Ground-cherry
Physalis virginiana T
Virginia Ground-cherry
Pityopsis aspera
Sticky Golden-aster
Pityopsis graminifolia T
Grass-leaved Golden-aster
Polygala grandiflora
Showy Milkwort
Polygala mariana T ✳
Maryland Milkwort
Prenanthes autumnalis
One-sided Rattlesnake-root
Pycnanthemum flexuosum
Savanna Mountain-mint
Pycnanthemum tenuifolium ✳
Slender Mountain-mint

Pyxidanthera brevifolia ❁
  Sandhills Pyxie-moss
Rhexia alifanus ❁
  Savanna Meadow-beauty
Rhus copallinum
  Winged Sumac
Rhus glabra ❁
  Smooth Sumac
Rhus michauxii
  Michaux's Sumac
Rhynchosia reniformis
  Dollarweed;
  Roundleaf Snoutbean
Rhynchosia tomentosa
  Erect Snoutbean
Robinia nana ❁
  Dwarf Locust
Rubus cuneifolius ❁
  Sand Blackberry
Ruellia ciliosa
  Sandhill Wild-petunia
Sabatia brachiata
  Narrowleaf Sabatia
Sabatia quadrangula T ❁
  Four-angled Sabatia
Saccharum alopecuroides T ❁
  Foxtail Plumegrass
Salvia azurea var. *azurea*
  Azure Sage
Schizachyrium scoparium
  Little Bluestem
Schwalbea americana
  Chaffseed
Sericocarpus asteroides
  Toothed White-topped Aster
Sericocarpus linifolius T
  Slender White-topped Aster
Sericocarpus tortifolius
  Twistleaf White-topped Aster;
  Dixie White-topped Aster
Seymeria cassioides
  Senna Seymeria
Silene virginica ❁
  Fire Pink
Silphium compositum
  Rosinweed
Sisyrinchium fuscatum T
  Bristly Blue-eyed-grass
Sisyrinchium rufipes
  Sandhill Blue-eyed-grass

Smilax glauca ❁
  Sawbrier
Solidago arguta var. *caroliniana* ❁
  Vasey's Goldenrod
Solidago odora
  Fragrant Goldenrod
Solidago pinetorum T ❁
  Pineywoods Goldenrod
Solidago rugosa var. *aspera* T ❁
  Roughstem Goldenrod
Sorghastrum elliottii
  Nodding Indiangrass
Sorghastrum nutans
  Prairie Indiangrass;
  Yellow Indiangrass
Spiranthes praecox ❁
  Grass-leaved Ladies'-tresses
Spiranthes tuberosa
  Little Ladies'-tresses
Stillingia sylvatica
  Queen's Delight
Stylisma patens ssp. *angustifolia* T
  Narrowleaf Dawnflower
Stylisma patens ssp. *patens*
  Sandhill Morning-glory;
  Sandhill Dawnflower
Stylodon carneus
  Carolina Vervain
Stylosanthes biflora
  Pencil Flower
Symphyotrichum concolor
  Eastern Silvery-aster
Symphyotrichum patens ❁
  Skydrop Aster
Symphyotrichum walteri
  Walter's Aster
Tephrosia florida T
  Savanna Goat's-rue
Tephrosia spicata
  Tawny Goat's-rue
Tephrosia virginiana
  Common Goat's-rue
Tetragonotheca helianthoides
  Squareheads
Thaspium trifoliatum ❁
  Woodland Parsnip
Toxicodendron pubescens
  Poison Oak
Trichostema setaceum T ❁
  Slender Blue-curls

Vaccinium stamineum ✳
  Deerberry
Vaccinium tenellum
  Narrowleaf Blueberry
Vernonia acaulis
  Carolina Ironweed
Vernonia angustifolia
  Slender Ironweed
Viola pedata
  Bird's-foot Violet
Viola villosa ✳
  Southern Woolly Violet

Vitis rotundifolia ✳
  Muscadine Grape
Warea cuneifolia ✳
  Carolina Pineland-cress
Xyris caroliniana
  Carolina Yellow-eyed-grass
Yucca filamentosa ✳
  Adam's Needle
Zornia bracteata
  Viperina

ASTERACEAE: ASTER FAMILY
Savanna Barbara's-buttons
Marshallia obovata (Walter) Beadle & Boynton
var. *scaposa* Channell

Perennial, stems usually single, 4–18″ (10–45 cm) tall, unbranched. Leaves are few and occur in the lower quarter of the stem, or they may be strictly basal. Leaves are ascending to spreading, oblanceolate to elliptic, 1.2–4.8″ (3–12 cm) long and 0.25–1″ (5–25 mm) wide, tapered to a stalk. The single flower head grows terminally atop stem, hemispherical, about 1″ (2.5 cm) wide, disc flowers white, rays absent.

With so few leaves, Savanna Barbara's-buttons looks like it is composed merely of a few basal leaves and a flower atop a simple stem—a botanical condition called "scapose." Chauncey Beadle and Frank Boynton were botanists and horticulturalists at the Biltmore Estate in NC; Robert Channell was a botany professor at Vanderbilt University.

Inhabits dry to seasonally moist, loamy sand soil of flats, pea swales, and savannas within longleaf pinelands. Ranges from c NC to c GA, nw FL, and se AL.

LATE APR.–MAY

ASTERACEAE: ASTER FAMILY
Mabry's Wild-quinine
Parthenium integrifolium L.
var. *mabryanum* Mears

Perennial from tuberlike roots, the stem single and usually unbranched, 1–2.5′ (30–75 cm) tall, smooth to pubescent. Leaves are alternate, the basal ones lanceolate, 4–8″ (10–20 cm) long and 0.8–1.6″ (2–4 cm) wide, acute-tipped, tapering to the base, smooth or with short, appressed, roughish hairs, margins toothed, in some plants also deeply lobed. Midstem and upper leaves are much smaller and sessile. Flower heads grow in flat-topped clusters on branches from upper leaf axils, about 0.3″ (8 mm) across, ray flowers white, about 2 mm long, disc flowers creamy white.

As its name suggests, this plant (and its close relatives) was used medicinally to treat fevers, including malaria, and to reduce inflammation of the urinary tract. Typical Wild-quinine (*P. integrifolium* var. *integrifolium*) is primarily a Piedmont plant; it is larger in all dimensions.

Inhabits dry longleaf pinelands, rights-of-way, and sometimes roadsides. Ranges on the Coastal Plain from se VA to nc SC.

LATE MAY–EARLY NOV., BLOOMING STRONGLY IN RESPONSE TO FIRE

ASTERACEAE: ASTER FAMILY
Small-leaved White Snakeroot
Ageratina aromatica (L.) Spach
[*Eupatorium aromaticum* L.]

Perennial, 10–24″ (30–65 cm) tall, branched from mid- and upper leaf bases, pubescent. Leaves are opposite, stalks 0.4–0.8″ (1–2 cm) long, blades ovate, 1.2–2.8″ (3–7 cm) long and 0.6–2″ (1.5–5 cm) wide, bluntly toothed. Convex or flattish inflorescences grow at tips of branches, each cluster with many tiny flower heads. Each head has short-pointed white bracts and 5 bright white disc flowers, rays absent.

Small-leaved White Snakeroot is closely related to eupatoriums, but it has much longer leafstalks; its leaves are a brighter green and its flowers a brighter white.

Inhabits loamy sandy soil within longleaf pinelands, mesic to moist pine savannas and flatwoods, and oak-hickory slopes. Ranges from e MA to OH south to n FL and se LA.

LATE AUG.–OCT.

ASTERACEAE: ASTER FAMILY
White Eupatorium
Eupatorium album L.

Pubescent perennial, stems erect or ascending, mostly 10–24″ (25–70 cm) tall. Leaves relatively few, opposite, 2–5″ (5–12 cm) long and 0.6–1.6″ (1.5–4 cm) wide, gradually reduced upward, lanceolate to elliptic, tapered basally, coarsely toothed. The stem is branched above into a flat-topped inflorescence of small flower heads, each with long-pointed white bracts and 5 white disc flowers, rays absent. The inflorescence is covered with short, white, downy hairs, in some plants also with dark glands.

This is our only eupatorium whose lower leaves are distinctly larger than the upper leaves; this feature gives it a distinct profile.

Inhabits dry sandy to loamy soils of pinelands (including bean dips) and oak-hickory woods. Ranges from CT to KY and AR south to FL and TX.

LATE JUNE–MID-SEPT.

ASTERACEAE: ASTER FAMILY
Roundleaf Eupatorium

Eupatorium rotundifolium var. *rotundifolium* L.

Pubescent perennial, mostly 1.5–3′ (0.5–1 m) tall. Leaves opposite, virtually sessile, rotund or broadly ovate, 1.25–3″ (3–7.5 cm) long and 1–2.25″ (2.5–5.5 cm) wide, crenate, with yellow resin dots beneath. The stem is opposite-branched above into a convex or flat inflorescence of tiny flower heads, each with short-pointed white bracts and 5 white disc flowers, rays absent.

Rough Eupatorium (*E. pilosum*) is very similar, and the two can co-occur in streamhead ecotones; it differs in its narrower, ovate leaves, which have short but distinct stalks, and its smaller, alternate-branched inflorescence.

Common in dry to moist soil of pinelands and oak-hickory woods, also moist streamhead margins and pine savannas. Ranges mostly on the Coastal Plain from se NY to c FL and e TX.

AUG.–OCT.

ASTERACEAE: ASTER FAMILY
Eastern False-boneset; Eastern False-eupatorium

Brickellia eupatorioides (L.) Shinners var. *eupatorioides*
[*Kuhnia eupatorioides* L.]

Perennial, stem solitary or several together, 1–4′ (1.2 m) tall, with downy hairs. Leaves are alternate, linear or lanceolate, 1–4″ (2.5–10 cm) long and 0.1–0.6″ (2–15 mm) wide (sometimes wider), tapered to tip, more or less sessile, toothed or not, with many resin dots beneath. Flower heads grow from tips of stem and short branches, each head narrow and cylindric, 0.25–0.3″ (6–8 mm) long, 10–12 flowered. Disc flowers are cream or ivory color, rays absent.

At any distance Eastern False-boneset looks like several of our eupatoriums (genus *Eupatorium*); but its leaves are alternate, the inflorescence is not flat-topped, and its flowers are creamy, not white. The genus *Brickellia* commemorates John Brickell, an Irish-born physician and naturalist who settled in Georgia in the latter half of the eighteenth century.

Inhabits dry longleaf pinelands and oak-hickory forests; away from the Sandhills also in prairie remnants, open rocky slopes, and semiwooded glades. Ranges from s NJ to IN south to c FL and e TX.

LATE JUNE–EARLY OCT.

ASTERACEAE: ASTER FAMILY
Toothed White-topped Aster
Sericocarpus asteroides (L.) B.S.P.
[*Aster paternus* Cronquist]

Perennial, stems single or several, 8–24″ (20–60 cm) tall, branched in upper half, pubescent. Basal leaves are present at flowering, mostly 1–4″ (2.5–10 cm) long, oblanceolate, tapered to a short stalk, tip acute, margins toothed and with fine pale hairs, surfaces more or less pubescent. Stem leaves are smaller, elliptical, sessile. Flowers grow 2–5 per cluster at ends of stem and branches, forming a roughly flat-topped inflorescence. The bracts at bases of flowering heads are distinctly green-tipped. The 3–7 ray flowers are white, 0.25″ (3–6 mm) long; the 9–20 disc flowers are dull white.

White-topped asters (*Sericocarpus*) are immediately distinguished from other asters by the very few ray flowers. Slender White-topped Aster (*S. linifolius*) has much longer rays, and its leaves are more numerous, all of them linear to narrowly elliptic; it occupies the same habitats. These two species are our earliest asters to flower.

Inhabits dry pinelands, pine-oak wood-lands, oak-hickory-dogwood forests. Ranges from ME to OH and KY south to FL and LA.

LATE MAY–MID-JULY

ASTERACEAE: ASTER FAMILY

Twistleaf White-topped Aster; Dixie White-topped Aster

Sericocarpus tortifolius (Michaux) Nees
[*Aster tortifolius* Michaux]

Perennial, stems single or a few together, 1.3–3′ (40–100 cm) tall, branched in the upper fourth, densely pubescent. Basal leaves are not present at flowering. Stem leaves are obovate, sessile, 0.4–1.6″ (1–4 cm) long, usually twisted on axis, tip acute, margins entire, surfaces pubescent. Flowers grow 2–4 per cluster at ends of the stem and branches, forming a roughly flat-topped inflorescence. The bracts at bases of flowering heads are distinctly green-tipped. The 2–5 ray flowers are white, 0.25″ (3–6 mm) long; the 6–11 disc flowers are dull white.

Twistleaf White-topped Aster differs from other white-topped asters by its greater height and short, twisted leaves; at first glance it may remind you of a *Eupatorium*. This Coastal Plain endemic blooms much later than the other two *Sericocarpus*, an example of how the endemic species of the longleaf pine ecosystem often differ markedly from their nearest relatives.

Inhabits dry longleaf pinelands. Ranges on the Coastal Plain from e NC to s FL and w LA.

MID-AUG.–EARLY OCT.

ASTERACEAE: ASTER FAMILY
Slender Daisy-fleabane
Erigeron strigosus Muhl. ex Willd. var. *strigosus*

Winter annual (basal leaves form a rosette in late fall, disappear by blooming time). Stem 1.3–3' (0.4–1 m) tall, branched above, with short, appressed hairs. Leaves are relatively sparse, narrow lance-shaped to narrow elliptic, widest toward tip, 0.1–0.75" (2–18 mm) wide, irregularly toothed or crenate. Flower heads grow in corymbs forming a flat-topped cluster, heads 0.5" (12 mm) across, rays very numerous, white, disc flowers yellow.

As a group, daisy-fleabanes (*Erigeron*) look like asters (*Doellingeria, Eurybia, Ionactis, Symphyotrichum*) but have about twice as many ray flowers per head—a distinctive feature. Fleabanes once were used as pillow stuffing, or simply put under bedcovers, to help control fleas. This is a widespread species with many named variations; the taxonomy is not fully worked out yet.

Inhabits longleaf pinelands and savannas, openings in oak-hickory woods, plus a wide variety of disturbed sites. Ranges from N.S. to WA south to FL and TX.

MAY–OCT.

FABACEAE: PEA & BEAN FAMILY
Summer Farewell
Dalea pinnata (Walter ex J. F. Gmelin)
   Barneby var. *pinnata*
[*Petalostemon pinnatum*
   (Walter ex J. F. Gmelin) Blake]

Perennial, stems glabrous, 1–2' (30–70 cm) tall, short-branched above to form a flattish inflorescence. Leaves numerous, pinnate with terminal leaflet, up to 0.75" (18 mm) long, leaflets 3–11, linear, glabrous. Flowers grow in dense heads, each head flat-topped and with a conspicuous cuplike involucre of overlapping, scalelike bracts. Calyx densely hairy, lobes feathery, silvery white; petals small and inconspicuous, white. Pod obovate, about 2.5 mm long, one-seeded.

At first glance, Summer Farewell does not look like a member of the bean family, due to the obvious bracts around each head and the inconspicuous petals—much like some members of the aster family. The showy calyx lobes remain bright as the plant darkens with fall frosts. Other varieties of this species occur in S GA to S FL and SE LA.

Inhabits dry to very dry longleaf pinelands and turkey oak scrub, especially where burned, also rights-of-way and clearings. Ranges on the Coastal Plain from SE NC to C GA and C FL.

AUG.–NOV.

FABACEAE: PEA & BEAN FAMILY
Erect Milkpea
Galactia erecta (Walter) Vail

Slender erect perennial, stem 8–16″ tall, sparsely hairy. Leaves few, divided into 3 narrow, glabrous leaflets, each 1–2″ (2.5–4 cm) long. Flowers grow in small clusters of 1–6 from leaf axils, white, pea-shaped, about 0.5″ (13 mm) long.

Erect Milkpea is one of many inconspicuous plants in the Sandhills that generously repay efforts to see them—it has lovely architecture. It is our only milkpea that stands erect and our only one with white flowers. The name milkpea and the genus name (from the Greek word *gala*, "milk") is a misnomer for U.S. plants, since none of them have milky latex.

Inhabits dry longleaf pinelands, especially where regularly burned. Ranges on the Coastal Plain from se NC to n FL and e TX.

MID-MAY–EARLY JULY

FABACEAE: PEA & BEAN FAMILY
Tawny Goat's-rue
Tephrosia spicata (Walter) Torrey & Gray

Perennial from a woody taproot, the stem erect to prostrate, with dense tawny hairs. Leaves are few, to 5″ (12 cm) long, divided into 9–17 leaflets. Each leaflet is narrowly elliptic or oblanceolate, 0.5–1″ (12–25 mm) long and 0.25–0.5″ (6–12 mm) wide, more or less hairy. One to several flowers grow at tips of long (longer than leaves) cylindrical stalks from leaf axils. Flowers are pea-shaped, 0.5–0.75″ (12–20 mm) long, white, quickly turning pink and then maroon.

Savanna or Smooth Goat's-rue (*T. florida*) is very similar, but the stem is glabrate or has very short whitish hairs, and flower stalks are flattened lengthwise. It prefers moister habitats such as savannas and streamhead ecotones.

Inhabits dry to mesic longleaf pine communities, oak-hickory woods, roadsides, clearings, and rights-of-way. Ranges on the Coastal Plain and Piedmont from DE to KY south to FL and LA.

JUNE–AUG.

FABACEAE: PEA & BEAN FAMILY
Narrowleaf Bush-clover
Lespedeza angustifolia (Pursh) Elliott

Perennial, stems slender, 1–3′ (0.3–1 m) tall, occasionally taller, with dense, short, appressed hairs. Leaves are very short-stalked; leaflets 3, narrowly elliptic or linear, 0.8–1.6″ (2–4 cm) long and up to 0.25″ (2–6 mm) wide, surfaces usually with dense, short, appressed hairs, tip acute. Flowers grow densely in short-cylindric or roundish clusters (racemes) from axils of upper leaves, the racemes up to 1.2″ (3 cm) long on stalks 0.4–2″ (1–5 cm) long. The calyx has dense, short, spreading hairs; petals are yellowish white, 0.25″ (5–7 mm) long, the banner with a central purple spot.

Bush-clovers as a group often get a bad rap, but that is primarily due to a few invasive alien species. Narrowleaf Bush-clover is quite elegant in its architecture and proportions. Seeds of native bush-clovers are important in the diet of bobwhite quail. Some bush-clovers look similar to some tick-trefoils (*Desmodium*), but bush-clover pods have a single segment (vs. multiple), and all bush-clovers have a stipule (small slender to ovate bract) at the base of each leafstalk (vs. none).

Inhabits dry to moist pine-wiregrass communities and savannas. Ranges on the Coastal Plain from se MA to c FL and s MS; w NC; n GA; ec TN.

AUG.–OCT.

FABACEAE: PEA & BEAN FAMILY
Silvery Bush-clover
Lespedeza capitata Michaux

Perennial, stems single or several, 1.5–5′ (0.5–1.5 m) tall, with dense, short, appressed, silvery hairs; branches normally are few and erect-ascending. Leaves grow on stalks 0.2″ (2–5 mm) long; the 3 leaflets are narrowly elliptic, 0.8–1.4″ (2–3.5 cm) long and 0.25–0.5″ (6–12 mm) wide, the surfaces usually with dense, short, appressed, silvery hairs, tip blunt. Flowers grow densely in elliptical clusters (racemes) from axils of upper leaves, raceme stalks longer than leaves. Petals are yellowish white, 0.3–0.5″ (8–12 mm) long; the banner has a central purple spot. The pod is elliptical with a short point, appressed hairy, single-seeded.

With its striking foliage color, Silvery Bush-clover is a handsome plant. It has a tendency to inhabit moister soils than those preferred by other bush-clovers and is often found near streamheads. Round-leaf Bush-clover (*L. hirta*) has much rounder flower clusters; its hairs are tawny and spread out from the stem (pilose); it has broader leaflets (elliptic to roundish); and it occupies dry habitats. A coastal plain variety, *L. hirta* var. *curtissii*, has silvery hairs on leaves, but they are not as striking as in Silvery Bush-clover, and leaflets are rotund.

Inhabits moist or seasonally moist longleaf pinelands and streamhead margins. Ranges from s ME to s Ont. and sD south to nw FL and TX.

AUG.–OCT.

FABACEAE: PEA & BEAN FAMILY
Dwarf Indigo-bush
Amorpha herbacea Walter var. *herbacea*

Perennial shrub, single- or multistemmed, to 4.5′ (1.5 m) tall, densely pubescent. Leaves are compound, up to 10″ (24 cm) long. Leaflets are numerous, opposite plus a terminal leaflet, elliptic, 0.4–1″ (1–2.5 cm) long, pubescent, with many glandular dots (use 10x hand lens). Flowers are small but very numerous in terminal spikes up to 8″ (20 cm) long, white, anthers yellow or orange-yellow.

Dwarf Indigo-bush is a frequent member of the sc Sandhills and the eastern part of the GA Sandhills but is curiously rare in the NC Sandhills (only two populations known).

Inhabits longleaf pinelands and flatwoods where burned periodically. Ranges on the Coastal Plain from e NC to e GA to c FL.

MID-MAY–EARLY JULY

APIACEAE: CARROT FAMILY
Downy Angelica
Angelica venenosa (Greenway) Fernald

Perennial from a taproot, stem 1–2.5′ (30–80 cm) tall, occasionally taller, usually unbranched, upper parts pubescent. Leaves are few, well-spaced, bipinnate (twice pinnately divided), with elliptic or lance-shaped leaflets up to 2″ (5 cm) long and 0.8″ (2 cm) wide, finely toothed. The base of the leafstalk is expanded around the stem. Flowers occur in twice-divided umbels that bear tiny white flowers. That is, the main stalk is split at its tip into numerous shorter stalks (rays), each ray 1–2″ (0.8–5 cm) long and split at its tip into very short rays tipped with flowers.

Downy Angelica is uncommon in our area, since it is primarily a Piedmont and Mountain plant. As in the similar Queen-Anne's-Lace (*Daucus carota*), the individual flowers are tiny, but the whole umbel is showy. However, Angelica grows only in natural woodlands, not disturbed roadsides and fields.

Inhabits loamy soils of flats and bean dips in longleaf pinelands and oak-hickory forests. Ranges from w MA to s MN south to nw FL, s MS, and s AR.

MID-JUNE–AUG.

APIACEAE: CARROT FAMILY
Rattlesnake Master; Button Snakeroot

Eryngium yuccifolium Michaux var. *yuccifolium*

Perennial, plants solitary or forming clumps of several together. Stem single, to 3.5′ (1.2 m) tall (sometimes taller), branched above. Lower leaves very stiff, parallel-veined, broadly linear, to 27″ (0.8 m) long, 0.4–1.2″ (1–3 cm) wide, tip acuminate, margins with bristly spines arranged singly (not two together); stem leaves much smaller. Flowers grow densely in heads subtended by sharp-tipped leafy bracts. Heads are rounded, about 0.4–0.8″ (10–20 mm) across, petals 5, greenish white.

The Latin name comes from the close resemblance of the leaves to those of yucca plants (*Yucca* spp.). The origin of the common names is obscure; perhaps their clumped leaves provide temporary shelter for snakes.

Inhabits dry to seasonally moist long-leaf pinelands and savannas, oak-hickory woods and openings. Ranges from NJ to MN south to FL and TX.

JUNE–AUG.

LAMIACEAE: MINT FAMILY
Savanna Mountain-mint

Pycnanthemum flexuosum (Walter) B.S.P.

Perennial, stems 4-angled, 1.3–3.5′ (0.4–1.1 m) tall, with white hairs, upwardly branched. Leaves are opposite, well-spaced, broadly lanceolate to elliptic, 0.6–2″ (1.5–5 cm) long, tip acute, base short-tapered, each margin with 1–4 blunt teeth, leafstalks up to 0.25 (5 mm) long. Flowers grow in a flat-topped inflorescence of headlike clusters 0.8–1.6″ (2–4 cm) wide, each cluster with several leafy, pointed bracts at base. Individual flowers have 5 sharp calyx lobes about 0.3″ (7 mm) long, the 5 petals white, about 0.25″ (5 mm) long, the 3 lower petals forming a lip and spotted with pale lavender.

Close inspection of mountain-mint flowers reveals intricate shapes (like an orchid) and bold spotting. This species differs from others in our region by its lack of (or faint) pungent minty odor and by its headlike flower clusters.

Inhabits dryish to moist longleaf pine-lands, savannas, and streamhead margins. Ranges on the Coastal Plain from se VA to n FL and s AL; disjunct to sw NC; c TN.

LATE JUNE–SEPT.

EUPHORBIACEAE:
EUPHORBIA & SPURGE FAMILY
White Sandhill-spurge
Euphorbia curtisii Engelmann

Perennial, very slender, hairless plant
from a thick rootstock, sap milky white.
Stem up to 18″ (50 cm), widely branched,
lower branches alternate, upper branches
opposite. Lower leaves are reduced and
bractlike; upper leaves are linear to
lanceolate, 0.4–2.4″ (1–6 cm) long and
0.1–0.75″ (1–15 mm) wide, opposite. Flowers grow on long stalks at ends of branches
and from leaf axils, petals absent, replaced
by tiny (1 mm), white, modified glands
that look like petals, 0.1–0.2″ (2–4 mm)
broad.

This plant was named for Moses Ashley
Curtis, a nineteenth- century botanist and
clergyman from NC. Purple Sandhill-
spurge (*E. exserta*) is very similar, but
the plant is gray-green and the petal-like
glands are purple or maroon; it grows in
similar habitats. The thick storage roots
of these species ensure survival following
fire.

Inhabits dry longleaf pinelands and
turkey oak scrub, especially where burned.
Ranges from se NC to nw FL.

LATE MAR.–EARLY JUNE

EUPHORBIACEAE:
EUPHORBIA & SPURGE FAMILY
Southern Flowering-spurge
Euphorbia pubentissima Michaux

Perennial from a thick rootstock, sap
milky white. Stems up to 2′ (60 cm) tall
(occasionally taller), branched above,
smooth to densely pilose. Lower leaves
alternate, middle and upper leaves mostly
opposite, linear to elliptic, 0.8–2.4″ (2–6
cm) long and 0.2–1.2″ (5–30 mm) wide,
nearly sessile. Flowers grow on long
stalks at ends of branches and from leaf
axils, 0.2–0.4″ (3–8 mm) broad, petals
absent, replaced by small (less than 0.2″,
1–4 mm), white, modified glands that
look like petals.

Although all spurges produce flowers,
the "petals" of this one are large enough
to attract attention. In autumn, the foliage
often turns bright red.

Inhabits dry longleaf pinelands,
oak-hickory woods, rights-of-way, and
clearings. Ranges from MD to TN south
to nw FL and s MS.

LATE MAR.–JULY

VERBENACEAE
Carolina Vervain

Stylodon carneus (Medikus) Moldenke
[*Verbena carnea* Medikus]

Perennial, the stems 4-angled, erect, ascending, or trailing and with the terminal portion erect, usually unbranched, 1–2.3′ (30–70 cm) tall (occasionally taller), densely glandular-pubescent terminally. Leaves are opposite, oblanceolate to elliptic, 1.6–3.6″ (4–9 cm) long and 0.5–1.2″ (1.2–3 cm) wide, tip blunt to acute, base tapered, margins toothed. Flowers grow in a long terminal spike 6–16″ (15–40 cm) long, the erect flower tube pink to lavender-pink and curved; the 5 white flaring lobes are 0.25″ (4–6 mm) long, the lowest lobe longest.

Carolina Vervain is the sole species in its genus, differing from the large genus *Verbena* in details of seeds and flowers; unlike the latter, it has become adapted to fire-maintained habitats.

Inhabits longleaf pinelands, pine-oak woodlands, and savannas, often in loamy sand soil. Ranges on the Coastal Plain from se NC to c FL and e TX.

LATE APR.–EARLY JULY

ORCHIDACEAE: ORCHID FAMILY
Little Ladies'-tresses

Spiranthes tuberosa Rafinesque

Perennial, slender, fleshy-textured, stems mostly 10–28″ (25–70 cm) tall, slender, glabrous. Leaves are linear, erect, 1–2.5″ (2.5–6.5 cm) long and 0.25–0.6″ (6–15 mm) wide, glabrous, reduced in size upward, the basal ones often withered by blooming period. Flowers grow in a loose to dense, twisted spiral up to 6″ (15 cm) long (usually half that). The 3 sepals and 3 petals are less than 0.2″ (2–3.5 mm) long (lip petal longest and widest), curved outward at tip, white. The lip is ovate to broadly elliptic, 1.5–2 mm wide, strongly curved downward, the margin minutely frilled.

The flowers of Little Ladies'-tresses are incredibly small, especially when we realize it is an orchid, yet hundreds of orchid flowers the world over are even smaller! It occupies the driest habitats of any of our orchids.

Inhabits dry longleaf pinelands, mixed pine-oak-hickory woods, sometimes even turkey oak barrens. Ranges from MA to OH and MO south to s FL and e TX.

JUNE–SEPT.

CONVOLVULACEAE:
MORNING-GLORY FAMILY
Sandhill Morning-glory;
Sandhill Dawnflower

Stylisma patens (Desr.) Myint ssp. *patens*

Trailing, perennial, nonclimbing vine
without tendrils. The few to many stems
are prostrate, up to 4′ (1.2 m) long. Leaves
are elliptic to narrowly elliptic, up to 2″
(5 cm) long and 0.4″ (1 cm) wide, with
short, appressed hairs. Flowers grow singly on erect slender stalks from leaf axils.
The 5-parted calyx is pubescent; the 5
white petals form a funnel-shaped corolla
about 0.75″ (2 cm) across, subtended by
two short bracts.

Dawnflowers are diminutive relatives of
familiar morning-glories (genus *Ipomoea*)
of roadsides and cropfields. Narrowleaf
Dawnflower (*S. patens* ssp. *angustifolia*)
is similar but has linear leaves (often
oriented vertically) and a glabrous calyx;
it occurs in the same habitats.

Inhabits dry to very dry longleaf pinelands and sandhills, especially where
wiregrass is abundant and fire-managed.
Ranges discontinuously from e NC to n FL
and s MS.

JUNE–AUG.

ERICACEAE: BLUEBERRY & AZALEA FAMILY
Trailing Arbutus

Epigaea repens L.

Perennial, prostrate shrublet with trailing branches, most of plant with brown,
stiffish (hispid), spreading hairs. Leaves
alternate, evergreen (but develop brown
patches in winter), elliptic, 1.2–3.2″ (3–8
cm) long and 0.8–1.6″ (2–4 cm) wide.
Leaves often with the tip or one margin
oriented upward, leafstalks 0.4–2″ (1–5
cm) long. Flowers grow in terminal clusters, each flower from a short stalk, petals
white or pinkish, forming a tube 0.25–0.5″
(6–10 mm) long with spreading lobes,
sweetly fragrant.

Everyone loves Trailing Arbutus but
seldom sees it flowering because it blooms
so early. A pity, for the fragrance is like
Lily-of-the-Valley (*Convallaria* spp.)—
kneel down to savor it! *Epigaea* is a small
but far-flung genus, with a second species
in Japan and a third in the Caucasus
Mountains.

Inhabits dry longleaf pinelands and
oak-hickory woods. Ranges from Newf.
to Sask. south to n FL, MS, and IA.

LATE FEB.–EARLY APR.

ERICACEAE: BLUEBERRY & AZALEA FAMILY
Narrowleaf Blueberry

Vaccinium tenellum Aiton

Perennial, colonial, woody shrub, 4–20″ (10–50 cm) tall, much-branched, the twigs densely pubescent. Leaves are deciduous, oblanceolate, 0.6–1.6″ (1.5–4 cm) long and 0.25–0.8″ (6–18 mm) wide, tip acute and with a tiny sharp point. Leaf surfaces are dull (not lustrous); undersides have scattered, gland-tipped hairs; and margins are finely toothed. Flowers grow in clusters of 5–15, or several clusters grow on a long terminal shoot, just prior to or with leaf-out. Each flower is short-stalked, cylindrical, the 5 petals reddish to whitish, 0.25–0.3″ (5–8 mm) long, tips acute and curled back. Berries are black, glaucescent, 0.25–0.3″ (5–8 mm), juicy, and sweet.

Narrowleaf Blueberry is one of our most common plants, often forming large patches. It tolerates fire very well. See Hillside Blueberry for how to tell the two apart. Dwarf Huckleberry (*Gaylussacia dumosa*) can look very similar, but its leaves are lustrous above and have golden resin dots on both surfaces.

Inhabits dry to moist soils of pine flatwoods, longleaf pine–wiregrass uplands, and upper margins of streamheads. Ranges on the Coastal Plain and lower Piedmont from se VA to sc GA and se MS.

LATE MAR.–EARLY MAY

ASTERACEAE: ASTER FAMILY
Eastern Greeneyes

Berlandiera pumila (Michaux) Nuttall var. *pumila*

Perennial from thick, fleshy roots, stems single or several from a crown, 1.3–3′ (0.4–1 m) tall, pubescent. Leaf blades are ovate to elliptical from a short stalk, 2.4–5.2″ (6–13 cm) long and 0.8–2.8″ (2–7 cm) wide, margins wavy, crenate (with small rounded teeth, or scalloped), base cordate or squared off, blade densely pubescent beneath. Flower heads grow singly from long stalks, each head with wide, thick-textured bracts at base. Ray flowers are yellow, 0.4–1.2″ (1–3 cm) long and with a notched tip. Disc flowers are green, turning yellowish or reddish.

Greeneyes gets it common name from the green center of the flower head, a rare feature among our members of the aster family. Jean Louis Berlandier (1805–51) was a Belgian botanist and explorer of the Louisiana Territory and Texas.

Inhabits dry longleaf pinelands, oak barrens, and roadsides. Ranges on the Coastal Plain from n SC to wc GA (Taylor County) to n FL, se TX, se OK, and sw AR.

LATE MAY–OCT.

ASTERACEAE: ASTER FAMILY
Rosinweed

Silphium compositum Michaux var. *compositum*

Glabrous perennial, the stem 2–6′ (0.6–2 m) tall, fleshy textured. Basal leaves are prostrate or ascending, the blades broadly ovate to round, 4–12″ (10–30 cm) long, slightly less wide, the base cordate, veins usually reddish. Leaf margins are deeply lobed, each lobe often toothed. Stem leaves are absent, or there might be just a few small ones, nearly sessile. Flower heads grow in small groups at tips of short to long branches from the top of the stem; usually only one flower per group blooms at a time. Ray flowers are 0.4–0.8″ (1–2 cm) long and 0.2″ (3–5 mm) wide, yellow; disc flowers are dull yellow. The bracts of the head are broad, green, and succulent.

With its deeply lobed, rhubarblike leaves, naked stem, and spreading flowering branches, Rosinweed seems to have come from another planet. In fact, it is the easternmost representative of a mostly midwestern group of plants with names like Prairie Dock, Cup Plant, and Compass Plant.

Inhabits dry to very dry longleaf pinelands, roadsides, rights-of-way, and even fallow fields. Ranges on the Coastal Plain and Piedmont from se VA to se GA.

EARLY JUNE–MID-SEPT.

ASTERACEAE: ASTER FAMILY
Whorled Tickseed; Whorled Coreopsis

Coreopsis major Walter var. *rigida*
  (Nuttall) Boynton

Glabrous or glabrate perennial, stems 1–2.5′ (0.3–0.8 m) tall. Leaves opposite and sessile, each pair appearing to be a whorl of 6 "leaves" due to the division of each leaf into 3 segments. Leaf segments are narrowly to broadly lance-shaped, 1.2–3″ (3–8 cm) long and 0.25–0.8″ (5–20 mm) wide, tapered to the tip, margins toothless. Flower heads are produced on erect, slender stalks forming a flattish array, ray flowers yellow, 0.8–1.5″ (2–4 cm) long, disc flowers dull yellow or brownish red.

Whorled Tickseed is one of our showiest flowers, especially when found in a dense grouping. Although quite tolerant of fire, it is by no means restricted to such environments. Its beauty and long blooming period have earned it a place in horticulture.

Inhabits dry to moist longleaf pinelands and savannas, oak-hickory forests, rights-of-way, and roadsides, as well as rocky slopes in the Piedmont. Ranges from VA to KY south to FL and LA.

LATE MAY–AUG.

ASTERACEAE: ASTER FAMILY
Purpledisc Sunflower

Helianthus atrorubens L.

Perennial, stem solitary (sometimes a few), 2.5–5′ (0.7–1.5 m) tall, hispid hairy basally, less so above, not much branched. Basal and lower stem leaves are crowded, opposite, ovate to rhombic, 2.4–8″ (6–20 cm) long and 1.2–4″ (3–10 cm) wide, surfaces scabrous, margins crenate, leaf-stalk widely winged. Mid- to upper stem leaves are much smaller, sparse, alternate, similarly scabrous. Flowering heads are terminal; disc flowers are dark purple, about 0.6″ (15 mm) across; ray flowers are bright yellow, 1.2–2″ (3–5 cm) long.

The name *atrorubens* means "black red," alluding to the deep purple or deep maroon disc flowers. Some plants have so few stem leaves that at first glance they appear to lack them.

Inhabits dry to moist longleaf pinelands, pine savannas, oak-hickory woodlands, and roadsides. Ranges from VA to w TN south to nw FL and se LA.

LATE JULY–OCT.

ASTERACEAE: ASTER FAMILY
Squarehead

Tetragonotheca helianthoides L.

Perennial from a thick taproot, stem solitary or a few together, erect to ascending, 1–3′ (30–90 cm) tall, few-branched, pubescent. Leaves are opposite, elliptic to ovate, 4–7″ (10–17 cm) long and mostly 1.6–4.5″ (4–11 cm) wide, margins toothed, tip acute, base abruptly narrowed to a short, winged stalk. Upper stem leaves are sessile. Flower heads are solitary and terminal, the outer 4 bracts angular-ovate, up to 1.2″ (3 cm) long and 1″ (2.5 cm) wide. There are 6–14 yellow rays, well-separated from one another, 1.2–2″ (3–5 cm) long; disc flowers are yellow.

Squarehead gets its name from the 4 outer bracts just beneath the flower head, which form a square pattern when viewed from above. The bracts and the well-spaced ray flowers give this plant an unmistakable look.

Inhabits loamy sand soil of longleaf pineland flats and bean dips, occurring down to the upper margins of streamheads. Ranges on the Coastal Plain from se VA to c FL and s MS; scattered inland to w NC, w SC, n GA, and e TN.

MAY–JUNE

ASTERACEAE: ASTER FAMILY
Maryland Golden-aster

Chrysopsis mariana L.
[*Heterotheca mariana* (L.) Shinners]

Perennial, often several stems are clumped together; stems erect, up to 2′ (0.7 m) tall. Lower leaves are oblanceolate to elliptic, tapered to a stalk, toothed, 1.5–4.5″ (3.5–11 cm) long, gradually smaller up the stem and becoming stalkless. Stems and leaves are moderately to sparsely covered with cobwebby white hairs. Flower heads grow at stem tips; each head is 1.5–2″ (3.5–5 cm) across, composed of dark yellow disc flowers and lighter yellow ray flowers.

Maryland Golden-aster is very adaptable and has spread into many human-disturbed habitats. Vegetative parts are far less hairy than Gossamer Golden-aster, and stems are erect, never prostrate.

Inhabits dry longleaf pinelands, oak-hickory forests, old fields, roadsides, rights-of-way, and yards. Ranges from s RI to s OH south to c FL and e TX.

LATE JUNE–OCT.

ASTERACEAE: ASTER FAMILY
Sticky Golden-aster

Pityopsis aspera (Shuttleworth ex Small) Small
[*Heterotheca adenolepis* (Fernald) Ahles;
    H. graminifolia (Michaux) Shinners, in part]

Perennial from a rhizome, the stem slender, to 1.5′ (0.5 m) tall, stem and branches with dense, gland-tipped hairs. Leaves are numerous and grasslike, the lower ones 2–10″ (5–25 cm) long and less than 0.5″ (12 mm) wide, rapidly reduced in size up the stem. All leaves are silky pubescent, which imparts a silvery sheen. Flower heads are produced on long branches from upper part of stem, each head 0.5″ (12 mm) wide, discs and rays yellow, the flower stalk and flower bracts with dense gland-tipped hairs.

Grass-leaved Golden-aster (*P. graminifolia* var. *latifolia*) is similar but larger in all dimensions; it lacks gland-tipped hairs on stems and flower stalks and usually grows in dense clonal patches.

Common in very dry to dry sandy soils of longleaf pinelands, turkey oak scrub, and ancient dunes. Ranges on inner Coastal Plain and Piedmont from c VA to ne AL south to n FL and se MS.

LATE JULY–OCT.

ASTERACEAE: ASTER FAMILY
Maryland Hawkweed

Hieracium marianum Willdenow

Perennial, stems 8–24″ (20–60 cm) tall, widely branched above, densely hairy below but becoming glabrate above, sap milky white. Basal leaves several at ground level, oblanceolate or elliptic, 1.6–5″ (4–12.5 cm) long and 0.4–1.7″ (1–4.5 cm) wide, pilose on upper surface, margins more or less toothed. The upper surface of the basal leaves sometimes shows purplish veins. Stem leaves vary from one to several, reduced in size up the stem. Flower heads grow at ends of branches to form a broad flattish corymb, the heads 0.5–0.75″ (12–18 mm) across, composed only of yellow ray flowers, disc flowers absent.

Beaked Hawkweed (*H. gronovii*) is very similar but blooms in the fall; the inflorescence forms a narrow panicle, and its stem is hairy throughout.

Inhabits dry, often disturbed sandy or gravelly soils of pinelands, oak-hickory forests, roadsides, yards, and fields. Ranges from NH to OH south to FL and MS.

LATE APR.–JULY, OCCASIONALLY LATER

ASTERACEAE: ASTER FAMILY
Slender Flat-topped Goldenrod

Euthamia caroliniana (L.) Greene
[*Solidago microcephala* (Greene) Bush]

Perennial from long rhizomes, often forming colonies. Stem single, 1–2.5′ (0.3–0.8 m) tall, branched above to form a flat-topped inflorescence. Leaves numerous, linear, 0.8–2.8″ (2–7 cm) long and 1–3 mm wide, 1-veined, usually curved, with fascicles (clusters) of small leaves in axils. Heads 8–12 flowered, about 0.25″ (4 mm) wide, ray and disc flowers yellow.

In contrast with other goldenrods (*Solidago* spp.), those in the genus *Euthamia* produce a distinctive flat-topped inflorescence of small flowers and are immediately recognizable.

Inhabits a wide range of soils and situations, from dry longleaf pinelands to seasonally wet depressions to wet flat-woods; also weedy in abandoned fields, rights-of-way, etc. Ranges on the Coastal Plain and lower Piedmont from S ME to S FL and se LA.

LATE AUG.–OCT.

ASTERACEAE: ASTER FAMILY
Fragrant Goldenrod
Solidago odora Aiton

Glabrate perennial, stems 1.5–3′ (0.5–1 m) tall (taller where not burned), leaning or erect, the upper portion arching, unbranched. There are no basal leaves. Stem leaves are lanceolate, 1.2–4″ (3–10 cm) long and 0.2–1″ (5–25 mm) wide, tip acuminate, base short-tapered or rounded, sessile, with odor of anise when crushed. Flowers grow in a terminal, branched inflorescence, pyramid-shaped. Ray flowers are yellow, less than 0.2″ (2–4 mm) long; disc yellow.

Fragrant Goldenrod is one of our most common goldenrods, found in a wide variety of habitats. Crushed leaves delight people with the scent of licorice or anise.

Inhabits dry to moist longleaf pinelands, pine flatwoods, oak-hickory woods, clearings, and rights-of-way. Ranges from NH to OH and MO south to FL and TX.

AUG.–OCT.

FABACEAE: PEA & BEAN FAMILY
Carolina Wild-indigo
Baptisia cinerea (Rafinesque) Fernald & Schubert

Perennial from a thick rhizome, most of the plant covered with short, appressed, silvery-tawny hairs. Stems single or several together, 1–2′ (30–70 cm) long, leaning or sprawling, wide-branched, with relatively few leaves. Leaves have long petioles (leafstalks); the 3 leaflets are elliptic, up to 3.5″ (9 cm) long and about 1″ (2.5 cm) wide. Flowers form dense, more or less cylindrical, terminal clusters at tips of stems and branches. The corolla is pea-shaped, bright yellow, 1″ (2.5 cm) long. Pods are 1–1.25″ (about 3 cm) long, round in cross section, tapered at the tip.

Carolina Wild-indigo is one of the showiest plants of the Carolinas, and fortunately it is quite common. After frost, the plant turns silvery gray and acts like a tumbleweed in winter. Lanceleaf Wild-indigo (*B. lanceolata*) replaces Carolina Wild-indigo in GA and southward. It is similar but grows taller, has much longer, lance-shaped leaflets, and blooms a month earlier; it ranges from S SC to SW GA and N FL.

Inhabits dry longleaf pinelands and turkey oak barrens. Ranges on the Coastal Plain from SE VA to S SC.

MAY–MID-JUNE

FABACEAE: PEA & BEAN FAMILY
Northern Wild-indigo

Baptisia tinctoria (L.) R. Brown

Perennial from a thick rhizome, glabrous, stem mostly 2–3′ (0.6–1 m) tall, erect, bushy-branched. Leaves are divided into 3 leaflets, each leaflet obovate, 0.25–0.8″ (6–20 mm) long. Flowers grow in few-flowered racemes at branch tips, the petals 0.4–0.6″ (9–16 mm) long, bright yellow. Pods are roundish, less than 0.4″ (10 mm) long.

Many species of *Baptisia* yield a dark juice that has been used as an inferior substitute for indigo dye (*Indigofera tinctoria* L.), an African plant formerly cultivated in the outer Coastal Plain. Native Americans used extracts of Northern Wild-indigo as a purgative and to heal wounds and treat toothaches.

Inhabits dry pinelands and oak-hickory forests. Ranges from s ME to MN south to n FL and LA.

APR.–AUG.

FABACEAE: PEA & BEAN FAMILY
Viperina

Zornia bracteata Walter ex J. F. Gmelin

Perennial, stems several to many, radiating erratically from a central point, erect or ascending or trailing, 8–32″ (20–80 cm) long. Leaves are palmately divided into 4 (sometimes 3 or fewer) leaflets. Each leaflet is linear to elliptical, 0.4–1.2″(1–3 cm) long, glabrous or with short, appressed hairs on midvein, acute. Three to 10 pea-shaped flowers grow in spikes 1.2–6″ (3–15 cm) long, each flower enveloped by a pair of ovate, appressed bracts 0.3–0.6″ (7–15 mm) long. Petals are deep yellow, 0.4–0.6″ (9–14 mm) long. The pod is 0.4–0.8″ (1–2 cm) long, with 2–6 segments, bristly hairy.

The sprawling stems, deep yellow flowers, and large flower bracts make this plant distinctive, but it occurs sporadically on the landscape. *Zornia bracteata* is the northernmost of some 75 species in the genus, most occurring in the tropics.

Inhabits dry longleaf pinelands, turkey oak scrub, and roadsides. Ranges on the Coastal Plain from se VA to s FL and c TX.

JUNE–AUG.

FABACEAE: PEA & BEAN FAMILY
Pursh's Rattlebox
Crotalaria purshii DC.

Perennial, 8–19″ (20–50 cm) tall, with
dense, upwardly appressed hairs. Leaves
are unlobed, the upper ones narrowly
lance-shaped, 1.2–2.4″ (3–6 cm) long and
0.2–0.4″ (4–10 mm) wide, the lower ones
broader. Stipules (paired appendages at
base of leaf) form wings on stem, their
sharp tips pointing upward. Several flowers grow on a stalk to 4.8″ (12 cm) long,
petals yellow, about 0.4–0.5″ (6 mm) long.
Pod 1–1.6″ (2.5–4 cm) long and 0.4″ (1 cm)
thick.

No other plant in our area has such
distinctive, arrow-shaped stipules. Pursh's
Rattlebox is named for Frederick Pursh,
early nineteenth-century botanist and
explorer. It has not yet been found in the
GA Sandhills.

Inhabits dry longleaf pinelands
(including bean dips) and openings in
oak-hickory forests; sometimes found on
roadsides. Ranges mostly on the Coastal
Plain from se VA to n FL and se LA, scattered inland to se TN, w NC, w SC, n GA.

MAY–MID-JULY

FABACEAE: PEA & BEAN FAMILY
Rabbitbells; Low Rattlebox
Crotalaria rotundifolia Walter ex J. F. Gmelin

Perennial, stems few to many, prostrate
to ascending, 4–16″ (10–40 cm) tall, with
dense spreading hairs. Leaves unlobed,
oval to rounded, 0.4–1.2″ (1–3 cm) long;
stipules usually absent. Several flowers
grow on a stalk to 6″ (15 cm) long, petals
pale to medium yellow, about 0.5″ (14 mm)
long. Pod 0.8–1.2″ (2–3 cm) long and 0.4″
(1 cm) thick.

Rabbitbells is easily distinguished from
Pursh's Rattlebox by its reclining stems
and lack of prominent stipules. The name
rattlebox is derived from the dried pods,
whose seeds make a rattling sound when
shaken.

Inhabits dry longleaf pinelands, openings in oak-hickory woods, and sometimes roadsides and rights-of-way. Ranges
from se VA to c FL and se LA; Mex.

LATE APR.–AUG.

FABACEAE: PEA & BEAN FAMILY
Dollarweed; Roundleaf Snoutbean
Rhynchosia reniformis DC.

Short-stemmed (appearing stemless) perennial, stem densely hairy, leaves less so. Leaves are closely spaced, often appearing to be just a basal rosette, the blades rounded to kidney-shaped, 0.75–2″ (2–5 cm) long and wide, undivided, long-stalked. Flowers are pealike, bright yellow, about 0.5″ (12 mm) long, growing densely in leaf axils and terminally. Flower stalks are short (1.5–3 mm) and exceeded by a slender bract. Pods are densely hairy, 0.4–0.7″ (1–1.8 cm) long, with only 2–3 peas within.

Dollarweed is instantly recognizable by its rotund or kidney-shaped, undivided leaves about the size of a silver dollar, set close to the ground, and its very short pods. "Snoutbean" is derived from the genus name; *rhynchos* is Greek for "beak."

Inhabits a variety of longleaf pine and pine-oak communities in dry to mesic soils. Ranges on the Coastal Plain from se NC to s FL and e TX; disjunct to e TN.

JUNE–SEPT.

FABACEAE: PEA & BEAN FAMILY
Erect Snoutbean
Rhynchosia tomentosa (L.) Hooker & Arnott

Erect perennial, stems densely to sparsely hairy. Leaves are relatively few, short- to long-stalked, 3-parted. The leaflets are ovate to rhombic or elliptic, 0.75–2.7″ (2–7 cm) long and about half as wide, velvety hairy beneath, veins prominent. Flowers are pealike, yellow, about 0.5″ (12 mm) long, growing densely in leaf axils and also terminally. Flower stalks are short (1.5–3 mm) and exceeded by a slender bract. Pods are densely hairy, 0.4–0.7″ (1–1.8 cm) long, with only 2–3 peas within.

Rhynchos means "beak" or "snout" in Greek, in reference to the short, pointy tip on each pod. The legume family is fourth in number of species in most southeastern U.S. habitats, after the aster family, grasses, and sedges. Legumes are vitally important as nitrogen-fixers in soil and as food for animals.

Inhabits dry to mesic soils of longleaf pine and pine-oak communities. Ranges on the Coastal Plain and Piedmont from DE to TN south to n FL and LA.

JUNE–AUG.

FABACEAE: PEA & BEAN FAMILY
Pencil Flower
Stylosanthes biflora (L.) B.S.P.

Perennial, stems vary from single to many, ascending to erect, to 20″ (50 cm) tall, glabrate to hairy. Leaves are well-spaced, on short stalks, divided into 3 lanceolate to broadly linear leaflets 0.6–1.6″ (1.5–4 cm) long, the terminal leaflet longest, the tip with a projecting point. Prominent stipules clasp the junction of leafstalks and stem; they are 0.4–0.6″ (10–15 mm) long with a needlelike tip, finely pubescent. One to several flowers grow terminally, pea-shaped, the petals yellow to deep yellow, the standard 0.2–0.3″ (5–9 mm) long.

The name Pencil Flower has an obscure origin, but perhaps it derives from the generic name *stylos*, Greek for "column," which refers to the shape of the calyx tube; *stylo* is a common French term for pen or pencil. A tropical genus of some 25 species, this is our only one.

Inhabits dry pinelands, pine-oak woodlands, and turkey oak scrub, as well as roadsides and disturbed ground. Ranges from S NY to KS south to C FL and TX.

LATE MAY–AUG.

FABACEAE: PEA & BEAN FAMILY
Sensitive Partridge-pea;
Wild Sensitive-plant
Chamaecrista nictitans (L.) Moench
[*Cassia nictitans* L.]

Annual herb from a slender taproot, to 18″ (0.5 m) tall, with spreading branches. Leaves are finely divided into 20–36 linear to narrowly elliptic leaflets. Each leaflet is 0.3–0.7″ (6–15 mm) long and less than 0.2″ (1–4 mm) wide, more or less sensitive to touch. Flowers grow in axils, mostly solitary, not pea-shaped, the 5 yellow petals very unequal, the largest 0.3–0.35″ (6–8 mm) long, stamens 5. Pods are 0.8–1.6″ (2–4 cm) long and 0.2–0.25″ (3–6 mm) wide.

Sensitive Partridge-pea is about half the size of Common Partridge-pea. It also is weedy but often inhabits natural communities.

Inhabits lightly burned pinelands and openings, roadsides, rights-of-way, cropfields, yards, and logging roads; also shores of depression ponds and vernal pools. Ranges from MA to OH and KS south to FL and TX; Mex.

MID-JUNE–EARLY OCT.

HYPERICACEAE: ST. JOHN'S-WORT FAMILY
St. Andrew's Cross
Hypericum hypericoides (L.) Crantz

Perennial slender shrub to 3′ (1 m) tall, with several branches, bark reddish brown and shreddy. Leaves opposite and sessile, lance-shaped to narrowly elliptic, 0.3–1″ (8–25 mm) long and 0.1–0.3″ (2–7 mm) wide, tip acute or blunt, base tapered. Flowers grow singly or a few together on a stalk (less than 0.25″ [1–5 mm]) from leaf axils. The 2 outer sepals are ovate, 0.25–0.5″ (6–12 mm) long and 0.2–0.3 (4–7 mm) wide, acute; the 2 inner sepals are very small or absent. The 4 petals are yellow, 0.25–0.4″ (6–10 mm) long. Capsules are brown, dry, persisting into winter.

Unlike our other *Hypericum* species, this and St. Peter's Cross have only 4 petals, arranged in an X pattern. St. Andrew is the patron saint of Scotland, and the X pattern is retained in the national flag. Both are common plants with wide ecological tolerances.

Inhabits dry to moist pinelands, oak-hickory woods, and flatwoods, but sometimes also in wetter situations such as seepage slopes and cypress-gum swamps. Ranges from NJ to KY and MO south to s FL and e TX; West Indies; Mex.; Central America.

LATE MAY–SEPT.

HYPOXIDACEAE: STARGRASS FAMILY
Pineland Stargrass
Hypoxis wrightii (Baker) Brackett

Stemless perennial from a small bulb and fleshy roots. Leaves grasslike, up to 12″ (30 cm) long and 0.25″ (5 mm) wide, usually folded lengthwise, tip attenuate, sparsely to moderately pubescent. One to 2 flowers grow atop a stalk less than half as long as the leaves. The 3 petals and 3 sepals are alike, yellow, mostly 0.2–0.3″ (4–8 mm) long and 0.2″ (2–3 mm) wide. Fruit is a green capsule 0.2–0.3″ (4–8 mm) long, with dark brown seeds covered with short pointed bumps (tuberculate).

Pineland Stargrass often is overlooked because its flower(s) grows on such a short stalk—sometimes only half an inch—that it is nearly hidden. It responds rapidly to burning and may bloom while the ground is still charred black.

Inhabits dry to moist longleaf pinelands. Ranges on the Coastal Plain from e NC to s FL and e TX; West Indies.

LATE MAR.–APR.

XYRIDACEAE: YELLOW-EYED-GRASS FAMILY
Carolina Yellow-eyed-grass
Xyris caroliniana Walter

Slender perennial, stem solitary or several together, mostly 1–2.5′ (30–75 cm) tall, twisted into a spiral, its base deep into the soil and swollen. Leaves are all basal, erect to spreading, 2-ranked, linear, twisted, 8–20″ (20–50 cm) long and about 0.2″ (2–4 mm) wide. Leaf surfaces are smooth, margins minutely bumpy (papillose), the basal portion brownish and lustrous. Flowers grow 1–3 at a time from a narrowly elliptical, conelike head atop the stem, the head tapering to both ends, 0.4–1.2″ (10–30 mm) long and composed of overlapping brown scales. The 3 petals are yellow, obovate, 0.3–0.4″ (8–10 mm) long, opening in afternoon.

Yellow-eyed-grasses are not grasses (family Poaceae) but belong to an unrelated family. They are instantly recognizable due to the conspicuous yellow flowers on a scaly "cone" atop a naked stem. With some 25 species, the U.S. Coastal Plain is a center for diversity in *Xyris*. Carolina Yellow-eyed-grass inhabits drier sites than our other species and blooms earlier.

Inhabits dry to moist longleaf pinelands and savannas, and upper margins of streamheads. Ranges on the Coastal Plain from se VA to S FL and e TX; S NJ; ne AL; w Cuba.

JUNE–JULY

LINACEAE: FLAX FAMILY
Savanna Flax
Linum floridanum (Planchon) Trelease
   var. *floridanum*

Slender, glabrous perennial, stems 1–3, in our region 1–2′ (30–60 cm) tall, potentially taller elsewhere. Leaves are numerous, overlapping, erect against the stem, alternate (lower ones may be opposite), 0.4–0.6″ (10–15 mm) long and 1–2 mm wide, acute. Flowers grow on stiffly ascending branches, usually opening one at a time per branch, flower stalks 2–3 mm long. The 5 petals are pale yellow, obovate, 0.25–0.4″ (5–10 mm) long. Fruit is a capsule, oval in outline, 3–4 mm long, green with a purplish, short-pointed tip.

The original flax of commerce, from which linen is made, is *Linum usitatissimum* from Eurasia; it has large blue flowers and is a rare weed in our states. Spreading or Texas Flax (*L. medium* var. *texanum*) is similar to Savanna Flax, but leaves are less crowded, the flowering branches spread widely, and the fruit has no pointy tip; it generally occurs on roadsides and in rights-of-way.

Inhabits moist longleaf pinelands, flatwoods, and seepage slopes; it does best where frequently burned. Ranges on the Coastal Plain from se VA to S FL and e TX; Jamaica.

MID-JUNE–EARLY SEPT.

ONAGRACEAE: EVENING-PRIMROSE FAMILY
Savanna Seedbox

Ludwigia virgata Michaux

Perennial, stem unbranched or with a few strongly ascending branches, mostly 1–2′ (30–60 cm) tall, normally glabrous. Leaves are alternate, sessile, erect, lance-shaped or narrowly elliptic, 0.8–1.2″ (2–3 cm) long and 0.4″ (1 cm) wide, acute to blunt. A few to many flowers grow in one-sided racemes, the flower stalks 0.25–0.4″ (6–10 mm) long. The 4 sepals are bent backward (reflexed), the 4 petals yellow, obovate, 0.4–0.7″ (10–16 mm) long.

This handsome wildflower puts on quite a show in longleaf pine habitats in the first growing season following a fire. The flowers come into bloom progressively up the stem. Rafinesque's Seedbox (*L. hirtella*) is very similar but is densely pubescent and its sepals spread sideways, not reflexed; it occupies the same habitats.

Inhabits moist longleaf pinelands, savannas, margins of streamheads, and seepage slopes. Ranges on the Coastal Plain from se VA to s FL and se MS.

MID-JUNE–EARLY SEPT.

ONAGRACEAE: EVENING-PRIMROSE FAMILY
Southern Sundrops

Oenothera fruticosa L. var. *fruticosa*

Perennial, pubescent, mostly 8–28″ (20–70 cm) tall, branched or not. Leaves are lanceolate to narrowly elliptic, up to 4″ (10 cm) long and 1″ (2.5 cm) wide, acute-tipped, short-tapered to base, margins smooth or crenate, leafstalks up to 0.4″ (10 mm) long. The leaves are reduced in size up the stem and are gray-green in color. Flowers grow terminally and from upper leaf axils on stalks to 0.8″ (2 cm) long. The sepals form a narrow tube 0.3–0.6″ (7–15 mm) long with 4 lobes 0.3–0.7″ (8–18 mm) long; the 4 petals are yellow, 0.4–0.8″ (10–20 mm) long and wide, each with a shallow notch at tip.

The bright yellow flowers glow like drops of sunlight, hence the common name. It prefers sunny situations to shade and is tolerant of fire. Native species of *Oenothera* in our region bloom during the day; alien species open their flowers late in the day and are called evening-primroses.

Inhabits dry longleaf pinelands and openings within dry oak-hickory woods. Ranges from CT to IN south to FL and LA.

MAY–JUNE, SOMETIMES LATER

SOLANACEAE: TOMATO & POTATO FAMILY
Sandhills Ground-cherry

Physalis lanceolata Michaux

Perennial from a rhizome, the stem is semierect, less than 10″ (25 cm) tall, with a few wide-spreading branches; most of the plant is covered with roughish hairs. Leaves are lanceolate to narrowly ovate, 1.5–3″ (3.5–7 cm) long and about 1″ (2.5 cm) wide, often with wavy margins. Flowers are solitary on drooping stalks from leaf axils, bell-shaped, about 0.75″ (18 mm) across, dull yellow with faint brownish markings basally. The fruit is a berry, contained within a loose, conical envelope.

Virginia Ground-cherry (*P. virginiana*) is similar, but its leaves are broadly ovate and its flowers have bold brownish markings basally; it usually avoids the very dry soils preferred by Sandhills Ground-cherry.

Inhabits dry longleaf pinelands, turkey oak scrub, roadsides, and rights-of-way. Endemic to the Sandhills region, from SC NC to EC GA (Augusta area).

LATE MAY–JULY

OROBANCHACEAE: BROOMRAPE FAMILY
Senna Seymeria

Seymeria cassioides (J. F. Gmelin) Blake

Annual, generally 2–3′ (60–100 cm) tall, much branched and shrublike, the stem pubescent to glabrate. Leaves are abundant, opposite, pinnately divided into filiform segments mostly less than 0.4″ (1 cm) long and 0.5 mm wide, pale green. Flowers grow singly from leaf axils, the corolla with 5 spreading lobes 0.25–0.3″ (6–8 mm) long, straw-yellow, usually with a red triangle at the base of the 3 lower lobes.

In our area this is an unmistakable plant, with its small and finely dissected leaves, its beautifully marked petals, and its overall shrubby shape. Senna Seymeria is parasitic on roots of pines. The names Senna and *cassioides* refer to a fanciful resemblance to plants in the genus *Cassia* (ours now in *Chamaecrista*), which also have pinnately dissected leaves and red-marked petals.

Inhabits dry to moist longleaf pine communities, especially where periodically burned. Ranges on the Coastal Plain from E NC to C FL, E TX, and SE AR; SE TN; NW Bah.

AUG.–MID-OCT.

EUPHORBIACEAE:
EUPHORBIA & SPURGE FAMILY
Queen's Delight

Stillingia sylvatica Garden ex L. ssp. *sylvatica*

Glabrous perennial with milky juice, several to many stems arising from a root crown, up to 2.5′ (80 cm) tall. Leaves are elliptic, 1.6–3.6″ (4–9 cm) long and 0.4–1.6″ (1–4 cm) wide, margins finely crenate, with short stalks less than 0.2″ (0–4 mm) long. Flowers grow in thickish terminal spikes 2–5″ (5–12 cm) long. The lower flowers are female, the upper flowers male, sepals yellow, petals none. The surfaces of the spike have large sessile glands. The fruit is a 3-lobed capsule 0.3–0.4″ (8–10 mm) long and wide; after falling, it leaves a triangular disc that persists on the plant through winter.

The name Queen's Delight is of uncertain origin but perhaps due to two of its many medicinal uses: women used it as an additive to bathwater when experiencing irregular periods and after giving birth. Plants senesce to gray "skeletons" over winter and are identifiable by the persistent fruit discs. The genus commemorates Benjamin Stillingfleet (1702–71), English naturalist.

Inhabits dry longleaf pinelands and turkey oak scrub. Ranges from se VA to KS south to c FL and NM.

MAY–JULY

ANACARDIACEAE: CASHEW & SUMAC FAMILY
Winged Sumac

Rhus copallinum L.

Perennial shrub or small tree to 23′ (7 m) tall, often forming clones via long rhizomes, the branches densely pubescent. Where frequently burned, plants seldom exceed 5′ (1.5 m). Leaves are pinnate, the rachis (extension of the leafstalk) winged. The 9–11 (or more) leaflets are sessile, oblong to elliptic, 1.2–2.4″ (3–6 cm) long and 0.4–1.2″ (1–3 cm) wide, entire to crenate, lustrous above, glabrous to pubescent beneath. Flowers grow in large terminal clusters up to 10″ (25 cm) long and wide, the 4–5 sepals and 4–5 petals dull yellow to straw-colored, a few mm long. Fruits are dull red, rounded, 0.2″ (3–4 mm) across, pubescent.

A very successful plant, Winged Sumac occupies a wide geographical range and many habitats; it is able to thrive in many soil types and even tolerates fire. Leaves turn dull purple to red in fall. Native Americans used the bark to stimulate milk flow; berries were chewed to treat mouth sores.

Inhabits dry to moist longleaf pine communities, oak-hickory forests, clearings, roadsides, old fields, and rights-of-way. Ranges from ME to s Ont. and NE south to FL and TX.

MID-AUG.–MID-SEPT.

ANACARDIACEAE: CASHEW & SUMAC FAMILY
Michaux's Sumac

Rhus michauxii Sargent

Densely pubescent perennial shrub, stem
solitary and unbranched, potentially to
3′ (1 m) tall, usually forming loose clones
via rhizomes. Leaves radiate out from the
stem at an angle, pinnate, with a wingless
or narrowly winged rachis. The 9–13
leaflets are sessile, broadly elliptic, 1.6–3.6″
(4–9 cm) long and 1.2–2″ (3–5 cm) wide,
margins toothed. Flowers grow in a
terminal cluster up to 6″ (15 cm) long, the
4–5 sepals and 4–5 petals dull yellowish
green, a few mm long. Fruits are dull red,
rounded, about 3 mm across.

Michaux's Sumac is federally endangered and has declined greatly in the past
50 years due to development and general
habitat loss; NC currently has 25 populations, GA has 2 populations, VA 1, SC none.
In most populations females comprise
only a small percent, which may contrib-
ute to overall rarity. It requires mechanical
and/or fire disturbance to reduce canopy
cover and to promote germination. The
leaves turn bright scarlet in fall.

Inhabits dry longleaf pinelands, especially in loamy sand soil of bean dips; also
oak-hickory forests in the lower Piedmont. It survives rather well in disturbed
soil situations, such as roadsides and
where topsoil has been scraped. Ranges
from SC VA to WC GA (Muscogee County).

MID-JUNE–EARLY JULY

ANACARDIACEAE: CASHEW & SUMAC FAMILY
Poison Oak

Toxicodendron pubescens P. Miller
[*Rhus toxicodendron* L.]

Perennial, pubescent dwarf shrub, forming loose to dense colonies via underground runners. Stems range from 8″–2′
(20–60 cm) tall, potentially taller where
not burned. Leaves are divided into 3
leaflets, each leaflet ovate, mostly 1.6–4″
(4–10 cm) long, dull above (not shiny),
densely pubescent beneath, tip blunt,
margins with 1 or 2 (rarely 0) large teeth.
Flowers grow in slender, elongate, spreading clusters from the lower leaf axils, the
4–5 sepals and petals greenish yellow.

Poisonous! This plant causes dermatitis
in most people, and people can also get a
rash from pet fur that has been in contact
with plant juices, as well as smoke from
burning plants. Poison Oak is common in
our region, so people need to learn to recognize it. Keep pantlegs tucked into socks
and it will rarely be a problem. Leaves
turn bright orange-red in fall; birds eat
the fruits.

Inhabits dry to very dry pinelands,
turkey oak scrub, oak-hickory woods.
Ranges on the Coastal Plain from S NY
to N FL and E TX; scattered inland to WV,
TN, MO, KS.

MID-APR.–MAY

MYRICACEAE: BAYBERRY FAMILY
Dwarf Wax-myrtle

Morella pumila (Michaux) Small
[*Myrica cerifera* L. var. *pumila* Michaux]

Perennial shrub, less than 3′ (1 m) tall (half that in frequently burned sites), forming colonies via subsurface rhizomes. Leaves are semievergreen (slowly deciduous), short-stalked, oblanceolate, mostly 1.2–2″ (3–5 cm) long and 0.4–0.6″ (1–1.5 cm) wide, usually few-toothed above the middle, both surfaces with resin dots, fragrant when crushed. Flowers are tiny and yellow-brown, densely packed in catkins on last year's twigs. The fruits are roundish, about 0.2″ (2.5–3 mm), covered with pale gray wax.

Dwarf Wax-myrtle is a specialized plant of dry to moist soil in frequently burned habitats. Common Wax-myrtle (*M. cerifera*) is much taller (5–20′), has longer and broader leaves, and inhabits wet to moist soils. It is uncommon in our region and occurs mostly in disturbed places or has been planted. Common Wax-myrtle has been used for centuries as a source for candle wax.

Inhabits frequently burned, dry longleaf pinelands and dry to moist flatwoods and savannas. Ranges on the Coastal Plain from se VA to s FL and se LA.

LATE MAR.–MID-APR.

APOCYNACEAE: DOGBANE & MILKWEED FAMILY
Sandhill Orange Milkweed

Asclepias tuberosa L. var. *rolfsii*
   (Britton ex Vail) Shinners

Perennial, up to 1.5′ (45 cm) tall, normally several stems grow together (but may be single), coarsely hairy, without milky sap. Leaves are nearly sessile, 2–3″ (5–8 cm) long, 0.5″ (12 mm) wide, with undulate margins and blunt tips, the bases more or less clasping the stem. Flowers are intricately shaped, with reflexed (turned back) corolla lobes and erect "hoods" within which are modified styles and stamens. Flowers vary in color from orange to yellow.

The majority of our plants are the pale-flowered subspecies *rolfsii*, a Coastal Plain endemic that is partial to the Sandhills region. The widespread Common Orange Milkweed or Common Butterfly-weed (*A. tuberosa* var. *tuberosa*), is taller, has wider and longer nonclasping leaves, and has deep orange to red-orange flowers; it is rare to uncommon in our region. Both subspecies attract many butterflies.

Found in dry longleaf pinelands and dry sandhills. Ranges on the Coastal Plain from c NC to c FL to s MS.

MID-MAY–MID-JULY

ASTERACEAE: ASTER FAMILY
Long-bracted Blazing-star

Liatris squarrosa (L.) Michaux var. *squarrosa*

Perennial from a hard, roundish rootstock. Stem usually solitary, erect, 12–20″
(30–80 cm) tall, pubescent or glabrate.
Leaves are numerous, the lowest ones
oblanceolate, mostly 4–9″ (10–22 cm) long
and up to 0.5″ (12 mm) wide, reduced in
size up the stem, glabrate. Flower heads
grow singly or in a loose, few-headed
raceme (heads on short stalks), the heads
facing upward. The bracts around the
heads form a thick cylindrical involucre
0.5–0.8″ (12–20 mm) long and half as
wide; bracts are triangular with tips that
are acuminate and bent outward. Disc
flowers number 20–30 per head, purple-
pink, with 5 short spreading lobes, rays
absent.

The relatively few heads per plant, the
large number of flowers per head, and the
long-pointed bracts readily identify this
blazing-star. It resembles chaffheads (*Carphephorus*), a closely related genus whose
heads grow in branched arrangements
rather than spikes or racemes. Note the
early flowering period compared to other
blazing-stars.

Inhabits dry longleaf pinelands, often in
loamy sand soil; also oak-hickory woods
that receive fire. Ranges from DE to S MI
and e MO south to n FL and AL.

LATE JUNE–AUG.

ASTERACEAE: ASTER FAMILY
Earle's Blazing-star

Liatris squarrulosa Michaux
[*Liatris earlei* (Greene) K. Schumann]

Perennial from a hard, roundish rootstock. Stem usually solitary, erect, 10–20″
(25–80 cm) tall, unbranched, pubescent.
Leaves are numerous, the lowest ones
oblanceolate to narrowly elliptic, mostly
4–9″ (10–22 cm) long and up to 1″
(25 mm) wide, gradually reduced in size
up the stem, glabrate. Flower heads grow
in a loose to dense, short spike (heads
without stalks) or raceme (heads on short
stalks), the heads oriented at right angles
to stem. The bracts around the heads are
usually purple tinged and form a cuplike
involucre 0.3–0.6″ (8–15 mm) long and
about as wide, each bract obovate, its tip
somewhat recurved. Disc flowers number
11–20 per head, purple or purple-pink,
with 5 short spreading lobes, rays absent.

With its relatively large number of
flowers per head, the heads at right angles
to the stem, and the blunt recurved bracts,
Earle's Blazing-star is easily identified—
and beautiful! Named for Franklin S. Earle
(1857–1929), botanist of the Gulf Coast
and adjacent areas.

Inhabits dry longleaf pinelands in
loamy sand soil; also oak-hickory woods
that are repeatedly burned. Ranges from
S WV to MO south to nw FL and e TX.

LATE AUG.–MID-OCT.

ASTERACEAE: ASTER FAMILY

Savanna Elephant's-foot; Pineland Elephant's-foot

Elephantopus nudatus Gray

Perennial from a basal rosette, stems 1–3, 8–24″ (20–60 cm) tall, pubescent, widely branched above. Leaves essentially all basal and set flat on ground (1–2 small leaves may be on stem), oblanceolate to elliptic, 6–12″ (15–30 cm) long and 1.2–2.8″ (3–7 cm) wide, tip blunt, tapered to base, sparsely pubescent beneath. Flowers grow in heads at ends of branches, each head with 3 triangular leafy bracts 0.5–0.9″ (10–20 mm) long. Heads are about 0.5″ (12 mm) across, disc flowers pink to pale purple, rays absent.

Upland or Woodland Elephant's-foot (*E. tomentosus*) is very similar but has longer and denser hairs, especially on undersides of leaves. It inhabits dry soils, generally in the shade of oak-hickory forests, and extends well into the Piedmont.

Inhabits moist soils in sunny pinelands, flatwoods and savannas, streamhead margins, and roadside ditches. Ranges on the Coastal Plain from DE to C FL, e TX, and S AR.

LATE JULY–SEPT.

ASTERACEAE: ASTER FAMILY

Sandhill Thistle

Cirsium repandum Michaux

Biennial, forming a flat basal rosette the first year then a thick stem the second, stem to 2′ (0.7 m) tall, with cobwebby hairs. Leaves spread widely, to 6″ (15 cm) long and 1.25″ (3 cm) wide, the blade with cobwebby hairs, wavy-margined and irregularly lobed, the divisions prickle-tipped. One to 5 stalked heads grow at top of stem, the bracts tight and with short prickles, heads about 1.5″ (3.5 cm) across, disc flowers bright purple or purple-pink, rays absent.

Fruiting heads spread out to reveal abundant whitish floss that acts like a parachute to disperse the small seeds; goldfinches often feed on the seeds and use the floss to line nests. Virginia Thistle (*C. virginianum*) is similar but usually taller; its leaves are white beneath with very dense short hairs (not cobwebby), and it inhabits seepages and margins of streamheads, blooming in fall.

Inhabits dry to very dry longleaf pine-lands and turkey oak scrub, also roadsides and rights-of-way. Almost endemic to the Carolinas, it barely reaches into se VA and the Augusta region of GA.

MID-MAY–JULY

ASTERACEAE: ASTER FAMILY
One-sided Rattlesnake-root

Prenanthes autumnalis Walter

Biennial, the stem erect or leaning, 1.5–4′ (0.5–1.2 m) tall, glabrous. Leaves are lobed and cut like dandelion leaves, up to 1′ (30 cm) long, 1.2–4″ (3–10 cm) wide, mostly below midstem, lower leaves longest. Flower heads grow in a long, one-sided, spikelike raceme up to 2′ (70 cm) long and 2″ (5 cm) wide, all flowers nodding. Ray flowers 0.6–0.8″ (1.5–2 cm) long and 2–4 mm wide, spreading outward, pink to lavender; disc flowers absent.

Generally an uncommon plant—populations often consist of only a few individuals—One-sided Rattlesnake-root is one of the most appealing of our plants, with its long, graceful wand of a dozen or more flower heads.

Inhabits dry to somewhat moist longleaf pinelands, including bean dips. Ranges on the Coastal Plain from s NJ to s SC and ne FL. Not yet known from the GA Sandhills.

LATE SEPT.–OCT.

FABACEAE: PEA & BEAN FAMILY
Upland Slender Tick-trefoil; Pineland Tick-trefoil

Desmodium strictum (Pursh) DC.

Perennial, 1.3–3′ (0.4–1 m) tall, sparsely to densely pubescent with short hooked hairs and straight hairs. Leaves 3-parted, leaflets linear, 1.2–2″ (3–5 cm) long, sparsely pubescent with short straight hairs. Flowers grow on short to long branches and branchlets, these with short hooked hairs, flowers purple-pink, on short 0.25–0.5″ (6–11 mm) stalks. Pods composed of 1–2 (–3) broadly elliptical or roundish segments, each one 0.2–0.3″ (4–6 mm) long and with a straight or slightly concave upper margin.

Savanna Slender Tick-trefoil (*D. tenuifolium*) is very similar, differing in its moist to wet habitats (streamhead margins, seepage slopes), and in its pod segments, which have convexly curved upper margins.

Inhabits dry to very dry sandy soils of longleaf pinelands and turkey oak scrub. Ranges on the Coastal Plain from s NJ to c FL and w LA.

AUG.–OCT.

DRY LONGLEAF PINELAND **75**

FABACEAE: PEA & BEAN FAMILY
Littleleaf Tick-trefoil

Desmodium ciliare (Muhlenberg ex Willdenow) DC.

Perennial, 1.3–3′ (0.4–1 m) tall, moderately pubescent with short hooked hairs and straight hairs. Leaves 3-parted, leaflets ovate to elliptic, 0.4–1.2″ (1–3 cm) long, with short straight hairs on both surfaces. Flowers grow on short to long branches and branchlets, these with short hooked hairs, flowers pealike, purple-pink, on short 0.2–0.4″ (4–9 mm) stalks. Pods are composed of 1–2 (–3) broadly elliptical or roundish segments, each segment 0.2–0.3″ (3.5–6 mm) long.

Get to know this common plant so you can compare it with other species in this genus—there may be half a dozen species in one location. Maryland Tick-trefoil (*D. marilandicum*) is very similar, differing mainly in its glabrate stems and leaves, its much longer flower stalks, and its moist soil habitats.

Inhabits sandy and loamy sand soils of longleaf pinelands (including pea swales), oak-hickory woods, and roadsides. Ranges from MA to se KS south to FL and TX; Cuba.

AUG.–OCT.

FABACEAE: PEA & BEAN FAMILY
Smooth Tick-trefoil

Desmodium laevigatum (Nuttall) DC.

Perennial, 2–4.5′ (0.6–1.3 m) tall, glabrous or with very sparse, short, hooked hairs. Leaves 3-parted, leaflets ovate, 2–3.5″ (5–9 cm) long, glabrous or essentially so, glaucescent beneath. Flowers grow on long spreading branches and branchlets, these with short hooked hairs, flowers pink to purple-pink, on stalks 0.3–0.75″ (7–19 mm) long. Note the pale green "eyes" on the standard; they occur in all of our tick-trefoils but are especially prominent in this species. Pods are composed of 2–5 diamond-shaped segments, each segment 0.25–0.4″ (5–8 mm) long.

In a difficult genus (there may be half a dozen species in one location) this is an easy one, due to its large smooth leaves, long spreading branches, and angular pod segments. Velvet Tick-trefoil (*D. viridiflorum*) is similar in size, differing in its broader, almost diamond-shaped leaves and its stems and leaves that have abundant short hooked hairs that easily stick to clothing like Velcro.

Inhabits sandy and loamy sand soils of longleaf pinelands (including pea swales), oak-hickory woods, and roadsides. Ranges from s NY to MO south to n FL and TX.

AUG.–OCT.

FABACEAE: PEA & BEAN FAMILY
Nuttall's Tick-trefoil
Desmodium nuttallii (Schindler) Schubert

Perennial, 2.2–4.4' (0.7–1.3 m) tall, densely pubescent with short hooked hairs and straight hairs. Leaves 3-parted, leaflets ovate to elliptic-ovate, 2–4″ (5–10 cm) long, densely hairy beneath with hooked and straight hairs. Flowers grow on long, ascending branches and branchlets, these with hooked and straight hairs, flowers pink to purple-pink, on stalks 0.2–0.3″ (3–7 mm) long. Pods are composed of 2–4 elliptical segments, each segment 0.2–0.25″ (4–5 mm) long.

Nuttall's Tick-trefoil, like all tick-trefoils, has evolved to disperse its pods via mammals: the hooked hairs stick like Velcro to passing fur—and clothing! Leaflets of Nuttall's and Velvet Tick-trefoils are equally adherent and can be worn as a sort of badge on one's shirt.

Inhabits sandy and loamy sand soils of longleaf pinelands (including pea swales), oak-hickory woods, and roadsides. Ranges from s NY to IN south to n FL and AR.

AUG.–OCT.

FABACEAE: PEA & BEAN FAMILY
Trailing Wild Bean; Sandhill Bean
Phaseolus sinuatus Nuttall ex Torrey & Gray

Perennial from a large, thick (1–2″ [2.5–5 cm]), branched rootstock. Stems few to many, prostrate, radiating from a central point, up to 14′ (4 m) long, unbranched. Leaves are produced at intervals; the 3 leaflets are ovate or diamond-shaped, margins are more or less sinuate, upper surface with greenish-white mottling. Flower stalks grow singly from leaf axils, erect, 4–8″ (10–20 cm) long. Flowers are single or a few, purple-pink, about 0.4″ (10 mm) long, the keel spirally coiled and splitting the wing petals.

Sandhill Bean is one of our most unusual plants, with its remarkably long trailing stems, variegated leaves, and spirally coiled keel. It is in the same genus as our familiar edible beans: green, red, kidney, pole, snap, string, bush, and lima. Although edible, the pods of Sandhill Bean are not abundant enough to harvest.

Inhabits dry longleaf pinelands, particularly in loamy soil of bean dips. Ranges on the Coastal Plain from sc NC to wc GA (Taylor and Muskogee Counties) and c FL.

EARLY JULY–EARLY SEPT.

FABACEAE: PEA & BEAN FAMILY
Creeping Bush-clover
Lespedeza repens (L.) Barton

Perennial, stems few to many, trailing, slender, 1–2.7′ (30–80 cm) long, with sparse to dense, upwardly appressed hairs. Leaves are alternate, well-spaced on stem, short-stalked. The 3 leaflets are elliptic or obovate, 0.4–1″ (1–2.5 cm) long and about half as wide, the surfaces sparsely to densely appressed pubescent, tip blunt. Flowers grow in racemes of 4–6 flowers from axils of upper leaves, the stalks 1.6–3.2″ (4–8 cm) long and upwardly appressed pubescent. Petals vary from pinkish white to pale purple, 0.25–0.3″ (6–8 mm) long. The pod is broadly elliptical, pointed, one-seeded.

Trailing Bush-clover (*L. procumbens*) is very similar but has denser hairs that spread out from the stem (pilose); it is rare in our region, being more of a Piedmont plant.

Inhabits dry longleaf pinelands (including pea swales) and oak-hickory woodlands. Ranges from CT to s WI and KS south to n FL and c TX.

JULY–SEPT.

FABACEAE: PEA & BEAN FAMILY
Smooth Milkpea; Common Milkpea
Galactia regularis (L.) B.S.P.

Perennial, glabrate, trailing or weakly climbing, to 5′ (1.5 m) long, sometimes many stems grow from a single rootstalk. Leaves numerous, divided into 3 leaflets that are elliptic or lance-shaped, 0.8–1.7″ (2–4 cm) long. Few to numerous flowers grow on spreading stalks 1.25–5″ (3–13 cm) long. Petals are purple-pink or rosy, the standard reflexed (swept back) nearly to 180 degrees.

Learn this common plant well as a basis for comparing other milkpeas. In clearings it may form large, multistemmed mounds with abundant flowers, but in natural habitats it produces a few trailing stems. Twining or Downy Milkpea (*G. volubilis*) is very similar but almost always climbs up coarse herbs and shrubs; its stems are noticeably hairy, and the standard is spread no more than 90 degrees.

Inhabits a variety of longleaf and other pine-oak communities. Ranges from se PA to MO south to s FL and se TX. Twining Milkpea occurs in much the same range but also in the Piedmont and low Mountains.

EARLY JUNE–AUG.

FABACEAE: PEA & BEAN FAMILY
Soft Milkpea

Galactia mollis Michaux

Perennial, densely soft hairy, trailing or weakly climbing, to 5′ (1.5 m) long. Leaves are relatively sparse, divided into 3 leaflets that are elliptic or broadly lance-shaped, 0.8–2″ (2–5 cm) long. One to 6 flowers grow at tips of long (4–8″ [10–20 cm]) erect stalks. Petals are purple-pink or lavender-pink, the standard is cream colored on the back and weakly erect.

Well-named, Soft Milkpea has leaves and stems that feel like velvet. It is rare in NC. In the GA sandhills it has been documented only from Richmond County.

Inhabits loamy sands of well-burned longleaf pinelands (including bean dips). Ranges on the Coastal Plain from se NC to ec GA, sw GA, and c FL.

MID-MAY–EARLY JULY

FABACEAE: PEA & BEAN FAMILY
Common Goat's-rue

Tephrosia virginiana (L.) Persoon

Perennial from slender, almost woody roots, the stem sparsely to densely hairy. Leaves grow to 6″ (15 cm) long; the 15–25 leaflets are narrowly elliptic, 0.5–1″ (12–25 mm) long and 0.25–0.5″ (5–12 mm) wide, hairy. Flowers grow in a showy terminal cluster, each pea-shaped, about 0.75″ (20 mm) long. The corollas are bicolored: the standard is ivory to creamy yellowish, the keel and wings pinkish rose.

This lovely wildflower is widespread and relatively common. It was named for its toxicity to goats and other grazing animals, for it contains rotenone, a proven insecticide that is injurious to mammals if ingested in quantity. Native Americans used it as a fish poison and insecticide but also to enhance male potency.

Inhabits dry to mesic longleaf pine communities, oak-hickory woodlands, roadsides, clearings, and rights-of-way. Ranges from NH to MN south to FL and TX.

MAY–JUNE

FABACEAE: PEA & BEAN FAMILY
Eastern Sensitive-brier

Mimosa microphylla Dryander
[*Schrankia microphylla* (Dryander) Macbride]

Perennial, prostrate or weakly clambering over low vegetation. The stems usually are 3–6′ (1–2 m) long, brownish to greenish, and densely short-prickly. Leaves are evenly bipinnate with 6–16 pinnae 0.8–2″ (2–5 cm) long, each pinna with 20–32 pinnules (ultimate leaflets) 0.2–0.3″ (2–8 mm) long. The pinnules close against the branchlets after being touched. Numerous flowers grow in dense spherical heads 0.8″ (2 cm) across, the flowers tubular and with 5 slender lobes, pink or pale rose with prominent yellow anthers.

What child (and adult!) hasn't watched with humor and wonder as a whole leaf closes its leaflets in response to touch? For your next cocktail party conversation, you can boast that Eastern Sensitive-brier exhibits a "thigmotropic reaction," that is, a positive response to touch.

Inhabits dry longleaf pinelands, openings or burned areas within oak-hickory woods, fallow fields, and roadsides. Ranges from DE to MO south to FL and TX.

JUNE–AUG.

GENTIANACEAE: GENTIAN FAMILY
Narrowleaf Sabatia

Sabatia brachiata Elliott

Glabrous annual, stems single or several, 6–19″ (15–50 cm) tall, slightly angled, opposite-branched above, the branches strongly ascending. Several basal leaves grow in a flattish rosette. Stem leaves are opposite, lanceolate to elliptic, 0.8–2″ (2–5 cm) long and 0.2–0.4″ (4–10 mm) wide, tip acute to obtuse. Flowers grow at ends of branches to form a more or less cylindric inflorescence up to 1′ (30 cm) long. The 5 petals are pink to rosy pink (occasionally white) with yellow bases outlined with red, elliptic, 0.4–0.8″ (1–2 cm) long.

The genus *Sabatia* is one of the showiest in North America; because of their beauty, sabatias attract attention wherever they grow. Bitterbloom (*S. angularis*) is similar, but its branches spread widely, its stems are distinctly winged lengthwise, the inflorescence is not cylindrical, and its basal leaves usually are absent at flowering; it is more often found in the Piedmont.

Inhabits dry to moist longleaf pinelands, occasionally roadsides and clearings. Ranges on the Coastal Plain from se VA to s GA, w LA, and se MO; c TN.

LATE MAY–JULY

LAMIACEAE: MINT FAMILY
Spotted Beebalm
Monarda punctata L. var. *punctata*

Perennial, stems 16–36″ (0.4–1 m) tall, usually branched, 4-angled, with very short and longer hairs mixed. Leaves are opposite, lanceolate to narrowly elliptic, 1.2–3.6″ (3–9 cm) long and 0.25–0.6″ (5–17 mm) wide, tip acute, margins toothed, leafstalk 0.25–1″ (5–25 mm) long. Flowers grow in several whorl-like clusters separated by short sections of stem, each cluster with several large, leafy, pink bracts. Each flower is 0.6–0.8″ (15–20 mm) long, yellow with purple spots, strongly 2-lipped, the upper 2 petals and stamens arching forward.

Spotted Beebalm is one of our most spectacular wildflowers, both in shape and color. Take time to look closely at the intricate pattern and coloring—no wonder folks often think it is a fancy tropical orchid! There are several beebalms in North America, but none as intricately patterned as this. Native Americans used Spotted Beebalm to treat stomach cramps, coughs, and bowel ailments; country doctors used it for indigestion and as a diuretic.

Inhabits disturbed places within long-leaf pinelands, roadsides, rights-of-way, and old fields. Ranges from se NY to FL and LA, mostly on the Coastal Plain.

LATE JULY–EARLY SEPT.

PLANTAGINACEAE: PLANTAIN FAMILY
Downy Beardtongue
Penstemon australis Small

Perennial, stems 8–28″ (20–70 cm) tall, downy, branched above midstem, the branches nearly erect. Basal leaves are prostrate, downy, oblanceolate, 2–4″ (5–10 cm) long and 0.6–1″ (1.5–2.5 cm) wide. Stem leaves are opposite, downy, lanceolate, 1.2–4″ (3–10 cm) long and 0.4–1″ (1–2.5 cm) wide, margins toothed. Flowers grow in panicles, the flower clusters few-flowered and on long stalks, each flower on a shorter stalk; stalks vary from glabrate to dense with gland-tipped hairs. Flowers are tubular with 5 short lobes at the tip, the upper lobes recurved, 0.6–1″ (15–25 mm) long, pale lavender or pinkish with purple lines.

Smooth Beardtongue (*P. laevigatus*) is similar but taller and essentially hairless; the leaves are larger, and the pinkish purple (varying to whitish) flowers lack lines. It is a Piedmont plant uncommon in our area.

Inhabits dry longleaf pinelands; also in oak-hickory woods and on roadsides. Ranges mostly on the Coastal Plain from se VA to n FL, c TX, and AR; scattered inland to n GA, TN, n AL.

MAY–EARLY JULY

POLYGALACEAE: MILKWORT FAMILY
Showy Milkwort
Polygala grandiflora Walter var. *grandiflora*

Perennial from a taproot, the stem single or several from one point, 8–20″ (20–50 cm) tall, usually branched, with appressed or spreading hairs. Leaves are oblanceolate, 0.6–2″ (15–50 mm) long and 0.25–0.6″ (5–15 mm) wide, tip acute. Flowers grow loosely in narrow terminal clusters 2–5″ (5–12.5 cm) long (much longer in fruit), pink to rosy, the spread wings about 0.6″ (15 mm) across.

Individually, the flowers of Showy Milkwort are larger than those of our other milkworts, and the wings are noticeably rounded in shape. It is uncommon and local in our area, listed as rare in NC.

Inhabits dry, loamy sand soil of slight depressions and upland flats in longleaf pinelands. Ranges on the Coastal Plain from se NC to s FL and se LA.

MID-MAY–EARLY JULY

POLEMONIACEAE: PHLOX FAMILY
Pineland Phlox
Phlox nivalis Loddiges ex Sweet var. *nivalis*

Perennial, semiwoody dwarf shrub, stems spreading along the ground and sending up flowering shoots 2–5″ (5–12.5 cm) tall. Leaves are opposite or in clusters of several leaves per node, crowded, more or less evergreen, needle-like, 0.2–0.5″ (4–12 mm) long and less than 1.5 mm wide, margins with fine bristly hairs. From one to several flowers grow terminally, the corolla tube 0.4–0.6″ (10–16 mm) long, the 5 lobes 0.3–0.5″ (8–12 mm) long, widest toward tip, pink, rosy, or lavender-pink (occasionally white), with a narrow red base.

A spectacular wildflower, Pineland Phlox is especially showy following a fire, each plant forming a brilliant patch of color against the blackened earth. A second variety (*P. nivalis* var. *hentzii*) differs in being taller and larger-leaved; it occurs primarily in the Piedmont, occasionally in our region.

Inhabits dry longleaf pinelands and turkey oak scrub, persisting best where regularly burned. Ranges on the Coastal Plain and adjacent Piedmont from c NC to wc GA and nw FL.

MID-MAR.–MAY

ASTERACEAE: ASTER FAMILY
Carolina Ironweed

Vernonia acaulis (Walter) Gleason

Perennial, with large basal leaves in a
rosette and small stem leaves, the stems
2–4′ (0.6–1.2 m) tall, branched from the
uppermost portion. The 3–8 basal leaves
are elliptic to oblanceolate, 4–8″ (10–20
cm) long and 0.8–4″ (2–10 cm) wide, tip
acute, tapered basally, margins irregularly
toothed, surfaces pubescent to roughish hairy. The 2–7 stem leaves are linear
to elliptic, less than half the size of basal
leaves. Flowers grow at ends of branches
in a flat-topped cluster, the heads about
0.5″ (12 mm) across, disc flowers purple,
ray flowers absent.

The genus is named for William Vernon
(16??–1711), English botanist who collected
in the Middle and North Atlantic states.
Elephant's-foots (*Elephantopus tomentosus*
and *E. nudatus*) are similar but have a distinct 3-parted bract just below each flower
head.

Inhabits dry to moist soils of longleaf
pinelands and margins of streamheads.
Ranges from c NC to sc GA.

LATE JUNE–AUG.

ASTERACEAE: ASTER FAMILY
Slender Ironweed

Vernonia angustifolia Michaux var. *angustifolia*

Perennial, lacking basal leaves, stems
single or several, 2–4′ (0.6–1.2 m) tall,
branched from the uppermost portion.
Leaves are numerous, linear, 2–5″ (5–12
cm) long and up to 0.25″ (1.5–6 mm) wide,
tip acute, short-tapered basally, margins
usually curled under (revolute). Flowers
grow at ends of branches in a flat-topped
cluster, the heads about 0.5″ (12 mm)
across, disc flowers purple, ray flowers
absent.

When growing in a group, Slender
Ironweed is one of our handsomest plants.
Wider-leaved varieties grow farther south
and west of our region.

Inhabits dry soils of longleaf pinelands
(including pea swales) and pine savannas.
Ranges on the Coastal Plain from se NC to
s GA.

LATE JUNE–EARLY SEPT.

APOCYNACEAE: DOGBANE & MILKWEED FAMILY
Wavy-leaved Milkweed

Asclepias amplexicaulis J. E. Smith

Glabrous perennial with milky sap, stem usually solitary, stout, 1.4–3′ (0.4–1 m) tall. Leaves occur in 3–6 pairs, opposite, sessile and clasping, broadly ovate or elliptic, 3–6″ (8–15 cm) long and 1.5–3″ (4–8 cm) wide, margins strongly wavy. Numerous flowers grow in a single, terminal, round cluster about 3″ (7–9 cm) across, dull rose or greenish purple, spicy fragrant.

Like most milkweed species, Wavy-leaved Milkweed occurs in small numbers, generally 1–5 individuals per population. The flowers are deliciously fragrant, reminiscent of cloves.

Inhabits dry sandy soil of pinelands, roadsides, and clearings. Ranges from NH to MN and KS S to C FL and TX.

MAY–EARLY JULY

ASTERACEAE: ASTER FAMILY
Rayless Blanket-flower; Sandhills Gaillardia

Gaillardia aestivalis (Walter) H. Rock
    var. *aestivalis*

Perennial, sometimes annual, pubescent. Stem ribbed lengthwise, 4–20″ (10–50 cm) tall. Leaves alternate, entire to sparsely toothed, oblanceolate, 0.6–2.8″ (1.5–7 cm) long and 0.2–0.6″ (2.5–14 mm) wide. Heads grow singly at ends of stalks 0.4–4″ (1–10 cm) long, disc red-purple and hemispheric, about 0.6″ (1.5 cm) across, rays absent (occasionally present, short and yellow).

This rather homely blanket-flower is closely related to Beach Blanket-flower (*G. pulchella* var. *drummondii*) of oceanside interdunes, which has showy red and yellow rays. The genus is named for M. Gaillard, eighteenth-century French patron of botanists. In nc and sc Rayless Blanket-flower occurs only in the Sandhills region, but it occurs throughout the Coastal Plain in GA. Rare in NC.

Inhabits dry longleaf pinelands and dry pine savannas. Ranges mostly on the Coastal Plain from sc nc to C FL, C TX, C OK, and AR.

JULY–OCT.

OROBANCHACEAE: BROOMRAPE FAMILY
Chaffseed

Schwalbea americana L.

Perennial, 1–2′ (30–60 cm) tall (occasionally shorter), unbranched, most parts with dense, woolly hairs. Leaves are elliptic to lanceolate, 0.8–1.6″ (2–4 cm) long and 0.25–0.4″ (6–10 mm) wide, gradually reduced in size up the stem, sessile, margins smooth. Flowers grow in a terminal, spikelike raceme, each flower from the axil of a leaflike bract. Sepals are 0.6–0.7″ (14–18 mm) long, tubular with 2 unequal lips; the 5 petals are yellowish or purplish with darker purple lines, about twice the length of sepals, forming a tube with 2 slightly unequal lips.

Chaffseed is federally endangered due to fire suppression and loss of habitat. Chaffseed apparently needs fire every 1–2 years to germinate and grow properly, conditions rarely met today. As a result it now survives in only 6 of its original 16 states, with most populations in SC. In the Sandhills region, it is known only from the NC Sandhills; Sumter County, SC; and Baldwin and Pike Counties, GA.

Inhabits frequently burned, loamy sand soil of longleaf pinelands and upper ecotones of streamheads. Original range: se MA to c FL and w LA; c TN; se KY; current range: NJ, NC, SC, GA, FL, AL, LA.

LATE MAY–JULY

FABACEAE: PEA & BEAN FAMILY
Sandhills Milkvetch

Astragalus michauxii (Kuntze) F. J. Hermann

Perennial, 1–3′ (0.3–1 m) tall, stem erect, pubescent above. Leaves are rather sparse, pinnate, with 15–30 elliptic leaflets about 0.6″ (15 mm) long and 0.25″ (6 mm) wide. The inflorescences are 2–5″ (5–12.5 cm) long, each from a long stalk. Flowers can be sparse or numerous, 0.5–0.75″ (12–18 mm) long, pinkish lavender or pinkish white, shaped like typical pea flowers.

Sandhills Milkvetch is one of our showiest legumes but has become scarce in the absence of fire and now is rare throughout its range. Most members of this huge genus (hundreds of species) are very short or tufted plants of prairies and steppes; ours is highly distinct and not closely related to them.

Inhabits dry to very dry longleaf pine communities, including bean dips and loamy flats in longleaf pinelands, turkey oak scrub, rosemary sandhills, and old riverine dunes. Ranges from sc NC to se GA, mostly on the inner Coastal Plain.

LATE APR.–LATE MAY

FABACEAE: PEA & BEAN FAMILY
Spurred Butterfly-pea
Centrosema virginiana (L.) Bentham

Perennial herbaceous vine to 6′ (2 m) long from a long taproot, trailing or twining on herbs and shrubs. Leaves are divided into 3 ovate to narrowly ovate leaflets 0.7–2.7″ (2–7 cm) long; they usually show vein reticulation on the undersides. Flowers grow from leaf axils, one to several from slender stalks, each flower 1–1.5″ (2.5–3.5 cm) wide and long. The corolla is bluish purple or lavender purple, and the standard is spread flat, the wings and keel much shorter and tightly curved to form a knob.

The wide, spreading petals of the standard are like the wings of a butterfly, giving this common plant its name. Its adaptability has brought it to dooryards, fencelines, roadsides, and other disturbed places.

Occurs in a wide variety of habitats, including natural longleaf pine-oak woodlands. Most often seen in disturbed and ruderal places. Ranges from NJ to KY and AR south to S FL and TX.

LATE JUNE–EARLY SEPT.

FABACEAE: PEA & BEAN FAMILY
Butterfly-pea
Clitora mariana L.

Perennial herbaceous vine to 4′ (1.2 m) long from a long taproot, trailing or weakly climbing on herbs and low shrubs. Leaves are divided into 3 ovate to narrowly ovate leaflets 0.7–2.7″ (2–7 cm) long that do not show vein reticulation on the undersides. One to 3 flowers grow on slender stalks from leaf axils, 1.6–2.2″ (4–5.5 cm) long, pale purplish pink or bluish pink to lavender. The standard forms a scoop (not spread flat), the wings and keel much shorter, curved and twisted.

This and Spurred Butterfly-pea are very similar, but note the spoon or scoop shape to the standard of Butterfly Pea vs. the flattened, platterlike standard of Spurred Butterfly-pea.

Occurs in a wide variety of habitats, including natural longleaf pinelands, where it is fairly common in loamy soil; also disturbed places, rights-of-way, and roadsides. Ranges from se NY to S OH and MO south to S FL and TX.

LATE JUNE–EARLY SEPT.

ACANTHACEAE: ACANTHUS FAMILY
Sandhill Wild-petunia
Ruellia ciliosa Pursh

Pubescent perennial, stemless or very short-stemmed, to 7″ (17 cm) tall; in the Sandhills region most plants are stemless. Leaves form a basal rosette (or also with a few on the stem), each oblanceolate to obovate, up to 3″ (7.5 cm) long and 1.5″ (3.5 cm) wide, lustrous, often strongly tinged brown. One or a few flowers arise from the center of the rosette or atop a short stem, erect with the mouth of the flower facing up. The calyx lobes are linear, the corolla lavender to pale purple, 1–1.5″ (2.5–3.5 cm) long, funnel-shaped with 5 spreading but united lobes.

With its virtually stemless aspect and brownish leaves, Sandhill Wild-petunia is like no other plant. It is uncommon or rare in our region, in part because it naturally occurs in small numbers and in part because it favors fire-managed communities.

Inhabits dry longleaf pinelands, including loamy sand soils of bean dips. Ranges on the Coastal Plain from sc NC to c FL and se LA; not yet known from the GA Sandhills.

JUNE–AUG.

IRIDACEAE: IRIS FAMILY
Dwarf Iris
Iris verna L. var. *verna*

Perennial from a long and scaly rhizome, stem 0.8–2″ (2–5 cm) tall, hidden by 5–9 overlapping and sheathing bracts. Leaves are all basal, grasslike, 4–18″ (10–45 cm) long (they continue to grow well past blooming) and mostly 0.2–0.3″ (3–8 mm) wide. Flowers are usually solitary atop the stem, fragrant, the corolla tube 0.8–2.4″ (2–6 cm) long and enclosed by green bracts. There are 3 sepals, 0.8–2.4″ (2–6 cm) long and 0.3–0.8″ (8–20 mm) wide, violet-blue with orange-yellow central band; 3 petals, similar to sepals but wholly violet-blue, erect and arching.

One of the wonders of the longleaf pine ecosystem is the appearance of Dwarf Iris a few weeks after a fire, the flowers brilliant against the blackened earth. Such a delicate beauty seems so incongruous in such a harsh environment. An important resource to the plant is the long rhizomes that can produce new plants at tips.

Inhabits dry to moist longleaf pinelands and turkey oak scrub. Ranges on the Coastal Plain and lower Piedmont from se VA to nw FL.

LATE MAR.–EARLY MAY

ASTERACEAE: ASTER FAMILY
Slender Wild-lettuce

Lactuca graminifolia Michaux
var. *graminifolia*

Biennial, 1.5–3′ (0.5–1 m) tall, glabrous, sap milky. Leaves alternate, mostly basal, broadly linear to oblanceolate, 4–12″ (10–30 cm) long, 0.4–2″ (1–5 cm) wide, tip acute, base clasping, leaves much reduced up stem. Leaves are irregularly lobed, with the terminal lobe about a third the length of the whole leaf blade. The upper half of the stem is widely branched, each branch terminated by a flower head. Heads are about 0.4″ (10 mm) across, ray flowers numerous, blue to violet, disc flowers absent. Seeds disperse via a "parachute" of white hairs.

The long, slender leaves give this plant its common name; indeed, *graminifolia* means "grass-leaved."

Inhabits dry longleaf pinelands and savannas. Ranges on the Coastal Plain from se NC to s FL and c LA; s NJ.

LATE APR.–JULY

ASTERACEAE: ASTER FAMILY
Eastern Silvery-aster

Symphyotrichum concolor (L.) Nesom
var. *concolor*
[*Aster concolor* L.]

Perennial, stems solitary or several, mostly 1.5–4′ (0.4–1.3 m) tall, erect to ascending, often leaning on other plants, unbranched, pubescent. Leaves are sessile, elliptic, 0.4–1.6″ (1–4 cm) long, erect and usually overlapping, the surfaces with silvery appressed hairs giving an overall grayish tone. Flower heads grow in a narrow, cylindrical, 1-sided inflorescence up to 8″ (20 cm) long, each head on a short to longish stalk. Ray flowers are violet to blue-violet or lavender, 0.4–0.8″ (1–2 cm) long; disc flowers yellow.

Few wildflowers are as elegant as Eastern Silvery-aster; with its ethereal blue-violet rays and bold yellow discs, it brightens autumn pinelands. It blooms best in the first growing season following a fire.

Inhabits dry longleaf pinelands, pine savannas, loamy soil pea swales; occurs in other habitats away from the Sandhills region. Ranges from se MA to KY south to FL and LA.

LATE SEPT.–OCT.

ASTERACEAE: ASTER FAMILY
Walter's Aster

Symphyotrichum walteri (Alexander) Nesom
[*Aster squarrosus* Walter]

Glabrate perennial, the stem usually solitary, erect, ascending, or sprawling, 8–20″ (20–50 cm) tall, branches few to several, elongate. Leaves are abundant, ovate-triangular, up to 0.6″ (15 mm) long and 0.3″ (7 mm) wide, sessile, bent abruptly downward, tip acute. One or a few flower heads grow at ends of branches; the bracts of heads are appressed. Rays are 0.4–0.8″ (1–2 cm) long, pale blue or pale blue-violet; disc flowers yellow.

With its numerous, sharply reflexed leaves, Walter's Aster is unique in our flora—another example of the extraordinary diversity of growth forms found in plants of the Coastal Plain.

Inhabits dry to mesic soil of longleaf pinelands. Ranges on the Coastal Plain from e NC to sc GA (Dooly and Laurens Counties) and c FL.

LATE SEPT.–EARLY NOV.

ASTERACEAE: ASTER FAMILY
Stiff Aster; Spruce Aster

Ionactis linariifolia (L.) Greene
[*Aster linariifolius* L.]

Perennial, with few to many stems 8–19″ (20–50 cm) tall, occasionally taller. Leaves are alternate, sessile, crowded, stiff, linear, coniferlike, mostly 0.4–1.2″ (1–3 cm) long and less than 0.2″ (3 mm) wide, minutely toothed. The inflorescence is comprised of one to many heads from short branches; the bracts around the head are whitish with a green midrib or all green, appressed, rough-margined. Ray flowers 7–15, lilac-blue to violet-blue, 0.4–0.8″ (1–2 cm) long, disc flowers bright yellow.

Stiff Aster gets it name from the sprucelike leaves that are rigid and not easily bent. Although a common species and often passed by, it is one of our most beautiful asters with its intensely yellow disc and lilac-blue rays.

Inhabits longleaf pinelands, oak-hickory woods, and turkey oak scrub. Ranges from ME to Que. and WI south to n FL and e TX.

LATE SEPT.–MID-NOV.

VIOLACEAE: VIOLET FAMILY
Bird's-foot Violet

Viola pedata L.

Glabrous perennial. Leaves are erect, the blades 1–2″ (2.5–5 cm) long, palmately and deeply divided into 3 principal lobes, these usually again dissected into 3 narrow parts, the leafstalk about as long as the blade. Some plants produce only unlobed, elliptical, or obovate leaf blades that are shallowly dissected into toothlike segments. Flowers grow on slender stalks independent of leaves, 1.2–1.8″ (3–4.5 cm) across. The 5 petals spread widely, blue-violet or lavender, the lowest petal larger and forming a lip plus a backward-pointing blunt spur. The stamen tips are orange and project forward.

Bird's-foot Violet is just about everyone's favorite spring plant—and with justification, for the large flowers are a beautiful hue, set off by the bright orange stamens. The peculiar form with shallowly cut leaves is restricted to the Sandhills region; both forms can occur together, and other than leaf shape the plants are identical.

Inhabits dry soil of well-burned longleaf pinelands and turkey oak scrub. Ranges from s NH to s Ont. and MN south to n FL and e TX.

MID-MAR.–APR.

LAMIACEAE: MINT FAMILY
Azure Sage

Salvia azurea Michaux ex Lamarck var. *azurea*

Perennial, stem single or a few together, 4-angled, 2.4–5′ (0.7–1.5 m) tall, erect or leaning, sparsely branched above, glabrous. Leaves are opposite, linear to narrowly elliptic, 1.6–3.4″ (4–8.5 cm) long and up to 1.2″ (3 cm) wide, tapered to both ends, margins crenate. Leafstalks and stem nodes are tinged dull violet. Flowers grow in a row along the ultimate branches, pale blue, about 0.6″ (1.4 cm) long, tubular with 2 flaring lobes, the lower lobe forming a drooping lip.

Azure Sage is widespread and fairly common in sc and GA, but it barely reaches NC, where it is a rare species. A second variety occurs in the Midwest.

Inhabits dry to mesic longleaf pinelands, from hilltops down almost to streamhead margins. Ranges on the Coastal Plain and lower Piedmont from sc NC to nw FL and e TX.

LATE AUG.–SEPT.

IRIDACEAE: IRIS FAMILY
Sandhill Blue-eyed-grass

Sisyrinchium rufipes Bicknell

Glabrous perennial, stems few to many
in a clump, mostly 6–12″ (15–30 cm)
tall, 0.6–1.2 mm wide, narrowly winged,
branched 1–2 times. Plant bases have
abundant pale brown or reddish brown fibers, which are remains of previous years'
leaves. Leaves are basal only, erect, grasslike, about as long and wide as stems, tip
acuminate. Flowers grow terminally, one
or a few in a single cluster that is partly
enclosed by 2 spathelike bracts 0.5–0.6″
(1.2–1.5 cm) long. The 3 sepals and 3 petals
are alike, blue with a yellow base, 0.3″ (7–9
mm) long, each with tiny point at the tip.

This plant is named for its preference
for very dry sandy soil and also for its reddish brown fibers at the plant base. Eugene
P. Bicknell (1859–1925) was a New York
lawyer by profession but also a remarkably
astute botanist. Bristly Blue-eyed-grass
(*S. fuscatum*) differs in its broader leaves
and stems (more than 1.5 mm wide); it
also has abundant bristles at the base of
the stems. These bristles are believed to
provide some protection to the tender
portion of the stem from fire.

Inhabits dry to very dry longleaf pinelands, sandhills, and turkey oak barrens.
Ranges on the Coastal Plain from se NC
to ec GA (Richmond County), n FL, and
s AL.

APR.–MID-JUNE

FABACEAE: PEA & BEAN FAMILY
Buckroot

Pediomelum canescens (Michaux) Rydberg
[*Psoralea canescens* Michaux]

Perennial from a thick, sometimes
globose, tuber. The stem grows to 3′ (1 m)
tall, pubescent, much-branched to form
a rounded crown. Leaves are divided
into 3 leaflets, each elliptic to obovate,
generally 1.5″ (35 mm) long and 0.75″
(18 mm) wide, glandular-dotted above and
beneath. Flowers grow in racemes about
1–2″ (2.5–6 cm) long, 4–8 per raceme. The
calyx is densely downy, the petals dull blue
or blue-violet, 0.3–0.6″ (8–15 mm) long;
the standard leans out over the keel and
wings, straw-colored on its upper surface.

Buckroot is a sparsely distributed plant
and not showy, so it can be hard to find
despite its large size. Look for a gumdrop-
shaped crown on a single stem. The
starchy tuber is edible but not flavorful.

Inhabits dry to very dry longleaf
pine-oak sandhills and turkey oak scrub,
especially where burned; also roadsides
and rights-of-way. Ranges on the Coastal
Plain from se VA to c FL and sw AL.

MAY–JULY

COMMELINACEAE: DAYFLOWER FAMILY

Pineland Dayflower; Sand Dayflower

Commelina erecta L. var. *angustifolia* (Michaux) Fernald

Perennial, to 14″ (30 cm) tall in our region (but can be taller elsewhere), somewhat succulent. Leaves are few, with conspicuous sheaths around the stem that have a bristly fringe. Leaf blades are narrow, long-pointed, 1.5–4″ (4–10 cm) long and 0.25–0.75″ (5–15 mm) wide. Flowers grow from within broad, fused bracts (called spathes) that sheath the stem. There are 2 blue petals plus a third that is white and much smaller, each flower 0.6–1.25″ (1.5–3 cm) across.

This is one of the jewels of our pinelands, with its bright blue flowers and succulent stems that seem out of place in a frequently burned environment. In the Piedmont and low Mountains occurs var. *erecta*, a larger plant of rocky slopes and ledges. A few other species of dayflowers occur on roadsides and in cropfields, but they are aliens to North America.

Inhabits dry longleaf pinelands, clearings, and roadsides. Ranges from e NC to s FL and TX, mostly on the Coastal Plain but also scattered inland.

JUNE–EARLY OCT.

FABACEAE: PEA & BEAN FAMILY

Sandhill Scurfpea; Lupine Scurfpea

Orbexilum lupinellum (Michaux) Isely
[*Psoralea lupinellus* Michaux]

Glabrate perennial from a slender rhizome, the stems usually many, 6–15″ (15–37 cm) tall, branches widely spreading and creating a bushy aspect. Leaves are palmately divided into 5–7 linear segments, each segment 1.25–3.2″ (3–8 cm) long and less than 1.5 mm wide, widest toward tip, with resin dots. Flowers grow terminally in small clusters atop a stalk 1.6–3.2″ (4–8 cm) long, the flowers pea-shaped, deep blue or violet. The pods have only a single segment, the surface with many raised lines.

Sandhill Scurfpea is another plant that deserves a close look to appreciate the architecture of its unique leaves, its richly colored flowers, and its lined pods. It is uncommon in NC, rare in SC, but known from many counties in s GA, apparently not quite reaching the GA Sandhills.

Inhabits dry pinelands and turkey oak barrens. Ranges on the Coastal Plain in three areas: from sc nc to nc SC; s SC to c FL and sw AL; c AL.

MAY–EARLY JULY

GENTIANACEAE: GENTIAN FAMILY
Autumn Gentian;
Pine-barren Gentian
Gentiana autumnalis L.

Perennial, 6–24″ (15–70 cm) tall. The leaves are sparse, opposite, linear, 2–3″ (5–7.5 cm) long and less than 2 mm wide, curved parallel to the ground so that when viewed from above they resemble whirling "helicopter blades." The single flower (rarely 2–3) is about 2″ (5 cm) long with 5 spreading lobes, deep blue, usually speckled with pale green dots.

Autumn gentian is one of the glories of the fall season, and its intensely blue flowers always generate interest and wonder. Petals open on sunny days but close when the sky is overcast. Once thought to be rare nationally, it has been found to be locally common in the Carolinas and NJ.

Inhabits dry to moist longleaf pinelands and savannas. Ranges throughout the Coastal Plain of NC south to Clarendon County, SC; SE VA, S DE, S NJ.

LATE SEPT–EARLY DEC.

BORAGINACEAE: BORAGE FAMILY
Virginia Marbleseed
Onosmodium virginianum (L.) A. DC.

Perennial, hispid (rough hairy), 1–2′ (30–80 cm) tall, branched in upper portion of stem. Leaves are oblanceolate, 1.2–5″ (3–13 cm) long, the lower ones tapered to base, all leaves short-tapered to tip, strongly veined. Flowers grow terminally and from upper axils in one-sided coils (technically a helicoid cyme), the lowest flowers blooming first, the coils also bearing small leaflike bracts. Corollas are pale yellow or greenish, tubular, 0.3–0.4″ (7–10 mm) long, with 5 short lobes that spread somewhat. Fruits are hard, white, smooth, glossy, ovoid nutlets, 0.2″ (2–2.8 mm) long.

Virginia Marbleseed is unique in our flora; nothing else combines its physical features of strongly veined leaves and shiny white nutlets. The coils unroll only one or a few flowers at a time. It has become rare north of NC.

Inhabits loamy sand soils of longleaf pinelands, including bean dips and upland flats. Ranges on the Coastal Plain from MA to FL and LA, with scattered stations inland to KY and TN.

LATE APR.–EARLY SEPT.

POACEAE: GRASS FAMILY
Carolina Wiregrass
Aristida stricta Michaux var. *stricta*

Tussock-forming, perennial grass from hardened bases that are clothed in remnants of old leaves. Leaves are abundant, radiating in all directions and forming a tussock. Leaves are rounded in cross section, 1–1.5′ (30–45 cm) long, tapered to a sharp point, smooth except some wispy hairs near the base. Flowering stems grow to 3′ (1 m) tall, with many flowers in the upper half; each flower has 3 wide-spreading awns up to 1″ (2.5 cm) long.

Wiregrass is the single most important component of the longleaf pine ecosystem, due to its abundance and ability to carry low-temperature fire through the community. It is so closely tied with fire that it normally will not flower or fruit until burned; then it produces abundant culms and turns a beautiful straw color in fall. Where fire is suppressed, wiregrass tussocks can survive for decades but eventually get shaded out by hardwoods. In central South Carolina there is a gap where wiregrass mysteriously does not occur; south of this zone it is replaced by Southern Wiregrass (*A. stricta* var. *beyrichiana*), which has a dense row of hairs near each leaf base.

Inhabits a broad range longleaf pine communities. Ranges on the Coastal Plain from e NC to c SC. Variety *beyrichiana* ranges from s SC to ec GA (Richmond County) to c FL and se MS.

JUNE–AUG.

POACEAE: GRASS FAMILY
Big Bluestem; Turkeyfoot
Andropogon gerardii Vitman

Tall perennial grass from a short, knotty rhizome, stems 3–6 feet (1–2 m) tall, smooth. Leaves grow up to 20″ (50 cm) long and 0.25 inch (5 mm) wide, smooth. Two to 5 flower spikes, each 3–4″ (7–10 cm) long, grow from the tip of the stem and spread somewhat, resembling a turkey's foot.

Big Bluestem is one of the primary grasses of midwestern tallgrass prairies, along with Switchgrass and Yellow Indiangrass, both of which also inhabit the Sandhills region. Their ability to withstand periodic fires serves them well in the Sandhills ecology. Big Bluestem often occurs in patches, suggesting vegetative clones rather than sexual reproduction.

Inhabits bean dips and loamy soil areas within longleaf-wiregrass pinelands, and openings in oak-hickory forests. Ranges from s Que. to s Sask. south to FL and AZ.

LATE SEPT.–MID-NOV.

POACEAE: GRASS FAMILY
Silvery Bluestem; Splitbeard Bluestem

Andropogon ternarius Michaux

Perennial from a short, knotty rhizome, stems 2.2–4.5′ (0.7–1.5 m) tall, smooth. Leaves grow up to 12″ (30 cm) long and 0.2 inch (3.5 mm) wide, smooth. Two to 3 flower spikes, each 0.8–2″ (2–5 cm) long, grow on long stalks at intervals along the stem. Each spike soon splits in 2, revealing densely and conspicuously white hairy flowers. As in all grasses, the flowers lack petals.

Silvery Bluestem is a beautiful, late fall grass whose silvery white spikes stand out against other vegetation. Oldfield Bluestem or Oldfield Broomsedge (*A. virginicus*) is very similar, but its flowering spikes grow on short stalks and are hardly showy. There are several other species of bluestems that you may find in our area; consult a more technical work.

Inhabits dry to mesic longleaf-wiregrass pinelands and also in oak-hickory forests. Ranges from DE to KY and MO south to FL and TX.

LATE SEPT.–MID-NOV.

POACEAE: GRASS FAMILY
Little Bluestem

Schizachyrium scoparium (Michaux)
  Nash var. *scoparium*
[*Andropogon scoparius* Michaux]

Perennial grass, stems solitary or forming small clumps, 2.2–4.5′ (0.7–1.5 m) tall, smooth. Leaves grow up to 10″ (25 cm) long and 0.2 inch (3.5 mm) wide, smooth; leaf sheaths are more or less hairy. Flower spikes are solitary, 0.8–2.4″ (2–6 cm) long, from long stalks at intervals along stem, the spike slender, not splitting in 2, white hairy.

Little Bluestem is a very important grass throughout much of North America. It is a major component of shortgrass prairies, and in our region it is prominent in a number of natural habitats as well as a pioneer in abandoned fields and disturbed woodlands.

Other species of bluestems are in the genus *Andropogon*; a few are included in this book. In *Andropogon*, each flower spike splits into 2 identical racemes.

Inhabits dry longleaf pinelands (especially where disturbed), oak-hickory woodlands, roadsides, old fields, and rights-of-way. Ranges from N.B. to Alb. south to FL and TX; Mex.

AUG.–OCT.

POACEAE: GRASS FAMILY
Silky Oatgrass
Danthonia sericea Nuttall

Perennial grass, forming small clumps of few to several stems with basal leaves that tend to curl and twist with age. Leaves grow up to 6″ (15 cm) long and 0.1–0.2″ (2–4 mm) wide, hairy beneath. Stems are 1.3–3′ (0.4–1 m) tall, with a few leaves on lower part, a few to several terminal branchlets with 6–10 flowering spikes, each flower densely hairy and with a more or less twisted awn 0.4–0.5″ (10–12 mm) long.

Silky Oatgrass is a common spring flowering grass that adds a dash of elegance to our woodlands and clearings. It is not related to cultivated oats (*Avena sativa*); the inflorescences merely bear a fanciful resemblance.

Inhabits a wide range of upland woodlands from longleaf pinelands to oak-hickory forests, especially where burned or disturbed; also found in openings and clearings and along roadsides. Ranges from s NJ to nw FL and se LA, inland to KY and TN.

APR.–EARLY JUNE

POACEAE: GRASS FAMILY
Upland Muhly
Muhlenbergia capillaris (L.) Trinius

Perennial tussock-forming grass. Leaves are very numerous, to 16″ (40 cm) long and less than 0.2″ (1–3 mm) wide, tip long attenuate and more or less involute (margins rolled under). Flowering stems are 1.5–3.5′ (0.5–1.2 m) tall, the inflorescence occupying half of it. The abundant and threadlike branches of the inflorescence form an open, elliptical panicle, the whole of it red-tinged. Each branch is terminated by a single flower, 0.2″ (4–5 mm) long and with an awn 0.2–0.5″ (3–13 mm) long.

Upland Muhly is one of our most beautiful grasses, due to the pale red, delicate, and airy inflorescences. When back-lit, a colony is truly spectacular! It is a close relative of the maritime dune grass called Sweet Grass (*M. sericea*), used for making baskets and in horticultural plantings.

Inhabits dry longleaf pine–wiregrass sites and pine savannas, especially in loamy sand of bean dips and upland flats. Ranges from MA to IN and KS south to FL and TX.

SEPT.–OCT.

POACEAE: GRASS FAMILY
Nodding Indiangrass
Sorghastrum elliottii (C. Mohr) Nash

Tall perennial grass to 6′ (2 m) tall, in tufts, loose colonies, or solitary. Leaves are all basal and near-basal, to 2′ (60 cm) long and 0.4″ (10 mm) wide, erect or ascending. Flowers grow in narrow, terminal, arching, or nodding inflorescences up to 12″ (30 cm) long and 1–2″ (2.5–5 cm) wide, lustrous brown with dull yellow anthers. Flower awns are brownish and twisted.

Nodding Indiangrass is one of the most graceful of plants and would make a great garden border. It often grows with Yellow Indiangrass in loamy soil areas that are especially rich in beans, composites, and grasses.

Inhabits longleaf pinelands, favoring loamy soil flats and bean dips; also openings in oak-hickory woods, rights-of-way, and roadsides. Ranges from MD to TN and OK south to n FL and TX.

SEPT.–OCT.

POACEAE: GRASS FAMILY
Prairie Indiangrass; Yellow Indiangrass
Sorghastrum nutans (L.) Nash

Tall perennial grass to 8′ (2.5 m) tall, in tufts or colonies. Leaves are all basal and near-basal, to 2′ (60 cm) long and 0.6″ (15 mm) wide, erect or ascending, sometimes glaucescent. Flowers grow in a narrowly elliptical, terminal, erect inflorescence up to 16″ (40 cm) long and 1.2–2″ (3–5 cm) wide, tawny or pale brown with bright yellow prominent anthers The flower awns are yellowish and twisted.

Yellow Indiangrass is one of the primary components of the tallgrass prairies of the Midwest, yet it is equally at home here because of its fire tolerance and need for abundant sunlight. When flowering, it is one of our most attractive plants.

Inhabits longleaf pinelands, favoring loamy soil flats and bean dips; also openings in oak-hickory woods, rights-of-way, and roadsides. Ranges from s Que. to s Man. south to c FL and AZ; Mex.

SEPT.–OCT.

CYPERACEAE: SEDGE FAMILY
Starburst Flatsedge;
Plukenet's Flatsedge

Cyperus plukenetii Fernald

Perennial from a cormlike base. Stem single, mostly 2–3' (0.7–1 m) tall, with several grasslike, pleated leaves at base with scabrous (rough) margins. The summit of the stem is divided into a few long, leafy bracts and several to many horizontally spreading or somewhat arching branches up to 1' (30 cm) long, each branch terminated by a flowering spike. Spikes are strongly obovate or top-shaped, 0.4–0.8" (1–2 cm) long, dark brown, composed of many sharp, backward-oriented scales. Reduced flowers (lacking petals) and seeds are produced singly among the scales.

As its name suggests, Starburst Flatsedge has wonderful architecture—like a miniature fireworks display. The spiny scales efficiently attach to fur or clothing for dispersal of the seeds.

Inhabits well-burned longleaf pinelands, generally avoiding the driest soils. Ranges mostly on the Coastal Plain from s NJ to c FL, e TX, and se MO.

JULY–OCT.

TURKEY OAK SCRUB

Turkey Oak Scrub, also called Turkey Oak Barrens, used to be common on upper slopes, hilltops, and ridges throughout our region, but it has been severely reduced by development, conversion to pine plantations, and fire suppression. Deep sandy soils and fairly frequent fires (originally by lightning and Native Americans) place high stresses on plants; some have evolved thick underground perennial rhizomes, while others are annuals dependent on a seed-bank. Dominants are Longleaf Pine (*Pinus palustris*), Turkey Oak (*Quercus laevis*), and Wiregrass (*Aristida stricta*, two varieties), but cover is sparser in all layers as compared with Dry Longleaf Pine-lands. Dwarf Post Oak (*Q. margarettae*), Bluejack Oak (*Q. incana*), and Persimmon (*Diospyros virginiana*) usually also occur and may be common. Herbs are sparsely to moderately distributed and include Threadleaf Gerardia (*Agalinis setacea*), Sheathed Bluestem (*Andropogon gyrans*), Slender Roseling (*Cuthbertia graminea*), Sandhill Chaffhead (*Carphephorus bellidifolius*), Rosemary (*Ceratiola ericoides*), Sandhill Thistle (*Cirsium repandum*), Tread-softly (*Cnidoscolus stimulosus*), White Sandhill-spurge (*Euphorbia curtisii*), Dwarf Huckleberry (*Gaylussacia dumosa*), Sandhills Blazing-star (*Liatris cokeri*), Georgia Beargrass (*Nolina georgiana*), Carolina Sandwort (*Minuartia caroliniana*), and Wire-plant (*Stipulicida setacea*). Sandhills Pyxie-moss (*Pyxidanthera brevifolia*) is nearly restricted to this community. Fire suppression produces dense oak thickets with sparse Longleaf Pines and reduced Wiregrass cover; eventually all but the oaks disappear.

Dry, nutrient-poor soils support Turkey Oaks and widely spaced Longleaf Pines.

At extreme sites, patches of bare sand are prominent, while pines and wiregrass are sparse.

Species List

The color after a name indicates the primary natural community or habitat.

T = mentioned in text of another species; not pictured.

Agalinis setacea
  Threadleaf Gerardia
Amsonia ciliata
  Fringed Bluestar; Sandhill Bluestar
Aristida stricta ✳
  Wiregrass
Asclepias amplexicaulis ✳
  Wavy-leaved Milkweed
Asclepias humistrata
  Fleshy Milkweed
Asclepias tomentosa
  Hairy Milkweed
Asclepias tuberosa ssp. *rolfsii* ✳
  Sandhill Orange Milkweed
Astragalus michauxii ✳
  Sandhills Milkvetch
Aureolaria pectinata
  Sticky False-foxglove;
  Southern Oakleach
Baptisia cinerea ✳
  Carolina Wild-indigo
Baptisia lanceolata T ✳
  Lanceleaf Wild-indigo
Baptisia perfoliata
  Gopherweed; Catbells
Berlandiera pumila ✳
  Eastern Greeneyes
Carphephorus bellidifolius
  Sandhill Chaffhead
Ceratiola ericoides
  Rosemary; Sand Heath
Chrysopsis gossypina var. *gossypina*
  Gossamer Golden-aster;
  Cottonleaf Golden-aster
Cirsium repandum ✳
  Sandhill Thistle
Cnidoscolus stimulosus
  Tread-softly; Spurge-nettle;
  Bull-nettle
Crataegus uniflora
  One-flowered Hawthorn
Crocanthemum canadense
  Canada Frostweed; Canada Sunrose
Cuthbertia graminea
  Slender Roseling; Grassleaf Roseling
Danthonia sericea ✳
  Silky Oatgrass

Elliottia racemosa
  Georgia Plume
Eriogonum tomentosum
  Sandhill Wild-buckwheat
Euphorbia curtisii ✳
  White Sandhill-spurge
Euphorbia ipecacuanhae
  Carolina Ipecac; Wild Ipecac
Euphorbia pubentissima ✳
  Southern Flowering-spurge
Galactia regularis ✳
  Smooth Milkpea
Gaylussacia dumosa
  Dwarf Huckleberry
Hypericum gentianoides ✳
  Pineweed
Hypericum hypericoides ✳
  St. Andrew's-cross
Ionactis linariifolius ✳
  Stiff Aster
Liatris cokeri
  Sandhills Blazing-star
Liatris secunda T
  One-sided Blazing-star
Liatris tenuifolia
  Slender Blazing-star
Lithospermum caroliniense
  Sandhill Puccoon
Lupinus diffusus
  Sandhill Lupine
Minuartia caroliniana
  Carolina Sandwort
Morella pumila ✳
  Dwarf Wax-myrtle
Nolina georgiana
  Georgia Beargrass
Opuntia humifusa
  Prickly Pear
Orbexilum lupinellum ✳
  Sandhill Scurfpea
Pediomelum canescens ✳
  Buckroot
Phlox nivalis ✳
  Pineland Phlox
Physalis lanceolata ✳
  Sandhills Ground-cherry

Pityopsis aspera ❋
  Sticky Golden-aster
Pityopsis pinifolia ❋
  Sandhills Golden-aster
Polygonella americana
  Showy Jointweed
Polygonella gracilis T
  Slender Jointweed
Polygonella polygama
  October-flower
Pyxidanthera brevifolia
  Sandhills Pyxie-moss
Robinia nana
  Dwarf Locust
Rubus cuneifolius ❋
  Sand Blackberry
Ruellia ciliosa ❋
  Sandhill Wild-petunia
Schizachyrium scoparium ❋
  Little Bluestem
Sericocarpus asteroides ❋
  Toothed White-topped Aster
Silphium compositum ❋
  Rosinweed
Sisyrinchium rufipes ❋
  Sandhill Blue-eyed-grass

Stillingia sylvatica ❋
  Queen's Delight
Stipulicida setacea
  Wire-plant
Stylisma patens ssp. *angustifolia* T ❋
  Narrowleaf Dawnflower
Stylisma patens ssp. *patens* ❋
  Sandhill Morning-glory;
  Sandhill Dawnflower
Stylisma pickeringii
  Pickering's Morning-glory;
  Pickering's Dawnflower
Tephrosia virginiana ❋
  Common Goat's-rue
Toxicodendron pubescens ❋
  Poison Oak
Vaccinium arboreum ❋
  Sparkleberry
Vernonia angustifolia ❋
  Slender Ironweed
Viola pedata ❋
  Bird's-foot Violet
Warea cuneifolia
  Carolina Pineland-cress

EUPHORBIACEAE: EUPHORBIA & SPURGE FAMILY
Tread-softly; Spurge-nettle; Bull-nettle

Cnidoscolus stimulosus (Michaux)
Engelmann & Gray

Perennial, erect to reclining, up to 1.5 feet (0.5 m) tall, entire plant covered with stinging hairs. Leaves single or a few together, palmately lobed, margins toothed, leafstalks about half as long as blades. Flowers grow in terminal clusters, normally 1 or a few blooming at one time, sepals showy, white, the 5 lobes spreading 0.8–1.2″ (2–3 cm) across; petals absent.

Tread-softly is a well-named plant, for its stinging hairs are guaranteed to get your attention! Each hair is hollow but filled with a chemical brew that causes a burning sensation that lasts for many minutes and produces a rash in most people.

Inhabits dry sandy soil of turkey oak scrub and longleaf pinelands; also roadsides and disused cropfields. Ranges primarily on the Coastal Plain but also into the Piedmont, from se VA to FL and se LA.

LATE MAR.–AUG.

ROSACEAE: ROSE FAMILY
One-flowered Hawthorn

Crataegus uniflora Muenchhausen

Perennial woody shrub to 10′ (3 m) tall but usually a third to half that, twigs ascending, with thorns 0.4–2″ (1–5 cm) long. Leaves are obovate or elliptic, 0.8–2.4″ (2–6 cm) long and 0.3–1.25″ (7–30 mm) wide, tip often slightly lobed, base tapered, glabrate above, pubescent below, margins doubly serrate and with gland-tipped teeth. One to 3 flowers grow from leaf bases, their stalks up to 0.8″ (20 mm) long and hairy. The sepal margins are serrate with gland-tipped teeth; the 5 petals are white. Fruits look like tiny red-brown apples.

Hawthorns (genus *Crataegus*) are a difficult group to sort to species without experience, but One-flowered Hawthorn is common and readily identified by its small stature, very few flowers per cluster, and preference for very dry soil.

Inhabits turkey oak scrub, dry longleaf pinelands, clearings, roadsides, and rocky slopes. Ranges from NJ and e PA south to n FL, e TX, and s MO, mostly in the Coastal Plain and Piedmont.

APR.–MAY

CARYOPHYLLACEAE:
PINK & SANDWORT FAMILY
Carolina Sandwort
Minuartia caroliniana (Walter) Mattfield
[*Arenaria caroliniana* Walter]

Perennial from a thickened root. Stems several to many, spreading on ground or forming tufts, up to 1′ (30 cm) long. The leaves are densely spaced, overlapping, awl-like, up to 0.5″ (12 mm) long and 1 mm wide, lacking fascicles of smaller leaves in axils. Flowers grow at ends of long, slender, branching stalks, about 0.75″ (18 mm) across, petals 5, white, separate to base.

Sandwort ("sand plant") is a good name for this species, as it grows out of seemingly sterile sand. The thick root stores food and water to last through droughts and hot fires. Vegetatively, Carolina Sandwort is very similar to Pineland Phlox, but the latter has bristly leaf margins and has fascicles of small leaves in the leaf axils.

Inhabits very dry sandy soil of turkey oak scrub, longleaf pinelands, roadside banks, and rights-of-way. Ranges on the Coastal Plain from sw RI and se NY to nw FL.

APR.–JUNE, SOMETIMES LATER

DIAPENSIACEAE:
DIAPENSIA & PYXIE-MOSS FAMILY
Sandhills Pyxie-moss
Pyxidanthera brevifolia Wells

Perennial, evergreen, prostrate shrublet with more or less hairy stems and leaves, the entire plant no more than 16″ (40 cm) in diameter. Leaves are crowded, lanceolate or narrowly oblanceolate, 0.2–0.25″ (2–5 mm) long, sessile, acute, dark green and often purple-tinged, with white hairs beneath and sometimes also above. Flowers grow singly at ends of numerous short branches, sepals 5, united basally, usually pink; petals 5, white, with obovate lobes about 0.2″ (3–4 mm) long.

Sandhills Pyxie-moss is endemic to the Sandhills region, discovered and named by ecologist B. W. Wells of North Carolina State University. When not flowering, both species of pyxie-moss can be mistaken for patches of moss; when flowering, both look like patches of snow, so densely covered with flowers are they. Common Pyxie-moss (*P. barbulata*) inhabits perennially moist soil; its plants are broader-spreading; it has larger, greener, and nearly hairless leaves; and its flowers are slightly larger than those of Sandhills Pyxie-moss.

Inhabits dry to very dry soil of turkey oak barrens and longleaf pinelands. Endemic to a 6-county area of the Sandhills of sc NC and nc SC.

EARLY MAR.–MID-APR.; SPORADICALLY IN JAN.–FEB.

CARYOPHYLLACEAE:
PINK & SANDWORT FAMILY

Wire-plant

Stipulicida setacea Michaux

Extremely slender annual or short-lived perennial, glabrous. The single stem grows up to 5″ (12 cm) long, widely forked above into wirelike segments. Basal leaves are spatulate, produced in autumn; they over-winter and then disappear. Stem leaves are tiny, bractlike, only 1–2 mm long. Flowers are terminal, about 0.25″ (5 mm) across, the 5 tiny petals white.

When not in flower, Wire-plant is easily overlooked, as its minuscule leaves and threadlike branches don't attract attention. Yet it is just these features that help it withstand midsummer's blazing heat reflected from the bare sand of its chosen habitat. And what great architecture!

Inhabits very dry, bare sandy soil of turkey oak barrens, longleaf pinelands, and Carolina bay rims. Ranges on the Coastal Plain from se VA to s FL and se LA; w Cuba.

MAY–AUG.

CONVOLVULACEAE: MORNING-GLORY FAMILY

Pickering's Morning-glory; Pickering's Dawnflower

Stylisma pickeringii (Torrey ex M. A. Curtis) Gray
var. *pickeringii*

Sprawling, perennial, nonclimbing vine without tendrils. Stems are numerous, more or less prostrate, up to 7′ (2.1 m) long, usually forming sprawling low mounds with radiating arms. Leaves are linear, oriented vertically, up to 2.25″ (5.5 cm) long and 0.15″ (3 mm) wide. One to 3 flowers grow on erect slender stalks from leaf axils. The 5-parted calyx is pubescent; the 5 white petals are spread out nearly flat, about 0.75″ (2 cm) across, subtended by 2 long, linear bracts.

Nothing looks quite like this plant, with its many long, skinny stems radiating out like a huge pinwheel. Although showy in flower, all traces disappear in late fall. Its protracted flowering period and unusual form would make it a novelty in a dry garden. Named for Charles Pickering (1805–78), Philadelphia physician, naturalist, and member of the Wilkes Exploring Expedition to the southern oceans.

Inhabits semistable sands of riverside terraces and river-deposited dunes; also adapted to open roadsides and scrapes. Ranges discontinuously from s NJ to s GA and c AL.

JUNE–AUG.

ERICACEAE: BLUEBERRY & AZALEA FAMILY
Dwarf Huckleberry

Gaylussacia dumosa (Andrews) Torrey & Gray

Perennial, small, colonial shrub from long horizontal rhizomes. Stems grow up to 1.5′ (0.5 m) tall but are much shorter where repeatedly burned. Leaves are elliptic to oblanceolate, up to 1.5″ (3.5 cm) long, shiny above, with many gland-tipped hairs and golden resin dots on both surfaces (best seen beneath). Small but showy clusters of short, white, tubular flowers 0.25″ (5–7 mm) long grow from branches that have prominent leaflike bracts. Berries are black, shiny, with gland-tipped hairs.

The large berries of this common plant are tantalizing but have little flavor and large seeds. Plants of Southern Blueberry (*Vaccinium tenellum*) can sometimes be confusingly similar; distinguish it by nonshiny leaves, lack of yellow resin dots, lack of leaflike bracts on floral branches, and hairless berries.

Inhabits dry to moist pinelands, turkey oak scrub, flatwoods, and savannas. Ranges from VA to FL and LA, mostly on the Coastal Plain but occasionally in the Piedmont and Mountains.

MID-MAR.–EARLY MAY

ERICACEAE: BLUEBERRY & AZALEA FAMILY
Georgia Plume

Elliottia racemosa Muhlenberg ex Elliott

Woody shrub or small tree to 30′ (9 m) tall (but normally less than half that), clonal and thicket-forming. Leaves alternate, deciduous, mostly 2–5″ (5–12 cm) long and 1–2″ (2.5–5 cm) wide, tapered at both ends, bristle-tipped, dark green above, gray-green beneath with dense pubescence. Flowers grow at branch tips in elongate clusters to 12″ (30 cm) long; petals 4–5, about 0.5″ (12 mm) long, white, recurved, the long style projecting straight out.

Georgia Plume is unique; nothing else closely resembles it. Honeycups (*Zenobia pulverulenta*) may look similar at a distance, but its leaves are much broader and its flowers are cup-shaped. The genus *Elliottia* is named for Stephen Elliott (1771–1830), author of the two-volume *A Sketch of the Botany of South Carolina and Georgia* in 1821–24. In the Sandhills region it grows only in the vicinity of Augusta, GA.

Inhabits dry to moist woodlands, sand ridges, and outcrops of serpentine rock. A Georgia endemic, found only in the southeastern third of the state (historically one site in SC). A Georgia rare plant.

JUNE–JULY

**POLYGONACEAE:
SMARTWEED & BUCKWHEAT FAMILY**
Sandhill Wild-buckwheat

Eriogonum tomentosum Michaux

Perennial, stem 1.3–3′ (0.4–1 m) tall,
much-branched above, hairy. Basal leaves
are numerous and form a rosette, elliptical, 2.8–4.8″ (7–12 cm) long and up to 1.6″
(4 cm) wide, tapering to a long stalk, glabrous above, densely tomentose beneath
with white or tan hairs. Stem leaves are
smaller, well-spaced, in whorls of 3 or 4.
Flowers grow at ends of branches, in tight
clusters of 10–20. Petals absent, sepals
petal-like, white to pinkish, about 0.2″
(3–4 mm) long at first, eventually reaching 0.3″ (7–8 mm).

Eriogonum is a large genus out West
(hundreds of species), but just a few occur
in the East. Sandhills Wild-buckwheat is
fairly common in sc and GA but collected
only once in NC in the 1890s.

Inhabits very dry sandy soil in turkey
oak scrub, longleaf pinelands, and Carolina bay rims. Ranges on the Coastal Plain
from se NC to c FL and se AL.

LATE JULY–SEPT.

**POLYGONACEAE:
SMARTWEED & BUCKWHEAT FAMILY**
Showy Jointweed

Polygonella americana (Fischer & Meyer) Small

Perennial, mostly 1.5–2.6′ (50–80 cm)
tall, with numerous short branches in
the upper third. Stems and branches
have slightly swollen nodes encircled by
short-tubular sheaths (in this family called
ocreae). Stem leaves are linear to oblinear,
0.4–0.8″ (1–2 cm) long, the tips translucent; branch leaves are smaller. Flowers
are numerous, the 5 sepals white, about
0.2″ (3 mm) long and broad, 3 of them
erect and 2 bent back; petals absent.

In a family not known for its beautiful
wildflowers, Showy Jointweed is an exception with its masses of brilliant white.
Moreover, it appears to be one of those
species whose original habitat remains
in question, for it is not found in natural
habitats. Slender Jointweed (*P. gracilis*) is
an annual with slender stems; it has few
or no branches, its leaves are up to 2.8″
(6.5 cm) long, and it has smaller flowers
in slender spikes. Slender Jointweed is
very rare in the Sandhills region, known
from Talbot and Taylor Counties, GA, and
Hoke County, NC.

Inhabits roadsides, dry old fields, and
disturbed turkey oak scrub, in all cases
benefiting from occasional fire or mechanical disturbance. Ranges from s NC
to TN and NM south to s GA and TX.

JUNE–JULY, OCCASIONALLY LATER

POLYGONACEAE:
SMARTWEED & BUCKWHEAT FAMILY
October-flower

Polygonella polygama (Ventenat)
   Engelmann & Gray

Perennial, bushy-branched to form small, rounded shrubs to 1.5′ (50 cm) tall. Stems and branches have slightly swollen nodes encircled by short-tubular sheaths (in this family called ocreae). Leaves are oblanceolate, 0.2–0.5″ (4–13 mm) long and 0.5–1.5 mm wide. Flowers are numerous, the 5 sepals white or creamy, about 1 mm long and broad, 3 of them erect and 2 bent back; petals absent.

October-flower forms gumdroplike mounds on sterile sand, for much of the year looking moribund, but come cooler fall days it bursts into bloom, each plant turning into a mass of creamy white flowers.

Inhabits roadsides, turkey oak scrub, dry longleaf pinelands, and Carolina bay rims. Ranges from se NC to ec GA (Augusta area), s FL, and se TX.

SEPT.–OCT.

RUSCACEAE:
MAYFLOWER & RUSCUS FAMILY
Georgia Beargrass

Nolina georgiana Michaux

Perennial from a basal tuft of leaves. The numerous leaves are all basal or near-basal, arching out and down, grasslike, linear, 1–1.5′ (30–45 cm) long and no more than 0.25″ (6 mm) wide, glaucescent. The stem grows 1–5′ (0.3–1.7 m) tall with branches that form a panicle bearing numerous flowers. The flowers grow 1–3 per node, short-stalked, the 3 petals and 3 sepals alike, white or ivory, about 0.2″ (2–4 mm) long.

No other plant in our region resembles Georgia Beargrass. The discoverer was André Michaux (1746–1802), a French horticulturist and plant explorer who was sent to the United States to find woody plants suitable for cultivation in Europe. He traveled widely and under difficult conditions, collected prodigiously, and established growing gardens in Charleston, SC, and in NJ from which he exported thousands of individual plants.

Inhabits dry to very dry turkey oak scrub and longleaf pinelands. Ranges from nc SC to c GA and se GA.

LATE MAY–JUNE

ASTERACEAE: ASTER FAMILY
Gossamer Golden-aster; Cottonleaf Golden-aster

Chrysopsis gossypina (Michaux) Elliott
[*Heterotheca gossypina* (Michaux) Shinners]

Perennial, stems one to several, up to 2′ (0.7 m) long, radiating from a central point and creeping along the ground, the outer portions erect. Leaves are broadly lance-shaped, gradually smaller up the stems; stems and leaves are covered with cobwebby white hairs. Showy flower heads grow at stem tips, each 1.5–2″ (3.5–5 cm) across, ray and disc flowers yellow.

Nothing else in our area looks quite like this plant, with its dense, cottony white hairs and low, spreading habit. It is another example of a plant with great architecture. Flowers of Maryland Golden-aster look very similar, but its stems are erect and much less hairy.

Inhabits dry to very dry longleaf pinelands and turkey oak scrub; tolerant of disturbance, it is often found on roadsides, rights-of-way, and similar areas. Ranges on the Coastal Plain from se VA to n FL.

SEPT.–OCT.

FABACEAE: PEA & BEAN FAMILY
Gopherweed; Catbells

Baptisia perfoliata (L.) R. Brown ex Aiton f.

Perennial from a thick rhizome, plant glabrous and glaucescent, stem 1.5–3′ (0.4–1 m) tall, erect or leaning, branched. Leaves are simple, perfoliate, rounded, up to 4″ (10 cm) long and wide. Flowers grow singly in leaf axils, bright yellow, 0.5″ (12 mm) long. Pods are tough, semiwoody, roundish, less than 0.75″ (18 mm) long.

With its unique architecture and undivided leaves, Gopherweed is one bizarre plant, but it is just one of many species in our region that have evolved odd shapes. The name refers to the fact that this plant often grows near burrows of Gopher Tortoises (*Gopherus polyphemus*); the animals apparently graze on the pods and void seeds outside their burrows.

Inhabits dry turkey oak scrub, sandhills, and longleaf pinelands. Ranges on the Coastal Plain from sw SC to e GA to C FL.

APR.–MAY

OROBANCHACEAE: BROOMRAPE FAMILY
Sticky False-foxglove; Southern Oakleach

Aureolaria pectinata (Nuttall) Pennell

Annual, nearly all parts with short, gland-tipped hairs, parasitic on roots of the black oak group. Stems grow to 3′ (1 m) tall, much-branched to form a bushy aspect. Leaves are numerous, opposite, lanceolate, 0.8–2.4″ (2–6 cm) long and 0.3–0.8″ (8–21 mm) wide, pinnately or bipinnately divided into narrow, usually toothed segments. Flowers are solitary in leaf axils, their stalks 0.3–0.6″ (8–16 mm) long. The 5 yellow petals form a tubular corolla with flaring lobes, 1.2–1.8″ (3–4.5 cm) long and nearly as broad. The whole plant turns blackish in autumn.

The large yellow flowers and gumdrop shape of Sticky False-foxglove make it very attractive. It is named for its abundant, viscid hairs, the function of which is unknown. Hapless insects are sometimes caught, but the plant obtains no nutrient benefit, as do sundews (*Drosera*).

Inhabits dry to very dry soil of turkey oak scrub and longleaf pinelands. Ranges from NC to S MO south to C FL and LA.

LATE MAY–SEPT.

CISTACEAE: ROCKROSE FAMILY
Canada Frostweed; Canada Sunrose

Crocanthemum canadense (L.) Britton
[*Helianthemum canadense* (L.) Michaux]

Perennial, 4–14″ (10–35 cm) tall, stem often tinged purple-brown, pubescent. Leaves 10–20, ascending, lance-shaped to elliptical, 0.4–1.2″ (1–3 cm) long and 0.2–0.4″ (4–8 mm) wide, leafstalks less than 0.2″ (3 mm) long. Leaves are densely pubescent with very short, stellate hairs beneath, much less so above. One or 2 flowers grow at tip of stem on stalks up to 0.4″ (10 mm) long, the 5 yellow petals 0.4–0.6″ (10–15 mm) long. The anthers usually are red.

Canada Frostweed is one of 8 species that occur in our 3 states, none of which is particularly common, and only 2 enter the Sandhills region. In addition to spring-blooming yellow flowers, frostweeds also produce "hidden" (cleistogamous) flowers without petals later in the season. These flowers actually are highly fertile and produce many viable seeds. Canada Frostweed is rare in GA.

Inhabits dry to very dry pinelands, turkey oak scrub, roadbanks, rights-of-way, and other disturbed areas. Ranges from N.S. to MN south to N AL and MO.

MID-APR.–MID-MAY

CACTACEAE: CACTUS FAMILY
Prickly Pear
Opuntia humifusa (Rafinesque) Rafinesque

Perennial from rather slender roots. The stems are prostrate to ascending, segmented, flattened yet very thick and fleshy, green and photosynthetic. Each segment is elliptical or broadly lanceolate, up to 7″ (18 cm) long and 3″ (7.5 cm) wide. Segments have scattered nodes or bumps that produce tufts of short, tawny, irritating hairs and sometimes also a single spine about 1″ (2.5 cm) long. Flowers grow on thick shoots, one to several flowers each, yellow, waxy, about 2.5″ (6 cm) across. Fruits are thick, purple-red berries up to 2″ (5 cm) long, full of seeds and fleshy pulp.

Cacti have fascinated people ever since the discovery of the New World, with large and colorful flowers and odd plant shapes, not to mention potent spines. The thick stems store large amounts of water—a feature very useful to native peoples living in desert regions. Fruits of many species of *Opuntia* are tasty and juicy; they are sold in Mexican *tiendas* under the Spanish name *tuna*.

Inhabits dry sandy soil of longleaf pinelands and turkey oak barrens; also roadsides, rights-of-way, and rock ledges. Ranges from MA to e IA south to n FL and c TX.

LATE MAY–MID-JUNE

EUPHORBIACEAE:
EUPHORBIA & SPURGE FAMILY
Carolina Ipecac; Wild Ipecac
Euphorbia ipecacuanhae L.

Perennial, hairless plant from a long, thick rootstock, sap milky white. Stem single, sometimes multiple, spreading and/or branching beneath ground, at soil level dividing again to produce prostrate (occasionally erect) branches up to 1′ (30 cm) long. Leaves opposite, linear to elliptic or oblanceolate, 0.4–2.8″ (1–7 cm) long and up to 0.8″ (1–20 mm) wide, green to purplish. Flowers grow on long stalks from leaf axils, about 0.2″ (2.5–4 mm) broad, petals absent, replaced by tiny (less than 0.5 mm), greenish, yellowish, or reddish modified glands that look like petals.

As one author aptly said, "hopelessly variable"; indeed, plants often look very different from one another, but the general aspect of prostrate plants with no main stem aboveground gives them away. Sometimes all one sees is a single pair of leaves and a flower! Widely used by Native Americans as an emetic and laxative. The original ipecac of commerce is a Brazilian shrub well-known for its purgative properties.

Inhabits dry longleaf pinelands and turkey oak barrens, especially where burned. Ranges on the Coastal Plain from c CT and se NY to e GA (Burke and Richmond Counties).

MID-MAR.–JUNE

BORAGINACEAE: BORAGE FAMILY
Sandhill Puccoon

Lithospermum caroliniense
(Walter ex J. F. Gmelin) MacMillan

Rough-haired perennial from a thick taproot, the stem simple or branched, 1–3′ (0.3–1 m) tall. Leaves are numerous, broadly linear to narrowly elliptic, blunt-tipped. Flowers grow in a row along branches arising from the upper leaf bases, the branches coiled at first and gradually unrolling. Corollas are orange or orange-yellow, funnel-shaped, 0.5–1″ (13–25 mm) long, with 5 spreading lobes. Fruits are dry hard capsules, white, smooth, about 0.2″ (3–3.5 mm) long.

"Sandhill" here refers to the habitat, for this plant extends well beyond the Sandhills region of the Coastal Plain. "Puccoon" is a Native American word for the roots of this and related plants, which were dried and beaten into a red powder used for swellings, aches, and body decoration. The bright white seeds are very hard and give the plant another common name, Stoneseed, which is what the Latin genus *Lithospermum* means.

Inhabits dry pine sandhills, turkey oak scrub, and roadsides. Ranges on the Coastal Plain from s sc to FL and e TX; also se VA.

APR.–JUNE

ASTERACEAE: ASTER FAMILY
Sandhill Chaffhead   *or Cat's Head?*

Carphephorus bellidifolius (Michaux)
Torrey & Gray

Perennial, one to several stems grow to 1.7′ (52 cm) tall, glabrous or appressed pubescent. The numerous basal leaves are prostrate, up to 8″ (20 cm) long and 1.25″ (3 cm) wide, long-stalked, each blade elliptic and blunt-tipped, glabrous or nearly so. Stem leaves are rapidly reduced upward in size, eventually stalkless. The inflorescence is about as broad as long, much-branched, with many heads. Each head is 0.5–.75″ (12–18 mm) wide, the bracts blunt and more or less reflexed, disc flowers deep pink to rose-purple, rays absent.

Sandhill Chaffhead is a characteristic plant of the dry Sandhills of NC and SC, entering GA only in the Augusta area. As with other purple fall flowers, Sandhill Chaffhead attracts many butterflies, especially skippers. Individual plants bloom for long periods and would make good garden subjects.

Inhabits turkey oak scrub and dry longleaf pinelands, even in relatively bare sand. Ranges on the Coastal Plain from se VA to ec GA (Richmond County).

LATE AUG.–EARLY NOV.

ASTERACEAE: ASTER FAMILY
Sandhills Blazing-star
Liatris cokeri Pyne & Stucky
[*Liatris regimontis* (Small) K. Schumann]

Perennial from a hard, roundish root-stock. Stems solitary or a few together, ascending or arching, sometimes erect, to 2.7′ (0.8 m) long, unbranched. Leaves are numerous, linear, 2–7″ (5–18 cm) long and less than 0.2″ (2–5 mm) wide, gradually reduced in length up the stem. Leaves are densely punctate on both surfaces; the margins have fine hairs near the base. Flower heads grow in a dense spike (heads without stalks) or raceme (heads short-stalked), the spike often one-sided. The bracts of the heads form a cone-shaped involucre 0.2–0.4″ (5–10 mm) long, their tips dense with resin dots. Each head is composed of 4–9 disc flowers, pink to rosy, up to 0.3″ (7 mm) long, with 5 short spreading lobes, rays absent.

Sandhills Blazing-star is named for William C. Coker, longtime professor of botany at the University of North Carolina at Chapel Hill and for whom the herbarium and the arboretum are named. For decades it was misidentified as another species, but in 1990 research-ers from North Carolina State University described it as distinct. One-sided Blazing-star (*L. secunda*) is very similar but has stems with short hairs, and its whitish or pale pink flowers only grow on one side of the stem (a condition called secund); it ranges from s NC to nw FL and s AL and inhabits the same communities.

Inhabits turkey oak scrub and dry long-leaf pinelands. Endemic to the Sandhills region of NC and SC, from Wayne County to Kershaw County.

AUG.–OCT.

ASTERACEAE: ASTER FAMILY
Slender Blazing-star
Liatris tenuifolia Nuttall

Perennial from a hard, roundish root-stock. The stem is usually solitary, erect, to 6′ (2 m) tall, unbranched. Leaves are numerous, linear, 2–6″ (5–15 cm) long and up to 1.5 mm wide, much reduced in length up the stem, glabrous. Flower heads grow in a dense, long, spikelike raceme (heads on very short stalks); the bracts form a short-cylindric involucre about 0.25″ (5–7 mm) long, with fine hairs. Disc flowers usually number 5 per head, lavender-pink or rosy, about 0.25″ (5–8 mm) long, with 5 short spreading lobes, rays absent.

Slender Blazing-star is a survivor extraordinaire, able to eke out an existence in the most barren of habitats in nutrient-poor, acidic sand. Yet it carries itself with a grace that defies its inhospitable environment.

Inhabits dry turkey oak barrens and scrub; also sand rims of Carolina bays. Ranges on the Coastal Plain from nc SC to wc GA (Taylor County), c FL and s AL.

LATE AUG.–EARLY OCT.

FABACEAE: PEA & BEAN FAMILY
Dwarf Locust
Robinia nana Elliott

Perennial, single-stemmed shrub 1–3′ (0.3–1 m) tall (to 6′ [2 m] in absence of fire), from spreading rhizomes. Young plants are pubescent, but mature plants are nearly smooth. Leaves grow near top of stem, 4–8″ (10–20 cm) long, divided into 7–15 elliptical leaflets up to 1.5″ (4 cm) long. Flowers grow in arching or drooping clusters about 4″ (10 cm) long, up to 10 flowers per cluster, pea-shaped, pink or rosy pink, about 1″ (2–3 cm) long.

Dwarf Locust is one of the showiest members of our flora, as it flowers prolifically. However, it rarely sets fruit, apparently reproducing vegetatively via rhizomes. It sprouts vigorously following fire. Bristly Locust (*R. hispida* var. *hispida*) is similar, but stems are densely bristly with brownish hairs; it is often planted and has escaped to roadsides and rights-of-way.

Inhabits very dry to mesic longleaf pinelands, turkey oak scrub, clearings, and roadsides. Ranges on the Coastal Plain from e NC to wc GA; scattered in the Piedmont from NC to ne AL.

MID-APR.–LATE MAY

APOCYNACEAE:
DOGBANE & MILKWEED FAMILY
Fleshy Milkweed
Asclepias humistrata Walter

Glabrous perennial with milky sap, stems stout, more or less prostrate, several to many in a circle or semicircle, 1–2.5′ (30–70 cm) long. Leaves occur in 5–8 pairs per stem, opposite, sessile, broadly ovate, 2.5–4.5″ (6–11 cm) long and 1.7–3.3″ (4.5–8.5 cm) wide. Note the pale grayish green surfaces with pinkish red veins, the thick texture, and the blades oriented sideways. Numerous flowers grow in 2–5 clusters from the upper stem nodes, 1.3–2″ (3–5 cm) across, flowers white with pale rosy reflexed petals.

With its circular arrangement of prostrate stems, its leaves held sideways as if to avoid the sun, and its unique coloring, Fleshy Milkweed is unmistakable.

Inhabits very dry sandy soil of longleaf pinelands, turkey oak scrub, roadsides, and clearings. Ranges on the Coastal Plain from se NC to s FL and se LA.

EARLY MAY–JUNE

BRASSICACEAE: MUSTARD FAMILY
Carolina Pineland-cress
Warea cuneifolia (Muhlenberg) Nuttall

Glabrous annual, stems mostly 1–2′ (30–60 cm) tall, widely branched above. Leaves are oblanceolate, 0.8–1.6″ (2–4 cm) long and 0.2–0.4″ (5–10 mm) wide, tip blunt, tapered to base, margins entire, leafstalk less than 0.2″ (1–5 mm) long. Flowers grow terminally in a headlike cluster about 0.4–0.8″ (10–20 mm) across, the 4 petals 0.25–0.4″ (7–10 mm) long, pink to whitish, spreading, abruptly narrowed basally. The stamens extend well beyond the petals. The fruit is a slender, curved pod 1.6–2.4″ (4–5 cm) long.

Despite its delicate appearance, Carolina Pineland-cress survives in our harshest habitats in poor soil and extreme heat. It relies on producing copious seeds to survive through unfavorable periods. The genus is named for Nathaniel A. Ware (1789–1853), South Carolina teacher. Three other species occur south of our region. Rare in NC.

Inhabits low-nutrient sandy soil of turkey oak scrub and longleaf pinelands. Ranges on the Coastal Plain from sc NC to wc GA and nw FL.

LATE JULY–SEPT.

OROBANCHACEAE: BROOMRAPE FAMILY
Threadleaf Gerardia

Agalinis setacea (J. F. Gmelin) Rafinesque

Much-branched, delicate-looking annual, 8–24″ (20–60 cm) tall. Principal leaves are opposite, linear, to 1.2″ (3 cm) long and 1 mm wide, often curved. Flowers grow on outer portions of branches, the flower stalks 0.6–1″ (15–25 mm) long. The corolla is horn-shaped (petals form a short tube with 5 flaring lobes), 0.6–1″ (15–25 mm) long, rosy pink, speckled inside with purple and with 2 pale yellow lines.

All members of this genus are parasitic while young on other plants' roots, but later they sever all connections. Threadleaf Gerardia flowers prolifically and can be common enough to color small patches of longleaf pinelands. Stems blacken with age, even before autumn frosts.

Inhabits dry longleaf pinelands, turkey oak scrub, Carolina bay rims, and poor soil of roadsides and rights-of-way. Ranges on the Coastal Plain from se NY to c FL; also scattered on dry rocky slopes in the Piedmont.

SEPT.–LATE OCT.

COMMELINACEAE: DAYFLOWER FAMILY
Slender Roseling; Grassleaf Roseling

Cuthbertia graminea Small
[*Tradescantia rosea* Ventenat var. *graminea* (Small) Anderson & Woodson]

Glabrous perennial to 1′ (30 cm) tall, numerous stems and leaves growing in a dense tuft. Leaves grasslike, mostly 6–9″ (15–22 cm) long and 2 mm wide, acuminate (long tapering). Each stem produces 3–10 rose-colored, 3-petaled flowers 0.5–0.75″ (12–18 mm) across.

From late spring to summer Slender Roseling brightens the pinelands and sand ridges with its vivid color. It is a wonder that such a delicate-looking plant can survive in the harsh conditions of droughty sterile soil and frequent fires. The genus is named for Alfred Cuthbert (1857–1932), a keen naturalist who collected plants in GA, SC, and FL. The type location (place of discovery) of *C. graminea* is Augusta, GA.

Inhabits dry longleaf pine sandhills, turkey oak scrub, and Carolina bay rims. Frequent in the Carolinas, uncommon in GA. Ranges on the Coastal Plain from se VA to ec GA and c FL.

MID-MAY–JULY

APOCYNACEAE:
DOGBANE & MILKWEED FAMILY

Fringed Bluestar;
Sandhill Bluestar

Amsonia ciliata Walter

Perennial from a thick rootstock, plant
with milky sap. Stems single or several
together, 1–2′ (30–70 m) tall, densely
hairy, branched in upper part, very leafy.
Leaves are alternate, linear or narrowly
lance-shaped, up to 3″ (7.5 cm) long and
0.25″ (5 mm) wide, densely hairy. Flowers
grow in a terminal cluster, pale blue, each
forming a slender tube with 5 spreading
lobes. Each flower is about 0.75″ (2 cm)
across and star-shaped. Fruits are paired
slender pods 4–7″ (10–17 cm) long, erect.

The dense hairs make each leaf appear
to be fringed, hence the name. Flowers
begin opening while the plant's unfurling
branches are lax, a curious but beautiful
effect.

Inhabits turkey oak barrens, dry
pinelands, roadsides, and rights-of-
way. Ranges on the Coastal Plain from
SC NC to C FL to S AL.

APR.

FABACEAE: PEA & BEAN FAMILY

Sandhill Lupine

Lupinus diffusus Nuttall

Densely hairy biennial from a thick
taproot, several to many stems radiate
outward and upward, 8–16″ long. Leaves
are grayish green due to the appressed
silvery hairs, elliptic, 2.5–4.7″ (6.5–12 cm)
long and 0.8–2″ (2–5 cm) wide, generally
held erect. Flowers grow in dense cylindrical racemes 4–12″ (10–30 cm) long, pale to
medium blue with a creamy white spot on
the standard. Pods are numerous, erect,
1.25–2″ (3–5 cm) long and about 0.3″ (7–9
mm) wide, with dense, appressed hairs.

Each plant produces leaves the first
growing season; these overwinter and
produce flowers in the spring. The whole
plant turns blackish brown and dies after
fruiting. Sundial Lupine (*L. perennis*) has
leaves divided into a circle of narrow segments, and its flowers are a deeper blue or
purple-blue; very uncommon in our area.

Inhabits dry to very dry soils of
longleaf pine sandhills, turkey oak scrub,
roadsides, and rights-of-way. Ranges on
the Coastal Plain from SE NC to S FL and
SE MS.

LATE MAR.–EARLY MAY

APOCYNACEAE:
DOGBANE & MILKWEED FAMILY
Hairy Milkweed

Asclepias tomentosa Elliott

Short-haired perennial with milky sap, stem single or a few together, 7–19″ (20–50 cm) tall. Leaves occur in 3–6 pairs, opposite, stalked, lance-shaped to broadly elliptical, 2.2–3.3″ (5.5–8.5 cm) long and 0.6–1.4″ (1.5–3.5 cm) wide, tip pointed, margins more or less wavy. Flowers grow in 2–6 clusters from upper leaf axils, 1.3–2″ (3–5 cm) across, flowers pale green or yellowish green.

Hairy Milkweed is a very uncommon species and seems to occupy only a fraction of suitable habitat. It has been reported from GA but without specimen documentation; it should be sought in the Augusta area.

Inhabits dry sandy soil of longleaf pine sandhills, turkey oak barrens, and clearings. Ranges on the Coastal Plain in 3 areas: SC NC to SC SC; southern peninsular FL to nw FL; e TX.

MAY–JUNE

ERICACEAE: BLUEBERRY & AZALEA FAMILY
Rosemary; Sand Heath

Ceratiola ericoides Michaux

Perennial shrub 1.5–8′ (0.5–2.5 m) tall, densely and widely branched, bark on older plants gray and shreddy, young twigs gray and with short, matted hairs. Leaves are abundant, alternate or whorled, sessile, like conifer needles, 0.25–0.75″ (5–15 mm) long, margins curled under. Sexes are on separate plants, the flowers sessile in leaf axils, the 2 sepals and 2 petals yellowish to brownish, about 1.5 mm long. The 2 stamens have red-brown anthers; the stigma has 4–5 lobes.

Rosemary is unique in many ways, not the least of which is its rather pungent but pleasing odor. It also is the sole species in its genus (thus a monotypic genus). Finally, although filled with highly flammable compounds (like many of our fire-adapted plants), Rosemary inhabits places that burn relatively infrequently. This may be a long-term survival strategy, as seeds germinate following fire even though adults may be killed. It is Rare in GA and SC.

Inhabits the driest, sandiest turkey oak sandhills and barrens, where wiregrass is uncommon or even absent. Ranges on the Coastal Plain from ne SC to ec GA (Richmond and Burke Counties) south to s FL and se MS.

OCT.–NOV.

OAK-HICKORY FOREST

This community is restricted to relatively fire-protected areas, such as steep slopes along creeks and rivers. Such places are often called "fire shadows" because fires burn unevenly or poorly through them, due to constant high humidity and relatively sparse herb and shrub layers. Some examples may originally have been Dry Longleaf Pineland communities that have been fire-suppressed for many decades. In all cases, soil nutrients and minerals build up to support a mix of oaks, hickories, and pines: Southern Red Oak (*Quercus falcata*), White Oak (*Q. alba*), Post Oak (*Q. stellata*), Black Oak (*Q. velutina*), Blackjack Oak (*Q. marilandica*), Mockernut Hickory (*Carya alba*), Sand Hickory (*C. pallida*), Longleaf Pine, Loblolly Pine (*Pinus taeda*), and Shortleaf Pine (*P. echinata*). Other trees may include Sourwood (*Oxydendrum arboreum*) and Upland Black Gum (*Nyssa sylvatica*). Understory trees include Dogwood (*Cornus florida*) and Witch Hazel (*Hamamelis virginiana*). Wiregrass is sparse or even absent, and herb diversity is low to moderate. A number of species intolerant of high fire frequencies occur in this habitat, such as White Milkweed (*Asclepias variegata*), Spotted Wintergreen (*Chimaphila maculata*), and Little Brown Jug (*Hexastylis arifolia*).

Many of the plants that occur in this habitat are much more common in the Piedmont than in the Coastal Plain; in fact, we often refer to them as "piedmont plants" from our point of view here in the Sandhills. On steep riverside bluffs, a variant of this community can take on a very Piedmont aspect indeed. In addition to some of the woody and herbaceous plants mentioned above, there may be Mountain Laurel (*Kalmia latifolia*), Fringetree (*Chionanthus virginicus*), Galax (*Galax urceolata*), and Hillside Blueberry (*Vaccinium pallidum*).

Oaks, hickories, and pines form a closed canopy, with Flowering Dogwood beneath. Leaf litter is slow to decompose.

Species List

The color after a name indicates the primary natural community or habitat.

T = mentioned in text of another species; not pictured.

Andropogon ternarius ❋
  Silvery Bluestem
Antennaria plantaginifolia
  Plantain-leaved Pussytoes

Arnica acaulis
  Leopard's-bane; Southeastern Arnica
Asclepias tuberosa ssp. *tuberosa* T ❋
  Common Butterfly-weed

Asclepias variegata
White Milkweed
Asclepias verticillata
Whorled Milkweed
Aureolaria virginica
Downy False-foxglove;
Virginia Oakleach
Baptisia tinctoria ✳
Northern Wild-indigo
Callicarpa americana
Beautyberry; French Mulberry
Ceanothus americanus
New Jersey Tea
Chimaphila maculata
Spotted Wintergreen;
Striped Pipsissewa
Clinopodium georgianum
Georgia Calamint
Coreopsis verticillata
Cutleaf Tickseed;
Threadleaf Coreopsis
Croomia pauciflora
Croomia
Desmodium ciliare ✳
Littleleaf Tick-trefoil
Desmodium laevigatum ✳
Smooth Tick-trefoil
Desmodium nuttallii ✳
Nuttall's Tick-trefoil
Desmodium paniculatum
Panicled Tick-trefoil
Desmodium viridiflorum T ✳
Velvet Tick-trefoil
Elephantopus tomentosus T ✳
Upland Elephant's-foot
Epigaea repens ✳
Trailing Arbutus
Eupatorium album ✳
White Eupatorium
Eupatorium hyssopifolium
Hyssopleaf Eupatorium
Eupatorium rotundifolium var.
rotundifolium ✳
Roundleaf Eupatorium
Galactia volubilis T ✳
Twining Milkpea
Gaura filipes
Threadstalk Gaura
Goodyera pubescens
Downy Rattlesnake-plantain

Helianthus atrorubens ✳
Purpledisc Sunflower
Helianthus divaricatus
Woodland Sunflower
Hexastylis arifolia
Little Brown Jug;
Arrowhead Heartleaf
Hieracium gronovii T ✳
Autumn Hawkweed
Hieracium marianum ✳
Maryland Hawkweed
Hieracium venosum
Rattlesnake Hawkweed
Houstonia caerulea ✳
Bluets
Houstonia purpurea
Summer Bluet
Hylodesmum nudiflorum
Naked Tick-trefoil
Hypericum lloydii
Piedmont St. John's-wort
Hypoxis hirsuta
Common or Upland Stargrass
Isotria verticillata
Large Whorled Pogonia
Lactuca canadensis ✳
Yellow Wild Lettuce
Lespedeza hirta T ✳
Roundleaf Bush-clover
Lespedeza procumbens T ✳
Trailing Bush-clover
Lespedeza repens ✳
Creeping Bush-clover
Lespedeza stuevei T
Stueve's Bush-clover
Lespedeza virginica
Slender Bush-clover;
Virginia Bush-clover
Liatris squarrulosa ✳
Earle's Blazing-star
Lilium michauxii
Carolina Lily
Lobelia puberula
Downy Lobelia
Lonicera sempervirens
Coral Honeysuckle
Luzula echinata
Hedgehog Woodrush
Lysimachia quadrifolia
Whorled Loosestrife

Malaxis unifolia
Green Adder's-mouth
Medeola virginiana
Indian Cucumber-root
Mitchella repens ❋
Partridge-berry
Monotropa uniflora
Indian Pipes
Nestronia umbellula
Nestronia
Oxalis stricta ❋
Common Yellow Wood-sorrel
Pedicularis canadensis
Wood Betony; Lousewort
Penstemon laevigatus T ❋
Smooth Beardtongue
Physalis virginiana T ❋
Virginia Ground-cherry
Polygonatum biflorum
Solomon's-seal
Potentilla canadensis ❋
Dwarf Cinquefoil
Pycnanthemum pycnanthemoides
Woodland Mountain-mint
Pycnanthemum tenuifolium
Slender Mountain-mint
Rhododendron periclymenoides
Wild Azalea;
Pinxter-flower
Rhus copallinum ❋
Winged Sumac
Rhus glabra
Smooth Sumac
Rosa carolina ❋
Carolina Rose
Ruellia caroliniensis
Carolina Wild-petunia
Sabatia angularis T ❋
Bitterbloom
Sabatia quadrangulata T ❋
Four-angled Sabatia
Saccharum alopecuroides T ❋
Foxtail Plumegrass
Sanicula canadensis
Canada Sanicle
Scutellaria elliptica
Elliptic-leaved Skullcap
Silene caroliniana var. *caroliniana*
Carolina Pink; Wild Pink
Silene virginica
Fire Pink

Smilax glauca
Sawbrier; Wild Sarsparilla
Solidago arguta var. *caroliniana*
Vasey's Goldenrod
Solidago caesia
Bridle-wreath Goldenrod;
Bluestem Goldenrod
Solidago odora ❋
Fragrant Goldenrod
Solidago pinetorum T
Pineywoods Goldenrod
Solidago rugosa var. *aspera* T ❋
Roughstem Goldenrod
Sorghastrum elliottii ❋
Nodding Indiangrass
Sorghastrum nutans ❋
Prairie Indiangrass
Spiranthes tuberosa ❋
Little Ladies'-tresses
Stewartia malacodendron ❋
Silky Camellia
Symphyotrichum grandiflorum
Rough Aster; Large-headed Aster
Symphyotrichum patens
Skydrop Aster
Tephrosia spicata ❋
Tawny Goat's-rue
Thaspium trifoliatum
Woodland Parsnip
Tipularia discolor
Cranefly Orchid
Trichostema dochotomum ❋
Common Blue-curls
Uvularia puberula var. *nitida*
Coastal Plain Bellwort
Vaccinium arboreum
Sparkleberry
Vaccinium pallidum
Hillside Blueberry
Vaccinium stamineum
Deerberry
Viburnum prunifolium
Black Haw; Nannyberry
Viola villosa
Southern Woolly Violet
Vitis aestivalis T
Summer Grape
Vitis rotundifolia
Muscadine Grape; Scuppernong
Yucca filamentosa
Adam's Needle; Curlyleaf Yucca

ASTERACEAE: ASTER FAMILY
Plantain-leaved Pussytoes

Antennaria plantaginifolia (L.) Richardson

Perennial from a rosette of leaves; also producing long subsurface runners that develop new plants at their tips, thus forming colonies. Blades of the rosette leaves are elliptical or obovate, up to 3″ (8 cm) long and 1″ (2.5 cm) wide, tapered to long stalks, gray green above and very densely coated with short, white, woolly hairs beneath. Leaves persist into winter before withering. Flowers grow in clusters of small heads on separate male and female plants (the species is thus dioecious), at top of stems up to 16″ (40 cm) tall with reduced leaves, disc flowers whitish, rays absent.

The soft flowering heads—like a cat's paw—give this plant part of its name; the other part comes from the leaves, which resemble plantains (genus *Plantago*). The gray-green color of the leaves is due to whitish hairs lying flat against the green surface.

Inhabits oak-hickory woodlands and sometimes loamy soil areas within dry longleaf pinelands. Ranges from N.S. to Sask. south to FL, AR, and OK.

LATE MAR.–EARLY MAY

ASTERACEAE: ASTER FAMILY
Hyssopleaf Eupatorium

Eupatorium hyssopifolium L.

Perennial, 1.5–3′ (0.5–1 m) tall, pubescent. Leaves in whorls of 4, linear, 1.2–3.2″ (3–8 cm) long and about 0.25″ (5 mm) wide, tapered at both ends, toothed or not, with tiny resin dots beneath. Middle and upper leaf whorls have some short leaves in axils. The stem is branched above into a flat-topped cluster of tiny flower heads, each with white bracts and 5 white disc flowers, rays absent. The inflorescence is covered with short, white, downy hairs.

From other eupatoriums, this one stands out with its slender whorled leaves and its fascicles of small leaves in the axils of most whorls.

Inhabits dry oak-hickory woods, road-sides, and loamy soil areas within longleaf pinelands. Ranges from se MA to n FL and e TX; inland to TN.

LATE JULY–OCT.

APOCYNACEAE:
DOGBANE & MILKWEED FAMILY
White Milkweed

Asclepias variegata L.

Glabrate to minutely pubescent perennial with milky sap, stem solitary, stout, 8–30″ (20–80 cm) tall. Leaves occur in 2–5 pairs, opposite, ovate or elliptic, 2–5.5″ (5–14 cm) long and 1.2–2.7″ (3–7 cm) wide. The lowermost leaves are much the smallest. Numerous bright white flowers grow in 1–4 rounded clusters about 1.3–2.5″ (3–6 cm) across, terminal and from upper leaf axils.

In our area White Milkweed shuns fire-dependent habitats; it is most often found on north-facing slopes that are in "fire shadows"—areas that generally lack wiregrass and do not carry fire well.

Inhabits dry to mesic sandy loam soils of oak-hickory forests and pine-oak woodlands. Ranges from sw CT to s IL and e OK south to nw FL and e TX.

MID-MAY–JUNE

APOCYNACEAE:
DOGBANE & MILKWEED FAMILY
Whorled Milkweed

Asclepias verticillata L.

Perennial with milky sap, stem solitary, slender, sometimes branched, pubescent in lines, 10–24″ (25–70 cm) tall. Leaves are numerous, whorled, linear, 1.2–2.8″ (3–7 cm) long and 1–2 mm wide, sparsely pubescent. The small flowers grow in clusters about 1.5″ (3–5 cm) across, from 2–8 upper leaf axils, dull white or greenish white. Pods are slender, only 0.25″ (4–6 mm) wide, long-tapered and smooth.

Mostly a Piedmont and Mountain species, Whorled Milkweed occurs in our better soils, such as loamy sands. It makes up for an inconspicuous nature with a long blooming period.

Inhabits dry to mesic loamy sand soils of oak-hickory woodlands and bean dips in longleaf pinelands and rocky slopes. Ranges from MA to Man. s to FL and e TX.

JUNE–SEPT.

RHAMNACEAE: BUCKTHORN FAMILY
New Jersey Tea

Ceanothus americanus L.

Perennial woody shrub to 3′ (1 m) tall, with widely spreading branches. Leaves are narrowly ovate, 1.2–3.2″ (3–8 cm) long and 0.4–1.6″ (1–4 cm) wide, finely toothed, pubescent, strongly 3-veined beneath. Flowers grow in dense oval clusters at ends of long stalks from the leaf bases, each flower on a long white stalk. The 5 petals are slender with an expanded tip, about 2 mm long, white. Fruits are 3-lobed, about 0.2″ (3–4 mm) long and 0.25″ (4–5 mm) wide, persisting into winter.

During the American Revolution, leaves were gathered in great quantity to serve as a poor substitute for tea during the trade embargo. Long before then, Indians made a root tea for fever, stomachache, and snakebite and as a blood tonic.

Inhabits oak-hickory forest and loamy soil areas within longleaf pinelands. Ranges from c ME to s Man. south to n FL and e TX.

MAY–JUNE

LAMIACEAE: MINT FAMILY
Slender Mountain-mint

Pycnanthemum tenuifolium Schrader

Perennial, stems 4-angled, 1.3–3′ (0.4–1 m) tall, glabrous, bushy-branched. Leaves are glabrous, opposite, linear or narrowly lanceolate, 0.8–2″ (2–5 cm) long and less than 0.2″ (1–4 mm) wide, tip acuminate, margins entire, nearly sessile. Flowers grow in terminal clusters, each cluster with several leafy, pointed bracts at base. Individual flowers have 5 sharp calyx lobes about 0.2″ (4 mm) long, the 5 petals white to pinkish, about 0.2″ (4 mm) long, the 3 lower petals forming a lip and spotted with lavender.

Close inspection of mountain-mint flowers reveals intricate shapes (orchidlike) and bold spotting. Slender Mountain-mint's leaves possess a mildly pungent, minty odor that is refreshing.

Inhabits longleaf pinelands, oak-hickory woodlands, roadsides, and rights-of-way. Ranges from s ME to s MN and KS south to n FL and TX.

LATE JUNE–AUG.

LAMIACEAE: MINT FAMILY
Woodland Mountain-mint

Pycnanthemum pycnanthemoides
(Leavenworth) Fernald

Perennial, stems 4-angled, 3–6′ (1–2 m) tall, with white hairs, upwardly branched. Leaves are softly downy, opposite, well-spaced, elliptic to narrowly ovate, 1.2–4″ (3–10 cm) long and 0.6–1.6″ (1.5–4 cm) wide, the tip acute to acuminate, the base short-tapered or rounded, margins toothed, stalks up to 0.5″ (12 mm) long. Upper leaves are strikingly whitened with dense, appressed hairs. Flowers grow in domed clusters 0.6–1.8″ (1.5–4.5 cm) wide, each cluster with several leafy, pointed bracts at base. Individual flowers have 5 sharp calyx lobes about 0.2″ (4 mm) long, the 5 petals white to pale lavender, about 0.3″ (8 mm) long, the 3 lower petals forming a lip and spotted with purple.

Close inspection of mountain-mint flowers reveals intricate shapes (orchid-like) and bold spotting. Woodland Mountain-mint leaves and stems possess a strong, pungent, minty odor that is very refreshing.

Inhabits oak-hickory woodlands and openings. Ranges from VA to IL south to C GA and AL.

LATE JUNE–AUG.

ONAGRACEAE: EVENING-PRIMROSE FAMILY
Threadstalk Gaura

Gaura filipes Spach

Perennial, stems to 5′ (1.5 m) tall, pubescent, with slender spreading branches above. Leaves are crowded below but sparse on branches, linear to lance-shaped, to 2.4″ (6 cm) long and 0.25″ (6 mm) wide. Leaves are tapered to a stalkless base, acute-tipped, toothed or wavy-margined. Flowers grow terminally in a row, sepals reflexed (swept back), petals 0.2–0.3″ (4–7 mm) long, white turning pink, stamens prominent.

There are half a dozen gauras in our 3 states; this is the one most likely to be seen in the Sandhills region. Flowers open in the evening and wither the next morning.

Inhabits dry, sandy pine-oak and oak-hickory woodlands, clearings, and old fields. Ranges from NC SC to KY and S IN south to N FL and E LA.

LATE APR.–JULY

ERICACEAE: BLUEBERRY & AZALEA FAMILY
Spotted Wintergreen; Striped Pipsissewa
Chimaphila maculata (L.) Pursh

Perennial subshrub with a long-lived, semiwoody stem, often connected to other plants via rhizomes; stems may grow to 8″ (20 cm) tall. Leaves are evergreen, technically alternate but often appearing whorled, lance-shaped, 0.8–2.4″ (2–6 cm) long and 0.4–0.9″ (1–2.3 cm) wide. Leaves are deep green with a central blaze and some whitish veins, thick-textured, margins remotely toothed, leafstalks up to 0.3″ (2–8 mm) long. One to 5 flowers grow atop stalks up to 4″ (10 cm) long, the 5 white petals waxy-textured, 0.25–0.3″ (5–8 mm) long, broadly elliptical.

Spotted Wintergreen is a favorite of many people, as the plants brighten dreary winter days and remind them of woodland retreats. The generic name means "winter lover," in reference to its evergreen leaves; the name pipsissewa is Native American meaning "to make water," in reference to its diuretic property.

Inhabits oak-hickory forests, less often in pure pinelands; also roadsides and yards. Ranges from ME to s Ont. south to nw FL and c AL.

MAY–JUNE

ERICACEAE: BLUEBERRY & AZALEA FAMILY
Indian Pipes
Monotropa uniflora L.

Perennial, waxy-textured plants without chlorophyll, white to various shades of pinkish or reddish, stems 2–8″ (5–20 cm) tall. Leaves are short and scalelike, narrowly ovate, up to 0.6″ (15 mm) long, sessile, tip acute. The single flower is terminal, tubular, 0.6–1.2″ (1.5–3 cm) long, nodding during the blooming period but turning erect in fruit. The 5 petals are minutely downy on the inner surface.

Indian Pipes is a classic example of a micotroph—a plant that derives its nutrients from the decay of other plants via an association with fungi. The fungi do not cause death but merely take nutrients from already-dead material just below the ground surface; nutrients are then transferred to the rootlets of the Indian Pipes. A number of medicinal uses have been attributed to it, including calming nerves, soothing aches, and as a sedative.

Inhabits dry to moist oak-hickory woods and forested slopes along streams; elsewhere it occurs in a broader range of habitats. Ranges from Lab. to AK south to s FL and c CA; Mex., n South America, se Asia.

MID-JUNE–OCT.

ERICACEAE: BLUEBERRY & AZALEA FAMILY
Sparkleberry

Vaccinium arboreum Marshall

Perennial woody shrub or small tree, potentially to 1′ (30 cm) in diameter but less than 5″ (13 cm) in our area, to 33′ (10 m) tall but less than half that here, widely branched above and forming a roundish crown. The bark is gray-brown, flaking off to reveal cinnamon inner bark. Leaves are numerous, dark green, slowly deciduous over time. Leaves are elliptic to obovate, 0.8–2.8″ (2–7 cm) long and 0.4–1.6″ (1–4 cm) wide, lustrous above, pale and dull beneath, margins smooth to finely toothed. Flowers are abundant in leafy racemes from previous year's twigs. Each flower is long-stalked, cup-shaped, the 5 white petals 0.25–0.3″ (5–8 mm) long, tips acute and curled back. Berries are black, lustrous, 0.25–0.3″ (5–8 mm), not juicy or sweet.

Sparkleberry is a common shrub, and when in bloom it is one of our showiest plants. Unfortunately the berries are dry and mealy, for they are produced in great abundance.

Inhabits dry to very dry soils of oak-hickory woods, turkey oak scrub, longleaf pinelands, and rocky slopes. Ranges from VA to se KS south to n FL and c TX.

LATE APR.–MID-JUNE

ERICACEAE: BLUEBERRY & AZALEA FAMILY
Hillside Blueberry

Vaccinium pallidum Aiton
[*Vaccinium vacillans* Torrey]

Perennial woody shrub, 8″–2′ (20–60 cm) tall, much-branched, the twigs glabrate. Leaves are deciduous, elliptic to ovate, 1–2.4″ (2.5–6 cm) long and 0.6–1.4″ (1.5–3.5 cm) wide. The leaf tip is acute and with a tiny sharp point, the surfaces dull, underside glaucescent, margins entire (sometimes finely toothed). Flowers grow in clusters of 4–10, just prior to or with leaf-out, on short stalks. Corollas are short-cylindrical, the 5 petals greenish white or pink-tinged, 0.25–0.3″ (5–8 mm) long, tips acute and curled back. Berries are blue, glaucescent, 0.25–0.3″ (5–8 mm), juicy and sweet.

Hillside Blueberry, one of the lowbush blueberries, is uncommon in our area and found mainly on cool, north-facing slopes; it lives mostly in the Mountains and Piedmont. Note the different leaf shape and lack of gland-tipped hairs on leaves (vs. *V. tenellum*).

Inhabits dry soils of oak-hickory forests, often on slopes above streams. Ranges from N.S. to s Ont. and ne IA south to wc GA (Harris County), n AL, and n AR.

MAR.–APR.

ERICACEAE: BLUEBERRY & AZALEA FAMILY
Deerberry
Vaccinium stamineum L.

Perennial woody shrub, 1–5' (0.3–1.5 m)
tall, much-branched, the twigs glabrous or
pubescent. Leaves are deciduous, elliptic
to oblanceolate, 1.2–4" (3–10 cm) long
and 0.6–1.8" (1.5–4.5 cm) wide, tip acute
and with a tiny sharp point, surfaces
dull. Leaves vary from green to glaucous
beneath, their margins more or less entire
(may be gland-toothed basally). Flowers
grow in elongate leafy clusters just prior
to or with leaf-out, each on a long stalk.
The 5 petals are fused only about half of
their length and somewhat spreading,
white, 0.25–0.3" (5–8 mm) long, tips blunt,
stamens and style projecting. Berries are
greenish to purplish, usually glaucous,
0.3–0.6" (7–15 mm), dryish and bitter.

Deerberry is intermediate in stature between lowbush and highbush blueberries,
has uniquely shaped flowers that are not
tubular, and blooms later than other species. Leaves are extremely variable in size,
hairiness, color of the undersides, and
glaucousness, and there have been many
(unsatisfactory) attempts to split this species into distinct varieties.

Inhabits dry soils of oak-hickory
woods, longleaf pinelands, and rock
ledges. Ranges from MA to s Ont. south
to c FL and e OK.

APR.–MAY

ADOXACEAE: VIBURNUM & ELDERBERRY FAMILY
Black Haw; Nannyberry
Viburnum prunifolium L.

Perennial woody shrub, 4–10' (1.2–3 m)
tall, much-branched. Leaves are opposite,
elliptic, mostly 1.6–4" (4–10 cm) long and
0.8–2" (2–5 cm) wide, larger on sprout
shoots. The leaf tip is acute or forming a
short drip-tip, base short-tapered, leafstalk 0.2–0.6" (5–15 mm) long, margins
finely toothed or crenate, surfaces glabrous except for rusty-colored scaly hairs
on midrib. Flowers grow densely in flat-
topped umbels up to 3" (7.5 cm) across,
the 5 white petals forming a cup-shaped
corolla with spreading lobes, 0.2–0.3"
(5–8 mm) across. Fruits are elliptical,
about 0.3" (8–9 mm) long, compressed
lengthwise, black.

Black Haw's scientific name comes from
the resemblance of its leaves to members
of the genus *Prunus* (cherries, plums,
peaches, etc.). Although they look invit-
ing, the fruits of our viburnums are not
juicy or flavorful to humans.

Inhabits moist to dryish soils of oak-
hickory forests, slopes along streams, and
small floodplains. Ranges from NY to IA
and KS south to C GA and TX.

LATE MAR.–APR.

ORCHIDACEAE: ORCHID FAMILY
Downy Rattlesnake-plantain
Goodyera pubescens (Willd.) R. Brown

Perennial, basal leaves evergreen. Basal leaves are ovate to elliptical, short-stalked, 1.2–3.6″ (3–9 cm) long and 0.5–1.4″ (1.2–3.5 cm) wide, bluish green, with main veins and most cross veins white. Flowering stem solitary, to 18″ (45 cm) tall, with scattered, small, bractlike leaves, densely downy above, terminated by a dense raceme 1.2–4.8″ (3–12 cm) long. Flowers are dull white, roundish in outline, the sepals and petals about 0.25″ (5 mm) long, downy.

Some folks know this plant simply as a "terrarium plant," not realizing that the handsome evergreen leaves actually belong to a wild orchid. To see the flowers, however, you must brave the hottest days of summer. Leaves and roots were used by Native Americans to treat snakebites and various internal ailments.

Inhabits dry to moist oak-hickory-dogwood forests and margins of river floodplains. Ranges from N.B. to Ont. and MN south to FL, MS, and AR.

LATE JUNE–AUG.

AGAVACEAE: AGAVE & YUCCA FAMILY

Adam's Needle; Curlyleaf Yucca

Yucca filamentosa L.

Perennial from a subwoody base. Leaves are all basal in a multilayered rosette, evergreen, dark green, thick and succulent textured, rigid, broadly linear. Leaves are 8–23″ (20–60 cm) long and 0.8–2.4″ (2–6 cm) wide, sessile, tip acuminate and with sharp spine, surfaces smooth, margins with pale curly fibers. Flowers grow on branches of a stem 3–6′ (1–2 m) tall, the flower stalks 0.4–1.2″ (1–3 cm) long. The 3 sepals and 3 petals are alike, white, ovate to lanceolate, 1.2–2.4″ (3–6 cm) long, drooping. The stem slowly decomposes over winter.

This familiar plant has long been an ornamental and is often found around old home sites. Native Americans made extensive use of it for baskets, fish nets, twine, garments, and needles; also used medicinally to halt bleeding and reduce inflammation. Pollination is achieved only by a yucca moth adapted specifically to this plant.

Inhabits natural oak-hickory woods and loamy soil areas in longleaf pine uplands; also roadsides, former house sites, other and disturbed areas. Originally ranged from MD to GA and MS; now spread widely from there.

LATE APR.–MAY

APIACEAE: CARROT FAMILY
Canada Sanicle
Sanicula canadensis L.

Perennial, mostly 8″–2′ (20–60 cm) tall,
widely branched. Leafstalks of the lower
leaves are longer than blades; upper leaves
are progressively shorter-stalked. Leaf
blade outline is broadly ovate to rotund;
each blade is divided into 3–5 oblanceolate
to elliptical leaflets, each 0.8–2.4″ (2–6
cm) long and 0.6–1.4″ (1.5–3.5 cm) wide,
margins toothed. Flowers grow in small
umbels atop long stalks up to 4.8″ (12 cm)
long, terminally and from upper leaf axils.
Each umbel is composed of 3 perfect flowers (male and female in same flower) and
0–4 male flowers. The 5 petals are greenish
white, sitting atop a barrel-shaped ovary
with many hooked bristles, the styles
shorter than the bristles.

Plants with tiny greenish flowers are
usually overlooked, but this one leaves
calling cards of your visit: tiny hitchhiking
fruits whose hooked bristles catch onto
clothing and hair. Native Americans used
powdered roots to stimulate menses and
as an abortive. Other sanicles occur in
more nutrient-rich soils; consult technical
manuals.

Inhabits mid- to lower slopes of oak-
hickory forests, wooded slopes along
streams and rivers. Ranges from s VT to
s Ont. and SD south to nw FL and e TX.

APR.–MAY

RUSCACEAE: MAYFLOWER & RUSCUS FAMILY
Small Solomon's-seal
Polygonatum biflorum (Walter) Elliott var. *biflorum*

Glabrous perennial from long, white,
horizontal rhizomes, the stem single,
unbranched, arching, to 2′ (0.6 m) tall
(taller in richer soils away from Sandhills).
Leaves grow in 2 ranks, narrowly elliptical,
2–4″ (5–10 cm) long and 0.4–1.6″ (1–4 cm)
wide, tapered to both ends, sessile. One to
3 flowers grow from leaf axils on slender,
drooping stalks 0.4–1.6″ (1–4 cm) long.
The 3 sepals and 3 petals are alike, greenish white, forming a tube with 6 flaring
tips, 0.4–0.6″ (1–1.5 cm) long. Fruits are
rounded, berrylike, blue-black.

In our relatively poor soils, plants attain
small sizes; you can expect larger plants
in richer woods of the Piedmont. The
common name comes from the junction
of the stem and the subsurface rhizome:
the dislocated stem leaves a depression
with irregular marks, resembling an old-
fashioned "seal" like that of a signet ring.

Inhabits hardwood slopes along
streams and rivers and moist oak-hickory-
dogwood forests. Ranges from CT to
s Ont. and NE south to n FL and s AL.

LATE APR.–MAY

ASTERACEAE: ASTER FAMILY
Leopard's-bane;
Southeastern Arnica
Arnica acaulis (Walter) B.S.P.

Perennial, unbranched, densely beset
with sticky, gland-tipped hairs. The stem
is usually solitary and up to 2.5′ (0.8 m)
tall, growing from a rosette of 4–8 nearly
stalkless, broadly elliptic to broadly ovate
leaves 1.6–3.2″ (4–8 cm) long and 0.8–2.7″
(2–7 cm) wide. Stem leaves are much
smaller and narrower. Flower heads grow
on long stalks from the upper half of the
stem, disc flowers dark yellow, ray flowers
bright yellow and 0.8–1.2″ (2–3 cm) long.

   The name Leopard's-bane comes from
the fact that botanist Thomas Walter originally placed it in the genus *Doronicum*,
which includes the Leopard's-bane of
Europe. However, our plant is unrelated
to true Leopard's-bane and actually is the
southernmost representative of the boreal
and alpine genus *Arnica*.

   Inhabits openings in oak-hickory
forests, longleaf pinelands, roadsides, and
rights-of-way. Uncommon. Ranges on the
Coastal Plain and adjacent Piedmont from
se PA to ne FL.

MID-APR.–EARLY JUNE

ASTERACEAE: ASTER FAMILY
Cutleaf Tickseed;
Threadleaf Coreopsis
Coreopsis verticillata L.

Glabrous or glabrate slender perennial,
stems 10–24″ (25–70 cm) tall. Leaves
opposite and stalkless, each pair deeply
dissected 2–3 times into slender segments.
Flower heads are produced on erect,
slender stalks forming a flattish array, ray
flowers yellow, 0.6–1.2″ (1.5–3 cm) long,
disc flowers dull yellow.

   Cutleaf Tickseed is unique among our
members of the aster family in its finely
dissected leaves, much like those of Garden Cosmos. It is also in the horticultural
trade.

   Inhabits dry oak-hickory-pine forests,
longleaf pinelands, rights-of-way, and
roadsides; found on rocky slopes in the
Piedmont. Ranges in the lower Piedmont
and Coastal Plain from MD to SC.

LATE MAY–EARLY AUG.

ASTERACEAE: ASTER FAMILY
Woodland Sunflower

Helianthus divaricatus L.

Perennial from long rhizomes, forming colonial patches. Stems are 2.3–5′ (0.7–1.5 m) tall, smooth, with few or no branches. Leaves are opposite and sessile, evenly spaced on the stem, lance-shaped or narrowly triangular, 2–5″ (5–13 cm) long and 0.5–2″ (1.2–5 cm) wide, tip acuminate, upper surface rough (scabrous), lower surface pubescent. Flowering heads are few, terminal, disc dull yellow, about 0.7″ (10–20 mm) across, rays bright yellow, 0.6–1″ (1.5–2.5 cm) long.

Primarily a Piedmont plant, Woodland Sunflower in our region is confined to sites with loamy soils. There are about 25 native sunflowers in our 3 states, few of which tolerate the nutrient-poor Sandhills soils and fire ecology.

Inhabits dry to mesic oak-hickory forests, less often in loamy soil areas in longleaf-wiregrass uplands. Ranges from s ME to sw Que. and IA south to nw FL, LA, and OK.

LATE JUNE–AUG.

ASTERACEAE: ASTER FAMILY
Rattlesnake Hawkweed

Hieracium venosum L.

Perennial, stems 8–24″ (20–60 cm) tall, widely branched above, glabrate, sap milky white. Basal leaves several at ground level, oblanceolate or elliptic, 1.6–6″ (4–15 cm) long and 0.4–3.7″ (1–4.5 cm) wide, sparsely pilose on upper surface, margins more or less toothed. The upper surface is strongly veined with purple or red. Stem leaves 0–2, greatly reduced in size. Flower heads grow at ends of slender branches to form a broad, flattish corymb, the heads 0.5–0.75″ (12–18 mm) across, composed only of yellow ray flowers, disc flowers absent.

The intricately patterned red leaf veins give this plant an unmistakable look. As in other hawkweeds, the seeds are carried by the wind via feathery plumes that form miniature "parachutes."

Inhabits dry sandy or gravelly soils of oak-hickory forests, pine-oak uplands, and rocky slopes. Ranges from s ME to s Ont. and MI south to sw GA, MS, and e OK.

LATE APR.–JUNE

ASTERACEAE: ASTER FAMILY
Bridal-wreath Goldenrod; Bluestem Goldenrod

Solidago caesia L. var. *caesia*

Glabrous perennial, stems 1.5–3′ (0.5–1 m) tall, erect or arching, bluish gray, unbranched, or branched in upper third. There are no basal leaves. Stem leaves are 1.6–5″ (4–13 cm) long and 0.4–1.2″ (1–3 cm) wide, tip acuminate, base short-tapered, nearly sessile. Flowers grow in small clusters from many of the leaf axils. Ray flowers are yellow and less than 0.2″ (2–3 mm) long; disc yellow.

Bridal-wreath Goldenrod is one of our most distinctive and attractive plants. It prefers relatively high-nutrient soils and cannot tolerate fire, so it must be sought in protected situations. Goldenrods have a reputation for causing hay fever, but this is entirely false.

Inhabits moist oak-hickory woods and hardwood slopes above streams. Ranges from N.S. to s Ont. and WI south to FL and TX.

SEPT.–OCT.

ASTERACEAE: ASTER FAMILY
Vasey's Goldenrod

Solidago arguta Aiton var. *caroliniana* Gray

Perennial, stems 2–3′ (0.6–1 m) tall, erect to arching, slender, long-branched in the upper third or half of the stem. The few basal leaves are more or less diamond-shaped, 2–5″ (5–12 cm) long and 0.8–1.2″ (2–3 cm) wide, tip acuminate, base tapered to a winged stalk, margins toothed, surfaces glabrous. Stem leaves become gradually smaller upward and tend to be elliptic. Flowers grow from the stem branches in terminal inflorescences, each a narrow pyramid with arching branchlets, the flower heads occurring only on 1 side of the branchlets. There are 2–6 yellow ray flowers, about 0.2″ (4 mm) long; disc yellow.

Vasey's Goldenrod is named for George Vasey (1822–93) of the U.S. Department of Agriculture, an expert primarily in grasses. Pineywoods Goldenrod (*S. pinetorum*) is similar, but stems are glabrous, leaves are linear to lanceolate, the upper leaves have fascicles of small leaves in axils, and it blooms much earlier (early July–Aug.); it barely reaches sc from the north.

Inhabits oak-hickory woods and loamy soil areas within longleaf pinelands. Ranges from VA to MO south to FL and LA.

MID-AUG–SEPT.

HYPERICACEAE: ST. JOHN'S-WORT FAMILY
Piedmont St. John's-wort

Hypericum lloydii (Svenson) W. P. Adams

Perennial dwarf shrub with spreading and ascending branches, plant up to 1' (30 cm) tall (occasionally taller). Leaves linear, like conifer needles, 0.5–1" (13–25 mm) long and less than 1 mm wide, tip acute, base sessile. Flowers grow in small clusters at up to 5 nodes near ends of branches, flowers 0.4–0.5" (10–12 mm) across, petals 5, yellow.

This has a unique distribution for a St. John's-wort: a narrow zone comprised of the lower Piedmont and inner Coastal Plain (Sandhills region). In flower it is handsome and well worth searching out; it makes up for the small size of its flowers with numbers. Named for Dr. A. J. Lloyd of Alabama, who brought specimens to Dr. Roland Harper, who first recognized that the plant may be a new species.

Inhabits dry soils of openings within oak-hickory woodlands; also roadsides through oak-hickory-pine woods. Ranges from sc VA to c AL.

JUNE–JULY

HYPOXIDACEAE: STARGRASS FAMILY
Common or Upland Stargrass

Hypoxis hirsuta (L.) Coville

Perennial from a bulb and fleshy roots, plant with abundant (sometimes sparse) whitish hairs. Leaves grasslike, up to 18" (45 cm) long and 0.4" (10 mm) wide, pleated lengthwise, tip attenuate. Three to 7 flowers grow atop branched stalks shorter than the leaves. The 3 petals and 3 sepals are alike, yellow, mostly 0.25–0.4" (6–10 mm) long and 0.2" (2–4 mm) wide. The fruit is a green capsule 0.25–0.4" (5–10 mm long), with lustrous black seeds.

Common Stargrass is indeed common over most of its vast range, in a variety of dry habitats. Swamp Stargrass (*H. curtissii*) is very similar but is hairless; its leaves are even wider (to 15 mm), and it inhabits stream shores, riverbanks, and floodplain forests.

Inhabits oak-hickory forests, longleaf pine-oak-wiregrass uplands, and sometimes moist bottomlands. Ranges from s ME to se Sask. south to FL and TX.

APR.–JUNE

MYRSINACEAE:
MYRSINE & YELLOW LOOSESTRIFE FAMILY
Whorled Loosestrife

Lysimachia quadrifolia L.

Perennial from rhizomes, often forming small colonies, stems unbranched, 1–3′ (0.3–1 m) tall, pubescent. Leaves grow in whorls of 3–6 (mostly 4), broadly lanceolate to elliptic, 1.2–4.8″ (3–12 cm) long and 0.4–1.8″ (1–4.5 cm) wide, acuminate-tipped, rounded at the sessile base, smooth. Flowers are produced singly from the upper leaf axils, on long stalks. The 5 petals are yellow with a red basal patch, the tips acute; the spread flower is about 0.4″ (1 cm) across.

Whorled Loosestrife is easy to identify, with its multilayered look and jaunty flowers on long stalks. The word "loosestrife" was applied to other species in this genus due to their alleged ability to relieve strife or unruliness among oxen pulling a plow. During the American Revolution, this was one of several plants used as a tea substitute.

Inhabits oak-hickory woodlands and "fire-shadow" slopes within longleaf pinelands. Ranges from ME to MN south to C GA, AL, and TN.

LATE MAY–MID-JULY

LILIACEAE: LILY FAMILY
Indian Cucumber-root

Medeola virginiana L.

Perennial from a short rhizome, the stem 8–32″ (20–80 cm) tall, mostly covered by longish tangled hairs. Nonflowering plants form a single whorl of 6–10 elliptic to oblanceolate leaves atop the stem, each leaf 2–6.4″ (5–16 cm) long and 0.8–2″ (2–5 cm) wide, abruptly narrowed to a slender tip, the base sessile. Flowering plants have a second whorl well above the first, the 3 leaves roughly half as long as the first whorl of leaves, often reddish at base. Flowers are terminal, 3–7 (up to 10), on slender stalks that arch downward. Corollas are 6-parted, each segment about 0.3″ (6–8 mm) long and 0.2″ (2–4 mm) wide, dull yellow, spreading to reflexed. Fruits are bluish black berries 0.3″ (6–8 mm) across.

Indian Cucumber-root has fascinating architecture, and the floral details are well worth studying with a hand lens. The whitish rhizomes were reportedly eaten by Native Americans. Nonflowering plants closely resemble Large Whorled Pogonia (*Isotria verticillata*), but their leaves are thinner-textured and the stem is slender and hairy.

Inhabits moist oak-hickory woodlands and hardwood slopes along blackwater rivers. Ranges from Que. to MN south to nw FL and LA.

MID-APR.–MAY

APIACEAE: CARROT FAMILY
Woodland Parsnip
Thaspium trifoliatum (L.) Gray

Perennial, glabrate, the stem up to 2′
(60 cm) tall, branched above. Basal leaves
usually are unlobed, heart-shaped, mostly
1–2″ (2.5–5 cm) long, tip blunt, margins
finely toothed, the leafstalk longer than
the blade. Stem leaves are 3-parted, each
part on a short stalk, ovate to broadly
lanceolate, up to 2.8″ (7 cm) long, 0.4–1.4″
(1–3.5 cm) wide, tip acute, margins
toothed. Flowers grow in 1–2 terminal
umbels composed of widely spreading
stalks 0.4–1.2″ (1–3 cm) long that support
tiny umbels at their tips (these technically
umbellets). The 5 flower petals are tiny, all
yellow or all maroon.

Although named for a fanciful resemblance to the edible Parsnip (*Pastinaca
sativa*), our plants have no known
culinary value. Woodland Parsnip is
largely a Piedmont species, uncommon
in our region. The two flower colors may
represent different geographical varieties;
most of our plants are yellow-flowered.

Inhabits oak-hickory woodlands and
adjacent longleaf pine–oak slopes. Ranges
from s NY to s MN south to nw FL and
W LA.

APR.–MAY

OROBANCHACEAE: BROOMRAPE FAMILY
Downy False-foxglove; Virginia Oakleach
Aureolaria virginica (L.) Pennell

Perennial, parasitic on roots of the white
oak group. Stems can be single or a few
together, up to 5′ (1.5 m) tall, unbranched
or few-branched, densely downy. Leaves
are opposite, lanceolate, 2.4–4.8″ (6–12
cm) long and 0.6–1.8″ (1.5–4.5 cm) wide,
entire or sinuate or pinnately lobed. Flowers solitary in axils of midstem and upper
leaves, stalks less than 3 mm long, petals
5, yellow, forming a tubular corolla with
flaring lobes, 1.4–1.8″ (3.5–4.5 cm) long
and a little less broad. Plants turn blackish
brown in autumn.

As with all its close relatives, Downy
False-foxglove is parasitic on roots of
oaks, and the name "oakleach" suggests
that it extracts nutrients from its hosts.
But it is quite benign, posing no serious threat to the host tree. A few other
members of *Aureolaria* may occur in our
region, but they have glabrous stems.

Inhabits dry to mesic soil of oak-
hickory forests and riverside hardwood-
pine slopes. Ranges from MA to MI south
to FL and LA.

LATE MAY–JULY

OROBANCHACEAE: BROOMRAPE FAMILY
Wood Betony; Lousewort
Pedicularis canadensis L.

Perennial, the stem 4–16″ (10–40 cm) tall, with dense, transparent hairs. Most leaves occur near or at the base of the stem, on moderate to long stalks, the blades lanceolate, 2–6″ (5–15 cm) long and 0.6–2″ (1.5–5 cm) wide, pinnately lobed, the lobes finely toothed. Stem leaves are smaller. Flowers grow in a dense, terminal, headlike cluster, the flowers erect to spreading, about 0.8″ (20 mm) long. Corollas are dull yellow and usually tinged with red, tubular with 2 lips, the upper lip strongly arched over, the lower lip spreading.

Generally a Piedmont and Mountains plant, Wood Betony is uncommon in our region. Note that the leaves are often tinged brown. True Betony is an unrelated Old World plant in the mint family. In Europe, other louseworts were said to give lice to grazing cattle, but no such trait has been ascribed to our species. Native Americans used it as cough medicine and to treat digestive ailments.

Inhabits oak-hickory woods and hardwood-pine slopes along streams, normally in moist soil. Ranges from Que. to Man. south to FL and TX; Mex.

APR.–MAY

ANACARDIACEAE: CASHEW & SUMAC FAMILY
Smooth Sumac
Rhus glabra L.

Perennial shrub or small tree to 23′ (7 m) tall, often forming loose clones via rhizomes, the branches glabrous and glaucescent. Leaves are pinnate, the stalk and rachis glaucescent. The 15–19 leaflets are sessile, lanceolate to oblong, 2–6″ (5–15 cm) long and 0.4–1.6″ (1–4 cm) wide, tip acuminate, margins toothed, glabrous and glaucescent beneath. Flowers grow in pyramidal terminal clusters up to 10″ (25 cm) long and 4″ (10 cm) wide. The 4–5 sepals and 4–5 petals are dull yellow to straw-colored, a few mm long. Fruits are bright red, rounded, 0.2″ (3–4 mm) across, pubescent.

The bright red fruits and green leaves make this a handsome plant; also, leaves turn scarlet in fall. Native Americans chewed berries to stop bedwetting, while leaf and bark teas helped alleviate diarrhea, dysentery, and fever; it was also taken as a general tonic.

Inhabits dry to moist oak-hickory forests, clearings, roadsides, old fields, and rights-of-way; occasionally found in longleaf pine communities. Ranges from ME to s Que. and B.C. south to FL and CA; Mex.

LATE MAY–EARLY JULY

SANTALACEAE: SANDALWOOD FAMILY

Nestronia

Nestronia umbellula Rafinesque

Perennial, semiparasitic, colonial shrub 2–4′ (0.6–1.3 m) tall, sexes on separate plants (dioecious), stem and branch nodes swollen. Leaves are opposite, ovate to elliptical, 1.6–2.4″ (4–6 cm) long, with an acute tip. Flowers grow from leaf axils, the males in clusters of 3–11, sepals mostly 5, green, their tips recurved, petals absent. Female flowers grow singly from leaf axils, sepals mostly 4, dull yellow to green, their tips recurved, petals absent. The greenish fruit is nearly round, 0.4–0.6″ (1–1.5 cm) across, but seldom produced.

Nestronia looks like an intermediate-height blueberry bush, but with opposite leaves. It is parasitic on the roots of pines and perhaps other woody plants. Like some other colonial plants, fruits are not often produced, and reproduction is mainly by vegetative cloning. It is the sole member of its genus and considered to be of ancient age.

Inhabits moist soil on terraces of blackwater streams and rivers; also found on dry slopes in oak-hickory forests. It is very tolerant of fire. Ranges in the Piedmont and Sandhills from sc VA to sc KY south to c GA (including Burke, Muscogee, and Richmond Counties) and ec MS.

APR.–MAY

SMILACACEAE: GREENBRIER FAMILY

Sawbrier; Wild Sarsaparilla

Smilax glauca Walter

Perennial slender vine from tough underground runners, forming loose colonies, climbing via curly tendrils. The lower part of the stem is gray or gray-brown, densely beset with slender prickles; upper part of stem is glaucous and sparsely to moderately prickly. Leaves are tardily deciduous, ovate to roundish, thin-textured, tip acute, margins smooth, often mottled with pale areas above, glaucous beneath, short-stalked. Flowers grow in small umbels from leaf axils, the 3 sepals and 3 petals alike, 0.25″ (5–7 mm) long, yellowish. Fruits are berries, black, glaucescent, 0.2–0.3″ (5–8 mm) in diameter.

Sawbrier's surprisingly strong stems can easily trip a person, and the prickles readily cut skin. The runners smell and taste like sarsaparilla, which was originally derived from a Mexican species of *Smilax*. Native Americans used sawbrier tea for rheumatism, upset stomach, and muscle cramps.

Inhabits moist soil of oak-hickory woods, streamside slopes, streamhead margins, pine flatwoods, and blackwater river floodplains; also drier soil of pinelands and old fields. Ranges from se MA to s OH and se KS south to s FL and e TX.

LATE APR.–MAY

COLCHICACEAE:
MEADOW-SAFFRON & BELLWORT FAMILY
Coastal Plain Bellwort

Uvularia puberula Michaux var. *nitida* (Britton)
Fernald

Glabrous, noncolonial perennial, stems one to several, 4–16″ (10–40 cm) tall, usually with 1–2 branches. Leaves are relatively few, elliptic or ovate, mostly 1.6–3.2″ (4–8 cm) long and 0.4–1.5″ (1–3.5 cm) wide, tip acute, base sessile, margins smooth, surfaces lustrous. Flowers are few (usually 1–3), growing singly from upper leaf axils, drooping. The 3 sepals and 3 petals are alike, pale yellow, lanceolate, 0.7–1″ (1.7–2.5 cm) long, acute.

This plant seems to naturally occur in populations of only a few individuals, so finding it is always a special treat. It is apparently rare in GA but known historically from the Augusta area. A Mountain/upper Piedmont variety (*U. puberula* var. *puberula*) differs in having tiny appressed hairs on the stems and leaf undersides.

Inhabits moist lower slopes of oak-hickory woods, wooded riverside slopes, and river/stream terraces. Ranges on the Coastal Plain from se NY to ec GA.

LATE MAR.–APR.

LILIACEAE: LILY FAMILY
Carolina Lily

Lilium michauxii Poiret

Perennial from succulent, scaly bulb(s), stem mostly 16″–3′ (0.4–1 m) tall. Midstem leaves grow in 2–4 whorls of 4–10 leaves each, oblanceolate, 2.4–4.8″ (6–12 cm) long and up to 1″ (2.5 cm) wide, abruptly acute, lower surface pale and shiny. Upper stem leaves are solitary, ascending, smaller. One to 2 nodding (angled downward) flowers grow atop the stem on long stalks, sepals and petals are partly united and recurve so that tips touch each other. The 3 sepals and 3 petals are alike, 2.4–3.2″ (6–8 cm) long and 0.4–0.8″ (1–2 cm) wide, tapering to point, orange to yellow-orange, spotted with purple, sweetly fragrant; 6 stamens and 1 style are prominently exposed.

Carolina Lily is the official wildflower of North Carolina. The flowers closely resemble those of Sandhills Lily but are fragrant, and the leaves are a different shape and occur in fewer whorls; note also the distinct habitat difference.

Inhabits dry oak-hickory woodlands, treefall openings, rights-of-way, and roadsides. Ranges from s VA to e TN and c MS south to nw FL and s LA.

MID-JULY-MID-AUG.

RUBIACEAE: MADDER FAMILY
Summer Bluet
Houstonia purpurea L.

Perennial, stem narrowly winged, 4–12″ (10–30 cm) tall, branched. Basal leaves, produced in autumn, wither by flowering time. Stem leaves are opposite, sessile, ovate, 0.8–3.2″ (2–6 cm) long and 0.3–1″ (8–25 mm) wide, with 3–7 prominent veins. Flowers grow in small clusters from ends of branches, petals 4, pink, lavender, or whitish, corolla tube 0.25–0.3″ (5–7 mm) long, lobes shorter and not spreading much.

Summer Bluet is less well-known than Bluets (*H. caerulea*) but is no less handsome with its tidy foliage and numerous flowers.

Inhabits oak-hickory woodlands and hardwood slopes within longleaf pinelands. Ranges from s PA to s OH and s MO south to nw FL and e TX.

MID-MAY–JULY

LAMIACEAE: MINT FAMILY
Beautyberry; French Mulberry
Callicarpa americana L.

Perennial woody shrub 3–8′ (1–2.5 m) tall, twigs 4-angled, densely pubescent with stellate hairs. Leaves are opposite, ovate, 3–6″ (7–15 cm) long and 1.25–3″ (3–8 cm) wide, stellate-pubescent beneath, margins crenate or more sharply toothed, tip acute to acuminate, leafstalks 0.6–1.5″ (1.5–3.5 cm) long. Flowers grow in tight, rounded clusters at leaf bases, each flower about 0.25″ (3–5 mm) long. Petals are united basally, with 5 spreading lobes, lavender or pink, stamens extending beyond petals. Fruits form rounded clusters, bright magenta.

The garish fruits of Beautyberry are sure to attract attention, no matter how often you've seen them; there's nothing in our flora quite like that intense magenta color.

Inhabits oak-hickory forests (especially lower, moist slopes) and margins of river floodplains as well as clearings and roadsides. Ranges from MD to TN and OK south to FL and TX; West Indies; Mex.

JUNE–JULY

FABACEAE: PEA & BEAN FAMILY
Panicled Tick-trefoil

Desmodium paniculatum (L.) DC.

Perennial, stem 1.3–3′ (0.4–1 m) tall, often leaning or arching, usually with spreading branches, glabrate to moderately pubescent with short, hooked hairs. Leaves are sparse, long-stalked, 3-parted; leaflets are broadly linear to lance-shaped, 1.2–3.2″ (3–8 cm) long, glabrous or with sparse, short hairs. Flowers grow on short to long branches and branchlets, these with short, hooked hairs, flowers pink, on stalks 0.25–0.5″ (5–12 mm) long. Pods are composed of 3–6 diamond-shaped segments, each segment 0.25–0.3″ (5–7 mm) long.

The arching stems, spreading branches and sparse, slender leaves give this plant an elegant look.

Inhabits loamy sand soils of oak-hickory woods and flats and pea swales within longleaf pinelands. Ranges from s ME to s Ont. and e NE south to FL and TX.

AUG.–OCT.

FABACEAE: PEA & BEAN FAMILY
Naked Tick-trefoil

Hylodesmum nudiflorum (L.)
   H. Ahashi and R. R. Mill
[*Desmodium nudiflorum* (L.) DC.]

Perennial, with separate fertile and sterile stems, glabrate. Sterile stems are 4–12″ (10–30 cm) tall, with 4–7 leaves at summit, leaves divided into 3 leaflets, ovate to diamond-shaped, 1.6–4.8″ (4–12 cm) long, sparsely pubescent with hooked and straight hairs. Fertile stems are single or sometimes several, leafless, unbranched, 1.5–2.9′ (0.4–0.8 m) tall. Flowers are purple or pink, pea-shaped, on stalks 0.4–0.8″ (10–20 mm) long. Pods are composed of 2–4 diamond-shaped segments, each segment 0.25–0.35″ (6–8 mm) long.

This is our most distinctive tick-trefoil and also the least likely to be found in fire-managed habitats. Naked Tick-trefoil blooms a month earlier than our other tick-trefoils (genus *Desmodium*).

Inhabits loamy sand soils of oak-hickory woods. Ranges from s ME to s MN south to nw FL and e TX.

JULY–AUG.

FABACEAE: PEA & BEAN FAMILY

Slender Bush-clover; Virginia Bush-clover

Lespedeza virginica (L.) Britton

Perennial, stems single or a few, slender, 1–2.5′ (0.3–0.8 m) tall, with sparse to moderate, short appressed hairs, branches erect and often numerous. Leaves are alternate, very short-stalked; the 3 leaflets are narrowly elliptic or linear, 0.4–1″ (1–2.5 cm) long and about 0.2″ (2–5 mm) wide, surfaces usually have short appressed hairs, tip acute. Flowers grow mostly 4–10 in racemes from axils of most midstem and upper leaves, racemes are shorter than or equal to leaves, nearly stalkless. Petals are purple or rosy, 0.25″ (5–7 mm) long. The pod is elliptical with a short point, appressed hairy, 1-seeded.

The copious flowers give Slender Bush-clover a top-heavy look. Get to know this common species so you can learn other, less common species. Stueve's Bush-clover (*L. stuevei*) differs in its less-branchy aspect, its dense velvety hairs that stick straight out from the stem, its broader leaflets (elliptic), and its paler purplish flowers. It occupies the same habitats.

Inhabits loamy sand soils of oak-hickory woods and pea swales in long-leaf pinelands. Ranges from NH to IA south to nw FL and TX.

JULY–SEPT.

ERICACEAE: BLUEBERRY & AZALEA FAMILY

Wild Azalea; Pinxter-flower

Rhododendron periclymenoides (Michaux) Shinners
[*Rhododendron nudiflorum* (L.) Torrey]

Perennial shrub 3–6.5′ (1–2 m) tall (rarely to 3 m), with spreading to ascending branches that are glabrate or have appressed hairs. Leaves are very short-stalked, elliptic to oblanceolate, 1.2–3.2″ (3–8 cm) long and 0.6–1.2″ (1.5–3 cm) wide, glabrate above with appressed hairs on veins beneath, tip blunt, margins with appressed bristles. Flowers appear as leaves begin to unfold, in terminal clusters of several flowers, each on a stalk 0.2–0.5″ (4–12 mm) long. The flowers are faintly or not at all fragrant, the corolla tube 0.5–0.8″ (1.3–2 cm) long, reddish pink, with short, often gland-tipped hairs, the 5 pink lobes flare outward. The stamens and style are reddish and extend far beyond the petals.

Unlike Dwarf Azalea (*R. atlanticum*), Wild Azalea grows singly, is twice as tall, has all-pink flowers, and is not fragrant or only slightly so. It also is one of our showiest plants and in a garden would outshine almost all Asian azaleas.

Inhabits dryish to moist oak-hickory forests and mixed pine-oak woodlands, especially on river- and creekside slopes. Ranges from MA to s OH south to s GA and s AL.

EARLY APR.–EARLY MAY; OCCASIONALLY
ALSO IN MID-SEPT.–OCT.

CARYOPHYLLACEAE:
PINK & SANDWORT FAMILY
Carolina Pink; Wild Pink
Silene caroliniana Walter var. *caroliniana*

Perennial, several stems ascend from a group of basal leaves, 4–12″ (10–30 cm) tall. Basal leaves are spatulate, to 4″ (10 cm) long and 1.2″ (3 cm) wide, tip blunt to rounded, long-tapered to the leafstalk, upper surface with appressed white hairs. There are 1–2 pairs of stem leaves, much smaller than basal leaves. Flowers grow in dense terminal clusters, the 5 spreading petals 0.4–0.6″ (10–15 mm) long, pale pink, the tip broader than the base and notched. The calyx has hairs tipped with sticky glands.

Carolina Pink is an uncommon plant whose populations are small and scattered on the landscape; therefore, finding it is a challenge. It was named by Thomas Walter (1740–89), South Carolina farmer, horticulturist, and botanist who wrote the first account of the plants of the Carolinas.

Inhabits oak-hickory woods and hardwood slopes above streams. Ranges in the Piedmont and inner Coastal Plain from s NC to ec GA (Burke to Effingham Counties).

LATE APR.–JUNE

CARYOPHYLLACEAE:
PINK & SANDWORT FAMILY
Fire Pink
Silene virginica L.

Perennial, stems single or a few together, erect, to 27″ (70 cm) tall, often branched from near the base. Basal and stem leaves are sparse, opposite, lanceolate to spatulate, to 10″ (25 cm) long and 1.8″ (4.5 cm) wide, tip acute, tapered to the stalk. Flowers grow singly or a few in terminal clusters, the petals forming a tube with 5 widely spreading lobes. Each lobe is 0.6–1″ (15–25 mm) long, bright red, the tip about as wide as the base and notched. The flower stalks and the calyx are covered with dense, sticky, glandular hairs.

Fire Pink is an uncommon plant in our region, as it is primarily a Piedmont and Mountain species. But it tolerates fire and makes a fine addition to some longleaf pine woodlands. The intense red color is surpassed only by that of Cardinal Flower.

Inhabits oak-hickory woods, loamy soil areas within longleaf pinelands, and rocky slopes. Ranges from s NY to s Ont. and s MI south to nw FL and e OK.

APR.–MID-MAY

CAPRIFOLIACEAE: HONEYSUCKLE FAMILY
Coral Honeysuckle

Lonicera sempervirens L.

Perennial, low-climbing vine to about 15′ (5 m) long, glabrous. Leaves are opposite, eventually deciduous, narrowly elliptical to broadly obovate, 1.2–2.8″ (3–7 cm) long and 0.4–1.8″ (1–4.5 cm) wide, margins smooth, glaucous beneath. The leaves just below the flowers are the widest and are joined at the base (connate). Flowers grow in terminal clusters from a long stalk, red outside, usually yellow inside, 1.2–2″ (3–5 cm) long, tubular with 5 very short lobes, stamens and style barely projecting. Berries are red.

Coral Honeysuckle is a beautiful plant and should get wider use in the horticultural trade and in native plant gardens. The flowers are very attractive to Ruby-throated Hummingbirds, who seek their nectar after arriving from the wintering grounds.

Inhabits riverside slopes, oak-hickory woodlands, forest openings, and shrub thickets. Ranges from MA to IA south to FL and TX.

LATE MAR.–MID-MAY, SPORADICALLY LATER

LAMIACEAE: MINT FAMILY
Georgia Calamint

Clinopodium georgianum R. M. Harper
[*Satureja georgiana* (R. M. Harper) Ahles]

Perennial, subwoody, sprawling shrub with 4-angled, densely pubescent twigs, plant normally less than 1.5′ (45 cm) tall. Leaves are ovate to elliptic, 0.4–1.25″ (10–30 mm) long and 0.25–0.75″ (5–18 mm) wide, tip acute, base tapered to a leafstalk less than 0.3″ (2–7 mm) long, margins crenate, surfaces punctate. Flowers grow in terminal, elongate, branched clusters, each cluster composed of 3–9 flowers and leaflike bracts. Corollas are lavender or lavender-pink, about 0.5″ (10–14 mm) long.

Georgia Calamint was discovered and named by the indefatigable botanist Roland M. Harper (1878–1966), whose explorations in the southeastern U.S., especially southern Georgia, greatly increased our understanding of plant taxonomy and distribution. It is rare in NC.

Inhabits dry oak-hickory forests, longleaf pinelands, dry slopes along streams, and roadsides. Ranges in the Coastal Plain and Piedmont from s NC to ne GA, nw FL, and se LA.

JULY–SEPT.

ACANTHACEAE: ACANTHUS FAMILY
Carolina Wild-petunia
Ruellia caroliniensis (Walter) Steudel

Perennial, varying from unbranched plants with stems 5″ (12 cm) tall to robust plants 2′ (60 cm) tall with many widely spreading branches, more or less pubescent although some plants barely so. Leaves are opposite, lanceolate to ovate, up to 4″ (10 cm) long and 1.8″ (4.5 cm) wide. Flowers arise from bases of upper and terminal leaves, erect, the calyx lobes linear, the corolla purple-blue to lavender-blue, 1–1.75″ (2.5–4.5 cm) long, funnel-shaped with 5 spreading but united lobes.

Carolina Wild-petunia is widespread and fairly common. The great variability in plant size and shape may in part be due to the effects of different habitats and soil nutrients; a modern analysis is sorely needed. Garden petunias (genus *Petunia*) are members of the potato family (Solanaceae) and not related to *Ruellia*.

Inhabits moist soil in pinelands, mixed woodlands, floodplain margins, roadsides, and timber cuts; may also occur in drier soil. Ranges from NJ to s IN south to c FL and e TX.

MID-MAY–SEPT.

VIOLACEAE: VIOLET FAMILY
Southern Woolly Violet
Viola villosa Walter

Perennial. Leaves are more or less evergreen, prostrate and forming a rosette, their surfaces densely pubescent. Leaf blades are broadly ovate to rotund, mostly 1–2″ (2.5–5 cm) long, tip blunt, base cordate (heart-shaped), margins crenate, leafstalk up to 0.4″ (10 mm) long. Flowers grow on slender stalks independent of and usually shorter than leaves, 0.6–0.8″ (1.5–2 cm) across. The 5 petals are violet to blue-violet, the lowest one (the lip) slightly larger and with a backward-pointing blunt spur. The lowest 3 petals have a patch of short white hairs on the inside surface.

Southern Woolly Violet is uncommon in our region but not hard to find once you learn its specific habitat preferences. Its thick rootstalk helps protect it from pineland fires.

Inhabits dry loamy sand soil of oak-hickory woodlands, pine-oak-sourwood slopes along streamheads, and pea swales within longleaf pinelands. Ranges from se NC to n FL, e TX, and se OK.

MAR.–EARLY APR.

ASTERACEAE: ASTER FAMILY
Skydrop Aster
Symphyotrichum patens (Aiton) Nesom
[*Aster patens* Aiton]

Perennial, stem usually solitary, erect, mostly 1.3–3′ (0.4–1 m) tall (taller elsewhere), sparsely but long-branched in the upper third, more or less scabrous (with rough hairs). Leaves are well-spaced, lanceolate to oblanceolate, 1.2–5″ (3–13 cm) long and 0.4–1.6″ (1–4 cm) wide, sessile and clasping the stem, tip acute, surfaces and margins scabrous. Flower heads grow at ends of long, horizontal branches, these branches with small leaves, the bracts of the heads with appressed, glandular-hairy tips. Rays are 0.6–0.8″ (1.5–2 cm) long, violet (varying to bluish or purplish); disc flowers yellow turning maroon.

Skydrop Aster is more common on rocky slopes of the Piedmont but is also adapted to the fire-dependent ecosystem of the Sandhills region. The sparse, long, nearly horizontal branches with small leaves and few flowers are distinctive.

Inhabits dry soil of openings in oak-hickory woodlands, longleaf pinelands, roadsides, and rights-of-way. Ranges from s vt to se ks south to nw fl and c tx.

SEPT.–OCT.

CAMPANULACEAE:
BELLFLOWER & LOBELIA FAMILY
Downy Lobelia
Lobelia puberula Michaux

Perennial, densely pubescent with short, appressed hairs (some plants much less pubescent), stem usually unbranched, mostly 1.2–4′ (40–120 cm) tall. Leaves are well-spaced, elliptical to oblanceolate, 1.2–5″ (3–12 cm) long and mostly 0.4–1.6″ (1–4 cm) wide, sessile or tapering to a very short stalk, blunt-tipped, margins smooth or with tiny, knoblike teeth. Flowers grow in a dense to interrupted raceme of up to 30 flowers (seldom fewer than 10), each flower on a stalk 0.25″ (3–5 mm) long, subtended by a slender, leaflike bract. The corolla is blue with a white "eye" at the throat, 0.7–1″ (15–25 mm) long, tubular with 2 flaring lobes above and 3 below forming a lip.

This is our only lobelia that is noticeably hairy, though the hairs are very short. Linnaeus named this genus for Matthias de Lobel, Flemish physician to James I of England.

Inhabits dry to moist oak-hickory woodlands, roadsides, rights-of-way, and clearings; occurs in other habitats elsewhere in its range. Ranges from nj to il south to n fl, e tx, and se ok.

LATE JULY–EARLY OCT.

LAMIACEAE: MINT FAMILY
Elliptic-leaved Skullcap
Scutellaria elliptica Muhlenberg ex Sprengel

Perennial, stems 1–3, 8–32″ (20–80 cm) tall, 4-angled, simple or branched above, pubescent. Leaves are opposite, elliptic to ovate, 1.2–3.2″ (3–8 cm) long and 0.6–1.6″ (1.5–4 cm) wide, margins crenate, tip acute to blunt, base quickly narrowed to a short, winged stalk. Flowers grow in terminal spikelike racemes up to 3.2″ (8 cm) long, in opposite pairs subtended by leaflike bracts. The calyx is 2-lobed, the upper lobe crested; the corolla is blue to violet-blue, 0.5–0.8″ (1.2–2 cm long), tubular, 2-lipped, the upper lip 3-lobed, the basal part of the tube abruptly bent.

Flowers of skullcaps (genus *Scutellaria*) have a fanciful resemblance to an ancient European cap or helmet. The genus name is Latin for "little dish," referring to the platelike remnant of the fruit, which remains on the plant well into winter and is a distinctive clue to this genus of plants.

Inhabits oak-hickory woods and streamside slopes and is found occasionally in loamy soil areas within longleaf pinelands. Ranges from NY to MO south to nw FL and e TX.

LATE MAY–JUNE

ASTERACEAE: ASTER FAMILY
Rough Aster; Large-headed Aster
Symphyotrichum grandiflorum (L.) Nesom
[*Aster grandiflorus* L.]

Rough-pubescent perennial, stems solitary or several together, mostly 2–4′ (0.7–1.3 m) tall, usually widely branched to form a bushy aspect. Leaves are lanceolate to oblanceolate, 0.8–2.8″ (2–7 cm) long and 0.25–0.6″ (5–15 mm) wide, sessile and clasping the stem, tip acute, surfaces scabrous (very rough). Flower heads grow on branches with small leaves, the bracts of the heads with long, recurved tips. Rays are 0.8–1.4″ (2–3.5 cm) long, violet or purple-violet; disc flowers yellow.

Our 3 states are home to about 50 species of asters, 18 of them in the Sandhills region. They are all attractive plants, few more so than Rough Aster, with its very large and bright violet ray flowers. In our area it is found only in NC and SC.

Inhabits dry to moist soils of openings in oak-hickory woods, pine flatwoods, roadsides, and rights-of-way. Ranges from c VA to nc SC.

MID-SEPT.–OCT.

ORCHIDACEAE: ORCHID FAMILY
Large Whorled Pogonia

Isotria verticillata (Muhl. ex Willd.) Rafinesque

Perennial, more or less succulent, colonial from long, slender roots. Stem purplish brown, 4–14″ (10–35 cm) tall, unbranched, with a single whorl of 5–6 leaves at summit. Leaves are dark green, oblanceolate to obovate, 1.2–3.6″ (3–9 cm) long and 1–2″ (2.5–5 cm) wide, blunt-tipped or acute. A single flower, sometimes 2, grows from a stalk 1–2″ (2.5–5 cm) long. The 3 petals are yellowish green, elliptic, 0.8–1″ (2–2.5 cm) long, the lip petal curved down and streaked with purple. The 3 sepals spread outward, purple-green or purple-brown, linear, 1.4–2.6″ (3.5–6.5 cm) long, folded lengthwise. The fruit is a capsule, 0.8–1.4″ (2–3.5 cm) long, erect, green drying gray-brown.

Large Whorled Pogonia is one of our most striking orchids, with its rakish, spreading sepals and the single whorl of leaves. Nonflowering plants look like nonflowering plants of Indian Cucumber-root (*Medeola virginiana*), but leaves are dark (vs. light) green and thick- (vs. thin-) textured; also, stems are smooth (vs. matted-hairy).

Inhabits oak-hickory forests, especially lower slopes, and moist margins of swamp forests. Ranges from s ME to s Ont. and MI south to nw FL and e TX.

MID-APR.–MID-MAY

STEMONACEAE: STEMONA FAMILY
Croomia

Croomia pauciflora (Nuttall) Torrey

Perennial from underground rhizomes, often forming small colonies. Stems are roughly 6″ (15 cm) tall but may reach 12″ (30 cm), somewhat fleshy, hairless. Leaves 4–7, long-stalked, clustered atop stem and appearing whorled (but actually alternate), broadly ovate, about 3.2″ (8 cm) wide, with prominent parallel veins. Flowers grow from the stem below leaves, on stalks about 1″ (25 mm) long, 1 flower per stalk, about 0.4″ across; petals 3, pale green, lance-shaped to narrowly elliptical, stamens maroon.

Croomia is named for Hardy B. Croom, a North Carolina naturalist of the first third of the nineteenth century, who also owned a cotton plantation near Tallahassee, FL. He is renowned for discovering the famous Torreya Tree (*Torreya taxifolia*), now endangered. Croomia can be confused with immature or nonflowering plants of carrionflowers and greenbriers (genus *Smilax*) and wild yams (genus *Dioscorea*). *Smilax* leaves are either glaucous beneath, pubescent beneath, or have prickly margins; *Dioscorea* leaves have many cross veins as well as parallel veins.

Inhabits rich hardwood forests in ravines and bluffs in the Chattahoochee River drainage, in our area only in Chattahoochee, Harris, Muskogee, Talbot, and Taylor Counties, GA.

Ranges through much of Alabama; also cw and sw GA, nw FL, and sc LA.

APR.–MAY

VITACEAE: GRAPE FAMILY
Muscadine Grape; Scuppernong

Vitis rotundifolia Michaux

Perennial, woody, high-climbing vine, also scrambling across ground, spreading long distances via branching stems in the soil. The bark of stems is tight, not peeling. Either climbing tendrils or flower clusters are attached to the opposite side of the stem from the leaves, but are absent every third leaf. Tendrils are unbranched. Leaves grow up to 3.2″ (8 cm) long and wide, rounded in outline, base cordate, tip acute, margins toothed, glabrous above, glabrous or pubescent beneath on veins, leafstalks about as long as blade. Flowers grow in branched clusters 1.2–3.2″ (3–8 cm) long, the 5 petals 1–2.5 mm long, pale green. Fruits are round, 0.4–0.8″ (1–2 cm), violet-black, juicy, sweet.

Greenish-fruited cultivars, called Scuppernong Grapes, produce a distinctive taste and are an important commercial crop in our states. Summer Grape (*V. aestivalis*) has larger leaves that are often deeply 3–5 lobed, whitened (glaucous) beneath, and more or less woolly hairy beneath. Its tendrils are 3-branched. Its berries are half the size and grow in clusters 2–6″ (5–15 cm) long. Summer Grape is scattered in our region.

Inhabits dry to moist soil of oak-hickory forests, roadsides, suburban yards, and fire-suppressed areas in longleaf pinelands. Ranges from DE to S IN and S MO south to FL and e TX.

MAY–JUNE

ORCHIDACEAE: ORCHID FAMILY
Green Adder's-mouth

Malaxis unifolia Michaux

Perennial from a small bulb, the stem potentially up to 18″ (50 cm) tall but usually half that. There is only one leaf midway up the stem, broadly ovate to roundish, mostly 1.2–3.6″ (3–9 cm) long and 0.25–2.4″ (0.6–6 cm) wide, sessile and clasping the stem. Flowers grow in a terminal raceme of many flowers on slender stalks 0.2–0.4″ (5–10 mm) long, the upper part of raceme densely packed. Sepals and petals green, the sepals narrowly elliptic, about 0.2″ (1.8–3.5 mm) long, the lateral petals linear and a bit shorter than sepals, the lip triangular and with a forked tip.

Adder's-mouth orchids (the genus *Malaxis*) occur widely over the globe; the flowers of many of them have a fancied resemblance to a snake's forked tongue.

Inhabits dryish to moist ecotones where oak-hickory transitions into swamp forest or into streamheads. Ranges from Newf. to MN south to C FL and e TX.

JUNE–AUG.

ARISTOLOCHIACEAE: BIRTHWORT FAMILY
Little Brown Jug;
Arrowhead Heartleaf

Hexastylis arifolia (Michaux) Small var. *arifolia*

Perennial, stemless. Leaves radiate outward on long stalks, the blades triangular
or ovate with prominent angular basal
lobes, 2.4–6.4″ (6–16 cm) long and 2–6″
(5–15 cm) wide, dark green with light
mottling. One to many flowers grow just
beneath leaf litter, the sepals forming a
vase-shaped tube with a rounded base and
3 erect, blunt lobes, 0.75–1.5″ (18–36 mm)
long, pale brown or tan, petals absent.

The flowers of Little Brown Jug resemble old-time pitchers or vases. To see
them you need to brush away leaves; keep
trying, as not all plants of a population
may bloom. Flowers are pollinated by
terrestrial and near-terrestrial insects,
including thrips.

Inhabits dry to moist loamy soils of
oak-hickory woods, mixed hardwood-
pine slopes above streams and rivers, and
borders of cypress-gum swamps. Ranges
from s VA to s TN south to nw FL and
se LA.

MID-MAR.–EARLY MAY

ORCHIDACEAE: ORCHID FAMILY
Cranefly Orchid

Tipularia discolor (Pursh) Nuttall

Perennial from a horizontal series of
bulblike corms in the soil. The single leaf
grows at the base of the stem, is produced
in autumn, overwinters, then withers
in early summer. The leaf is dark green
above and often has small dark purple
blotches, entirely rich purple beneath,
broadly ovate, 2–4″ (5–10 cm) long and
1–2.5″ (2.5–6 cm) wide, tip acute to short-
acuminate. Flowers grow in a cylindrical
raceme, the flowers numerous but not
crowded, all parts very slender, brown,
bronze, or dull greenish yellow. The 3
sepals and 3 petals are 0.2–0.3″ (4–8 mm)
long, spreading; the lip is 3-lobed and has
a spur directed toward the stem. Capsules
are dry, about 0.4″ (1 cm) long and 0.2″
(5 mm) wide, drooping.

Cranefly orchid has a remarkable life
history: it blooms in mid- to late summer
using energy stored in the corms, then it
produces a leaf in the fall that photosyn-
thesizes through winter and spring (when
trees are leafless), thereby replenishing
the corms. The slender flowers somewhat
resemble long-legged craneflies (genus
Tipula); hence the name. Children (and
adults!) delight in turning leaves over to
see the rich purple underside.

Inhabits moist to dryish soil of oak-
hickory woods, upper margins of streamheads, and slopes and terraces along
rivers. Ranges from se MA to s MI south
to FL and TX.

MID-JULY–EARLY SEPT.

Hedgehog Woodrush

Luzula echinata (Small) Hermann

Perennial from knotty rhizomes, with grasslike basal leaves and a slender stem 8–16″ (20–40 cm) tall. Leaves are nearly all basal and form a tuft, 2–6″ (5–15 cm) long and about 0.25″ (3–7 mm) wide, margins with long wispy hairs; a few smaller leaves occur on the stem. Flowers grow in 4–15 oval or roundish heads on slender stalks, dull greenish brown to brown, the 3 sepals and 3 petals alike, 0.2″ (2.6–4 mm) long, anthers cream-colored, conspicuous during flowering period.

Woodrushes (genus *Luzula*) are a small group of four species in NC, SC, and GA; they are conspicuous members of the early spring woodland flora, then become inconspicuous as other vegetation develops. Hedgehog Woodrush is the commonest species in the Sandhills region; it gets its name from the sharp-tipped sepals and petals.

Inhabits middle and lower slopes in oak-hickory forests and on banks of streams and small rivers where not often flooded; also occurs on moist roadsides. Ranges from MA to WV and IA south to S GA and e TX.

MID-MAR.–APR.

STREAMHEADS AND SEEPAGE SLOPES

This vitally important natural community features permanently moist or wet soils derived from groundwater seepage. Here in the Sandhills region, clay soil layers often lie just beneath the sandy surface soil. Rainwater percolates down through the porous sand, hits the clay layer, and on slopes is forced sideways to the surface to form a seepage area, a streamhead, or both. The water remains close to or at the surface and therefore available to plants that require permanently moist soil. There are two major zones: the streamhead margin and the streamhead itself. In the Sandhills region, seepage areas are common and have been given various names by botanists and ecologists: streamhead ecotone, seepage bog, sandhill seep, hillside bog, and pitcher-plant bog. Stream-heads are most often called streamhead pocosin and baygall. However, examples in truly natural condition are now uncommon, except locally where fire management prevails.

Streamheads typically are densely shrubby, with tall trees above. Here we see Pond Pine (left), Atlantic White Cedar (right), Red Maple (foreground), and Tulip Poplar (background).

Well-burned ecotones or margins of streamheads support a diverse array of wildflowers, such as Savanna Meadow-beauty, Carolina Yellow-eyed-grass, and Toothache Grass.

Active seepage zones may support stands of Yellow Pitcher-plants.

Streamhead Margins and Seepage Slopes

The margin—or ecotone—between a streamhead and a longleaf pine/ wiregrass community is very dynamic and provides habitat for a great diversity of herbaceous plants, many of which occur in the ecotone but not in adjacent communities. Typically, the margin is narrow—several yards wide—but can be twenty or more yards wide where seepage water is plentiful. Almost without exception, there is a gradual shift of plant species from a drier upslope to the wetter downslope. The upslope portion is dominated by grasses, sedges, flowering herbs, and low shrubs. The downslope portion is dominated by taller shrubs and Switch Cane (*Arundinaria tecta*), perhaps with small openings where sphagnum moss, pitcher-plants, and sedges grow. Throughout the margin Longleaf Pine (*Pinus palustris*) and Pond Pine (*P. serotina*) are normally the only canopy species present, but trees from the adjacent streamhead may occur, such as Tulip Poplar (*Liriodendron tulipifera*) and Sourwood (*Oxydendrum arboreum*). The characteristics of a given margin can be highly variable, depending on soil moisture, fire intensity, and fire frequency. Particularly broad margins resemble pine savannas of the outer Coastal Plain, share many species, and are similarly rich in plant species. A large number of uncommon or rare plants occur in ecotones and seepage slopes; they are one of the features of this guide. Some margins are very wet and support extensive beds of sphagnum moss; others go nearly dry in periods of low rainfall. Fire is essential to maintain seepage slopes in healthy condition and to keep biodiversity high; in the absence of fire, shrubs and trees grow unrestricted and shade out the ground layer. In our three states, the rare Pine Barrens Treefrog (*Hyla andersonii*) is nearly restricted to streamhead margins and seepage slopes. Rights-of-way for power lines and gas lines that cross streamheads create similar conditions via mowing, and they can be very productive habitats.

Streamheads

Downslope of the margin is the streamhead proper. In the Sandhills region, streamheads support a small number of tree species, a dense shrub-catbrier layer below, and mosses and herbs at ground level. Trees include Pond Pine, Tulip Poplar, Swamp Black Gum (*Nyssa biflora*), Red Maple (*Acer rubrum*), Atlantic White Cedar (*Chamaecyparis thyoides*), and Sweetbay Magnolia (*Magnolia virginiana*). Numerous species of shrubs occur, many in the blueberry family, ranging up to 10 feet tall. Catbriers, notably Bamboo-vine (*Smilax laurifolia*), are common; these and the dense shrubs make passage difficult. Nonetheless, most streamheads have small areas within them that are relatively shrub-free and which support abundant mosses, some sedges, and scattered flowering plants, such as Primrose-leaved Violet (*Viola primulifolia*) and Clubspur Orchid (*Platanthera clavellata*). Rare or uncommon plants also occur in streamheads, particularly in association with Atlantic White Cedar.

The streamhead community continues downstream as long as there is sufficient seepage input from adjacent slopes; when water from flooding events becomes the dominant input, the community shifts to a floodplain forest or cypress-gum swamp.

Species List

The color after a name indicates the primary natural community or habitat.

T = mentioned in text of another species; not pictured.

Agalinis purpurea ✳
  Purple Gerardia
Aletris aurea
  Golden Colicroot
Aletris farinosa T
  White Colicroot
Amelanchier obovalis
  Pocosin Shadbush;
  Coastal Plain Shadbush
Andropogon glomeratus
  Bog Broomsedge;
  Clustered Bluestem
Aronia arbutifolia
  Red Chokeberry
Arundinaria tecta
  Switch Cane
Asclepias rubra
  Red or Bog Milkweed
Bartonia paniculata
  Screwstem; Twining Bartonia
Bartonia virginica T
  Common Bartonia
Bigelowia nudata
  Rayless Goldenrod
Buchnera floridana
  Savanna Bluehearts;
  Florida Bluehearts
Burmannia biflora ✳
  Blue Burmannia
Burmannia capitata
  White Burmannia
Calopogon pallidus
  Pale Grass-pink
Calopogon tuberosus
  Common Grass-pink
Carex glaucescens ✳
  Glaucescent Sedge
Carphephorus paniculatus T
  Panicled Chaffhead
Carphephorus tomentosus
  Sticky Chaffhead
Centella erecta
  False Pennywort
Chaptalia tomentosa
  Sunbonnets
Cirsium virginianum
  Virginia Thistle

Cleistes bifaria
  Small Spreading Pogonia
Cleistes divaricata T
  Large Spreading Pogonia
Clethra alnifolia var. *alnifolia*
  Sweet Pepperbush
Clethra alnifolia var. *pubescens* T
  Southern Sweet Pepperbush
Coreopsis falcata
  Carolina Tickseed
Coreopsis linifolia
  Savanna Tickseed
Ctenium aromaticum
  Toothache Grass
Cuscuta compacta
  Compact Dodder
Cyrilla racemiflora ✳
  Ti-ti
Desmodium marilandicum T ✳
  Maryland Tick-trefoil
Desmodium tenuifolium T ✳
  Savanna Slender Tick-trefoil
Dioscorea villosa
  Streamhead Yam;
  Common Wild Yam
Doellingeria sericocarpoides
  Streamhead Flat-topped Aster
Drosera brevifolia
  Dwarf Sundew; Early Sundew
Drosera capillaris
  Bog Sundew
Drosera rotundifolia T
  Roundleaf Sundew
Elephantopus nudatus ✳
  Savanna Elephant's-foot
Erigeron vernus
  Savanna Daisy-fleabane
Eriocaulon decangulare
  Hard Pipewort; Hatpins
Eriocaulon texense T
  Texas Pipewort
Eryngium integrifolium
  Savanna Eryngo
Eupatorium leucolepis
  Savanna Eupatorium
Eupatorium mohrii T
  Mohr's Eupatorium

Eupatorium pilosum T ❉
  Rough Eupatorium
Eupatorium resinosum
  Resinous Boneset;
  Resinous Eupatorium
Eurybia paludosa
  Savanna Grass-leaved Aster
Euthamia caroliniana ❉
  Slender Flat-topped Goldenrod
Fothergilla gardenii
  Dwarf Witch-alder
Gaylussacia frondosa
  Dangleberry
Gaylussacia tomentosa T
  Hairy Dangleberry
Gentiana catesbaei
  Catesby's Gentian
Hexastylis minor
  Little Heartleaf
Hexastylis undescribed T
  Streamhead Heartleaf
Hypericum canadense
  Canada St. John's-wort
Hypericum crux-andreae
  St. Peter's Cross
Hypericum setosum
  Downy St. John's-wort
Ilex coriacea
  Large Gallberry;
  Sweet Gallberry
Ilex glabra
  Gallberry; Inkberry
Ilex laevigata
  Smooth Winterberry
Juncus trigonocarpus
  Redpod Rush
Kalmia carolina ❉
  Carolina Sheep Laurel
Kalmia cuneata T ❉
  White Wicky
Lachnanthes caroliniana ❉
  Redroot
Lachnocaulon anceps
  Savanna Bog-buttons
Lespedeza capitata ❉
  Silvery Bush-clover
Leucothoe axillaris ❉
  Coastal Plain Doghobble
Liatris spicata var. *resinosa*
  Bog Blazing-star

Lilium catesbaei
  Catesby's Lily; Pine Lily
Lilium pyrophilum
  Sandhills Lily
Lindera subcoriacea
  Bog Spicebush;
  Streamhead Spicebush
Listera australis
  Southern Twayblade
Lobelia glandulosa
  Savanna Lobelia
Lobelia nuttallii
  Nuttall's Lobelia
Lobelia undescribed T
  Sandhills Lobelia
Ludwigia virgata ❉
  Savanna Seedbox
Lycopus cokeri
  Sandhills Bugleweed
Lyonia ligustrina var. *foliosiflora*
  Southern Maleberry
Lyonia lucida ❉
  Shining Fetterbush
Lyonia mariana
  Staggerbush
Lysimachia asperulifolia
  Roughleaf Loosestrife
Magnolia virginiana
  Sweet Bay;
  Sweetbay Magnolia
Marshallia graminifolia
  Grassleaf Barbara's-buttons
Mecardonia acuminata
  Axil-flower; Mecardonia
Melanthium virginicum
  Virginia Bunchflower
Mitreola sessiliflora
  Small-leaved Miterwort
Morella caroliniensis
  Evergreen Bayberry;
  Pocosin Bayberry
Orbexilum pedunculatum var.
    psoralioides
  Sampson's Snakeroot
Oxypolis filiformis T
  Water Dropwort
Oxypolis rigidior
  Cowbane; Pig Potato
Oxypolis ternata
  Savanna Cowbane

Panicum virgatum var. *cubense*
Savanna Panic-grass;
Coastal Plain Switchgrass
Parnassia caroliniana
Carolina Grass-of-Parnassus;
Savanna Parnassia
Pinguicula caerulea
Blue Butterwort
Pinguicula primuliflora
Clearwater Butterwort;
Primrose Butterwort
Platanthera blephariglottis
White Fringed Orchid
Platanthera ciliaris
Orange Fringed Orchid
Platanthera clavellata
Clubspur Orchid;
Streamhead Orchid
Platanthera cristata
Crested Fringed Orchid
Pogonia ophioglossoides
Rose Pogonia
Polygala cruciata var. *cruciata*
Cross-leaved Milkwort;
Drumheads
Polygala lutea
Orange Milkwort; Candyroot
Polygala ramosa
Savanna Milkwort
Pycnanthemum flexuosum ✳
Savanna Mountain-mint
Pyxidanthera barbulata ✳
Common Pyxie-moss
Rhexia alifanus
Savanna Meadow-beauty
Rhexia lutea
Yellow Meadow-beauty
Rhexia nashii
Nash's Meadow-beauty
Rhexia petiolata
Bog Meadow-beauty
Rhododendron viscosum
Swamp Azalea;
Swamp Honeysuckle
Sabatia difformis
Lanceleaf Sabatia
Sarracenia flava
Yellow Pitcher-plant; Trumpets
Sarracenia purpurea var. *venosa*
Southern Purple Pitcher-plant

Sarracenia rubra var. *rubra*
Red Pitcher-plant;
Sweet Pitcher-plant
Scutellaria integrifolia
Narrow-leaved Skullcap
Smilax glauca ✳
Sawbrier
Smilax laurifolia
Bamboo-vine; Bayvine;
Blaspheme-vine
Smilax pseudochina
Coastal Plain Carrion-flower
Solidago austrina
Graceful Goldenrod
Solidago patula var. *strictula*
Streamhead Goldenrod
Solidago rugosa var. *celtidifolia*
Hackberry-leaved Goldenrod
Solidago verna
Spring Goldenrod
Sophronanthe pilosa
Pilose Hedge-hyssop
Spiranthes cernua ✳
Nodding Ladies'-tresses
Spiranthes praecox
Grass-leaved Ladies'-tresses
Stenanthium densum
Crow Poison; Savanna Camass
Symphyotrichum dumosum
Rice-button Aster
Symplocos tinctoria
Sweetleaf; Horse-sugar
Tephrosia florida T ✳
Savanna Goat's-rue
Tofieldia glabra
Carolina Asphodel
Toxicodendron vernix
Poison Sumac
Triantha racemosa
Savanna Asphodel
Utricularia juncea
Slender Horned Bladderwort
Utricularia subulata
Zig-zag Bladderwort
Vaccinium crassifolium ✳
Creeping Blueberry
Vaccinium formosum ✳
Southern Highbush Blueberry
Vaccinium fuscatum T ✳
Black Highbush Blueberry

Viburnum nudum
  Possum Haw;
  Swamp Viburnum
Viola primulifolia
  Primrose-leaved Violet
Xyris ambigua T
  Savanna Yellow-eyed-grass
Xyris baldwiniana T
  Baldwin's Yellow-eyed-grass
Xyris chapmanii T
  Chapman's Yellow-eyed-grass

Xyris curtissii
  Curtiss's Yellow-eyed-grass
Xyris platylepis
  Bog Yellow-eyed-grass
Xyris scabrifolia
  Harper's Yellow-eyed-grass
Zenobia pulverulenta
  Honeycups; Zenobia
Zigadenus gleberrimus
  Bog Death-camass;
  Large Death-camass

ASTERACEAE: ASTER FAMILY
Rice-button Aster
Symphyotrichum dumosum (L.) Nesom
  var. *dumosum*
[*Aster dumosus* L.]

Perennial, mostly 2–4′ (0.7–1.2 m) tall, widely branched to form a bushy aspect. Stems and main branches have scattered, linear to narrowly elliptic leaves to 4″ (10 cm) long; the lesser branches and flower stalks have numerous tiny, ovate to elliptic, blunt leaves. Flower heads are 0.5–0.75″ (12–20 mm) across, with white or pale bluish rays and yellow to maroon discs.

A good character in recognizing this common species is the abundant tiny, blunt leaves on the branches; these are shaped unlike those of other asters, which tend to have pointed tips. Get to know Rice-button Aster well so as to compare it with other white-flowered species.

Inhabits a wide array of wet to moist habitats, including streamhead ecotones, pine flatwoods, savannas, beaver ponds, and swamp margins; also found in dry to moist pinelands and roadsides.

MID-AUG.–OCT.

ASTERACEAE: ASTER FAMILY
Streamhead Flat-topped Aster
Doellingeria sericocarpoides Small
[*Aster umbellatus* Miller
  var. *brevisquamus* Fernald]

Perennial, 1 to few stems grow from a root crown, 3–6′ (1–1.8 m) tall. Leaves numerous, alternate, elliptic to broadly lanceolate, 1.6–4.4″ (4–11 cm) long and 0.75–1.5″ (1.7–3.5 cm) wide. Flower heads are numerous in a branched, flat-topped inflorescence 5–10″ (12–25 cm) across; each head about 1″ (2.5 cm) across, rays 2–7, white, disc yellow turning purplish with age.

This tall aster is one of the characteristic plants of boggy streamheads, especially those that are periodically burned. Note the small number of rays, as in the white-topped asters (genus *Sericocarpus*) (compare to asters in the genus *Symphyotrichum*, which have many more rays). In the Georgia Sandhills, it has been found so far only in Richmond County.

Inhabits wet streamhead margins, openings in streamheads, and boggy seepage slopes. Ranges on the Coastal Plain from SC NC to N FL, E TX, and AR; disjunct to S NJ.

LATE JULY–OCT.

ASTERACEAE: ASTER FAMILY
Savanna Daisy-fleabane
Erigeron vernus (L.) Torrey & Gray

Perennial, stem 8–20″ (20–50 cm) tall,
smooth or with short, appressed hairs
above. Leaves are all (or nearly all) basal
and form a rosette, elliptic to oblanceolate,
0.8–3″ (2–8 cm) long and 0.25–1.2″ (0.6–3
cm) wide, irregularly toothed or entire,
tapered to base. Flower heads grow in a
corymb, heads 3–20, 0.75″ (18 mm) across;
rays 30 or fewer in number, white to pale
lavender, disc flowers yellow.

One of the delights of spring and
early summer in our longleaf pinelands,
Savanna Daisy-fleabane grows with sundews, pitcher-plants, orchids, milkworts,
and eupatoriums to form colorful swaths.

Inhabits moist to wet longleaf pinelands
and savannas, streamhead margins, and
seepage slopes. Ranges on the Coastal
Plain from se VA to S FL and SW LA.

LATE MAR.–JUNE

ASTERACEAE: ASTER FAMILY
Sunbonnets
Chaptalia tomentosa Ventenat

Perennial from a basal rosette of leaves;
stems 1 to few, 2–16″ (5–40 cm) tall, white
woolly, leafless. Basal leaves are elliptic
to oblanceolate, 2–7″ (5–18 cm) long and
0.4–1.6″ (1–4 cm) wide, with some tufts of
white woolly hairs above, densely matted
with white hairs beneath, margins with
tiny teeth, base of leaf tapered. Flower
heads grow singly, nodding at first,
eventually erect. Ray flowers are about
0.5″ (1–1.5 cm) long, white inside, deep
pink or purple outside; disc flowers are
cream-colored.

Sunbonnets is one of many Sandhills
plants that is so distinctive that it is
instantly learned—and appreciated, for
it grows among choice company such
as pitcher-plants, meadow-beauties,
sundews, and orchids. It responds well
to recurring burns and may begin blooming while the ground is still blackened.

Inhabits moist to wet streamhead mar-
gins, seepage slopes, and wet savannas.
Ranges on the Coastal Plain from e NC to
S FL and e TX.

LATE MAR.–MAY

ASTERACEAE: ASTER FAMILY
Savanna Eupatorium
Eupatorium leucolepis (DC.) Torrey & Gray

Perennial, 1.5–2.5′ (45–80 cm) tall. Leaves
are well-spaced, opposite, almost sessile,
lance-shaped, 1.5–3″ (3.5–7.5 cm) long
and about 0.5″ (12 mm) wide, margins
toothed. The stem is branched above into
a flat-topped cluster of tiny flower heads,
each with long-pointed white bracts and
about 5 white disc flowers, rays absent.
The inflorescence is covered with short,
white, downy hairs.

Learn this plant well so you can distinguish other eupatoriums that grow nearby.
Mohr's Eupatorium (*E. mohrii*) is similar; but the leaves are recurved, wedge-
shaped (widest toward the tip), 0.75–1″
(18–25 mm) wide, and it has blunt flower
bracts. It prefers depression ponds and
wetter streamhead ecotones. Narrowleaf
Eupatorium (*E. linearifolium*) has more
numerous and narrower leaves, the leaves
have fewer teeth, and the flower bracts are
blunt; it inhabits drier soils.

Inhabits moist pineland savannas
and streamhead ecotones but can also
be found in drier uplands. Ranges on the
Coastal Plain from se NY to n FL and e TX.

AUG.–OCT.

ASTERACEAE: ASTER FAMILY
Resinous Boneset;
Resinous Eupatorium
Eupatorium resinosum Torrey ex DC.

Perennial, 2–5′ (0.6–1.5 m) tall, stems
and inflorescence densely pubescent.
Leaves are well-spaced, opposite, sessile,
lance-shaped, 3–5″ (7.5–12.5 cm) long
and 0.4–1″ (1–2.5 cm) wide, tip acuminate, margins toothed. Note the dense
pubescence on leaf undersides and the
prominent golden resin dots. The stem is
branched above into a flat-topped cluster
of tiny flower heads, each with white
bracts and about 7 white disc flowers,
rays absent.

Resinous Boneset is a specialty of
Fort Bragg, NC, and environs, rarely
found elsewhere in the state and very
rare in northern sc (Chesterfield and
Dillon Counties). It was once a candidate
for federal listing, but a large number of
populations have been documented on
and near Fort Bragg. It fares best in wet
soils where regularly burned.

Inhabits wet streamheads and their
ecotones, boggy borders of impoundments, and wet roadside ditches. Restricted to the Coastal Plain of s NC
and n SC; disjunct to s NJ.

AUG.–OCT.

GENTIANACEAE: GENTIAN FAMILY
Lanceleaf Sabatia

Sabatia difformis (L.) Druce

Glabrous perennial from short rhizomes, the stem rounded or slightly angled, 1–3′ (0.3–1 m) tall, opposite-branched above; basal leaves absent. Stem leaves are opposite, lanceolate, up to 2″ (5 cm) long and 0.8″ (2 cm) wide, tip acute. Flowers grow at ends of branches to form a flat or convex top, the 5 petals white with a small greenish yellow base, about 0.7″ (1.5–2 cm) long.

Lanceleaf Sabatia is a good indicator that pitcher-plants and other seepage slope or savanna plants are present. Four-angled Sabatia (*S. quadrangula*) is very similar, but its stem is distinctly angled and narrowly winged lengthwise; it usually inhabits drier pine-oak woodlands and flatwoods of the Piedmont and is very uncommon in our area.

Inhabits wet to moist streamhead margins, seepage slopes, pine flatwoods and savannas, and roadside ditches. Ranges on the Coastal Plain from c NJ to c FL and s AL.

JUNE–AUG.

PARNASSIACEAE:
GRASS-OF-PARNASSUS FAMILY
Carolina Grass-of-Parnassus; Savanna Parnassia

Parnassia caroliniana Michaux

Perennial, glabrous, fleshy textured. Leaves are nearly all basal, broadly ovate, 0.8–2.4″ (2–6 cm) long and wide, with distinct, curving, parallel veins, the base more or less heart-shaped; 1–2 smaller leaves occur on flower stems. Flowers grow singly atop stems 8–20″ (20–50 cm) tall, the 5 petals white with prominent tan or dull green veins, ovate, 0.6–0.8″ (15–20 mm) long.

Those lucky enough to find this plant are in for a wonderful treat, for the flowers are among the most beautiful in our flora. The intricate veining on the pure white petals has to be seen to be appreciated. Grass-of-Parnassus refers to a related European species that Dioscorides described from Mount Parnassus in Greece; why he called it a "grass" is a mystery. Our species is unique in this north-temperate/arctic genus in occurring wholly within the Coastal Plain.

Inhabits wet margins of streamheads and wet savannas. Ranges on the Coastal Plain from se NC to c SC; disjunct to nw FL.

MID-SEPT.–EARLY NOV.

MAGNOLIACEAE: MAGNOLIA FAMILY
Sweet Bay; Sweetbay Magnolia
Magnolia virginiana L.

Perennial tree (or shrubby following fire) with smooth, pale gray bark. Branches are relatively sparse and short, forming a narrow crown. Leaves are semievergreen or deciduous, elliptic, 3–6″ (7.5–15 cm) long and 1–2.5″ (2.5–6 cm) wide, dark green above and glaucous beneath, glabrous or with short, silky hairs beneath. The flowers are globular in outline, 2–3″ (5–7.5 cm) across, white with many yellow stamens, fragrant.

Sweet Bay is included here because it flowers as a shrubby sprout following fire. One can then enjoy the flowers at nose level, especially in the evening when the scent is strongest. Bull Bay (*M. grandiflora*), the commonly planted street tree, differs in its much larger, very thick-textured leaves and in its huge flowers. Bull Bay is native in the Sandhills of southern SC and GA but found in the NC Sandhills only as a result of bird-dispersed seeds from cultivated trees.

Inhabits blackwater streamheads, baygalls, maple-gum and cypress gum swamps, and wet flatwoods. Ranges on the Coastal Plain from e MA to s FL, e TX, and s AR.

EARLY MAY–MID-JUNE

ADOXACEAE:
VIBURNUM & ELDERBERRY FAMILY
Possum Haw; Swamp Viburnum
Viburnum nudum L.

Perennial woody shrub, 4–10′ (1.2–3 m) tall, widely branched, young twigs and leafstalks with rust-colored, scaly hairs. Leaves are opposite, broadly to narrowly elliptic, mostly 2–5″ (5–12 cm) long and 1–2.5″ (2.5–6 cm) wide, larger on sprout shoots. The leaf tip is acute, base short-tapered, leafstalk 0.2–1″ (0.5–2.5 cm) long, margins entire to crenate, surfaces glabrate. Flowers grow densely in flat-topped umbels up to 6″ (15 cm) across, the 5 white petals forming a cup-shaped corolla with spreading lobes, 0.2–0.3″ (5–8 mm) across. Fruits are elliptical, about 0.3″ (8–9 mm) long, compressed lengthwise, glaucous blue.

With its large umbels of flowers, this common wetland shrub is very attractive. As fruits develop, they change from yellow-green to red-pink to glaucous blue. Indians made a tea from the bark to treat diabetes and as a diuretic and general tonic. Note: *Ilex decidua* is also called Possum Haw.

Inhabits wet soils of streamheads, seepage slopes, streambanks, floodplains, and cypress-gum swamps. Ranges on Coastal Plain and Piedmont from s CT to c FL, e TX, and e AR.

APR.–MAY

ROSACEAE: ROSE FAMILY
Pocosin Shadbush;
Coastal Plain Shadbush

Amelanchier obovalis (Michaux) Ashe

Perennial woody shrub to 5′ (1.5 m) tall, occasionally taller, from spreading rhizomes. Branches reach upward, spreading little. Leaves are elliptic or slightly wider toward the tip, 0.8–2.4″ (2–6 cm) long and 0.4–1.3″ (1–3.5 cm) wide, largest leaves on new shoots and sprouts, densely hairy beneath at first, later nearly smooth. Flowers grow in leafy clusters 2–3″ (5–7.5 cm) long at ends of twigs, the 5 petals white, about 0.4″ (1 cm) long. The fruit is blackish purple, rounded, about 0.3″ (8 mm), juicy.

Pocosin Shadbush is one of several showy, spring-flowering shrubs that brighten moist thickets; its fruits are sweet and make good preserves and pies—if you can beat the birds and deer to them!

Inhabits moist margins of streamheads, moist flatwoods, and margins of beaver ponds and impoundments. Ranges on the Coastal Plain from s NJ to s SC; GA reports need verification.

MID-MAR.–MID-APR.

ROSACEAE: ROSE FAMILY
Red Chokeberry

Aronia arbutifolia (L.) Persoon

Perennial woody shrub to 10′ (3 m) tall, colonial from spreading rhizomes. Branches are strongly ascending, not spreading. Leaves are elliptic or oblanceolate, 1.6–4″ (4–10 cm) long and 0.6–1.8″ (1.5–4.5 cm) wide, the largest ones on new shoots and fire sprouts. Leaves are dark green and glabrous above, densely white pubescent beneath, tip blunt, margins crenate. Flowers grow in leafless terminal clusters of up to 10 flowers, the 5 white petals about 0.25″ (4–7 mm) long, stamens 15–20 with red anthers. Fruits are dull red, rounded, about 0.3″ (6–9 mm), dryish.

Red Chokeberry's bright white flowers, set off by the red anthers, are very attractive; so too is the purplish-tinged fall foliage. This species might make a good garden border if kept trimmed.

Inhabits moist to wet streamheads and margins of beaver ponds and impoundments. Ranges from Newf. to WV and KY south to c FL and e TX.

MID-MAR.–MID-APR.

CLETHRACEAE:
CLETHRA & WHITE-ALDER FAMILY
Sweet Pepperbush

Clethra alnifolia L. var. *alnifolia*;
and var. *pubescens* Aiton

Perennial shrub to 7′ (2.2 m) tall, with densely pubescent twigs. Leaves are alternate, oblanceolate or obelliptic, tapered toward the base, 1–4″ (2.5–10 cm) long and 0.75–2″ (1.8–5 cm) wide. Flowers grow densely in terminal cylinders, each flower white, very fragrant, about 0.7″ (15 mm) across, with 5 waxy-textured petals and prominent styles and stamens.

The sweet fragrance of this plant is one of the joys of sultry summer days. Two varieties occur in our region: var. *alnifolia* has glabrous or sparsely white-hairy leaves and occurs from central SC northward; var. *pubescens* has thicker-textured, darker green leaves that are densely hairy beneath with pale, tawny hairs and occurs from northern SC through GA to the Gulf Coast.

Sweet Pepperbush is common and inhabits a wide variety of moist to wet soils, from clay slopes in pinelands to streamhead ecotones, pitcher-plant bogs, Carolina bays, and blackwater swamp forests. The aggregate species occurs on the Coastal Plain from s N.S. to n FL and e TX.

MID-JUNE–JULY

ERICACEAE: BLUEBERRY & AZALEA FAMILY
Dangleberry

Gaylussacia frondosa (L.) Torrey & Gray ex Torrey

Perennial shrub up to 3′ (1 m) tall with glabrous or glabrate twigs. The leaves are deciduous, oblanceolate, 1–2.5″ (2.5–6 cm) long and 0.6–1.25″ (1.5–3 cm) wide, glabrate, glaucescent, with conspicuous golden resin dots beneath. The flowers grow on long stalks in loose clusters, greenish white, similar to blueberry flowers but shorter and squat looking, 0.2″ (3–5 mm) long; the berries are pale blue, juicy.

Dangleberry's sweet berries make a delicious midsummer treat, although the seeds are rather large. It is widespread and common in NC and northern SC. In southern SC and eastern GA grows Hairy Dangleberry (*G. tomentosa*), which is very similar but has densely pubescent twigs and leaves; it apparently is uncommon in the Sandhills region.

Inhabits moist borders of streamheads, seepage slopes, moist pinelands, and even relatively dry oak-hickory uplands. Ranges on the Coastal Plain and lower Piedmont from s NH to c SC. Hairy Dangleberry ranges from c SC to c FL and sw AL.

LATE MAR.–APR.

ERICACEAE: BLUEBERRY & AZALEA FAMILY
Southern Maleberry

Lyonia ligustrina (L.) DC.
  var. *foliosiflora* (Michaux) Fernald

Perennial rhizomatous shrub forming
loose colonies, stems to 3′ (1 m) high
(taller where fire has been suppressed),
branches spreading, more or less pubescent. Leaves deciduous, pubescent above
and below, obovate to elliptic, 1.2–2.8″
(3–7 cm) long and 0.4–1.6″ (1–3.5 cm)
wide, acute, minutely toothed. Flowers
are numerous in terminal, elongate, leafy
branches. Petals are white, globose with
minute flaring lobes, 0.2″ (2.5–3 mm)
long and wide. The fruit is a rounded
capsule with pale sutures.

  The small and rather squat-looking
flowers in a branched, leafy inflorescence
give this shrub a distinctive appearance.
Northern Maleberry (*L. ligustrina* var.
ligustrina) reaches our states only in the
Mountains and Piedmont; its inflorescences have few or no leaves.

  Inhabits moist to wet margins of
streamheads and in flatwoods. Ranges
on the Coastal Plain from se VA to c FL,
e TX, and nc AR.

LATE APR.–MAY

ERICACEAE: BLUEBERRY & AZALEA FAMILY
Staggerbush

Lyonia mariana (L.) D. Don

Perennial rhizomatous shrub forming
loose colonies, stems to 5′ (1.5 m) high but
often only half that, branches spreading,
glabrous. Leaves are deciduous, glabrous,
elliptic to ovate, 1.6–3.6″ (4–9 cm) long
and 0.6–1.8″ (1.5–4.5 cm) wide, acute and
with a minute point, short-stalked, margins not toothed. Flowers grow in clusters
from the nodes of leafless branches,
each flower at the end of an arching or
drooping stalk. The corolla is white, elliptical with minute flaring lobes, 0.3–0.5″
(7–14 mm) long. The fruit is an ovoid
capsule with conspicuous pale sutures,
semiwoody.

  The flowers look like large versions
of Southern Highbush Blueberry flowers,
but note the arrangement along leafless
branches. The rigid, angular fruits have
a unique "boxy" look.

  Inhabits moist upper margins of
streamheads, in flatwoods, and up into
dry longleaf pinelands. Ranges on the
Coastal Plain from s RI to c FL and nw FL;
w LA to e TX and c AR; se MO.

APR.–MAY

ERICACEAE: BLUEBERRY & AZALEA FAMILY
Honeycups; Zenobia
Zenobia pulverulenta (Bartram) Pollard

Perennial shrub, more or less colonial
from rhizomes, 3–6′ (1–2 m) tall, branches
erect, ascending, or arched, glabrous,
twigs often glaucous white. Leaves are deciduous, elliptic to elliptic-ovate, 1.4–3.2″
(3.5–8 cm) long and 0.6–1.6″ (1.5–4 cm)
wide, glabrate, the leafstalks about 0.25″
(3–6 mm) long. Leaves vary from green to
pale blue-gray or even whitish above, and
green to glaucous white beneath, margins
crenate, tip blunt to acute. Numerous
flowers grow on straight to arching
branches, each flower drooping from a
stalk 0.4–1″ (1–2.5 cm) long. The corolla
is cup-shaped, the 5 white petals 0.3–0.5″
(7–12 mm) long, fragrant.

Honeycups comes in two color forms:
one with ordinary green leaves, twigs, and
flower stalks, and one with these parts
glaucous white to pale bluish gray; intermediates occur. The glaucous form is most
common in the Sandhills region and is
such a spectacular plant that it should be
in every garden. In addition, the flowers
are sweetly fragrant.

Inhabits streamhead margins, seepage
slopes, beaver ponds, and impoundments.
Ranges on the Coastal Plain from e NC to
se GA (Liberty County).

LATE APR.–MID-JUNE

ERICACEAE: BLUEBERRY & AZALEA FAMILY
Swamp Azalea;
Swamp Honeysuckle
Rhododendron viscosum (L.) Torrey

Perennial shrub 1.5–13′ (0.5–4 m) tall, with
spreading to ascending branches that are
shaggy hairy when young. Leaves are essentially sessile, dark green above and glaucescent beneath, elliptic to oblanceolate, 1–2.8″
(2.5–7 cm) long, glabrous above except for
midrib, with appressed bristles on midrib
beneath and on margins, tip blunt. Flowers
appear as the leaves unfold, in terminal
clusters of several flowers, each on a stalk
0.25–0.8″ (5–20 mm) long, sweetly fragrant.
The corolla tube is 0.6–1″ (1.5–2.5 cm) long,
white, with dense, gland-tipped hairs, the 5
lobes flaring, white. The stamens and style
extend far beyond the petals, whitish.

You often can smell Swamp Azalea
before you see it, such is the fragrance.
The principal variety (var. *viscosum*) is our
latest-flowering azalea. A second variety
(var. *serrulatum*) also grows here (at least
in nc and sc); it blooms 1–2 weeks earlier
and inhabits more open seepage slopes.
The inside of the corolla tube is glabrous
in var. *serrulatum*, hairy in var. *viscosum*.

Inhabits wet streamheads, shrubby seepage slopes, margins of beaver ponds, and
cypress-gum swamps. Var. *viscosum* ranges
from s ME to ne OH south to se SC; perhaps
also to n FL.

LATE MAY–JUNE; OCCASIONALLY ALSO IN MID-
SEP–OCT. THE VAR. *SERRULATUM* BLOOMS FROM
MID-MAY–EARLY JUNE AND RANGES ON THE
COASTAL PLAIN FROM SE VA TO C FL AND SE LA.

AQUIFOLIACEAE: HOLLY FAMILY
Gallberry; Inkberry
Ilex glabra (L.) Gray

Perennial, evergreen shrub from rhizomes, forming colonies. Stems 2–9′
(0.6–3 m) tall, but usually less than 6′
(2 m), twigs minutely hairy. Leaves are
oblanceolate to narrowly obovate, 1–2.5″
(2.5–6 cm) long, glabrous, lustrous above,
bluntly few-toothed near tip. Plants are
either male or female (dioecious), flowers
short-stalked, 1–3 (3–7 if male) from leaf
axils. Petals 5–8, white, waxy-textured,
0.25–0.4″ (6–8 mm) across, mildly fragrant. Fruit black, rounded, about 0.3″
(5–7 mm).

   Inkberry is one of our commonest
shrubs, forming thickets or patches in
moist soils of streamheads and seepage
slopes. A related species (Yaupon, *I. vomi-
toria*), was used by Native Americans
as an emetic; it naturally occurs on the
flat portion of the Coastal Plain but has
escaped from plantings in the Sandhills.
Its leaves have blunt teeth on the entire
margin and its fruits are red or yellow.

   Inhabits streamheads and their margins, seepage slopes, and creek and river
swamps; also found well upslope in clay
soils in pinelands. Ranges mostly on the
Coastal Plain from sw N.S. to s FL and
e TX; disjunct to nw GA.

LATE APR.–MID-MAY

AQUIFOLIACEAE: HOLLY FAMILY
Large Gallberry; Sweet Gallberry
Ilex coriacea (Pursh) Chapman

Perennial, evergreen shrub from rhizomes, colony forming. Stems grow 5–12′
(1.5–4 m) tall, twigs are minutely hairy.
Leaves are ovate to broadly elliptical,
1.4–2.8″ (3.5–7 cm) long and 0.6–1.6″
(1.5–4 cm) wide, glabrous, lustrous above,
margins with a few short spiny teeth (or
none). Plants are either male or female
(dioecious). Flowers are short-stalked, 1–3
(3–7 if male) from leaf axils, white, waxy,
petals 5–8, 0.25–0.4″ (6–8 mm) across,
mildly fragrant. Fruit black, lustrous,
rounded, about 0.4″ (7–10 mm).

   Large Gallberry is one of those tall,
densely tangled shrubs that gives people
pause before they enter a swamp or a
streamhead. Large Gallberry and its com-
panions—Shining Fetterbush (*Lyonia
lucida*), Bamboo-vine (*Smilax laurifolia*),
Ti-ti (*Cyrilla racemiflora*), Coastal Plain
Doghobble (*Leucothoe axillaris*), and
Poison Sumac (*Toxicodendron vernix*)—
seem to conspire to make your visit
unpleasant and brief.

   Inhabits blackwater streamheads, creek
margins, and river swamps. Ranges on the
Coastal Plain from se VA to c FL and e TX.

LATE APR.–MID-MAY

AQUIFOLIACEAE: HOLLY FAMILY
Smooth Winterberry
Ilex laevigata (Pursh) Gray

Perennial shrub, stems single or a few together, 5–12′ (1.5–4 m) tall, branches relatively few and not widely spreading, twigs glabrous. Leaves are deciduous, oblanceolate to narrowly obovate, 1.6–3.5″ (4–9 cm) long and 0.6–1.6″ (1.5–4 cm) wide, glabrous and lustrous above, margins crenate. Leaves may have some hairs on veins beneath, but never densely so. Plants are either male or female (dioecious), flowers short-stalked, 1–3 (3 to many if male) from leaf axils. There are 5–8 petals, white, waxy, 0.25–0.4″ (6–8 mm) across, mildly fragrant. Fruit bright red, lustrous, rounded, about 0.3″ (6–8 mm).

With its brilliant red fruits and lustrous leaves that turn yellow late in fall, Smooth Winterberry is a beautiful shrub, but too little known or appreciated. Downy Winterberry or Black Alder (*I. verticillata*) is similar in dimensions, but its leaves are densely to sparsely pubescent beneath, dull above, and rugose-textured. Flowers of both are very similar to Large Gall-berry, and the berries last through much of the winter.

Inhabits seepy blackwater streamheads and creek margins. Ranges mostly on the Coastal Plain from s ME to nc SC.

LATE APR.–MID-MAY

HAMAMELIDACEAE: WITCH-HAZEL FAMILY
Dwarf Witch-alder
Fothergilla gardenii Murray

Perennial shrub 1–3′ (0.3–1 m) tall. Leaves elliptic or obelliptic, mostly 1–2″ (2.5–5 cm) long and 0.75–1.5″ (1.8–3.5 cm) wide, usually blunt-tipped, base rounded to almost cordate, stellate-pubescent, margins toothed above middle (or not). Flowers are produced just prior to leaf-out in dense terminal spikes up to 2″ (5 cm) long and 1″ (2.5 cm) wide. Petals are absent, stamens numerous, white with yellow anthers. Fruit is a hard capsule, densely hairy.

When flowering, Dwarf Witch-alder's showy pom-poms on leafless stems are hard to miss, but later this shrub blends in with other co-occurring species and is easily overlooked. Dr. John Fothergill was a London physician and patron of early American botanists. Dr. Alexander Garden of Charleston, SC, sent the first specimens of this plant to Linnaeus; the genus *Gardenia* is also named after him.

Inhabits moist to wet streamhead ecotones, seepage slopes, and flatwoods, especially where burned. Ranges on the Coastal Plain from e NC to nw FL and s AL; disjunct to Macon and Taylor Counties, GA.

APR.–EARLY MAY

ORCHIDACEAE: ORCHID FAMILY
White Fringed Orchid

Platanthera blephariglottis (Willdenow) Lindley
[*Habenaria blephariglottis* (Willdenow) Hooker]

Perennial, glabrous, stem mostly 1.5–2.5′ (45–76 cm) tall. Leaves are strongly ascending, broadly lanceolate, 2–13″ (5–35 cm) long and 0.4–2″ (1–5 cm) wide, tip acuminate, parallel-veined, lowest leaves largest, upper ones much smaller. Flowers grow in a dense cylindrical raceme with leafy bracts, each flower white, on a stalk about 0.8″ (2 cm) long. The 3 sepals are elliptic to roundish, 0.2–0.4 (5–11 mm) long, the 2 upper petals are oblanceolate, 0.2–0.3″ (3–8 mm) long and 1–3 mm wide, the tip often with tiny teeth. The lip (lower petal) is elliptical, 0.25–0.5″ (6–13 mm) long, with slender fringing around the margin; the spur is more or less curved, 0.6–2″ (1.5–5 cm) long.

One of the jewels of the Sandhills region, White Fringed Orchid has sadly become rare due to fire suppression and conversion of streamheads to fish ponds and recreation lakes. Two entities (one with larger flowers and spurs) occur in our area, but details of their distribution have not yet been worked out; most current populations are of the larger form.

Inhabits boggy streamhead margins, seepage slopes, and pitcher-plant bogs. The larger form ranges on the Coastal Plain from NC to c FL and e TX; the smaller form is more northern, extending to Newf. and inland to MI.

MID-JULY–AUG.

ORCHIDACEAE: ORCHID FAMILY
Grass-leaved Ladies'-tresses

Spiranthes praecox (Walter) S. Watson

Perennial, slender, fleshy-textured, stems mostly 10–28″ (25–70 cm) tall, glabrate. Leaves are linear, erect, 4–10″ (10–25 cm) long and less than 0.25″ (1–5 mm) wide, glabrous, reduced in size upward. Flowers grow in a loose, gradually twisted spiral up to 6″ (15 cm) long. The 3 sepals and 3 petals are 0.25–0.4″ (5.5–11 mm) long and 1–2 mm wide (lip petal longest and widest), not curved outward at the tip, white, glandular-pubescent on the outside. The lip is elliptical, 0.25″ (4–6 mm) wide, strongly curved downward, margin frilled, inner surface with several green lines.

Grass-leaved Ladies'-tresses can be told by its lazy spiral of flowers, each with green or gray-brown lines on the lip. It is uncommon to rare in our area, perhaps due to fire suppression.

Inhabits moist to wet longleaf pine savannas, streamhead margins, and seepage slopes; sometimes found on blackwater river terraces. Ranges on the Coastal Plain from s DE to s FL, e TX, se OK, and s AR; nw GA.

MID-APR.–EARLY JULY

VIOLACEAE: VIOLET FAMILY
Primrose-leaved Violet
Viola primulifolia L.

Perennial, often colonial via runners in
the soil. Leaves are ascending or leaning,
glabrous to pubescent, narrowly ovate or
broadly lanceolate. The blades are mostly
1–4″ (2.5–10 cm) long, tip acute, base
tapered to the leafstalk, margins crenate,
leafstalk about as long as blade. Flowers
grow on slender stalks independent of
and overtopping the leaves, 0.4–0.8″ (1–2
cm) across. The 5 petals are white, the
lowest one (the lip) slightly larger and
with purple lines. The lip petal also has a
backward-pointing, blunt spur.

Primrose-leaved Violet is probably our
commonest violet, but you often need
to get your shoes wet to see it. Lanceleaf
Violet (*V. lanceolata*) also has white flowers, but its leaves are narrowly lanceolate
to almost linear and are long-tapered to
both ends.

Inhabits wet soil of streamhead margins, seepage slopes, and streambanks and
riverbanks. Ranges from Newf. to Ont.
south to c FL and e TX.

MID-MAR.–APR.

ERIOCAULACEAE: PIPEWORT FAMILY
Hard Pipewort; Hatpins
Eriocaulon decangulare L. var. *decangulare*

Perennial, terrestrial or semiaquatic.
Leaves all basal, ascending to erect, thick-
textured and stiff, mostly 5–12″ (12–30
cm) long and up to 0.4″ (10 mm) wide
(occasionally broader), acute. Stems single
or several, 12–32″ (30–80 cm) tall, ribbed
lengthwise, each topped by a domed head.
Heads white, 0.3–0.6″ (8–16 mm) wide,
hard, composed of tiny flowers.

Hard pipeworts are popular in flower
arrangements. A rare associate of Hard
Pipewort is Texas Pipewort (*E. texense*),
disjunct from the Gulf Coast to a handful of Sandhills region seepage bogs in
NC and SC. It is less than half the size of
Hard Pipewort, with a soft head only 0.25″
(5 mm) wide; its leaves are very short
and less than 0.25″ (6 mm) wide, and it
blooms late April–May.

Inhabits seepage slopes, streamhead
ecotones, wet flatwoods, boggy scrapes,
and beaver ponds, generally with sundews
and pitcher-plants. Ranges mostly on the
Coastal Plain from s NJ to s FL, e TX, and
s AR; many records inland; Mex.; Central
America.

LATE JUNE–SEPT.

ERIOCAULACEAE: PIPEWORT FAMILY
Savanna Bog-buttons
Lachnocaulon anceps (Walter) Morong

Perennial from a scaly rhizome, plants often forming patches or mats. Leaves are numerous, all basal, linear, 0.8–3.2″ (2–8 cm) long and less than 0.2″ (3 mm) wide, tip acuminate. Leaf surfaces have scattered wispy hairs; old leaf bases often persist as tan-colored remnants. Flowering stems grow singly or several together, 2–10″ (5–25 cm) long, twisted in a spiral, narrowly ridged lengthwise, with scattered wispy hairs. Flowers grow in a single, small, dense head atop each stem, heads roundish, about 0.25″ (4–7 mm) across, white or whitish.

This plant should remind you of a miniature Hard Pipewort (*Eriocaulon decangulare*), but note the wispy hairs on the stems and leaves. Both species can be found together in seepage slopes.

Inhabits seepage slopes, margins of streamheads, moist to wet savannas, and margins of beaver ponds. Ranges on the Coastal Plain from s NJ to s FL and e TX; ne AL to c TN; w Cuba.

MID-MAY–LATE SEPT.

DROSERACEAE: SUNDEW FAMILY
Bog Sundew
Drosera capillaris Poiret

Annual, leaves confined to a flat basal rosette 1.2–3″ (3–8 cm) across, blades elliptical to rotund, 0.25–0.5″ (5–12 mm) long, shorter than the stalks, strongly red-tinged when growing in full sun, covered with gland-tipped hairs. Flowering stem solitary, leafless, without gland-tipped hairs, 0.8–2.4″ (4–15 cm) tall, maroon or dull red. Flowers bloom one at a time as the upper stem uncoils, white or pale pink, petals 0.25–0.3″ (5–7 mm) long.

This is our commonest sundew. Like all sundews, it catches insects passively with its viscid hairs; the leaf then slowly curls around the prey and secretes digestive chemicals. Even tiny frogs have been unfortunate victims, but ants and small beetles are normal prey. Roundleaf Sundew (*D. rotundifolia*) is a rare member of the NC Sandhills on clay seepage walls of Little River and in sphagnum moss of several streamheads; it resembles Bog Sundew but is twice the size, its leaf blades are wider than long, and its blades are always green, never red.

Inhabits moist to wet seepage slopes, streamhead margins, pineland savannas, and shores of beaver ponds and impoundments. Ranges on the Coastal Plain from se MD to s FL and e TX; scattered through much of the neotropics.

LATE MAY–AUG.

DROSERACEAE: SUNDEW FAMILY
Dwarf Sundew; Early Sundew

Drosera brevifolia Pursh

Annual, leaves confined to a flat basal rosette 0.8–1.6″ (2–3 cm) across, blades obovate to obdeltoid to rotund, 0.25–0.4″ (5–10 mm) long, about as long as the leafstalks, strongly red-tinged when in full sun, covered with gland-tipped hairs. Flowering stem solitary, leafless, with numerous short gland-tipped hairs, 0.8–2.4″ (2–6 cm) tall, maroon or dull red. Flowers bloom one at a time as the upper stem uncoils, petals 5, pale pink or white, 0.3–0.4″ (7–9 mm) long.

Dwarf Sundew is named for its small rosettes and often short stem, but its dimensions overlap widely with those of Bog Sundew. Leaf blades normally are distinctly broader nearer the tip than the base, unlike Bog Sundew. If unsure, check the stem for the telltale glandular hairs of Dwarf Sundew. It is our earliest flowering sundew. Much less common than Bog Sundew and more likely to be overlooked.

Inhabits moist streamhead margins, seepage slopes, and pineland savannas and flatwoods. Ranges on the Coastal Plain from se VA to s FL, e TX, and s AR; locally in TN; also Cuba; s Mex.; Belize; s Brazil; Uruguay.

APR.–EARLY JUNE

BURMANNIACEAE: BURMANNIA FAMILY
White Burmannia

Burmannia capitata (Gmelin) Martius

Annual, stem very slender and threadlike, 1.25–6″ (3–15 cm) tall. Leaves are alternate, tiny and scalelike, 0.25″ (3–5 mm) long. Flowers number 1–20 in a dense terminal cluster or head, each flower 0.2–0.25″ (3–5 mm) long and about 1 mm wide, creamy white.

With luck, you may find both White Burmannia and Blue Burmannia (Bluethread) (*B. biflora*) together in the same seepage slope, along with pitcher-plants, sundews, and orchids. The genus and family were named for Johannes Burmann, Dutch botanist of the eighteenth century.

Inhabits wet streamhead margins, seepage slopes, and seasonally ponded depressions. Ranges on the Coastal Plain from c NC to s FL, e TX, and se OK; West Indies; Central America; South America.

JULY–OCT.

ARALIACEAE: GINSENG FAMILY
False Pennywort

Centella erecta (L.f.) Fernald
[*Centella asiatica* (L.) Urban]

Perennial, usually colonial, the plants connected by slender rhizomes. Leaves stand erect on pubescent stalks to 6″ (15 cm) long, the blade elliptical, with cordate base (heart-shaped sinus), 0.6–1.6″ (1.5–4 cm) long and slightly less wide, margins crenate or entire. Four to 9 flowers grow in dense clusters atop stalks that are shorter than leafstalks, petals 5, white, tiny, soon deciduous.

False Pennywort is closely related to true pennyworts of the genus *Hydrocotyle*, but its leaves are nonpeltate—its leafstalk is attached at the leaf margin rather than at the center. The name "pennywort" is especially apt for *Centella*, since the latter name is the diminutive of *centum*, Latin for "coin."

Inhabits streamhead margins, seepage slopes, margins of beaver ponds, and shores of depression ponds. Ranges from s DE to s FL and se TX; Mex.; West Indies; Central America.

JUNE–AUG.

LOGANIACEAE: LOGANIA FAMILY
Small-leaved Miterwort

Mitreola sessilifolia (J. F. Gmelin) G. Don

Annual, stem 4–20″ (10–50 cm) tall, not branched, glabrous or nearly so. Leaves are ovate to elliptic 0.25–1″ (5–25 mm) long and 0.2–0.8″ (3–20 mm) wide, nearly sessile, the uppermost pairs well-spaced. Flowers grow densely in short, terminal, spreading or recurved branchlets. The flowers are sessile, white, about 2 mm long, short-tubular with 5 tiny lobes.

Small-leaved Miterwort is an uncommon plant in our area; it is more numerous on the middle and outer Coastal Plain. The inflorescence of short curved branchlets crowded with tiny flowers is like no other Sandhills plant.

Inhabits seepage slopes, margins of streamheads, and vernal pools. Ranges on the Coastal Plain from se VA to s FL, e TX, and se OK; nw Bahamas.

LATE JUNE–AUG.

CONVOLVULACEAE:
MORNING-GLORY FAMILY
Compact Dodder

Cuscuta compacta Jussieu ex Choisy

Annual twining vine without roots, parasitic on various herbs and shrubs. Stems slender, orange to yellow, tightly twining and gripping via tiny suckers. Flowers grow in numerous multiflowered clusters that are closely packed along the stem. Flowers are sessile, white, ovate-tubular, about 0.25–0.3″ (5–5.5 mm) long, constricted at the base of petal lobes, the lobes spreading to reflexed.

Compact Dodder is one of about 10 species that occur in our 3 states, but it is the most numerous in the Sandhills region. Its fairly thick, "ropelike" flower clusters are quite distinct. The suckers penetrate host plant tissue and extract nutrients but do not kill the hosts. The flowers of all dodders have a semisucculent, waxy texture.

Inhabits moist to wet streamheads, blackwater river swamps, seepage slopes, flatwoods, and shrub thickets. Ranges from VT to Que. and NE, south to FL and TX.

AUG.–OCT.

GENTIANACEAE: GENTIAN FAMILY
Screwstem; Twining Bartonia

Bartonia paniculata (Michaux)
   Muhlenberg ssp. *paniculata*

Annual, the slender stem erect, ascending, or twining on adjacent plants, up to 18″ (45 cm) tall, often purplish-tinged. The tiny leaves are alternate or subopposite, scalelike, 0.1″ (1–3 mm) long. Flowers grow on slender stalks up to 1″ (25 mm) long in the upper half of the plant. The 4 petals are greenish or whitish, 0.2–0.25″ (3–5 mm) long, acute to acuminate, margins smooth.

Look for this inconspicuous plant in sphagnum moss under Atlantic White Cedar. Common Bartonia (*B. virginica*) is very similar, but the stem is thicker and noticeably 4-angled; its leaves are nearly always opposite, and its petals are not so taper-pointed (bluntly acute) and usually have a few tiny teeth on margins. Both species are apparently much rarer in the SC and GA Sandhills than in NC.

Inhabits mossy streamheads and their margins, especially under Atlantic White Cedar; also found along small blackwater rivers. Ranges on the Coastal Plain from MA to FL and TX, with scattered sites inland.

AUG.–OCT.

LAMIACEAE: MINT FAMILY
Sandhills Bugleweed

Lycopus cokeri Ahles ex Sorrie

Perennial from fibrous roots; plants also produce lateral stolons with small tubers at the ends. Stems grow 8–24″ (20–75 cm) tall, 4-angled, simple or branched from the upper nodes, moderately pubescent. Leaves are opposite, almost sessile, ovate to elliptical, 0.75–1.75″ (1.7–4.5 cm) long and 0.4–1″ (0.8–2.5 cm) wide, pointed, margins bluntly 2–6 toothed, the lower surface with tiny golden dots. Flowers grow in compact radial clusters in leaf axils, white, short-tubular with 4 pointed lobes, only a few mm long.

This mint has a limited range yet is common in appropriate habitat; it should be sought in the Augusta, GA, area. Virginia Bugleweed (*L. virginicus*) is similar but has larger leaves with long, winged leafstalks, longer leaf tips, and twice as many marginal teeth; it inhabits floodplains downstream of Sandhills Bugleweed.

Inhabits wet streamheads, shrubby seepage slopes, and boggy shores of impoundments. Endemic to the Sandhills region, from sc NC to sc SC.

JULY–OCT.

PLANTAGINACEAE : PLANTAIN FAMILY
Pilose Hedge-hyssop

Sophronanthe pilosa (Michaux) Small
[*Gratiola pilosa* Michaux]

Perennial, usually unbranched, 4–28″ (10–70 cm) tall, pilose (hairs stick straight out). Leaves are sessile, ovate, 0.5–0.8″ (12–20 mm) long and 0.2–0.5″ (5–12 mm) wide, margins smooth or irregularly toothed. Flowers occur singly at leaf bases, nearly sessile, with 2 leafy bracts at the base of the flower. The corolla is tubular with 5 spreading lobes, 0.25–0.3″ (6–8 mm) long, white, tinged lavender.

Hedge-hyssops (*Sophronanthe* and *Gratiola*) are mostly inconspicuous plants of wet habitats. There are 11 species in our 3 states but only 4 in the Sandhills region. Sticky Hedge-hyssop (*Gratiola viscidula*) is similar, but flowers grow on long stalks and stems are glandular-hairy; it occurs on shores of creeks and bottoms of beaver ponds.

Inhabits wet depressions, streamhead ecotones, seepage slopes, margins of beaver ponds, and wet savannas. Ranges mostly on the Coastal Plain from s NJ to s FL, e TX, and AR; scattered inland to w NC, nw SC, nc GA, TN, KY.

JUNE–SEPT.

PLANTAGINACEAE: PLANTAIN FAMILY
Axil-flower; Mecardonia
Mecardonia acuminata (Walter) Small

Glabrous perennial with a single stem
(sometimes multiple), branched or not,
4–18″ (10–50 cm) tall. Leaves are opposite,
narrowly elliptic, 0.4–1.7″ (1–4.5 cm) long
and 0.25–0.5″ (5–12 mm) wide, short-
tapered to both ends, nearly sessile, few-
toothed on margins. Flowers grow singly
from leaf axils in upper half of plant,
their stalks slender and curved upward
and outward, longer than the leaves. The
calyx is pale green, with 5 sharp lobes; the
corolla is white, tubular, 0.4″ (9–11 mm)
long, with 5 small flaring lobes.

It is hard to predict where one will find
Mecardonia, for it is absent from many
seemingly suitable places. So when you do
find it, enjoy this plant with its delightful
little flowers on jaunty stalks.

Inhabits moist margins of streamheads,
shores of rivers, moist roadside ditches,
borrow pits, and rights-of-way. Ranges
from DE to KY and MO south to S FL and
E TX.

JULY–SEPT.

APIACEAE: CARROT FAMILY
Cowbane; Pig Potato
Oxypolis rigidior (L.) Rafinesque

Glabrous perennial 2.5–5′ (0.75–1.5 m)
tall. Leaves are few and well-spaced, the
blades divided into 7–11 linear to narrowly
elliptical segments 2.5–5″ (6–12 cm) long
and 0.2–1.6″ (0.5–4 cm) wide, irregularly
few-toothed. Flowers grow in 1–3 flat-
topped umbels atop stalks 2.8–8″ (7–20
cm) long, terminal or from the upper leaf
axil. Umbels are composed of 12–25 stalks
(termed rays in this family) mostly 1.2–2″
(3–5 cm) long, each tipped by 1 flower
with 5 tiny white petals.

The leaflets are highly variable in width
and length, and slender plants may resemble Savanna Cowbane (*O. ternata*), so be
sure to check for teeth on the margins.
The name cowbane, meaning "poisonous to cows," derives from compounds
produced by the plant; *it is injurious to
humans if taken in quantity.*

Inhabits seepage slopes and boggy
margins of streamheads; away from the
Sandhills it grows in marshes and streamsides. Ranges from NY to MN south to FL
and TX.

LATE AUG.–OCT.

APIACEAE: CARROT FAMILY
Savanna Cowbane

Oxypolis ternata (Nuttall) A. Heller

Very slender glabrous perennial, 1.5–3′ (0.5–1 m) tall. Leaves are few and well-spaced, the stalks up to 1′ (30 cm) long, blades are divided into 3 linear or thread-like segments 0.3–7.5″ (8–20 cm) long and less than 0.2″ (3 mm) wide, sometimes undivided. Flowers grow in 1–3 flat-topped umbels atop stalks 1.6–6″ (4–15 cm) long, terminal or from the upper leaf axil. Umbels are composed of 5–11 stalks (termed rays in this family) 0.8–3.2″ (2–8 cm) long, each tipped by a tiny flower with 5 white petals.

This remarkable plant is so slender it is hard to see among neighboring grasses and sedges. But wherever it grows, you are sure to find other exciting plants, like pitcher-plants, sundews, meadow-beauties, and yellow-eyed-grasses. Water Dropwort (*O. filiformis*) is taller (up to 4.5′), with a much thicker stem, the undivided leaves round in cross section; it prefers wet savannas in the outer Coastal Plain and is rare in our area.

Inhabits seepage slopes and boggy margins of streamheads. Ranges disjunctly on the Coastal Plain from se VA to ne SC; se GA to nw FL.

SEPT.–OCT.

TOFIELDIACEAE: FALSE-ASPHODEL FAMILY
Savanna Asphodel

Triantha racemosa (Walter) Small
[*Tofieldia racemosa* (Walter) B.S.P.]

Perennial from short rhizomes. Leaves are mostly basal, rapidly reduced up the stem, grasslike but have a succulent texture, 3–12″ (7.5–30 cm) long and less than 0.3″ (8 mm) wide, acute. The stem grows up to 2′ (70 cm) tall, densely covered with grainy whitish glands. Flowers grow in groups of 3–7 at each node, about 0.4″ (10 mm) across. The 3 sepals and 3 petals are white, oblanceolate.

True asphodels belong to the related Mediterranean genus *Asphodelus* and are cultivated for their edible bulbs and as a source of dyes. Our Savanna Asphodel and Carolina Asphodel (*Tofieldia glabra*) often are found together but divide the resources (including pollinators) by blooming at different periods.

Inhabits streamhead ecotones, seepage slopes, and wet savannas. Ranges from s NJ to nw FL and se LA; e TX; c TN.

JUNE–EARLY AUG.

TOFIELDIACEAE: FALSE-ASPHODEL FAMILY
Carolina Asphodel

Tofieldia glabra Nuttall

Glabrous perennial from short rhizomes.
Leaves are mostly basal, erect, grasslike
but have a succulent texture, 3–12″ (7.5–30
cm) long and less than 0.3″ (8 mm) wide,
tip acute, rapidly reduced in size up the
stem. The stem grows up to 2′ (70 cm) tall.
Flowers grow singly at each node of the
inflorescence, about 0.4″ (10 mm) across,
the 3 sepals and 3 petals alike, white,
oblanceolate.

Unlike Savanna Asphodel (*Triantha
racemosa*), Carolina Asphodel has smooth
stems and only one flower per node, and it
blooms in the fall.

Inhabits streamhead ecotones, seepage
slopes, and wet savannas. Endemic to the
Coastal Plain of e NC and c SC.

LATE AUG.–OCT.

MELANTHIACEAE: BUNCHFLOWER FAMILY
Crow Poison; Savanna Camass

Stenanthium densum (Desr.) Zomlefer & Judd
[*Zigadenus densus* (Desr.) Fernald]

Glabrous, glaucescent perennial from a
bulblike base, the stems to 3′ (1 m) tall
(occasionally taller). Leaves are linear,
erect to ascending, shorter than the stem,
0.2–0.4″ (3–10 mm) wide, mostly basal.
A few short leaves grow partway up the
stem. Flowers grow in a terminal elliptic
or cylindric cluster, each flower on a stalk
from the axil of a bract. The 3 sepals and 3
petals are alike, white, fading to purplish,
ovate to elliptic, 0.25″ (4–5 mm) long.

Common names refer to its resemblance to plants (in different genera)
that are poisonous to grazing animals.
This lovely plant has declined greatly in
our region due to fire suppression and
conversion of habitat. When you find it,
be sure to return in late summer for Bog
Death-camass (*Zigadenus glaberrimus*),
which often accompanies it.

Inhabits periodically burned streamhead margins, seepage slopes, and pitcher-
plant bogs. Ranges on the Coastal Plain
from se VA to c FL and e TX; c TN.

APR.–EARLY JUNE

MELANTHIACEAE: BUNCHFLOWER FAMILY
Bog Death-camass, Large Death-camass
Zigadenus glaberrimus Michaux

Glabrous perennial, solitary or forming small colonies via slender rhizomes, the stems 20–32″ (50–80 cm) tall. Leaves are 2–3 ranked, linear, pleated lengthwise, 6–16″ (15–40 cm) long and 0.25–0.8″ (6–20 mm) wide, gradually smaller up the stem, tip acute to acuminate. Flowers grow in a spikelike terminal inflorescence and on ascending branches, the whole 6–16″ (15–40 cm) long. The 3 sepals and 3 petals are lanceolate, 0.4–0.6″ (10–16 mm) long and 0.2″ (3–5 mm) wide, white with 2 roundish yellow-green glands at the base.

Bog Death-camass is one of our showiest summer flowers, due to its tall stature and numerous flowers. Take a few minutes to examine the intricate flower design. Contains poisonous alkaloids, but their effects on humans is unknown. Other death-camasses are now in the genus *Anticlea*; our species remains as the sole member of *Zigadenus*, endemic to the Coastal Plain.

Inhabits seepage slopes, pitcher-plant bogs, margins, or streamheads. Ranges on the Coastal Plain from se VA to n FL and se MS.

LATE JUNE–AUG.

MELANTHIACEAE: BUNCHFLOWER FAMILY
Virginia Bunchflower
Melanthium virginicum L.

Perennial from a stout (even bulbous) rootstock that usually has fibrous remnants of old leaf bases. Stems are minutely but densely downy above, glabrous below, 3–6′ (1–2 m) tall. Leaves occur mostly in the lower half of stem, linear, 12–32″ (30–80 cm) long and (4–30 mm) wide, the largest basally, gradually smaller above, pleated lengthwise. Flowers are numerous on ascending branches and on the terminal portion of the stem. Corollas are 6-parted, the sepals and petals alike, cream-colored fading to pale green, narrowly ovate, about 0.25″ (5–8 mm) long, quickly tapered basally, each with 2 small glands toward the base.

Virginia Bunchflower normally occurs in small numbers and often occurs among dense shrubs, so it takes some persistence to locate. It benefits from occasional disturbance to its habitat to reduce shrub density.

Inhabits wet streamheads and boggy seepage slopes. Ranges from s NY to IA south to n FL and e TX.

JUNE–JULY

ASTERACEAE: ASTER FAMILY
Savanna Tickseed
Coreopsis linifolia Nuttall

Glabrous, pale green perennial, stems
1.5–3′ (0.5–1 m) tall. Leaves are all opposite
or the lower ones alternate, lower leaves
much larger than upper, margins toothless. Lower leaves are very long-stalked,
narrowly to broadly lance-shaped, 1.2–6″
(3–15 cm) long and 0.25–0.8″ (0.5–2 cm)
wide. Flower heads are produced on long,
erect, slender stalks forming a flat to
multilayered cluster, ray flowers yellow,
0.4–0.8″ (1–2 cm) long, toothed at tip,
disc flowers maroon-red.

Although fairly common in NC,
Savanna Tickseed is rare or absent in the
Sandhills region of SC and GA. A clinch-
ing identification character is the tiny dark
dots on the leaves as seen in transmitted
light.

Inhabits moist to wet pineland savannas, seepage slopes, and streamhead
margins. Ranges on the Coastal Plain
from SE VA to N FL and E TX.

MID-JULY–OCT.

ASTERACEAE: ASTER FAMILY
Carolina Tickseed
Coreopsis falcata Boynton

Glabrous, pale green or glaucescent
perennial, stems 1.6–5.5′ (0.5–1.7 m) tall.
Leaves sparse (mostly 3–7), the lower
much larger than the upper, long-stalked,
margins toothless. Lower leaves are narrowly elliptic, 1.6–6″ (4–15 cm) long and
0.4–1.5″ (1–3.5 cm) wide, often with 1–2
linear lobes near the base. Flower heads
are produced on long, erect, slender stalks
forming a flattish cyme, ray flowers yellow,
0.8–1.25″ (2–3 cm) long, toothed at tip,
disc flowers maroon-red.

With their brilliant yellow ray flowers,
tickseeds are among our handsomest
plants. The name tickseed comes from
the seed, which is flattened and has many
teeth around the margin that sort of resemble a tick's legs. Carolina Tickseed
is our only spring-flowering species.
Named by Frank E. Boynton, longtime
horticulturist at the Biltmore Estate in NC.

Inhabits wet seepage slopes, streamhead
margins, and pine savannas; sometimes
also found in borrow pits. Ranges on the
Coastal Plain from SE VA to SE SC.

MID-MAY–EARLY JULY

ASTERACEAE: ASTER FAMILY
Graceful Goldenrod

Solidago austrina Small
[*Solidago gracillima* Torrey & Gray, in part]

Perennial, stems 2–4.5′ (0.6–1.4 m) tall, erect to leaning, glabrous. The few to several basal leaves are erect, lanceolate, 2.5–6″ (6–15 cm) long and less than 1.2″ (3 cm) wide, tip acute, base long-tapered to stalk, margins minutely scabrous. Stem leaves rapidly become smaller upward; soon they are elliptic and 0.4″ (1 cm) long, margins minutely scabrous. Flowers grow in a terminal, one-sided inflorescence, often also with short arching branches. The 1–3 ray flowers are yellow, about 0.2″ (2–4 mm) long; disc yellow.

Graceful Goldenrod is remarkably slender and often leans on other vegetation for support. Wand Goldenrod (*S. stricta*) is very similar but even taller; its upper stem leaves are not scabrous and its inflorescence rarely is branched; it occurs only on the outer and middle Coastal Plain.

Inhabits streamhead margins and seepage slopes. Ranges in the lower Piedmont and Coastal Plain from se VA to nw FL and s AL.

SEPT.–MID-OCT.

ASTERACEAE: ASTER FAMILY
Streamhead Goldenrod

Solidago patula Muhl. ex Willd.
  var. *strictula* Torrey & Gray

Perennial, stems 3–6′ (1–2 m) tall, erect, glabrate, usually with long, ascending branches in the upper third. There are several basal leaves, ascending, ovate, 6–8″ (15–20 cm) long and 2–2.5″ (5–6 cm) wide, tip acute, base tapered to long winged stalk, margins serrate. Stem leaves become smaller upward and shorter-stalked, eventually elliptic and sessile; upper surfaces of all leaves are scabrous. Flowers grow in a terminal inflorescence, pyramidal with arching branches, the flower heads only on 1 side of the branches (secund). The 5–10 yellow ray flowers are less than 0.2″ (2 mm) long; disc yellow.

Streamhead Goldenrod is named for the habitat it occupies—open streamheads and their seepy margins, where fire is a recurring disturbance. Only Hackberry-leaved Goldenrod (*S. rugosa*) has leaves as rough as these.

Inhabits wet streamheads and seepage slopes. Ranges on the Coastal Plain from sc VA to nw FL, e TX, and s AR.

SEPT.–OCT.

ASTERACEAE: ASTER FAMILY
Hackberry-leaved Goldenrod

Solidago rugosa P. Miller
   var. *celtidifolia* (Small) Fernald

Perennial, stems 1–3′ (0.3–1 m) tall, erect, moderately hairy, the upper half of stem often arching, branches few or none. There are no basal leaves. Stem leaves are dark green, ovate, tip acute, base broad, margins crenate, upper surface scabrous, texture thick with prominent veins. Leaves become smaller up the stem, much smaller on branches. Flowers grow in terminal clusters on stem and branches, each cluster compact and usually with short branches. Flower heads occur only on 1 side of each branch (secund). The 5–9 ray flowers are yellow, less than 0.2″ (2 mm) long; disc yellow.

This goldenrod is named for the shape and roughness of its leaves—like those of hackberry trees (genus *Celtis*); note also the dark green color and thick texture. Roughstem Goldenrod (*S. rugosa* var. *aspera*) is similar but has medium green leaves that are lanceolate to elliptic, its leaves are more strongly toothed, its stems have coarser hairs, and it usually inhabits dry to moist soils.

Inhabits wet streamhead margins, seepage slopes, and edges of beaver ponds and impoundments. Ranges on the Coastal Plain and lower Piedmont from sc VA to n FL and e TX.

LATE SEPT.–EARLY NOV.

ASTERACEAE: ASTER FAMILY
Spring Goldenrod

Solidago verna M. A. Curtis

Perennial, stems 1–3′ (0.3–1 m) tall, erect to ascending, softly pubescent, usually branched in the upper third. The 5–9 basal leaves are prostrate to ascending, broadly ovate, 2–4″ (5–10 cm) long and 1.2–1.6″ (3–4 cm) wide, tip blunt, base rounded and abruptly merging with a winged stalk, margins toothed, surfaces softly pubescent. Stem leaves gradually become smaller upward, eventually just elliptic. Flowers grow in a terminal inflorescence with ascending and arching branches, the flower heads only on 1 side of branch (secund). The 7–12 ray flowers are yellow, about 0.25″ (4–7 mm) long; disc yellow.

As its name implies, Spring Goldenrod blooms earlier than any other goldenrod, a unique feature in this normally fall-flowering genus. Even when not in bloom, the soft, hairy, basal leaves are a good clue to identification. It is rare in NC and SC.

Inhabits streamhead margins, flatwoods, and moist savannas within longleaf pinelands; occasionally found on roadsides. Ranges on the Coastal Plain from se NC to nc SC.

MAY–MID-JUNE

ASTERACEAE: ASTER FAMILY
Rayless Goldenrod

Bigelowia nudata (Michaux) DC. ssp. *nudata*
[*Chondrophora nudata* (Michaux) Britton]

Perennial, hairless, stems 1–2′ (30–70 cm) tall, with ascending slender branches in upper third. Five to 15 basal leaves grow in a rosette, each leaf oblanceolate, 2–6″ (5–15 cm) long and 0.2–0.4″ (4–10 mm) wide, tapering to stalk. Stem leaves are few, much smaller, linear. All leaves have tiny glandular dots in pits (use 10x hand lens). Flowers grow at tips of branches forming a flat-topped inflorescence (in this case a corymb). Heads are numerous, slender (2 mm wide), 3–5 flowered, disc flowers deep yellow, rays absent.

Despite lacking ray flowers, this relative of goldenrods is plenty showy with its vibrant yellow disc flowers; it would make a great subject for a wet-soil garden.

Inhabits streamhead margins, seepage slopes, and moist to wet savannas. Ranges on the Coastal Plain from e NC to c FL and se LA; formerly s NJ.

AUG.–OCT.

HYPERICACEAE: ST. JOHN'S-WORT FAMILY
Canada St. John's-wort

Hypericum canadense L.

Annual or short-lived perennial, stem slender, 4–24″ (10–60 cm) tall, with ascending branches or none. Leaves opposite, sessile, linear, 0.25–1.2″ (6–30 mm) long and up to 0.2″ (3 mm) wide, 1–3 nerved, blunt-tipped, tapered to base. Flowers grow terminally in small groups, forming a more or less flat-topped inflorescence, petals 5, yellow, 0.2″ (2–3 mm) long.

Canada St. John's-wort is the slimmest of our wetland St. John's-worts. Dwarf St. John's-wort (*H. mutilum*) can appear similar, but its leaves are much wider. The genus *Hypericum* is well-developed in our region and challenging to professional botanists and amateurs alike; however, seeking them out will bring you into some wonderfully varied habitats.

Inhabits streamhead margins, vernal pools, and depression ponds. Ranges from Newf. to MN south to n FL and MS.

JULY–SEPT.

HYPERICACEAE: ST. JOHN'S-WORT FAMILY
St. Peter's Cross
Hypericum crux-andreae (L.) Crantz

Perennial slender shrub to 3′ (1 m) tall, with few branches, bark reddish brown and shreddy. Leaves are opposite, elliptic to ovate, 0.4–1.6″ (1–4 cm) long and 0.25–0.8″ (6–20 mm) wide, blunt-tipped, base rounded, somewhat clasping. Flowers grow singly or a few together on a stalk (0.2–0.4″, 4–10 mm) from leaf axils. The 2 outer sepals are broadly ovate, 0.4–0.75″ (10–18 mm) long and a little less wide, acute or blunt; the 2 inner sepals are lanceolate, 0.25–0.6″ (6–15 mm) long and 0.2″ (2–3 mm) wide, acute. Petals 4, yellow, 0.4–0.75″ (10–18 mm) long. Capsules brown, dry, persisting into winter.

This and St. Andrew's Cross (*H. hypericoides*) are very similar and may occur together, but St. Peter's Cross prefers wetter soils, and has larger petals, outer sepals, and leaves. Both species retain capsule husks well into winter.

Inhabits seepage slopes, streamhead margins, and margins of beaver ponds; sometimes also in drier situations. Ranges on the Coastal Plain from se NY to c FL and e TX; scattered inland to w NC, w SC, n GA, n AL, c TN, s KY, c AR.

JUNE–SEPT.

HYPERICACEAE: ST. JOHN'S-WORT FAMILY
Downy St. John's-wort
Hypericum setosum L.

Annual or biennial, 8–30″ (20–75 cm) tall, unbranched below inflorescence, densely pubescent. Leaves are opposite and sessile, ascending or spreading, lance-shaped to ovate, 0.2–0.7″ (3–15 mm) long and up to 0.3″ (8 mm) wide, densely pubescent. Flowers grow in clusters at ends of short ascending branches, petals 5, orange-yellow, 0.2″ (2.5–4.5 mm) long, stamens few.

Downy St. John's-wort is our only *Hypericum* with hairy stems and leaves; coupled with its orange-yellow flowers it is unmistakable.

Inhabits seepage slopes, streamhead margins, and wet ditches, less often in drier soils of pinelands. Ranges on the Coastal Plain from se VA to c FL and e TX.

LATE MAY–SEPT.

MELASTOMATACEAE:
MELASTOME & MEADOW-BEAUTY FAMILY

Yellow Meadow-beauty

Rhexia lutea Walter

Perennial, stems one or several, to 19″ (50 cm) tall but often much shorter, 4-angled, much-branched, pubescent. Leaves are opposite, dark green, sessile, lanceolate to narrowly elliptic, 0.8–1.2″ (2–3 cm) long and 0.25″ (6 mm) wide, tip acute, 3-nerved, with coarse yellowish hairs. Flowers grow in an elongate, branched inflorescence from upper leaf axils. The 4 petals are golden yellow, obovate to broadly elliptical, 0.4–0.6″ (10–15 mm) long, each petal oblique (lengthwise, one half is larger than the other), the 8 stamens and anthers yellow and straight. The fruit is a capsule shaped like an old cream pitcher, narrowed beyond middle to a short neck, then flared to the 4 persistent sepals.

Yellow Meadow-beauty is the only yellow-flowered *Rhexia* and so is easy to identify, but it is very uncommon in our region, occurring in high-quality, fire-managed communities.

Inhabits moist to wet streamhead margins, seepage slopes, pine savannas, and flatwoods; sometimes also in rights-of-way. Ranges on the Coastal Plain from e NC to n FL and e TX.

MAY–EARLY JULY

MYRSINACEAE:
MYRSINE & YELLOW LOOSESTRIFE FAMILY

Roughleaf Loosestrife; Pocosin Loosestrife

Lysimachia asperulifolia Poiret

Perennial from long slender rhizomes, usually forming colonies. Stems are slender, normally unbranched, 1–2.5′ (30–80 cm) tall, glabrous or with gland-tipped hairs in upper third. Leaves are dark green, in whorls of 3 (sometimes 4), lanceolate, 0.8–1.6″ (2–4 cm) long and 0.3–0.8″ (0.8–2 cm) wide, acute-tipped, squared-off at the sessile base, glabrous except for gland-tipped hairs toward base and along veins. Flowers are produced irregularly except following fires, when they grow in a terminal raceme 1.2–4″ (3–10 cm) long. The 5 petals are yellow, about 0.6″ (1.5 cm) across, acute, with gland-tipped hairs.

Roughleaf Loosestrife is one of only a handful of plants in our area that is federally endangered. It is endemic to the Carolinas, where it is one of a number of wetland plants that reproduce best following fires that reduce woody competition. Rare in NC and SC.

Inhabits wet streamheads and their margins, usually in the company of pitcher-plants; on the outer Coastal Plain also in boggy shrub pocosins. Restricted to se NC and ne SC.

LATE MAY–MID-JUNE

SARRACENIACEAE: PITCHER-PLANT FAMILY
Yellow Pitcher-plant; Trumpets

Sarracenia flava L.

Perennial, carnivorous. Leaves vary
from a few to many from a root crown,
deciduous, yellowish green, erect, tubular,
1–3′ (0.3–1 m) tall, with a narrow wing
lengthwise on ventral side. The leaf tip
is modified into an ascending hood, the
hood often blotched with maroon; the end
of the leaf tube is modified into a thickened shiny lip. The inside of the tube is
smooth, shiny, slick, and partly filled with
liquid and decaying insect parts. Flowers
grow singly atop leafless stems about as
long as leaves, nodding, the 5 yellow petals
2.2–3.2″ (5.5–8 cm) long, drooping, soon
falling and leaving the specialized "style
disc," 1.2–2.8″ (3–7 cm) diameter.

Imagine the first people to set eyes on
this fantastic plant! And what is more
amazing is that it catches insects and even
small vertebrates that crawl into the tube
and cannot escape, soon to be digested by
chemicals secreted by the leaves. Sadly,
Trumpets have greatly declined everywhere, victims of fire suppression and
land conversion.

Inhabits well-burned streamhead
margins, seepage slopes, and margins of
impoundments. Ranges on the Coastal
Plain from se VA to c GA (Bibb County),
nw FL, and sw AL.

APR.

POLYGALACEAE: MILKWORT FAMILY
Savanna Milkwort

Polygala ramosa Elliott

Glabrous biennial, stems often several
together, much-branched, 4–12″ (10–30
cm) tall. Several to many basal leaves
form a flattish rosette, each leaf spatulate,
up to 1.5″ (36 mm) long, often senescent
by second year. Stem leaves are linear, up
to 0.75″ (20 mm) long. Flowers grow in
dense terminal heads, together forming a
flattish or umbrella-shaped inflorescence,
bright yellow, the spread wings about
0.25″ (5 mm) across.

The brilliant yellow inflorescences
are sure to catch your eye and will amply
repay close inspection with a hand lens.
A second yellow-flowered species is Dwarf
Milkwort (*P. nana*), with oval or elliptical
flowering heads atop a short stem (maxi-
mum 5″), and with a prominent basal
rosette. It occurs locally in the GA and
sc Sandhills in seepage slopes.

Inhabits streamhead ecotones, seepage
slopes, wet savannas, and roadside ditches.
Ranges on the Coastal Plain from s NJ to
s FL and e TX.

JUNE–AUG.

LENTIBULARIACEAE: BLADDERWORT FAMILY
Slender Horned Bladderwort
Utricularia juncea Vahl

Perennial, terrestrial, the main stems occur slightly below the soil surface, the leaves with a few filiform (very slender) segments, with tiny insect-trapping bladders. The flowering stem is slender, up to 18″ (45 cm) tall, with 2–15 flowers on stalks less than 2 mm long. The flowers are mostly 0.3–0.6″ (8–15 mm) long, yellow, 2-lipped (upper lip much smaller), the spur 0.2–0.3″ (4–8 mm), pointed.

This attractive plant usually grows in colonies of many plants, growing with sundews (*Drosera* spp.) and pitcher-plants (*Sarracenia* spp.). Unlike aquatic bladderworts, this species captures soil-dwelling prey—a sensible strategy, since invertebrates are abundant in the soil as well as in water.

Inhabits wet, often peaty, sandy soil of seepage slopes, streamhead margins, wet savannas, and borrow pits. Ranges on the Coastal Plain from se NY to s FL, e TX, and s AR; West Indies; Central America; South America.

JULY–SEPT.

LENTIBULARIACEAE: BLADDERWORT FAMILY
Zig-zag Bladderwort
Utricularia subulata L.

Perennial, terrestrial, the primary stem subterranean or on the soil surface, its leaves with a few filiform segments, with or without bladders. The flowering stem is filiform, 1–6″ (2.5–15 cm) tall, with 1–8 flowers. Flowers are 0.25–0.4″ (6–10 mm) long, yellow, 2-lipped and spurred, the spur longer than the lower lip and blunt.

Named for the usually angular stem, Zig-zag Bladderwort is tiny but often makes up for that by being numerous. It almost always grows with sundews (*Drosera* spp.), milkworts (*Polygala*), meadow-beauties (*Rhexia*), and other colorful wildflowers.

Inhabits moist sand of open seepage slopes, streamhead ecotones, and wet savannas; also found in scrapes and ditches. Ranges from s N.S. to s FL, e TX, and s AR; West Indies; Central America; South America; Africa; Asia.

LATE MAR.–AUG.

NARTHECIACEAE: BOG ASPHODEL FAMILY
Golden Colicroot
Aletris aurea Walter

Perennial, a single unbranched stem grows from a flat basal rosette of elliptic to lance-shaped leaves 1.5–3″ (3.5–7.5 cm) long. The stem is 12–30″ (30–80 cm) tall, with a few greatly reduced leaves appressed to it. Flowers grow on very short stalks in upper half of stem in a spikelike raceme. The 3 petals and 3 sepals are alike, yellow, with a granular surface, forming a tube with 6 blunt points, 0.25–0.3″ (6–8 mm) long.

Golden Colicroot's leaves stay green for a short period, then turn yellowish. It is an excellent indicator of wet seepage slopes and boggy habitats, places where you should look for pitcher-plants and sundews. White Colicroot (*A. farinosa* L.) has slightly longer white flowers and its leaves turn orangish; it inhabits less wet margins of seepage slopes, plus drier uplands.

Inhabits seepage slopes, streamhead ecotones, wet flatwoods, and boggy margins of impoundments. Ranges on the Coastal Plain from se MD to nw FL, e TX, and se OK.

MID-MAY–MID-JULY

XYRIDACEAE: YELLOW-EYED-GRASS FAMILY
Bog Yellow-eyed-grass
Xyris platylepis Chapman

Perennial, stem single or a few together, mostly 1.5–3′ (45–90 cm) tall, twisted, base swollen (bulblike) and glutinous. Leaves are all basal, 2-ranked, linear, flattened, twisted, 6–12″ (15–30 cm) long and 0.25–0.5″ (5–12 mm) wide, surfaces and margins essentially smooth, basal portion deep pink to red and glutinous. Flowers grow 1–2 at a time from an elliptical, conelike head atop the stem, the head 0.4–1″ (10–25 mm) long and composed of overlapping brown scales. The 3 petals are yellow, obovate, about 0.25″ (5 mm) long, opening at midday or later.

Savanna Yellow-eyed-grass (*X. ambigua*) differs in its nontwisted leaves (usually forming a broad fan) that are pale pink or straw-colored basally; its flowers open in the morning. Both species occur in wet seepy places with pitcher-plants, hatpins, sundews, and other wonderful plants.

Inhabits seepage bogs, margins of streamheads, and wet savannas. Ranges on the Coastal Plain from se VA to s FL and e TX.

JULY–SEPT.

STREAMHEADS AND SEEPAGE SLOPES **193**

XYRIDACEAE: YELLOW-EYED-GRASS FAMILY
Harper's Yellow-eyed-grass
Xyris scabrifolia R. M. Harper

Perennial, stem usually solitary, mostly 10–32″ (25–80 cm) tall, more or less twisted, densely minutely bumpy (papillose), glaucescent, the base somewhat swollen. Leaves are all basal, 2-ranked, linear, flattened, more or less twisted, 8–20″ (20–50 cm) long and 0.2–0.4″ (3–10 mm) wide, surfaces and margins papillose, glaucescent, basal portion pink. Flowers grow 1–2 at a time from an elliptical, conelike head atop the stem, the head 0.4–0.7″ (10–17 mm) long and composed of overlapping brown scales. The 3 petals are yellow, obovate, about 0.2″ (3–5 mm) long, opening at midday or later.

Named by Roland M. Harper (1878–1966), tireless field botanist of the Deep South, who discovered this species in Meriwether County, GA. Chapman's Yellow-eyed-grass (*X. chapmanii*) differs in its shorter, narrower, nonglaucescent scape and leaves. Its leaves are maroon to deep pink basally, and it prefers wetter, boggier parts of streamheads.

Inhabits seepage bogs and margins of streamheads. Ranges on the Coastal Plain from se NC to nc SC; wc GA to nw FL and e TX.

AUG.–SEPT.

XYRIDACEAE: YELLOW-EYED-GRASS FAMILY
Curtiss's Yellow-eyed-grass
Xyris curtissii Malme

Perennial, stem usually solitary, mostly 3–8″ (7.5–20 cm) tall, 4-ribbed, and minutely bumpy (papillose). Leaves are all basal, 2-ranked and forming a fan-shaped pattern, linear, flattened, 2–5″ (5–12 cm) long and 0.2″ (2.5–4.5 mm) wide, surfaces and margins papillose, bases reddish. Flowers grow 1–2 at a time from an elliptical, conelike head atop the stem, the head about 0.25″ (5 mm) long and composed of overlapping brown scales. The 3 petals are yellow, obovate or obtriangular, about 0.2″ (4 mm) long, opening in morning.

Baldwin's Yellow-eyed-grass (*X. baldwiniana*) differs in its much longer and narrower leaves that do not form a fan; its scape is up to 18″ (45 cm) tall, and its petals angle upward. These two species were named for Allen H. Curtiss (1845–1907) and William Baldwin (1779–1819), early botanists of FL and GA, respectively.

Inhabits seepage bogs, margins of streamheads, and wet savannas. Ranges on the Coastal Plain from se VA to c FL, e TX, and s AR; Belize; Puerto Rico.

JULY–MID-SEPT.

ORCHIDACEAE: ORCHID FAMILY
Clubspur Orchid; Streamhead Orchid

Platanthera clavellata (Michaux) Luer
[*Habenaria clavellata* (Michaux) Sprengel]

Perennial, glabrous, the stem mostly 3.2–14″ (8–35 cm) tall. The single leaf (rarely 2) grows at midstem, oriented at an angle upward, oblanceolate, 2–7″ (5–18 cm) long and 0.4–1.6″ (1–3.5 cm) wide, blunt-tipped, parallel-veined. A few bractlike leaves occur up the stem. Up to 10 flowers grow in a short raceme with bracts, each flower on a stalk about 0.4″ (1 cm) long, creamy or dull greenish yellow. The 3 sepals are ovate, about 0.2″ (3–5 mm) long, the 2 upper petals ovate, about 0.2″ (3–5 mm) long and 2 mm wide, the lip (lower petal) elliptical, about 0.25″ (3–7 mm) long, blunt, the spur more or less curved, about 0.4″ (10 mm) long, thickened toward the end.

In our region, you will find this orchid hiding among the mosses, ferns, and shrubs of shady streamheads. With a little effort you will soon find that it is not a particularly rare plant. Note that the flowers are usually twisted at odd angles on their stalks.

Inhabits moist mossy streamheads and their margins, benefiting from occasional burns. Ranges from Newf. to ND south to n FL and e TX.

LATE JUNE–AUG.

DIOSCOREACEAE: YAM FAMILY
Streamhead Yam; Common Wild Yam

Dioscorea villosa L.

Perennial, slender twining vine to 13′ (4 m), stem smooth to densely pubescent, plants either male or female (dioecious). Leaves all alternate or the lowermost in a whorl of 3–4, blades ovate to broadly ovate, base heart-shaped, tip long-tapered, 2–4″ (5–10 cm) long, with dense short hairs beneath. Seven to 11 prominent nerves radiate from the base of the blade. Male flowers are tiny, greenish white or yellowish, 1–4 at each node of a branched inflorescence. There are 5–10 female flowers, alternate, on an unbranched stalk, flowers greenish, about 0.25″ long. Fruit a pale brown dry capsule, with 3 broad papery wings, the whole 0.7–1″ (16–25 mm) long.

As its name suggests, this is a relative of the edible yam (several species from the Old World), but not to the orange-colored "yam" or Sweet Potato (*Ipomoea batatas*), which is in the morning-glory family. The scientific name commemorates Dioscorides, Greek naturalist and physician. Native Americans used it for a wide range of cures, including relief of labor pains, morning sickness, asthma, and rheumatism. Contains diosgenin, used by pharmaceutical firms to make steroids, including progesterone.

Inhabits moist to wet streamheads, blackwater swamp forests, and openings in such habitats. Ranges from se MA to FL, mostly on the Coastal Plain.

EARLY MAY–JUNE

STREAMHEADS AND SEEPAGE SLOPES **195**

SMILACACEAE: GREENBRIER FAMILY
Bamboo-vine; Bayvine; Blaspheme-vine

Smilax laurifolia L.

Perennial, robust, thick-stemmed, high-climbing vine from large rhizomes, often forming dense thickets, climbing via curly tendrils. The lower parts of the stem can be up to 0.8″ (2 cm) thick, dark gray-brown, with abundant stout prickles to 0.5″ (1.2 cm) long; the upper part of the stem is pale green, flexuous, and sparsely to moderately prickly. Leaves are evergreen, narrowly to broadly elliptical, thick and leathery textured, tip acute, margins smooth, short-stalked. Flowers grow in small umbels from leaf axils, the 3 sepals and 3 petals alike, 0.25″ (5–6 mm) long, pale yellowish green. Fruits are berries, black, glaucescent, 0.25–0.3″ (6–8 mm) diameter.

Bamboo-vine is a common and characteristic member of our southern landscape, and people who spend time outdoors have stories to tell about their encounters with this formidable plant. It will rip your trousers to shreds if you are not careful! Having to negotiate through a patch of it is an effective way to learn patience and humility.

Inhabits wet soil of streamheads, seepage slopes, cypress-gum swamps, and Carolina bays. Ranges on the Coastal Plain from s NJ to s FL and e TX; also scattered inland locations; Cuba; Bahamas.

JULY–AUG.

SMILACACEAE: GREENBRIER FAMILY
Coastal Plain Carrion-flower

Smilax pseudochina L.

Perennial, slender-stemmed, herbaceous, usually solitary vine to 6′ (2 m) long, climbing over shrubs via curly tendrils. Stems are pale grayish green, varying to reddish brown, dying back to ground each year, without prickles. Leaves are deciduous, ovate to hastate, thin-textured, tip acute to blunt, margins usually wavy, grayish green above, paler beneath, short-stalked. Flowers grow in small umbels from leaf axils, the 3 sepals and 3 petals alike, yellowish green. Fruits are berries, black, 0.3–0.4″ (7–10 mm) diameter.

Unlike other *Smilax* in this guide, this one dies back to the ground each autumn and has no thorns. It is uncommon in our area and occupies a very narrow habitat range. It may occur with the similar-looking Streamhead Yam (*Dioscorea villosa*), but the yam has leaves with 7–11 prominent nerves and long-pointed tips (vs. only 3 prominent nerves and a short-pointed tip).

Inhabits moist soil of streamhead margins and seepage slopes. Ranges on the Coastal Plain from se NY to se GA.

MAY–EARLY JUNE

ANACARDIACEAE:
CASHEW & SUMAC FAMILY
Poison Sumac

Toxicodendron vernix (L.) Kuntze
[*Rhus vernix* L.]

Glabrous perennial shrub or small tree, stems mostly 3–13′ (1–4 m) tall in our region. Leaves grow in upper part of stem, elongate, pinnately divided into 7–13 leaflets. Each leaflet is oblanceolate to narrowly elliptic, 2–4.5″ (5–12 cm) long, tip acute to acuminate, margins without teeth. Flowers grow in branched, elongate, spreading to arching sprays from leaf axils, the 4–5 sepals and petals greenish yellow.

Poisonous! This plant causes dermatitis in most people, reportedly worse than Poison Ivy and Poison Oak; however, it is easy to avoid contact. Poison Sumac is a fairly common plant in our region, so people need to learn to identify it; look for it when you get near a streamhead. Unlike our nonpoisonous sumacs (genus *Rhus*), Poison Sumac lacks teeth on its leaflets and lives in wet habitats. Leaves turn bright orange-red in fall; birds eat the fruits.

Inhabits moist to wet soils of streamheads, seepage areas, and wooded slopes. Ranges from N.S. to s MN south to c FL and e TX.

MAY–EARLY JUNE

LAURACEAE: LAUREL FAMILY
Bog Spicebush;
Streamhead Spicebush

Lindera subcoriacea Wofford

Perennial dioecious shrub, stems single or several, to 12′ (3.5 m) tall, bark with small whitish lenticels; bruised twigs and leaves have a faint lemon odor. Leaves are oblanceolate, blunt, 1.5–3.5″ (3.5–9 cm) long and up to 1″ (2.5 cm) wide, glaucescent and minutely hairy below, margins without teeth. Numerous whorls of small flowers grow at intervals on the twigs, the 6 petals are a few millimeters long, yellow, stamens prominent. Fruits are oval in outline, bright red, about 0.25″ (6mm).

Bog Spicebush was newly described in 1983. It is easiest to detect in early spring when the bright flowers stand out against foliage of evergreen shrubs and trees. Fruiting plants resemble winterberry hollies (*Ilex verticillata* and *I. laevigata*) but lack marginal teeth on leaves. Bog Spicebush is related to Common Spicebush (*L. benzoin*), but that plant grows in brownwater river floodplains, has a broader crown, and has strongly fragrant twigs and leaves; its leaves grow up to 4.5″ long and have an abrupt drip-tip rather than a blunt tip.

Inhabits blackwater streamheads (often with Atlantic White Cedar, *Chamaecyparis thyoides*) downstream to where seepage influence is lost. Uncommon. Ranges on the Coastal Plain from se VA to nw FL and se LA.

LATE FEB.–MAR.

STREAMHEADS AND SEEPAGE SLOPES **197**

SYMPLOCACEAE: SWEETLEAF FAMILY
Sweetleaf; Horse-sugar

Symplocos tinctoria (L.) L'Heritier

Perennial woody shrub or small tree to 20′
(6 m) tall, but less than 6′ where burned
periodically. Leaves are dark green,
thick-textured, tardily deciduous (lasting
well into winter), elliptic to oblanceolate,
3.2–5″ (8–13 cm) long and 1–2″ (2.5–5
cm) wide, short-stalked. Leaf margins are
smooth (or crenate toward tip), tip short-
acuminate, and blades are minutely pubescent beneath. Flowers grow in ball-like
clusters in leaf axils (before leaf-out or as
leaves appear) along previous year's twigs,
nearly sessile. The 5 petals are pale yellow
or whitish, broadly ovate, 0.3″ (6–8 mm)
long; the yellow stamens are very numerous and much longer than the petals.

Sweetleaf derives its name from the
taste of the leaf midribs and adjacent tissue, which is attractive to browsing deer,
cattle, horses, and other mammals, but
only mildly sweet to humans. The flowers
are attractive to butterflies.

Inhabits seepage slopes, streamhead
margins, and wooded slopes along
streams and rivers; in the Sandhills region
it often occurs well upslope in clayey soil
of longleaf pinelands. Ranges from DE to
n FL, e TX, and se OK; inland to mountains of NC, SC, GA, AL.

MAR.–APR.

ORCHIDACEAE: ORCHID FAMILY
Orange Fringed Orchid

Platanthera ciliaris (L.) Lindley
[*Habenaria ciliaris* (L.) R. Brown]

Perennial, glabrous, stem mostly 10–24″
(25–62 cm) tall. Leaves are strongly
ascending, broadly lanceolate, 2–12″
(5–30 cm) long and 0.4–2″ (1–5 cm)
wide, tip acuminate, parallel-veined,
lowest leaves are the largest, upper ones
much smaller. Flowers grow in a dense
cylindrical raceme with leafy bracts, each
flower orange, on a stalk about 0.8″ (2 cm)
long. The 3 sepals are elliptic to roundish,
0.2–0.4 (4–9 mm) long, the 2 upper petals
are oblanceolate, 0.2–0.25″ (5–7 mm) long
and 1–2 mm wide, the tip with tiny teeth.
The lip (lower petal) is elliptical, 0.3–0.5″
(8–12 mm) long, with long slender fringing around the margin; the spur is more
or less straight, 0.8–1.2″ (2–3 cm) long.

Many books call this Yellow Fringed
Orchid, but the flowers are pure orange.
This spectacular plant sometimes occurs
near White Fringed Orchid (*P. blephariglottis*) but prefers less-wet soil; the two
may hybridize to produce yellow- or
cream-colored individuals.

Inhabits moist streamhead margins,
seepage slopes, rights-of-way, and roadsides. Ranges from s NH to MI and MO
south to c FL and e TX.

LATE JULY–EARLY SEPT.

ORCHIDACEAE: ORCHID FAMILY
Crested Fringed Orchid

Platanthera cristata (Michaux) Lindley
[*Habenaria cristata* (Michaux) R. Brown]

Perennial, glabrous, the stem mostly
8–18″ (20–45 cm) tall. Leaves are strongly
ascending, lance-shaped, 2–8″ (5–20
cm) long and 0.4–1″ (1–2.5 cm) wide, tip
acuminate, parallel-veined, the lowest
leaves are largest, the upper ones much
smaller. Flowers grow in a dense, short-
cylindrical raceme with leafy bracts,
each flower orange, on a stalk about 0.6″
(1.5 cm) long. The 3 sepals are elliptic to
roundish, about 0.2″ (3–5 mm) long, the 2
upper petals narrowly elliptic, about 0.2″
(2–4 mm) long and 1–2 mm wide, the tip
with a short fringe. The lip (lower petal)
is elliptical, about 0.25″ (3–6 mm) long,
with short slender fringing on the margin;
the spur is more or less straight, 0.2–0.4″
(5–10 mm) long.

This is an exquisite plant but not often
appreciated, since it often grows in tangly
streamheads and populations typically are
small. The flowers are half the size of our
other fringed orchids.

Inhabits moist streamheads and their
margins, seepage slopes, and rights-of-
way, preferably well-burned. Ranges on
the Coastal Plain from se MA to c FL,
e TX, and c AR; scattered inland to c TN,
e KY, w NC, w SC.

LATE JUNE–AUG.

POLYGALACEAE: MILKWORT FAMILY
Orange Milkwort; Candyroot

Polygala lutea L.

Glabrous biennial, branched or not,
mostly 5–15″ (12–35 cm) tall, rather
succulent-textured. Several to many spatulate basal leaves form a flattish rosette.
Stem leaves are oblanceolate to spatulate,
up to 1.5″ (35 mm) long and 0.4″ (10 mm)
wide, tip acute or blunt, reduced in size up
the stem. Flowers grow in dense terminal
heads 0.5–1.4″ (12–35 mm) long and 0.5–1″
(12–25 mm) wide, bright orange (rarely
yellow), the spread wings about 0.5″
(12 mm) across.

The brilliance of its orange flowers is
rarely matched in our native flora, and
a colony of Orange Milkwort is breath-
taking. The alternate name comes from
the licoricelike or aniselike odor and taste
of the roots.

Inhabits streamhead ecotones, seepage
slopes, wet savannas, and roadside ditches.
Ranges on the Coastal Plain from se NY to
s FL and se LA.

LATE APR.–JULY (OR LATER)

LILIACEAE: LILY FAMILY
Catesby's Lily; Pine Lily
Lilium catesbaei Walter

Perennial from succulent scaly bulb(s),
the stem mostly 18–28″ (45–70 cm) tall.
Basal leaves usually are absent (if present,
up to 3.2″ or 8 cm long and ascending);
middle and upper leaves are alternate,
narrowly elliptic, 0.8–1.6″ (2–4 cm) long
and up to 0.4″ (1 cm) wide, appressed to
the stem, blunt-tipped to acute. The flower
is solitary, erect (facing upward) with
spreading-recurved sepals and petals that
are separate to the base. The 3 sepals and
3 petals are alike, 2.8–4.8″ (7–12 cm) long,
the basal portion narrow, the middle portion abruptly widened, the tip tapered to a
long point. Sepals and petals are orange to
red-orange, the basal portion yellow with
purple spots; stamens 6, style 1.

Catesby's Lily is one of North America's
showiest flowers, practically unmatched
in its brilliant color and vaselike shape.
Named for Mark Catesby (1679–1749),
English naturalist who traveled the southeastern United States and the Bahamas
describing and painting hundreds of
plants and animals. Catesby's Lily is rare
in the Sandhills region of NC and SC, absent from the GA portion. It is pollinated
mostly by the Palamedes Swallowtail
butterfly.

Inhabits pitcher-plant bogs, seepage
slopes, and streamhead ecotones within
fire-maintained longleaf pinelands.
Ranges on the Coastal Plain from SE VA
to S FL and SE LA.

MID-JUNE–MID-SEPT.

LILIACEAE: LILY FAMILY
Sandhills Lily
Lilium pyrophilum M. W. Skinner & Sorrie

Perennial from succulent, scaly bulb(s),
stem mostly 2–5.3′ (0.6–1.6 m) tall. Midstem leaves grow mostly in 3–10 whorls of
4–11 leaves each, lanceolate, 1.6–4″ (4–10
cm) long and up to 1″ (2.5 cm) wide, ascending, acute. The upper and lower stem
leaves are solitary or in partial whorls,
erect or strongly ascending, smaller. One
to 5 nodding (angling downward) flowers
grow atop the stem on long stalks; sepals
and petals are partly united and recurve
so that tips touch each other. The 3 sepals
and 3 petals are alike, 2.8–3.6″ (7–9 cm)
long and 0.4–0.8″ (1–2 cm) wide, tapering
to a point, orange to red-orange or deep
red, spotted with purple, not fragrant;
6 stamens and 1 style are prominently
exposed.

Sandhills Lily was officially described
in 2002, although historical specimens
dated from 1928, misidentified as other
species. It is an excellent example of a species that requires perennially wet soil yet
benefits from recurring fires or mowing;
a number of Sandhills region plants share
these traits, but most have declined greatly
without frequent disturbance.

Inhabits wet to moist seepage slopes
and streamhead margins, also wet rights-
of-way. Almost endemic to the Sandhills
region of S NC and C SC; also SE VA.

LATE JULY–MID-AUG.

ASTERACEAE: ASTER FAMILY
Sticky Chaffhead
Carphephorus tomentosus (Michaux)
  Torrey & Gray

Perennial, 1 to few stems grow to 2′
(70 cm) tall, usually densely pubescent
but occasionally glabrate. The numerous
basal leaves are more or less prostrate,
up to 5″ (12.5 cm) long and 0.75″ (18 mm)
wide, long-stalked. Each blade is narrowly
elliptic and acute, glabrate to pubescent.
Stem leaves are rapidly reduced in size upward; most are without stalks and pressed
against the stem. The inflorescence is like
a cyme, composed of 3-many ascending
branches, each with 1 head. Heads are 0.5″
(12 mm) wide, the bracts acute, appressed,
sticky-glandular; disc florets pinkish
purple to rose-purple, rays absent.

Sticky Chaffhead is a handsome plant
but uncommon in our region, as much of
its habitat has been lost. The French botanist and horticulturist André Michaux
discovered this species in 1794 near Fayetteville, NC. A similar species, Panicled
Chaffhead (*C. paniculatus*), may occur
in the same habitats; its inflorescence is a
narrow raceme, so that the plant looks like
a wand, and the flowers are much smaller
and lavender-purple in tone.

Inhabits moist streamhead margins,
seepage slopes, and flatwoods. Ranges on
the Coastal Plain from se VA to se GA.

LATE AUG.–LATE OCT.

ASTERACEAE: ASTER FAMILY
Bog Blazing-star
Liatris spicata (L.) Willdenow
  var. *resinosa* (Nuttall) Gaiser

Perennial from a hard, roundish rootstock. Stem usually solitary, erect, to 5.5′
(1.7 m) high, unbranched. Leaves are
numerous, linear (the lowest ones lanceolate), 4–12″ (10–30 cm) long and up to
0.6″ (15 mm) wide, gradually reduced in
length up the stem, glabrate. Flower heads
grow in a dense, long spike (heads without
stalks); the bracts are purplish and form
a short-cylindric involucre 0.25–0.4″
(7–10 mm) long, and their outer surface
has dense resin dots. Disc flowers usually
number 8 per head, purple or deep rosy,
about 0.3″ (6.5–9 mm) long, with 5 short
spreading lobes, rays absent.

Bog Blazing-star is a very showy
member of our pitcher-plant bogs and
streamhead margins, blooming when the
fringed-orchids (*Platanthera blephariglottis* and *P. ciliaris*) are in flower.

Inhabits seepage slopes and boggy
streamhead margins. Ranges on the
Coastal Plain from s NJ to s FL and se LA;
reported c TN.

LATE JULY–EARLY SEPT.

ASTERACEAE: ASTER FAMILY
Grassleaf Barbara's-buttons
Marshallia graminifolia (Walter) Small

Perennial, stems single or several together, 16–32″ (40–80 cm) tall, branched or not. Leaves are numerous, the lower ones nearly erect, linear to narrowly elliptic, 2–8″ (5–20 cm) long and 0.2–0.7″ (5–15 mm) wide, tapered to both ends. Upper leaves are ascending, usually less than 1.2″ (3 cm) long and 2 mm wide. Flower heads grow terminally on slender stalks up to 4.8″ (12 cm) long, each head about 1″ (2.5 cm) wide. Disc flowers are pink to whitish, with lobes curled or twisted, rays absent.

The unkempt aspect of the flower heads and the grasslike leaves make this an easy plant to recognize. Moreover, it enjoys the company of showy wildflowers like White Fringed Orchid (*Platanthera blephariglottis*), Savanna Meadow-beauty (*Rhexia alifanus*), Orange Milkwort (*Polygala lutea*), and Bog Blazing-star (*Liatris spicata* var. *resinosa*). Grassleaf Barbara's-buttons is rare in GA.

Inhabits seepage slopes, streamhead margins, and wet savannas. Ranges on the Coastal Plain from e NC to se GA (Emanuel County).

LATE JULY–MID-SEPT.

ORCHIDACEAE: ORCHID FAMILY
Pale Grass-pink
Calopogon pallidus Chapman

Slender, glabrous perennial from a roundish corm (fleshy bulblike base in the soil), stem single, 9–24″ (22–70 cm) tall. The single leaf is erect, grasslike, 3″–1′ (7.5–30 cm) long and about 0.2″ (5 mm) wide, pleated lengthwise. Flowers grow in upper half of stem, opening successively upward. Each flower is short-stalked, pale pinkish white to rosy pink, a bit less than 1″ (2.5 cm) across, the lateral sepals strongly curved upward.

Much rarer than Common Grass-pink (*C. tuberosus*), with which it may grow, Pale Grass-pink is smaller and more delicate looking but has much elegance and grace.

Inhabits seepage slopes and wet savannas within pinelands. Ranges on the Coastal Plain from se VA to s FL and se LA.

LATE MAY–JULY

ORCHIDACEAE: ORCHID FAMILY
Common Grass-pink
Calopogon tuberosus (L.) B.S.P.

Glabrous perennial from a roundish corm (fleshy bulblike base in the soil), stem single, up to 3′ (1 m) tall. The single leaf is erect, grasslike, mostly 1–2′ (30–70 cm) long and 0.75–2″ (1.8–5 cm) wide, pleated lengthwise. Flowers grow in upper half of stem, opening successively upward, short-stalked. Each flower is about 1.5″ (3.5 cm) across, magenta-purple to rosy pink, often with a whitish tip to the lip, lateral sepals more or less straight.

Common Grass-pink is one of the glories of our seepage slopes and survives best when burned periodically. *Calopogon* means "beautiful beard," in reference to the patch of golden hairs on the lip. Unlike most of our orchids, the lips of grass-pinks point upward.

Inhabits seepage slopes, wet savannas, and wet roadsides. Ranges from Newf. to se Man. south to c FL and e TX.

LATE MAY–EARLY JULY

ORCHIDACEAE: ORCHID FAMILY
Small Spreading Pogonia
Cleistes bifaria (Fernald) Catling & Gregg

Perennial from a bulblike corm, stem and leaf glaucous. Flowering stem mostly 6–18″ (15–45 cm) tall, with a single (rarely 2) leaf at midstem 2–5.5″ (5–14 cm) long and 0.25–1″ (6–25 mm) wide, ascending to erect. The single flower faces sideways to somewhat downward, the 3 sepals flaring, brown-maroon, linear, 1–2″ (2.4–5.5 cm) long. The corolla is pink to rosy pink or whitish, tubular, 0.8–1.5″ (2.1–3.6 cm) long, with a 3-lobed lip.

A close relative, Large Spreading Pogonia (*C. divaricata*) differs in its longer petals (1.2–2.2″ [2.7–5.3 cm]) and longer sepals (1.25–2.7″ [3.1–6.5 cm]); it flowers about 2 weeks later than Small Spreading Pogonia. Both of these spectacular orchids are found in our region, but rarely; they have severely declined without fire management.

Inhabits seepage slopes, streamhead margins, and wet savannas, as well as wet rights-of-way. Ranges on the Coastal Plain from e NC to c FL and se LA; also mountains of WV to GA and AL.

MID-MAY–EARLY JULY

ORCHIDACEAE: ORCHID FAMILY

Rose Pogonia

Pogonia ophioglossoides (L.) Ker-Gawler

Perennial, glabrous, pale green, 3.2–18″ (8–45 cm) tall (rarely taller), often propagating via root runners. The single leaf grows at midstem, ovate to elliptic, 0.8–4″ (2–10 cm) long and 0.4–1.2″ (1–3 cm) wide, the tip blunt to acute, the base tapered. A single flower (occasionally 2 or 3) grows at the summit of the stem from a leafy bract 0.4–1.2″ (1–3 cm) long, rose or rose-pink, fragrant. The 3 sepals spread widely, are narrowly elliptical, 0.6–1″ (1.5–2.5 cm) long and about 0.25″ (3–6 mm) wide; the upper 2 petals are broadly elliptical, 0.5–1″ (1.3–2.5 cm) long and 0.25–0.4″ (5–11 mm) wide. The lip (lower petal) projects forward, elliptical, 0.6–1″ (1.5–2.5 cm) long, toothed at the tip, the upper surface prominently "bearded" with yellow and white fleshy bristles.

Rose Pogonia is one of the widest-ranging orchids in North America, in part due to its ability to reproduce vegetatively as well as sexually. The word *pogonia* is Greek for "bearded"; *ophioglossoides* means "like Ophioglossum," the genus of Adder's-tongue ferns that have remarkably similar, single leaves.

Inhabits seepage slopes, streamhead margins, wet seepy roadsides, and boggy beaver ponds and impoundments, usually in sphagnum moss. Ranges from Newf. to Man. south to FL and TX.

MID-MAY–JUNE

LENTIBULARIACEAE: BLADDERWORT FAMILY

Clearwater Butterwort; Primrose Butterwort

Pinguicula primuliflora C. E. Wood & Godfrey

Perennial. Leaves form a flat basal rosette, sessile, ovate to elliptic, 2.5–3.5″ (6–9 cm) long and up to 1″ (2.5 cm) wide, pale green to yellowish, sticky-viscous above. The single flower grows atop a narrow leafless stem; it is 5-lobed and has a downward-pointing spur. Petals are lavender to pinkish or pale violet, white basally, about 1″ (2.5 cm) long, notched at tip.

Clearwater Butterwort is a species of the East Gulf Coastal Plain, disjunct to the Sandhills region of GA, where it is found in Marion and Taylor Counties. The white bases of the petals form a pale "eye" in the open flower. Like all butterworts, it captures insects on the viscous leaves, slowly digesting them to obtain nutrients and minerals. Rare in GA.

Inhabits shady baygalls and seepy streamheads, in sphagnum or other mosses. Ranges from SW GA to NW FL and SE MS; WC GA; C AL.

MAR.–EARLY MAY

POLYGALACEAE: MILKWORT FAMILY
Cross-leaved Milkwort; Drumheads
Polygala cruciata L. var. *cruciata*

Glabrous annual, branched or not, the stem 4–18″ (10–45 cm) tall (usually less than 12″), narrowly winged. Leaves grow in whorls of 4, linear to oblanceolate, 0.5–2″ (1.2–5 cm) long and up to 0.3″ (8 mm) wide. Flowers grow in dense terminal heads to 1.3″ (3 cm) long and 0.6″ (1.6 cm) wide. The flowers are pink or whitish or greenish, the spread wings (2 sepals) nearly 0.4″ (1 cm) across and long- to short-pointed.

In most milkworts the petals are small, tubular, and inconspicuous, one of them forming a fringed "lip." The showy parts of the flower are the 2 "wings," which actually are colorful sepals. The shape of the inflorescence—like a miniature barrel or drum—gives this plant its alternate name.

Inhabits seepage slopes, pitcher-plant bogs, streamhead margins, and wet rights-of-way. Ranges on the Coastal Plain from se VA to c FL and e TX. A northern variety (not found in our region) ranges from ME and MN south to the mountains of GA and AL.

JUNE–SEPT.

MELASTOMATACEAE:
MELASTOME & MEADOW-BEAUTY FAMILY
Savanna Meadow-beauty
Rhexia alifanus Walter

Perennial, glabrous, mostly 1.5–3′ (0.5–1 m) tall, normally unbranched. Leaves are bluish green, opposite, 4-ranked, sessile, lanceolate to narrowly elliptic, up to 2.8″ (7 cm) long and 0.4″ (1 cm) wide, tip acute to acuminate, prominently 3-nerved. Flowers grow in a flat-topped, branched inflorescence terminally and from upper leaf axils. The 4 petals are rosy pink, obovate to broadly elliptical, 0.7–1″ (18–25 mm) long, each petal oblique (lengthwise, one half is larger than the other). The 8 stamens and anthers are bright yellow and curved. The fruit is a capsule shaped like an old cream pitcher, narrowed beyond the middle to a "neck," then flared to the 4 persistent sepals.

Savanna Meadow-beauty is one of the characteristic wildflowers of the longleaf pine ecosystem—and one of the most spectacular. *Rhexia* consists of 12 species restricted to eastern North America and the West Indies; all 12 occur in the southeastern United States.

Inhabits moist to wet streamhead margins, seepage slopes, and pine savannas, extending into dryish longleaf pinelands. Ranges on the Coastal Plain from e NC to c FL and e TX.

LATE MAY–LATE JULY, OCCASIONALLY LATER

MELASTOMATACEAE:
MELASTOME & MEADOW-BEAUTY FAMILY
Nash's Meadow-beauty
Rhexia nashii Small

Perennial, often colonial, potentially
to 3′ (1 m) tall but usually half that,
branched or not. Leaves are glabrate,
opposite, short-stalked or sessile, elliptic
to broadly lanceolate, 1.2–2.8″ (3–7 cm)
long, tapered to both ends, margins finely
toothed. Flowers grow in a branched
inflorescence from upper leaf axils. The
4 petals are bright rosy pink, obovate to
broadly elliptical, 0.8–1″ (20–25 mm) or
more long, each petal oblique (lengthwise, one half is larger than the other)
and with gland-tipped hairs on the
backside. The 8 stamens and anthers are
bright yellow and curved. The fruit is a
capsule shaped like an old cream pitcher,
narrowed beyond the middle to a long
neck, then flared to the 4 glabrous sepals.

Nash's Meadow-beauty was named
for George V. Nash (1864–1921), a botanist who specialized in grasses. Nash's
Meadow-beauty is similar to Maryland
Meadow-beauty (*Rhexia mariana* var.
mariana), but the latter has smaller and
duller pink petals that lack gland-tipped
hairs.

Inhabits wet margins of streamheads,
seepage slopes, and seepy roadside
ditches. Ranges on the Coastal Plain
from se VA to s FL and se LA.

JUNE–MID-SEPT.

MELASTOMATACEAE:
MELASTOME & MEADOW-BEAUTY FAMILY
Bog Meadow-beauty
Rhexia petiolata Walter

Perennial, to 2′ (60 cm) tall but often
half that, unbranched or few-branched
from the base. Leaves are opposite, sessile, broadly elliptic to ovate, 0.4–0.6″
(1–1.5 cm) long, acute, margins finely
toothed, the teeth bristle-tipped. Flowers
grow singly or a few together in a compact
cluster at the stem terminus. The 4 petals
are pink to rosy pink, ovate to broadly
elliptical, 0.4–0.8″ (10–20 mm) long, the
8 stamens and anthers yellow, erect and
straight. The fruit is a capsule shaped like
an old cream pitcher, narrowed beyond
the middle to a very short neck, then
flared to the 4 hairy sepals.

Bog Meadow-beauty is our only species
whose flowers always face upward to the
sky, rather than sideways. In its seepy wet
habitat, it may co-occur with four other
Rhexias.

Inhabits wet margins of streamheads,
seepage slopes, and pitcher-plant bogs.
Ranges on the Coastal Plain from s MD
to c FL and e TX.

JUNE–MID-SEPT.

ASTERACEAE: ASTER FAMILY
Virginia Thistle
Cirsium virginianum (L.) Michaux

Biennial, forming a flat basal rosette of
leaves the first year and then a thick stem
the second, stem to 5′ (1.5 m) tall, with
cobwebby hairs. Leaves spread widely,
to 6″ (15 cm) long and 2″ (5 cm) wide,
the blade lobed or not, divisions spine-
tipped, underside white with densely
matted pubescence. One to 5 stalked
heads grow at top of stem, the bracts
tight and with short spines. Each head
is about 1″ (2.5 cm) across, disc florets
bright purple, rays absent.

Fruiting heads spread out to reveal
abundant whitish floss that acts like a
parachute to disperse the seeds. Sandhill
Thistle (*C. repandum*) is similar but
shorter; its leaves have cobwebby hairs
(entangled) beneath, it inhabits dry
sandy soil, and it blooms in late spring.
Virginia thistle is rare in GA.

Inhabits wet to moist streamhead margins, seepage slopes, and savannas. Ranges
on the Coastal Plain from s NJ to ne FL.

AUG.–OCT.

APOCYNACEAE:
DOGBANE & MILKWEED FAMILY
Red or Bog Milkweed
Asclepias rubra L.

Glabrate perennial with milky sap, stem
solitary, 1.5–3′ (0.5–1 m) tall. Leaves grow
in 3-5 pairs, opposite, lance-shaped, 3.5–5″
(9–12 cm) long and 0.6–1.2″ (1.5–3 cm)
wide, margins wavy, sparsely hairy. Flowers grow in roundish clusters about 1.5″
(3–5 cm) across, terminal or from upper
leaf axil, rosy purple to pinkish purple,
spicy fragrant.

The loss of habitat from fire suppression and conversion of habitat to
ponds and plantations has caused losses
rangewide. Like many milkweeds, Red
Milkweed naturally occurs in small populations, usually 1–5 plants. A hand lens
will reveal the intricate structure of the
flower; refer to the drawing in this book
for names of the parts.

Inhabits wet boggy soil of streamheads,
seepage slopes, pitcher-plant savannas,
and beaver ponds. Ranges on the Coastal
Plain from se NY to nw FL and e TX.

JUNE–JULY

SARRACENIACEAE: PITCHER-PLANT FAMILY
Southern Purple Pitcher-plant

Sarracenia purpurea var. *venosa* (Raf.) Fernald

Perennial, carnivorous. Leaves vary from several to many from a root crown, lasting beyond a single growing year. Leaves are pale green to reddish green, ascending to spreading, short-tubular and "squat," 2–8″ (5–20 cm) long, with a broad wing lengthwise on the ventral side. The leaf tip is modified into an erect hood, the hood margins undulate, the end of the leaf tube modified into a thickened, shiny lip. The inside of the tube is smooth, shiny, slick, with downward-pointing hairs, filled with liquid and decaying insect parts. Flowers grow singly atop leafless stems 2–5 times as long as the leaves, nodding, the 5 petals purple or maroon, 1.6–2.4″ (4–6 cm) long, soon falling and leaving the specialized "style disc," 1.2–2″ (3–5 cm) diameter.

If insect-catching weren't enough to wonder about, the highly acidic water of the leaves is the only home for several species of mosquitoes in the genus *Wyeomia*. Southern Purple Pitcher-plant is still fairly numerous in NC and SC but apparently absent from the GA Sandhills. It is listed as rare in GA. Indians and doctors alike used extracts as a diuretic, laxative, and childbirth aid.

Inhabits well-burned streamhead margins, seepage slopes, and margins of impoundments. Ranges on the Coastal Plain from se VA to se GA.

APR.

SARRACENIACEAE: PITCHER-PLANT FAMILY
Red Pitcher-plant; Sweet Pitcher-plant

Sarracenia rubra Walter ssp. *rubra*

Perennial, carnivorous. Leaves vary from a few to many from a root crown, deciduous, yellowish green, often suffused with reddish, erect, slender-tubular, 4–20″ (10–50 cm) tall, with a narrow wing lengthwise on the ventral side. The leaf tip is modified into an ascending hood; the end of the leaf tube is modified into a thickened, shiny lip. The inside of the tube is smooth, shiny, slick, partly filled with liquid and decaying insect parts. Flowers grow singly atop leafless stems about as long as leaves, nodding, petals purple to maroon, 0.8–1.2″ (2–3 cm) long, drooping, soon falling and leaving the specialized "style disc," 0.4–1.2″ (1–3 cm) diameter.

In NC and SC this species is second to Southern Purple Pitcher-plant (*Sarracenia purpurea* var. *venosa*) in abundance, but in GA it is the most numerous, although both are rare in that state. Red Pitcher-plant often grows among shrubs in streamhead thickets, so it is not obvious from a distance. Three other subspecies occur south and west of our area.

Inhabits well-burned streamheads and margins, seepage slopes, and margins of impoundments. Ranges on the Coastal Plain from se NC to wc GA.

APR.–EARLY MAY

ORCHIDACEAE: ORCHID FAMILY
Southern Twayblade
Listera australis Lindley

Perennial from fibrous roots, stem up to
8″ (20 cm) tall but often half that, purplish
green. The 2 leaves are opposite and sessile, about midway up stem, ovate to elliptic, 0.6–1.2″ (1.5–3 cm) long and 0.2–0.8″
(0.5–2 cm) wide, dark green. Flowers grow
in a terminal raceme of 5–25 flowers on
slender stalks about 0.25″ (4–6 mm) long,
reddish purple. The sepals are ovate, about
1.5 mm long, the 2 upper petals elliptical,
about 1 mm long, the lip linear, 0.25–0.5″
(6–12 mm) long, deeply forked.

   Twayblades (meaning "two leaves")
are among our smallest orchids and are
a challenge to find. This genus of some
25 species of north temperate and boreal
regions was named for Martin Lister,
seventeenth-century English physician
and naturalist. Ours is the only species
found on the Coastal Plain.

   Inhabits wet streamheads and swampy
woods along small rivers, almost always
in moss. Ranges on the Coastal Plain
from se NY to c FL and e TX; also inland
in n NJ to w NY, w VT, se Ont., and s Que.;
disjunct to c TN.

EARLY APR.–JUNE

OROBANCHACEAE: BROOMRAPE FAMILY
Savanna Bluehearts;
Florida Bluehearts
Buchnera floridana Gandoger

Biennial or perennial, stem 10–24″ (25–
60 cm) tall, unbranched, pilose basally,
glabrate above. Leaves are opposite, lower
leaves elliptical, upper leaves linear. Leaves
of midstem are lanceolate or oblanceolate,
1–2.4″ (2.5–6 cm) long, blunt-tipped,
with a few blunt teeth or none, with 1
central and 2 smaller side veins. Flowers
grow in a raceme, on stalks only 1 mm
long, red-purple or violet-purple, 0.5–0.6
(12–15 mm) long, tubular with 5 flaring
lobes, calyx with short white hairs.

   Savanna Bluehearts has declined
dramatically in our area, due to a lack of
fire management in our pinelands. With
its simple stem and showy purple flowers
it is hard to mistake. It is semiparasitic on
various grasses and woody plants; that is,
it obtains some, but not all, of its nutrients
from the roots of other species.

   Inhabits moist streamhead margins and
seepage slopes within longleaf pine habitats. Also may occur on moist roadsides.
Ranges on the Coastal Plain from c NC to
s FL and e TX; Cuba; Bahamas.

MAY–SEPT.

FABACEAE: PEA & BEAN FAMILY
Sampson's Snakeroot

Orbexilum pedunculatum (P. Miller) Rydberg
  var. *psoralioides* (Walter) Isely
[*Psoralea psoralioides* (Walter) Cory
  var. *psoralioides*]

Glabrate perennial from a taproot, the stem usually 1–2′ (30–65 cm) tall, erect or leaning. Leaves are sparse and well-spaced on stem, the 3 leaflets lanceolate or narrowly elliptic, 1.25–2.75″ (3–7 cm) long and 0.25–0.75″ (5–15 mm) wide, glandular-dotted. Flowers grow in dense, narrow clusters (they look like inverted cones) atop a long stalk, flowers pea-shaped, pale purple-blue to violet-blue.

This plant can be numerous and showy following a fire; otherwise it occurs in small numbers. A second variety grows from the Southern Appalachian Mountains westward.

Inhabits moist to dry pine savannas, flatwoods, streamhead ecotones, mesic oak-hickory woods, and clearings. Ranges on the Coastal Plain and lower Piedmont from s MD to n FL.

MAY–EARLY JULY

APIACEAE: CARROT FAMILY
Savanna Eryngo

Eryngium integrifolium Walter

Perennial, somewhat succulent, stems 8–32″ (20–80 cm) tall, widely branched above. Basal leaves lance-shaped to ovate to obovate, 0.8–4″ (2–10 cm) long and up to 2″ (5 cm) wide, tapered to a stalk, margins crenate or serrate, leaf tip blunt. Stem leaves short-stalked or sessile, 1.2–2.8″ (3–7 cm) long, margins serrate to deeply cut, leaf tip pointed. Flowers grow densely in heads subtended by sharp-tipped leafy bracts. Heads are rounded, 0.25–0.4″ (5–10 mm) across; petals 5, tiny, blue to pale greenish blue.

Like many Sandhills region plants, Savanna Eryngo has become uncommon due to habitat conversion and lack of fire management. Look for it when you see Orange Milkwort (*Polygala lutea*).

Inhabits wet to moist streamhead ecotones, seepage slopes, and pine savannas. Ranges from se VA to TN and OK, south to FL and TX.

AUG.–OCT.

ASTERACEAE: ASTER FAMILY
Savanna Grass-leaved Aster

Eurybia paludosa (Aiton) Nesom
[*Aster paludosus* Aiton]

Perennial, usually single-stemmed,
7.5–30″ (20–80 cm) tall, slender, glabrous
or glabrate, branched above to form the
inflorescence. Basal leaves are produced
in spring, often withered by flowering
time, broadly linear to narrowly lanceolate, very long, up to 12″ (30 cm) and
0.6″ (15 mm) wide, long-tapered to base,
sparsely toothed. Stem leaves are similar
but smaller, linear. Up to 9 flower heads
grow in a terminal corymb (branches
form a relatively flat top), heads about
1–1.25″ (2.5–3 cm) across. Ray flowers are
violet-blue to lavender-blue, disc flowers
yellow, bracts are slightly recurved and
minutely hairy.

It's a pity this aster doesn't grow in
masses, for individuals are very showy
with their blue and yellow flower heads.
A great subject for a bog garden.

Inhabits wet streamhead margins, sandhill seeps, and wet pine savannas. Ranges
on the Coastal Plain from se NC to se GA.

LATE JULY–OCT.

GENTIANACEAE: GENTIAN FAMILY
Catesby's Gentian

Gentiana catesbaei Walter

Perennial, with pubescent stems up to
24″ (70 cm) tall. Leaves opposite, sessile,
elliptic to lanceolate, up to 3″ (7.5 cm) long
and 1.25″ (3 cm) wide. Flowers are blue
or violet-blue, in dense clusters of 1–9,
1.5″ (3.5 cm) or so long, narrow, funnel-
shaped, petals 5, the tips usually (but not
always) spreading.

This lovely plant is named for Mark
Catesby, eighteenth-century naturalist
who wrote some of the earliest descriptions of New World flora and fauna.
Striped Gentian (*G. villosa*) is similar
but has greenish or pale yellowish flowers
suffused with blue and occurs in drier
habitats.

Inhabits blackwater streamheads and
margins of cypress-gum swamps. Within
the Sandhills region, it is numerous in NC,
uncommon in SC, and rare in GA. Ranges
on the Coastal Plain from s NJ to n FL.

LATE SEPT.–MID-NOV.

TOP Savanna Lobelia
BOTTOM "Sandhills Lobelia"

CAMPANULACEAE:
BELLFLOWER & LOBELIA FAMILY
Savanna Lobelia

Lobelia glandulosa Walter

Glabrous perennial, stem erect or ascending, usually unbranched, mostly 1.5–3' (45–90 cm) tall. Leaves are well-spaced, linear to lanceolate, 1.2–6" (3–15 cm) long and less than 0.4" (1 cm) wide, nearly sessile, acute to acuminate, margins smooth or crenate, upper leaves smallest. Flowers grow in a one-sided, uncrowded raceme of up to 20 flowers (often fewer than 10), each flower on a stalk 0.25–0.5" (5–12 mm) long. Flower stalks and calyx tubes usually have whitish translucent hairs and are subtended by a slender leaflike bract with knoblike teeth on margins. The corolla is blue, 0.8–1.2" (2–3 cm) long, tubular with 2 flaring lobes above and 3 below forming a lip, base of lip densely white-pubescent.

Savanna Lobelia occurs mostly in the middle and outer Coastal Plain; it is uncommon or rare in our area. In the Sandhills region grows a closely similar but undescribed species that differs in its shorter stature and shorter flowers that lack hairs on the lip; it inhabits wet mossy streamheads and margins of beaver ponds. To date, this "Sandhills Lobelia" has been found only in the Sandhills of NC and SC, where it is frequent.

Inhabits wet pine savannas, flatwoods, and seepage slopes. Ranges on the Coastal Plain from SE VA to S FL and S AL.

LATE AUG.–EARLY OCT.

CAMPANULACEAE:
BELLFLOWER & LOBELIA FAMILY
Nuttall's Lobelia

Lobelia nuttallii Roemer & Schultes

Slender annual, branched or not, mostly
1–2′ (30–60 cm) tall. Basal leaves are
ovate to elliptic, 0.4–0.8″ (1–2 cm) long,
frequently absent at blooming time. Stem
leaves are well-spaced, linear to lanceolate,
0.4–1.4″ (1–3.5 cm) long and less than 0.2″
(1–4 mm) wide, margins smooth or with
tiny blunt teeth. Flowers grow well-spaced
in racemes of up to 20 flowers (often fewer
than 10), each flower on a short stalk,
subtended by a slender, leaflike bract with
knoblike teeth on margins. The delicate
corolla is pale blue to whitish, 0.3–0.4″
(8–11 mm) long, tubular with 2 flaring
lobes above and 3 below forming a lip.

  Nuttall's Lobelia is a common companion throughout much of the longleaf pine
region. It is named for Thomas Nuttall
(1786–1859), eminent botanist and ornithologist, who was one of the first naturalists to explore west of the Mississippi
River.

  Inhabits moist to wet pinelands, savannas, flatwoods, seepage slopes, streamhead margins, and vernal pools. Ranges
primarily on the Coastal Plain from se NY
to nw FL and sw AL; scattered inland to
the Piedmont and Cumberland Plateau.

MAY–EARLY OCT.

LAMIACEAE: MINT FAMILY
Narrow-leaved Skullcap

Scutellaria integrifolia L.

Perennial, stems 1 to several, 8–32″
(20–80 cm) tall, 4-angled, simple or
branched above, pubescent. Leaves are
opposite, the lowest ones triangular-ovate
and up to 1.4″ (3.5 cm) long, with a stalk
up to 1″ (2.5 cm) long. Midstem and
upper leaves are lanceolate, 1–2.4″ (2.5–6
cm) long, margins more or less smooth,
tip acute, base tapered to a winged stalk.
Flowers grow in terminal spikelike racemes up to 8″ (20 cm) long, in opposite
pairs subtended by small, leaflike bracts.
The corolla is blue to violet-blue, 0.5–1″
(1.3–2.5 cm long), tubular, 2-lipped, upper
lip 3-lobed, basal part of the tube abruptly
bent. Note that the upper lip is densely
pubescent on its outer surface.

  This is a common plant of various wet
soil situations, at times numerous enough
to form a patch of vibrant blue. Mad-dog
Skullcap (*S. lateriflora*) inhabits river
floodplains and beaver marshes; it has tiny
blue flowers only 0.25″ (5–7 mm) long on
very long axillary stalks. It was reputed to
cure bites of rabid dogs, but this has been
disproven.

  Inhabits streamheads, streamhead eco-
tones, beaver ponds, and river floodplains.
Ranges from MA to OH south to FL and
TX.

LATE MAY–JULY

LENTIBULARIACEAE:
BLADDERWORT FAMILY
Blue Butterwort

Pinguicula caerulea Walter

Perennial. Leaves form a flat basal rosette, sessile, ovate to elliptic, up to 2.5″ (6 cm) long and 1″ (2.5 cm) wide, pale green to yellowish, sticky-viscous above. The single flower grows atop a narrow leafless stem; it is 5-lobed and has a downward-pointing spur. Petals are pale violet to bluish lavender or whitish, with blue venation, 1–1.5″ (2.5–3.5 cm) long, irregularly notched or cleft.

Blue Butterwort has become rare in the Sandhills region due to its requirements of perennially moist soil and frequent fire. Clearwater Butterwort (*P. primuliflora*) has paler lavender or pinkish flowers with a central white "eye." Both species capture insects on their viscous leaves, slowly digesting them to obtain nutrients and minerals.

Inhabits open seepage slopes, streamhead ecotones, and wet savannas. Ranges from se NC to s FL and nw FL; in the Sandhills region it only occurs in s NC and n SC.

APR.–MAY

MYRICACEAE: BAYBERRY FAMILY
Evergreen Bayberry; Pocosin Bayberry

Morella caroliniensis (P. Miller) Small
[*Myrica heterophylla* Raf.]

Perennial shrub, generally 3–6′ (1–2 m) tall, widely branched. Leaves are more or less evergreen, short-stalked, broadly oblanceolate to elliptic, 2–4.5″ (5–11 cm) long and 0.8–2″ (2.2–5 cm) wide. Leaves are usually toothed above the middle, have resin dots beneath, and are scarcely or not fragrant. Flowers are densely packed in short catkins on last year's twigs, tiny and yellow-brown. Fruits are roundish, about 0.2″ (4 mm), covered with pale gray wax.

The name Pocosin Bayberry comes from the Native American word "pocosin," a shrub- and peat-dominated wetland with scattered pines. Common Wax-myrtle (*M. cerifera*) is taller (5–20′) and has narrower leaves with resin dots on both surfaces and fragrant foliage. All members of *Morella* have been used to treat fevers, as astringents, and for gastrointestinal tract disorders.

Inhabits streamheads, baygalls, and their margins; also in blackwater river forests, margins of beaver ponds, and impoundments. Ranges on the Coastal Plain from s NJ to n FL, e TX, and s AR.

LATE MAR.–MID-APR.

ARISTOLOCHIACEAE: BIRTHWORT FAMILY
Little Heartleaf

Hexastylis minor (Ashe) Blomquist

Perennial, stemless. Leaves radiate outward on long stalks; blades are broadly ovate with cordate (heart-shaped) base, 1.6–2.4″ (4–6 cm) long and 1.4–2.4″ (3.5–6 cm) wide, dark green with light mottling. A few to many brownish flowers grow just beneath leaf litter. The sepals form a cup with a flattish base and 3 spreading lobes about 0.3″ (6–9 mm) long; the lobes have crinkly hairs on the inside; petals are absent.

The above description is of Little Heartleaf, which apparently is restricted to the Piedmont. For decades the plants of the Sandhills region were thought to be Little Heartleaf, but Dr. L. L. Gaddy recently recognized them as a distinct entity (Streamhead Heartleaf); the Latin name has not been formally published. The new heartleaf (see photo) is endemic (restricted to) the Sandhills of southern NC and northern SC, but it should be looked for in the eastern GA Sandhills. It closely resembles Little Heartleaf but its sepal lobes are only 0.2″ (5 mm) long. It inhabits moist to wet streamheads and their margins.

Inhabits moist deciduous forests and slopes above creeks. Ranges from c VA to c SC and w SC.

MAR.–EARLY MAY

POACEAE: GRASS FAMILY
Bog Broomsedge; Clustered Bluestem

Andropogon glomeratus (Walter) B.S.P.
  var. *glomeratus*

Perennial from a short rhizome, stems 1.5–3′ (0.5–1 m) tall, with short rough hairs. Leaves grow up to 12″ (30 cm) long and 0.3 inch (7 mm) wide. Flower spikes, each about 3″ (7.5 cm) long, grow in a dense cluster at top of stem, like a tiny broom. These eventually split open to reveal the dense, long-haired flowers.

No other Sandhills grass looks quite like Bog Broomsedge, with its broom-like flower heads. They keep their shape through winter and are popular in dried arrangements. As with all bluestems, each seed has long hairs that act as a "parachute" for dispersal. There are a few other species of wetland bluestems that you may find in our area; consult a more technical work.

Inhabits wet seepage slopes, streamhead borders, margins of beaver ponds, and wet flatwoods, especially where periodically burned. Ranges from se MA to c FL and s MS, mostly on the Coastal Plain but with scattered inland populations to KY and TN.

LATE SEPT.–MID-NOV.

POACEAE: GRASS FAMILY
Switch Cane
Arundinaria tecta (Walter) Muhlenberg

Coarse, semiwoody, bamboolike grass, densely colonial via runners. Stems are generally 3–13′ (1–4 m) tall but usually less than 7′ (2.2 m) where frequently burned, tan or straw-colored, smooth, short-branched in the upper third. Leaves are narrowly lanceolate, to 8″ (20 cm) long and 1.5″ (4 cm) wide, acuminate, margins rough, the leafstalk forming a green sheath around the branch. Flowers grow on separate stalks and are normally produced following fire; the stalks are 1–2.5′ (30–75 cm) tall, dark brown, the flowers congested near the top, with prominent yellow anthers.

Switch Cane actually is a bamboo but is a native species, not to be confused with the introduced Golden Bamboo (*Phyllostachys aurea*) a much taller, robust, yellow-stemmed plant escaped to woodland borders. Prior to the era of fire suppression, Switch Cane used to form "canebrakes," dense swaths up to a mile long and a third as wide; they are now very rare.

A major component of streamheads and their margins, seepage slopes, wet savannas, pine flatwoods, blackwater floodplains, and cypress-gum swamps. Ranges mostly on the Coastal Plain from e MD to FL and s AL.

APR.–JULY, DEPENDING ON FIRE

POACEAE: GRASS FAMILY
Toothache Grass
Ctenium aromaticum (Walter) Wood

Perennial grass from a short rhizome covered by fibrous basal remnants of old leaves. Leaves lax, mostly basal and forming low clumps or tussocks, a few scattered up on stem, blades up to 16″ (0.4 m) long, 0.2–0.3″ (3–5 mm) wide, green above, glaucous below. Flowering stem 2–5′ (0.6–1.5 m) tall, with a terminal spike (sometimes 2) about 3″ (7.5 cm) long, at first straight but eventually curving, flowers abundant and occur only on one side of the spike, each with awns, looking comblike.

Many people know this plant, if not by name, then from its use in dried arrangements: as the spikes begin dropping their seed, they curl and twist into pig's-tails, spirals, curlycues, and other fanciful shapes. Its common name comes from the somewhat aromatic spike and especially the rhizome, which has a chemical compound that numbs the gums and tongue. *Ctenium* comes from the Greek word for "comb."

Inhabits moist to wet, fire-maintained, longleaf pineland savannas, streamhead margins, and seepage slopes. A Coastal Plain endemic, ranging from se VA to c FL and e TX.

JUNE–AUG.

POACEAE: GRASS FAMILY
Savanna Panic-grass; Coastal Plain Switchgrass

Panicum virgatum L. var. *cubense* Grisebach

Perennial grass from short, slender rhizomes, the stems clumped or solitary, 1.5–5' (0.5–1.5 m) tall, hairless. Leaves grow up to 1.5' (0.5 m) long and mostly 0.2–0.4" (3–10 mm) wide, tip acuminate, margins minutely toothed. Spikelets grow in a terminal, many-branched, open panicle, 5–12" (12–30 cm) long and 4–8" (9.5–20 cm) wide, the branches strongly ascending. Spikelets are purplish, becoming tan-colored (contrasting with the rest of the green plant), 0.2" (2.8–3.2 mm) long, narrowly oval, tip acute.

This is the Coastal Plain representative of Prairie Switchgrass (*P. virgatum* var. *virgatum*), one of the dominant members of original midwestern prairies and occasionally planted or adventive in our region on roadsides. Prairie Switchgrass is robust and much taller (up to 3 m); the leaves are glaucescent, and spikelets are 3.5–6 mm long with the tip acuminate.

Inhabits wet to moist margins of streamheads, seepage slopes, savannas, vernal pools, and depression ponds. Ranges on the Coastal Plain from se MA to s FL and s MS; Cuba. Also known from scattered locations in the Piedmont.

JUNE–SEPT.

JUNCACEAE: RUSH FAMILY
Redpod Rush

Juncus trigonocarpus Steudel

Perennial, usually several stems per plant, dark green with reddish bases. Stems and leaves are 2–3' (0.6–1 m) tall, rather stiff. Leaves are round in cross section, septate, sharp-pointed. Flowers grow in terminal, open, branched clusters, each branch ending in an angular group of 2–4 flowers. The 3 sepals and 3 petals are 0.2" (3–3.5 mm) long, greenish tan. Fruiting capsule is shiny dark red or red-brown, 3-angled, about twice as long as petals.

Redpod Rush is a common member of seepage bogs and streamhead margins, in company with pitcher-plants, orchids, meadow-beauties, and other showy plants. Canada Rush (*J. canadensis*) is very similar, but its flowers are more numerous in roundish groups, and its capsules are pale brown and not much longer than the petals.

Inhabits seepage slopes and streamhead margins, including those crossed by rights-of-way. Ranges on the Coastal Plain from se NC to nw FL, e TX, and s AR.

JUNE–SEPT.

MOIST PINE FLATWOODS AND RIVER TERRACES

Due to the hilly nature of the Sandhills region, areas that combine flat terrain and moist soil are uncommon. In the outer Coastal Plain with its low relief and high water table, "flatwoods" are a common feature of the landscape, but in our region they are restricted to terraces immediately adjacent to blackwater streams and rivers. Here, Longleaf Pine (*Pinus palustris*) and Loblolly Pine (*P. taeda*) are co-dominant, sometimes also with Pond Pine (*P. serotina*) in wetter sites, with scattered Water Oak (*Quercus nigra*), Southern Red Oak (*Q. falcata*), and Sweetgum (*Liquidambar styraciflua*) in the understory. With periodic burning, however, hardwoods are greatly reduced in size and number. Moisture-loving shrubs are a feature of flatwoods communities, and we commonly find Gallberry (*Ilex glabra*), Dangleberry (*Gaylussacia frondosa*), Narrowleaf Blueberry (*Vaccinium tenellum*), Elliott's Blueberry (*V. elliottii*), Southern Maleberry (*Lyonia ligustrina* var. *foliosiflora*), and Carolina Sheep Laurel (*Kalmia carolina*) competing for space with Wiregrass (*Aristida stricta*) and other herbaceous plants. Carolina Jessamine (*Gelsemium sempervirens*) is a common trailing and climbing vine in infrequently burned sites. In the Carolinas, Common Pyxie-moss (*Pyxidanthera barbulata*) and Creeping Blueberry (*Vaccinium crassifolium*) are most often found in moist flatwoods.

A dense layer of low shrubs is characteristic of flatwoods and rarely flooded river terraces. If frequently burned, river terraces may yield high species diversity.

In riverside terraces that receive occasional flooding, soils are relatively nutrient-rich and support a very high diversity of herbaceous species—sites in North Carolina have recorded some of the highest species counts anywhere within the longleaf pine ecosystem. Georgia Indigo-bush (*Amorpha georgiana*) is nearly restricted to this habitat variant.

Species List

The color after a name indicates the primary natural community or habitat.

T = mentioned in text of another species; not pictured.

Amorpha georgiana
   Georgia Indigo-bush
Cypripedium acaule
   Pink Lady's-slipper; Moccasin Flower
Gelsemium sempervirens
   Yellow Jessamine
Helianthus angustifolius ❋
   Narrowleaf Sunflower
Helianthus resinosus
   Resinous Sunflower
Ilex glabra ❋
   Gallberry
Kalmia buxifolia
   Sand Myrtle
Kalmia carolina
   Carolina Sheep Laurel;
   Wicky
Lobelia glandulosa ❋
   Savanna Lobelia
Lyonia ligustrina var. *foliosiflora* ❋
   Southern Maleberry
Lyonia mariana ❋
   Staggerbush
Nestronia umbellula ❋
   Nestronia

Pyxidanthera barbulata
   Common Pyxie-moss
Rhododendron atlanticum
   Dwarf Azalea
Ruellia caroliniensis ❋
   Carolina Wild-petunia
Sisyrinchium capillare
   Wiry Blue-eyed-grass
Solidago fistulosa
   Shaggy Pineywoods Goldenrod
Solidago stricta T ❋
   Wand Goldenrod
Solidago verna ❋
   Spring Goldenrod
Uvularia puberula var. *nitida* ❋
   Coastal Plain Bellwort
Vaccinium crassifolium
   Creeping Blueberry
Vaccinium elliottii
   Elliott's Blueberry; Mayberry
Vaccinium tenellum ❋
   Narrowleaf Blueberry
Vitis rotundifolia ❋
   Muscadine Grape

ERICACEAE: BLUEBERRY & AZALEA FAMILY
Sand Myrtle

Kalmia buxifolia (Bergius) Gift, Kron, & Stevens
[*Leiophyllum buxifolium* (Bergius) Elliott]

Perennial, evergreen shrub up to 5′
(1.7 m) tall, branches stiff and strongly
ascending. Leaves are alternate or opposite, crowded, elliptic, 0.4–1″ (1–2.5 cm)
long and 0.2–0.3″ (3–8 mm) wide, dark
green, lustrous, glabrate or with tiny
gland-tipped hairs. Flowers grow in dense
clusters on stalks with leafy bracts. The
5 petals are separate (not joined at all),
white, about 0.2″ (3–5 mm) long, stamens
10, as long as petals, the style a bit longer.
Fruit is a dry gray-brown capsule.

Sand Myrtle gets its common name
from inhabiting sandy (but moist underneath) soils. In our region it occurs on
bluffs and flatwoods along Rockfish Creek
near Fayetteville, NC, where it is quite
common. This is the only *Kalmia* with
separate petals.

Inhabits pine flatwoods and blufflike
slopes, very local in Sandhills region.
Ranges disjunctly in the Coastal Plain of
s NJ and se NC to c SC; also in Appalachians of w NC to w SC, ne GA, and e TN;
Whitely County, KY; Monroe County, PA.

APR.–MID-MAY

ERICACEAE: BLUEBERRY & AZALEA FAMILY
Elliott's Blueberry; Mayberry

Vaccinium elliottii Chapman

Perennial woody shrub, 3–8′ (1–2.5 m)
tall, much-branched, the twigs relatively
thin and arching outward and downward, pubescent. Leaves are numerous,
deciduous, elliptic, 0.6–1.4″ (1.5–3.5 cm)
long and 0.25–0.6″ (6–15 mm) wide. The
leaf tip is acute and with a tiny sharp
point, surfaces dull, margins crenate to
finely toothed. Flowers grow in clusters
of 3–5, just prior to leaf-out, short-stalked,
short-cylindrical, the 5 petals white or
pink-tinged, 0.25–0.3″ (5–8 mm) long, tips
acute and curled back. Berries are black,
0.25–0.3″ (5–8 mm), juicy and sweet.

This highbush blueberry is immediately distinguished from other highbush
species by its consistently small leaves and
flowers and earlier blooming period. It
is named for Stephen Elliott (1771–1830)
of SC, who wrote *A Sketch of the Botany
of South Carolina and Georgia*, in which
are described all of the native plants then
known.

Inhabits moist soils of riverbanks,
streambanks, and their terraces. Ranges
on the Coastal Plain from se VA to n FL,
e TX, and s AR; scattered in the Piedmont.

MID-MAR.–MID-APR.

ERICACEAE: BLUEBERRY & AZALEA FAMILY
Creeping Blueberry
Vaccinium crassifolium Andrews

Perennial, semiwoody, prostrate, and with long, trailing branches. Leaves are numerous, evergreen, elliptic, 0.3–0.8″ (0.7–2 mm) long and 0.2–0.4″ (3–10 mm) wide, dark green above, pale green beneath, tip with a short spiny point, margins smooth to crenate. Flowers grow in tight clusters of 3–7 on erect leafy shoots, the 5 petals white to reddish, 0.2″ (2–4 mm) long, forming a globular shape with a small opening. Berries are black, lustrous, 0.25″ (5–6 mm), juicy but not very sweet.

With its trailing stems and branches, Creeping Blueberry has the most unusual growth form of any of our blueberries. Rayner's Blueberry (*V. sempervirens*) is closely related but has much larger leaves and longer, ascending stems and branches; it occurs in a few boggy streamheads in Lexington County, SC.

Inhabits moist soil of pine flatwoods and margins of streamheads; also found on clay and sandstone hilltops. Ranges on the Coastal Plain from se VA to se GA (Effingham County).

APR.–MAY

DIAPENSIACEAE:
DIAPENSIA & PYXIE-MOSS FAMILY
Common Pyxie-moss
Pyxidanthera barbulata Michaux

Perennial, evergreen, prostrate shrublet with glabrate stems and leaves, the entire plant no more than 2.5′ (75 cm) in diameter. Leaves are crowded, oblanceolate, 0.2–0.3″ (4–8 mm) long, sessile, acute, dark green. Flowers grow singly at ends of numerous short branches, sepals 5, united basally, usually pink; petals 5, white, with obovate lobes about 0.25″ (4–5 mm) long.

This genus of 2 species is unique to the Atlantic Coastal Plain. When not flowering, both species of pyxie-moss can be mistaken for patches of moss, so look carefully! Common Pyxie-moss inhabits perennially moist soil, the plants are wider-spreading and less compact than Sandhills Pyxie-moss (*P. brevifolia*), the leaves are larger and nearly hairless, and it has slightly larger flowers.

Inhabits moist soil of streamhead margins and longleaf pine flatwoods. Ranges on the Coastal Plain from se NY to se NC and probably ne SC.

EARLY MAR.–MID-APR.

ASTERACEAE: ASTER FAMILY
Resinous Sunflower

Helianthus resinosus Small

Perennial, stem solitary or clumped together, 2.5–6′ (0.7–2 m) tall, hispid hairy (rarely smoothish), not much branched. Leaves are evenly spaced, the lower ones opposite, the upper ones usually alternate, lance-shaped to ovate, 2.4–8″ (6–20 cm) long and 1.2–3.25″ (3–8 cm) wide. The upper surface of leaves is scabrous, the lower surface densely soft-hairy (velvety), margins crenate to serrate, tapered to both ends. Flowering heads are terminal, disc dark yellow or brownish, about 1″ (2.5 cm) across, rays bright yellow, 1.2–2″ (3–5 cm) long.

The common name refers to the glandular dots on the leaf undersides; these are somewhat resinous (sticky to touch).

Inhabits moist soils of longleaf pine flatwoods and savannas, slopes above creeks, and occasionally roadsides. Ranges on the Coastal Plain from nc NC to nw FL and MS; inland to sw NC, n GA, and ne AL.

LATE JUNE–OCT.

ASTERACEAE: ASTER FAMILY
Shaggy Pineywoods Goldenrod

Solidago fistulosa P. Miller

Perennial, stems 1.5–5′ (0.5–1.5 m) tall (reportedly to 6.5′), erect, the lower part glabrate, the upper part densely pilose. There are no basal leaves. Stem leaves are elliptical or a bit narrower, 1.6–4″ (4–10 cm) long and 0.4–1.2″ (1–3 cm) wide, ascending, sessile and clasping, margins crenate, rough-pubescent above, pubescent beneath. Flowers grow on one-sided branches in a terminal inflorescence, triangular in shape. Ray flowers are yellow, about 0.2″ (2–4 mm) long; disc yellow.

With its numerous upward-directed leaves and hairy stem, this goldenrod is easy to identify. It occurs primarily in the outer part of the Coastal Plain, barely reaching our region. There are more than 50 species of goldenrods in our 3 states; they are a rewarding challenge to learn.

Inhabits moist pine flatwoods, river terraces, and savannas. Ranges on the Coastal Plain from s NJ to s FL and se LA.

SEPT.–OCT.

GELSEMIACEAE: JESSAMINE FAMILY
Carolina Jessamine

Gelsemium sempervirens (L.) J. St. Hilaire

Perennial vine; high climbing, clambering on low vegetation, or trailing. Leaves
grow from short stalks (0.2–0.3″ [3–7
mm]), evergreen, opposite, lanceolate to
elliptic, 1.2–2.8″ (3–7 cm) long and 0.4–1″
(1–2.5 cm) wide, acute to acuminate, dark
green. Flowers are solitary (occasionally
2–3) from leaf axils, tubular with 5 flaring
lobes, 0.8–1.5″ (2–3.8 cm) long, bright
yellow, fragrant.

   Who does not know and love Carolina
Jessamine? Spring-blooming, brightly
colored, and fragrant, it is welcomed in
our yards and along our streets. But in the
wild its local abundance can be a sign of
fire suppression and/or habitat alteration,
where it can form a dense ground cover to
the detriment of wildflowers. Medicinally,
in low doses it has been used as a sedative,
to reduce fever, and as an emetic; in high
doses it may cause respiratory failure.
Beware: all parts are potentially toxic.

   Inhabits mesic to moist pine flatwoods, streamside slopes and bluffs, and
oak-hickory woodlands, spreading with
clearing and fire suppression to other
habitats, including roadsides. Ranges from
VA to AR south to C FL and e TX; Mex.;
Guatemala.

MID-MAR.–EARLY MAY

ORCHIDACEAE: ORCHID FAMILY
Pink Lady's-slipper;
Moccasin Flower

Cypripedium acaule Aiton

Perennial from rhizomes. Leaves 2, basal,
dark green above, paler below with silvery
sheen, strongly ribbed below, 4–9.5″
(10–24 cm) long and 1.6–5″ (4–12.5 cm)
wide, pubescent. Flower stalk single, to
16″ (40 cm) tall, topped by a leafy bract
and a single flower (rarely 2) composed
of a nodding, pouchlike lip and brownish
green to yellowish green sepals and side
petals. The lip about 2″ (5 cm) long and
1.4″ (3.5 cm) wide, pink or rosy with red
veins, appearing as if inflated.

   Both common names refer to the slip-
perlike shape of the lip. This is a mostly
northern orchid, rare in our region and as
yet not known from the Georgia sandhills.

   Inhabits moist margins of blackwater
swamp forests and on river terraces, usually under loblolly pines; also found in
adjacent pine-oak flatwoods. Ranges from
Newf. to Alb. south to n GA, n IN, and
MN.

LATE APR.–LATE MAY

ERICACEAE: BLUEBERRY & AZALEA FAMILY
Dwarf Azalea

Rhododendron atlanticum (Ashe) Rehder

Perennial colonial shrub 1–2′ (0.3–0.7 m) tall, taller in unburned sites, with spreading branches that are shaggy hairy when young. Leaves are very short stalked, dark green, elliptic to narrowly obovate, 1–2.4″ (2.5–6 cm) long, pubescent above (lost with age), tip blunt, margins with bristle-like hairs. Flowers appear just before the leaves, usually in a circular, terminal cluster, on stalks 0.25–0.6″ (5–15 mm) long. They are sweetly fragrant, the corolla tube 0.6–1″ (1.5–2.5 cm) long, reddish pink to whitish, with abundant gland-tipped hairs, the 5 lobes flaring and white or pink. The stamens and style extend far beyond the petals, reddish.

Dwarf Azalea is one of our showiest plants and should get more attention from gardeners and horticulturists, due to its low growth and fragrant flowers. A colony in full flower is a marvelous sight. While frequent in the NC Sandhills, it progressively becomes scarcer southward in SC and is absent from the GA Sandhills.

Inhabits moist to dryish pine flatwoods and savannas, especially on riverside terraces. Ranges on the Coastal Plain from S NJ to SE GA.

EARLY APR.–EARLY MAY; OCCASIONALLY ALSO IN MID-SEPT.–OCT.

ERICACEAE: BLUEBERRY & AZALEA FAMILY
Carolina Sheep Laurel; Wicky

Kalmia carolina Small

Perennial, evergreen, colonial shrub up to 5′ (1.7 m) tall with pubescent twigs. Leaves are arranged in whorls of 3, lanceolate to narrowly elliptic, to 2.5″ (6 cm) long and 1″ (2.5 cm) wide. Leaves are coriaceous (thick-textured and firm), green with a bluish tinge, lustrous above, densely but minutely hairy below. Clusters of stalked flowers are produced in leaf axils of last year's leaves, flowers about 0.5″ (12 mm) across, petals 5, united, rose or rose-pink with a ring of reddish spots. Fruit is a dry capsule, cinnamon-brown, lasting through winter.

Carolina Sheep Laurel, like Mountain Laurel, has a special pocket in each petal that holds the recurved stamens until pollen is ripe and then releases them explosively onto pollinating insects. White Wicky (*K. cuneata*) is a rare inhabitant of streamhead ecotones and Carolina bay pocosins of NC and SC; its flowers are white and its leaves are deciduous.

Inhabits streamhead ecotones, moist to wet pine flatwoods, and Carolina bay pocosins. Ranges on the Coastal Plain from SE VA to C SC, disjunct to Taylor County, GA; also in the mountains from SW VA to NE GA.

MID-APR–MID-MAY

FABACEAE: PEA & BEAN FAMILY
Georgia Indigo-bush
Amorpha georgiana Wilbur

Perennial shrub, usually multistemmed, to 3′ (1 m) tall, glabrate. Leaves are compound, up to 7″ (18 cm) long. Leaflets are numerous, opposite plus a terminal leaflet, elliptic, about 0.5″ (1–1.5 cm) long, with many glandular dots (use 10x hand lens). Flowers are small but numerous in terminal spikes up to 2.5″ (6 cm) long, each one pea-shaped, bluish violet or reddish violet, anthers golden yellow.

Georgia Indigo-bush is a rare plant throughout its range, a victim of fire suppression and habitat conversion. It occurs sporadically in the Sandhills of NC and SC, but in GA it only occurs to the south of the Sandhills region. Tall Indigo-bush (*A. fruticosa* L.) may occur along the same rivers, but it inhabits wetter soils (riverbanks, marshes) and is about 3 times the size of Georgia Indigo-bush in nearly all dimensions.

Inhabits terraces of blackwater rivers, especially where burned periodically or where crossed by a right-of-way, thus keeping the canopy open. It does not tolerate prolonged flooding. Ranges on the Coastal Plain from se NC to se GA.

LATE APR.–LATE MAY

IRIDACEAE: IRIS FAMILY
Wiry Blue-eyed-grass
Sisyrinchium capillare Bicknell

Glabrous perennial, stems single or a few together, 8–20″ (20–50 cm) tall, wiry and not winged, 0.5–1 mm wide, branched 1–2 times. The plant base has many brownish fibers, which are remains of previous years' leaves. Leaves are basal only, erect, grasslike, about as long and wide as the stems, tip acuminate. Flowers grow terminally, from 1 to several in 2 clusters that are each partly enclosed by 2 spathelike bracts 0.4–0.6″ (1–1.5 cm) long. These bracts themselves are partly enclosed by a leaflike bract that extends far beyond the flowers. The 3 sepals and 3 petals are alike, whitish to pale blue with a pale yellow base, 0.3–0.5″ (8–12 mm) long, each with a tiny point at the tip.

Wiry Blue-eyed-grass is named for its thin and wiry stems and leaves; when not in flower the plant is hard to see among Wiregrass (*Aristida stricta*) and other plants. Among Sandhills region blue-eyed-grasses, the whitish blue flowers are distinctive.

Inhabits moist to dry longleaf pine flatwoods and savannas. Ranges on the Coastal Plain from se VA to n FL.

APR.–MID-MAY

BLACKWATER RIVERS AND CYPRESS-GUM SWAMPS

Blackwater rivers originate within the Coastal Plain—in our case right here in the Sandhills region, where they collect water from a myriad of streamheads. They are called "blackwater" because the water is very dark, ranging from the color of strong tea to black-ish. The deep hues derive from tannins leached from leaves, bark, and other organic matter that does not completely break down in the highly acidic water. This situation is in stark contrast to brown-water rivers, which originate in the Piedmont and Mountains and are tan to brownish in color. The contrast is further apparent in the high plant diversity found in the nutrient- and mineral-rich soils of brownwater floodplains versus the lower diversity found in the nutrient- and mineral-poor soils of blackwater floodplains.

Forest communities develop in two situations: (1) On low levees of deposited sand and silt and on lower portions of river-side slopes. Here flooding is of short duration. (2) On broader floodplains where floodwaters remain longer and where soils are permanently saturated; these typically are cypress-gum swamps.

In blackwater rivers, poorly degraded tannins are carried throughout the water column, resulting in a dark tea color.

Frequently inundated floodplains support swamps of Pond Cypress, Swamp Black Gum, Loblolly Pine, and American Holly.

Riverside Communities

Examples of the first type of community occur on shores, islands, and other river deposits. They tend to be commonest on smaller rivers but also occur on large rivers on elevated places. River Birch (*Betula nigra*), Water Ash (*Fraxinus caroliniana*), Ironwood (*Carpinus caroliniana*), Water Oak (*Quercus nigra*), Sweetgum (*Liquidambar styraciflua*), Red Maple (*Acer rubrum*), Loblolly Pine (*Pinus taeda*), and American Holly (*Ilex opaca*) are common trees. Overcup Oak (*Q. lyrata*) occurs in small pooches (depressions and backwaters) where water stands. Atlantic White Cedar (*Chamaecyparis thyoides*) is widespread in our region but tends to occur only along specific rivers and is absent from others. Climbing vines are common and include grapes (*Vitis*), Crossvine (*Bignonia capreolata*), Trumpet-vine (*Campsis radicans*), Climbing Hempweed (*Mikania scandens*), greenbriers (*Smilax*), and Climbing Dogbane (*Trachelospermum difforme*). The shrub layer ranges from sparse to dense, with Elliott's Blueberry (*Vaccinium elliottii*), Ti-ti (*Cyrilla racemiflora*), Sweetspire (*Itea virginica*), and Switch Cane (*Arundinaria tecta*) most prominent. Herbs are relatively sparse under the forest canopy but moderately diverse on river shores, sandbars, and marshy openings where more sunlight penetrates.

Cypress-Gum Swamps

The hilly topography and dense clay soil layers of the Sandhills region limit the width of blackwater river floodplains and therefore also the size of cypress-gum swamps. Nonetheless, even small examples of cypress-gum swamps may contain trees of impressive height and girth. Canoeing or kayaking is the best way to see such trees and to experience a bit of wilderness close to home. Pond Cypress (*Taxodium ascendens*) and Swamp Black Gum (*Nyssa biflora*) are the dominant trees, with Red Maple, Ironwood, Sweet Bay (*Magnolia virginiana*), Red Bay (*Persea palustris*), and Water Ash in the understory. Ericaceous shrubs, Buttonbush (*Cephalanthus occidentalis*), and Switch Cane can be sparse to locally dense. Wildflowers are generally sparse.

Species List

The color after a name indicates the primary natural community or habitat.
T = mentioned in text of another species; not pictured.

Aesculus pavia
  Red Buckeye
Alnus serrulata ✽
  Tag Alder
Amorpha fruticosa T ✽
  Tall Indigo-bush
Amorpha georgiana ✽
  Georgia Indigo-bush
Amsonia tabernaemontana
  Eastern Bluestar
Apios americana
  Groundnut; Indian Potato
Arundinaria tecta ✽
  Switch Cane
Bacopa caroliniana ✽
  Blue Water-hyssop
Bidens discoidea
  Little Beggar-ticks;
  Swamp Beggar-ticks
Bignonia capreolata
  Crossvine
Campsis radicans
  Trumpet-creeper; Trumpet-vine
Cephalanthus occidentalis ✽
  Buttonbush
Chionanthus virginicus
  Fringetree
Cicuta maculata

  Spotted Water-hemlock;
  Spotted Cowbane
Clematis crispa
  Leatherflower; Marsh Clematis
Conoclinium coelestinum
  Mistflower; Ageratum
Cyrilla racemiflora
  Ti-ti
Dulichium arundinaceum ✽
  Three-way Sedge
Elephantopus carolinianus
  Leafy Elephant's-foot;
  Riverside Elephant's-foot
Erechtites hieraciifolius ✽
  Fireweed
Eubotrys racemosa
  Swamp Sweetbells; Fetterbush
Euonymus americanus
  Heart's-a-Bustin'; Strawberry-bush
Eupatorium semiserratum
  Olive Eupatorium;
  Threeleaf Eupatorium
Eutrochium dubium
  Three-nerved Joe-Pye-weed
Eutrochium fistulosum T
  Hollow Joe-Pye-weed
Gelsemium sempervirens ✽
  Yellow Jessamine

Gentiana catesbaei ✳
  Catesby's Gentian
Geum canadense
  Canada Avens
Gratiola virginiana
  Swamp Hedge-hyssop
Gratiola viscidula T ✳
  Sticky Hedge-hyssop
Helianthus angustifolius ✳
  Narrowleaf Sunflower
Helianthus resinosus ✳
  Resinous Sunflower
Hexastylis arifolia ✳
  Little Brown Jug
Hibiscus moscheutos
  Eastern Rose-mallow
Hydrocotyle verticillata T ✳
  Whorled Pennywort
Hydrolea quadrivalvis ✳
  Waterpod
Hypericum galioides ✳
  Slender-leaved St. John's-wort
Hypericum nitidum
  Needle-leaved St. John's-wort
Hypericum nudiflorum
  Streamside St. John's-wort
Hypoxis curtissii T ✳
  Swamp Stargrass
Ilex amelanchier
  Sarvis Holly
Ilex coriacea ✳
  Large Gallberry
Ilex decidua
  Possum Haw
Ilex verticillata T ✳
  Downy Winterberry
Ipomoea lacunosa
  Small White Morning-glory
Iris virginica ✳
  Southern Blue Flag
Itea virginica
  Sweetspire; Virginia Willow
Juncus repens
  Creeping Rush; Water Rush
Kalmia latifolia
  Mountain Laurel
Leucothoe axillaris
  Coastal Plain Doghobble
Ligustrum sinense
  Chinese Privet
Lindernia dubia ✳

  False Pimpernel
Linum striatum
  Wetland Flax
Listera australis ✳
  Southern Twayblade
Lobelia cardinalis
  Cardinal Flower
Lobelia elongata
  Streamside Lobelia
Lonicera japonica ✳
  Japanese Honeysuckle
Lonicera sempervirens ✳
  Coral Honeysuckle
Luzula echinata ✳
  Hedgehog Woodrush
Lycopus virginicus T ✳
  Virginia Bugleweed
Macbridea caroliniana
  Carolina Birds-in-a-Nest;
  Carolina Bogmint
Magnolia virginiana ✳
  Sweet Bay
Mayaca fluviatilis ✳
  Bogmoss
Mecardonia acuminata ✳
  Axil-flower
Medeola virginiana ✳
  Indian Cucumber-root
Microstegium vimineum
  Japanese Stiltgrass;
  Microstegium
Mikania scandens
  Climbing Hempweed
Mimulus alatus
  Winged Monkey-flower
Mitchella repens
  Partridge-berry
Morella cerifera T ✳
  Common Wax-myrtle
Murdannia keisak
  Swamp Dewflower
Orontium aquaticum ✳
  Golden Club
Packera glabella
  Butterweed; Smooth Ragwort
Parthenocissus quinquefolia
  Virginia Creeper
Peltandra virginica ✳
  Arrow Arum
Persicaria longiseta
  Longbristle Smartweed

Persicaria pensylvanica T
  Pinkweed
Persicaria sagittata
  Arrowleaf Tearthumb
Persicaria setacea
  Swamp Smartweed
Phoradendron serotinum
  American Mistletoe
Pluchea camphorata T ✹
  Camphorweed
Pluchea foetida ✹
  Pallid Marsh-fleabane
Potentilla simplex T ✹
  Five-fingers
Ptilimnium capillaceum
  Mock Bishop's-weed
Ranunculus pusillus
  Low Spearwort
Ranunculus recurvatus
  Hooked Buttercup
Rhexia virginica ✹
  Virginia Meadow-beauty
Rubus argutus ✹
  Southern Blackberry
Sagittaria latifolia T ✹
  Broadleaf Arrowhead
Salvia lyrata ✹
  Lyre-leaved Sage
Sambucus canadensis
  Black Elderberry;
  Common Elderberry
Sanicula canadensis ✹
  Canada Sanicle
Silene catesbaei
  Fringed Campion
Sisyrinchium angustifolium
  Stout Blue-eyed-grass
Smilax bona-nox T
  Catbrier
Smilax rotundifolia
  Greenbrier; Horsebrier
Smilax smallii
  Jackson-brier
Smilax walteri ✹
  Coral Brier
Solidago altissima
  Tall Goldenrod
Solidago caesia ✹
  Bridal-wreath Goldenrod
Solidago gigantea T
  Late Goldenrod

Sparganium americanum ✹
  American Bur-reed
Spiranthes odorata T ✹
  Fragrant Ladies'-tresses
Stewartia malacodendron
  Silky Camellia
Styrax americanus
  American Snowbell; Storax
Symphyotrichum lateriflorum
  Calico Aster; Riverside Aster
Symphyotrichum novi-belgii ✹
  New York Aster
Symplocos tinctoria ✹
  Sweetleaf
Tipularia discolor ✹
  Cranefly Orchid
Toxicodendron radicans
  Poison Ivy
Trachelospermum difforme
  Climbing Dogbane
Triadenum virginicum ✹
  Pale St. John's-wort
Triadenum walteri T ✹
  Walter's St. John's-wort
Uvularia sessilifolia
  Wild Oats; Straw Lily
Vaccinium elliottii ✹
  Elliott's Blueberry
Vaccinium formosum
  Southern Highbush Blueberry
Vaccinium fuscatum T
  Black Highbush Blueberry
Vernonia noveboracensis ✹
  New York Ironweed
Viburnum dentatum var. *lucidum*
  Smooth Viburnum; Arrow-wood
Viburnum nudum ✹
  Possum Haw
Viola primulifolia ✹
  Primrose-leaved Violet
Vitis aestivalis T ✹
  Summer Grape
Wisteria frutescens
  American Wisteria
Xanthorhiza simplicissima
  Yellowroot
Xyris difformis
  Flatstem Yellow-eyed-grass
Zephyranthes atamasca
  Atamasco Lily

ASTERACEAE: ASTER FAMILY
Calico Aster; Riverside Aster

Symphyotrichum lateriflorum (L.) Löve & Löve
[*Aster lateriflorus* (L.) Britton]

Perennial, stems single or a few together, erect to arching, mostly 1.5–5′ (0.5–1.5 m) tall, usually widely branched, glabrous or glabrate. Leaves are elliptic to lanceolate, up to 2–6″ (5–15 cm) long and up to 1.6″ (4 cm) wide, tip acuminate to acute, margins toothed, more or less pubescent beneath. Flower heads are numerous and form 1-sided arrays on branches with small, long-pointed leaves; the heads grow on stalks less than 0.6″ (15 mm) long. Rays are white, 0.2–0.4″ (5–10 mm) long; disc flowers yellow turning brownish maroon.

Canoeists know this aster well, as it is a frequent companion along blackwater streams and rivers. Our other small white-flowered asters occur in drier soil in full sun, so they are not likely to be confused. Rice-button Aster (*S. dumosum*) may co-occur, but it has very small and blunt leaves on branches.

Inhabits wooded riverbanks, floodplain forests, cypress-gum swamps, and marshes. Ranges from ME to MN south to FL and AR.

SEPT.–OCT.

ASTERACEAE: ASTER FAMILY
Olive Eupatorium; Threeleaf Eupatorium

Eupatorium semiserratum DC.

Perennial, 2.2–5.5′ (0.7–1.7 m) tall, olive-green color, stems pubescent. Leaves are well-spaced, in whorls of 3 (or rarely 4 or opposite). Leaves are lance-shaped or narrowly elliptic, 2–3.2″ (4.5–8 cm) long and 0.4–1.25″ (1–3 cm) wide, tip acute, margins toothed in outer half, base tapered to leafstalks up to 0.4″ (10 mm) long. The stem is branched above into a flat-topped cluster of tiny flower heads, each with whitish bracts and about 5 white disc flowers, rays absent.

The olive-green color of this plant, coupled with its whorls of 3 leaves, sets it apart from other eupatoriums in our area.

Inhabits moist slopes, banks, and openings along blackwater streams and rivers; occasionally found in margins of beaver ponds. Ranges on the Coastal Plain from se VA to n FL, e TX, and s AR; c TN.

AUG.–OCT.

ASTERACEAE: ASTER FAMILY
Climbing Hempweed
Mikania scandens (L.) Willdenow

Perennial vine, usually clambering over shrubs and coarse herbs (not up trees), the stems extending to 10′ (3 m) or more, pubescent. Leaves opposite, ovate to triangular-ovate, 1.6–4.8″ (4–12 cm) long and 0.8–3.6″ (2–9 cm) wide, tip acuminate, base cordate, margins smooth to wavy, leafstalks up to 4″ (10 cm) long. Flower heads grow in broad clusters 0.8–3.2″ (2–8 cm) wide on long stalks from leaf axils. The disc flowers are pale pink to white, ray flowers absent.

Climbing Hempweed is easily recognized as the only climbing member of the aster family in our region. It favors open sunny places and can often be found at streamside bridge crossings. Some 400 other species of *Mikania* occur in the tropics worldwide, mostly in Central and South America.

Inhabits riverside marshes and banks and margins of beaver ponds and impoundments. Ranges from ME to s Ont. and MO south to s FL and s TX; tropical America.

LATE JULY–EARLY OCT.

ERICACEAE: BLUEBERRY & AZALEA FAMILY
Mountain Laurel
Kalmia latifolia L.

Perennial, evergreen shrub up to 10′ (3 m) tall with stems to 4″ (10 cm) thick. Leaves are alternate, elliptic, to 4.5″ (11 cm) long and 1.5″ (3.5 cm) wide, coriaceous, glabrous. Flowers are produced in large terminal clusters, each about 1″ (2.5 cm) across, petals 5, united, white (or pink or rose-tinged) with a ring of reddish spots. Fruit is a dry capsule, cinnamon-brown, overwinters.

In the Sandhills region, Mountain Laurel is more often seen by canoeists than by botanists, for it prefers cool, steep, streamside slopes that mimic its mountain haunts. In early May, thickets of laurel put on showy flowering displays. In *Kalmia*, each petal has a special pocket that holds the recurved stamens until the pollen is ripe; then it releases them explosively onto insects. Old-time herbalists used it to treat fever, jaundice, syphilis, and inflammation.

Inhabits cool streamside bluffs and slopes. Ranges from s ME to OH south to n FL and se LA.

LATE APR.–MID-MAY

ERICACEAE: BLUEBERRY & AZALEA FAMILY
Coastal Plain Doghobble
Leucothoe axillaris (Lamarck) D. Don

Perennial, colonial, woody shrub to 3′ (1 m) high. Leaves are evergreen, very dark green, pubescent beneath or glabrous, lance-shaped or narrowly ovate, 2–5″ (5–13 cm) long and 0.6–2″ (1.5–5 cm) wide, margins finely toothed, tip acute or short acuminate. Flowers grow in dense, elongate clusters 1–2.8″ (2.5–7 cm) long from leaf axils. Corollas are tubular with 5 small spreading or recurved lobes, 0.25″ (5–7 mm) long, white. Fruits are dry capsules the shape of a depressed sphere, 0.25″ (5–6 mm) broad.

Doghobble is well-named, for thickets of it can easily halt the progress of dogs and people alike. Its leaves are among the darkest shade of green of any of the plants in the Sandhills region.

Inhabits blackwater river floodplains, cypress-gum swamps, moist banks of streams, and streamheads. Ranges on the Coastal Plain from se VA to c FL and c LA.

LATE MAR.–EARLY MAY

ERICACEAE: BLUEBERRY & AZALEA FAMILY
Swamp Sweetbells; Fetterbush
Eubotrys racemosa (L.) Nuttall
[*Leucothoe racemosa* (L.) Gray]

Perennial shrub 3–10′ (1–3 m) tall, widely branched. Leaves elliptic to ovate, 1.2–3.6″ (3–9 cm) long and 0.4–1.6″ (1–4 cm) wide, glabrate, margins sharp-toothed, tip acute, leafstalks less than 0.2″ (1–3 mm) long. Flowers grow single file in straight to somewhat curved rows, petals 5, white, forming a tube with tiny curled lobes, about 0.3″ (7 mm) long, fragrant.

Swamp Sweetbells is one of several shrubs that deserves better recognition in the horticultural trade, first for its deliciously fragrant flowers and second for the purple tinge to its fall leaves.

Inhabits blackwater streamheads, creekbanks and riverbanks, and cypress-gum swamps; also found in wet pine flatwoods. Ranges on the Coastal Plain and Piedmont from e MA to c FL and se TX; scattered sites inland.

APR.–MAY

ERICACEAE: BLUEBERRY & AZALEA FAMILY
Southern Highbush Blueberry

Vaccinium formosum Andrews
[*Vaccinium corymbosum* L., in part]

Perennial woody shrub, 3–10′ (1–3 m) tall, much-branched, the twigs arching outward and downward, glabrous. Leaves are deciduous, glabrous, elliptic to ovate, 1.6–3.2″ (4–8 cm) long and 0.6–1.6″ (1.5–4 cm) wide, tip acute, underside glaucescent, margins smooth. Flowers grow in clusters of a few to many just prior to leaf-out. Each flower is short-stalked, cylindrical, the 5 white petals 0.3–0.4″ (8–11 mm) long, tips acute and curled back. Berries are blue, glaucescent, 0.3–0.4″ (7–10 mm), juicy and sweet.

Southern Highbush Blueberry is the species from which our cultivated blueberries are derived, but flavor and sweetness vary a lot in wild bushes. Black Highbush Blueberry (*V. fuscatum*) differs in its pubescent twigs and leaf undersides, usually red-tinged flowers, and black berries. The two often occur together and will hybridize.

Inhabits moist to wet soils of blackwater river floodplains, cypress-gum swamps, streamheads, and seepage slopes. Ranges on the Coastal Plain from s NJ to n FL and e TX.

LATE MAR.–LATE APR.

CYRILLACEAE: TI-TI FAMILY
Ti-ti

Cyrilla racemiflora L.

Perennial woody shrub or small tree with leaning trunk(s), to 25′ (8 m) tall, bark reddish brown. Leaves semievergreen, alternate, oblanceolate, to 4″ (10 cm) long and 1.6″ (4 cm) wide, tapered to short leafstalk (1–6 mm), leathery, lustrous above. Flowers grow densely in slender, fingerlike racemes 2–6″ (5–15 cm) long that angle downward. Petals 5, white, about 0.25″ (3–5 mm) long, stamens shorter than petals.

Ti-ti (pronounced "tie-tie") is a common plant of wetlands and very showy in bloom. It is a constant companion of blackwater canoeists. The reticulate venation of leaves is quite distinctive once learned, although difficult to describe accurately. In fall, many leaves turn bright scarlet or red-orange. In the West Indies, Ti-ti grows to be a canopy tree with trunks 3′ (1 m) in diameter.

Inhabits margins and banks of blackwater rivers and shores of impoundments and beaver ponds; also found in streamheads. Ranges on the Coastal Plain and lower Piedmont from se VA to s FL and e TX; West Indies; Mex., Belize, northern South America.

LATE MAY–JULY

ITEACEAE: SWEETSPIRE FAMILY
Sweetspire; Virginia Willow
Itea virginica L.

RUBIACEAE: MADDER FAMILY
Partridge-berry
Mitchella repens L.

Perennial woody shrub 3–6′ (1–2 m) tall, erect or leaning over water. Leaves are alternate, elliptic or obovate, 1.2–3.6″ (3–9 cm) long and 0.4–1.6″ (1–4 cm) wide, hairless or nearly so, acute, finely toothed, leafstalks up to 0.4″ (10 mm) long. Flowers grow densely in a terminal, cylindrical raceme 2–6″ (5–15 cm) long. Each flower grows on a pubescent, very short stalk to 0.2″ (3.5 mm) long; petals 5, white, about 0.2″ (3.5–4.5 mm) long. Fruits are small, dark brown capsules.

Sweetspire is a handsome shrub of wet habitats, familiar to canoeists, fishermen, gardeners, and horticulturalists. The capsules remain on the inflorescence well into winter. Formerly placed in the saxifrage family (Saxifragaceae), this genus of 27 species is now in its own family; the other 26 species occur in Asia and Africa.

Inhabits riverbanks and streambanks, impoundments, beaver marshes, and cypress-gum swamps. Ranges from s NJ to s IL and se MO south to FL and e TX.

MAY–MID-JUNE

Perennial, the stem prostrate, creeping on ground and rooting at nodes, often covering small patches of ground. Leaves are opposite, dark green, evergreen, ovate to roundish, 0.3–0.8″ (8–20 mm) long, blunt, on very short stalks. Flowers grow in pairs at tips of short, erect branchlets, the bases fused. Corollas are white, tubular with 4 (occasionally 3, 5, or 6) flaring lobes, 0.5–0.75″ (12–18 mm) long, hairy on inner surface, fragrant. The fruits develop into pairs of fused scarlet berries.

Partridge-berry is familiar to many people as a field companion year-round, with its evergreen leaves, small but showy flowers, and intriguing fused fruits. The fruits are edible but have little taste. The genus was named for John Mitchell (1676–1768), Virginia physician; a second species occurs in Japan.

Occurs in moist streamsides, lower slopes of oak-hickory forests, and margins of cypress-gum swamps. Ranges from N.S. to Ont. and MN south to c FL and e TX.

MAY–JUNE

ROSACEAE: ROSE FAMILY

Common Avens

Geum canadense Jacquin

Perennial, stems 1.2–2.5′ (40–80 cm) tall, appressed to spreading white-hairy (varying to glabrate). Basal leaves several, more or less flat on ground, long-stalked, the blade usually 3–5 lobed, often with paler blue-gray markings, margins toothed. Lower stem leaves are similar but much shorter stalked; upper leaves smaller yet, sessile, 3-lobed or unlobed. Flowers grow singly from long stalks, sepals triangular, reflexed, pale green, petals 5, white, each flower about 0.6″ (15 mm) across. Fruits are aggregated into a sphere about 0.6″ (15 mm) wide, with dozens of bristly beaks.

Common Avens is a widespread plant of eastern North America, but in our area it is uncommon due to our generally poor soils. Tiny hooks on the fruit easily catch on animal fur—and on clothing—and so disperse widely.

Inhabits moist slopes of oak-hickory-dogwood forests and margins of cypress-gum swamps; also found in floodplain forests along rivers. Ranges from N.S. to ND south to c GA and e TX.

MAY–JULY

CONVOLVULACEAE: MORNING-GLORY FAMILY

Small White Morning-glory

Ipomoea lacunosa L.

Annual twining vine, sparsely pubescent, climbing on coarse herbs and shrubs, sometimes a short height up small trees or fenceposts. Leaves are alternate, ovate, entire or with 2 basal lobes, 1.6–3.2″ (4–8 cm) long and 1–2.6″ (2.5–6.5 cm) wide, the base cordate (with notch or sinus), tip acuminate. One to 3 flowers grow from leaf axils, corolla more or less bell-shaped, 0.6–0.9″ (1.5–2.3 cm) long, white.

Compared with most other morning-glories, the flowers are surprisingly small; moreover, the flowers usually are not numerous and so make this plant a bit of a challenge to find.

Inhabits moist streamsides, especially where there is an opening such as a road or power line crossing. Ranges from NJ to IL and KS south to FL and e TX.

SEPT.–OCT.

240 NATURAL COMMUNITIES

MALVACEAE: MALLOW FAMILY
Eastern Rose-mallow
Hibiscus moscheutos L. ssp. *moscheutos*

Perennial, with multiple stems rising to 6′ (2 m), stems with branched hairs. Leaves are narrowly to broadly ovate, the blades 3.2–9″ (8–22 cm) long and 1.6–4″ (4–10 cm) wide, rarely with pointed lateral lobes. Leaves are pubescent above, with dense whitish or gray hairs beneath, leafstalk 1.2–6″ (3–15 cm) long, margins toothed. Flowers grow in upper leaf axils from stalks 0.4–2.8″ (1–7 cm) long, white with red center, about 6″ (15 cm) across.

Eastern Rose-mallow has the largest flowers of any of our herbaceous plants and is therefore hard to miss. Like all members of the mallow family, the numerous pollen-bearing stamens are united to form a tube around the female style.

Inhabits nutrient-rich marshes, beaver ponds, impoundments, and river shores. Ranges from MD to IN south to FL and e TX.

JUNE–EARLY SEPT.

THEACEAE: TEA FAMILY
Silky Camellia
Stewartia malacodendron L.

Perennial, woody, tall shrub or small tree, the stem usually single but sometimes multiple, mostly 8–20′ (2.5–6 m) tall, widely branched. Leaves are broadly elliptic, 2–4″ (5–10 cm) long and 1–2″ (2.5–5 cm) wide, tip acute and forming a small "drip-tip," base short-tapered to a stalk 0.2″ (2–4 mm) long, margins with tiny teeth, pubescent beneath. Flowers grow singly from leaf axils, the 5 white petals are obovate, 0.8–1.8″ (2–4.5 cm) long and a bit less wide, the margins irregularly crenate, the purple stamens abundant.

This grand wildflower is known by more gardeners than naturalists and botanists, for it is an uncommon and sparsely distributed species with small populations in the wild. Listed rare in GA. In this same family are tea, various camellias, Loblolly Bay (*Gordonia lasianthus*), and the Franklinia Tree (*Franklinia alatamaha*).

Inhabits moist hardwood or hardwood-pine slopes along streams and rivers. Ranges on the Coastal Plain from se VA to nw FL, e TX, and s AR; also scattered occurrences inland.

MAY–JUNE

STYRACACEAE: STORAX FAMILY
American Snowbell; Storax

Styrax americanus Lamarck var. *americanus*

Perennial woody shrub to about 10′
(3 m) tall, often much shorter. Leaves are
oblanceolate to obovate, 1.2–2.8″ (3–7 cm)
long and 0.4–1.6″ (1–4 cm) wide, short-
stalked, quickly narrowed to a pointed
tip, margins smooth or weakly toothed,
glabrous or glabrate, pale green beneath.
Flowers grow in clusters of 2–4 at leaf
axils, fragrant, the 5 petals white, 0.3–0.5″
(8–12 mm) long. The recurved portion
of each petal is broadly linear, the yellow
stamens prominently exposed.

Flowers of American Snowbell are
generally numerous, making this a showy
plant and one worthy of garden borders.
A second variety, var. *pulverulentus*,
occurs on the lower Coastal Plain south
of our range; its leaves and leafstalks are
densely stellate-pubescent.

Inhabits perennially wet soil of floodplain forests, cypress-gum swamps, beaver
ponds, streamheads, and shorelines of
impoundments. Ranges from s PA to s MO
south to c FL and e TX.

APR.–MAY

APIACEAE: CARROT FAMILY
Spotted Water-hemlock; Spotted Cowbane

Cicuta maculata L.

Perennial from fibrous roots, often also
with small tubers. Stems 2–6.5′ (0.6–2 m)
tall, usually mottled with purple in
the lower third. Leaves are 2 or 3 times
pinnate, the segments lance-shaped to
narrowly elliptic, to 2.8″ (7 cm) long and
1″ (2.5 cm) wide, toothed. The leafstalks
boldly clasp the stem. Flowers grow in
rounded compound umbels from the tip
of the stem and from leaf axils; primary
umbels with 15–30 rays about 1.5″ (3–5 cm)
long, these in turn support numerous secondary rays tipped with tiny flowers. The
5 petals are white, about 3 mm across.

A cousin of Poison Hemlock (*Conium
maculatum*, with which Socrates was put
to death), Spotted Water-hemlock is perhaps equally deadly, especially the tuber-
ous roots. *Warning: All parts of the plant
are poisonous to humans and livestock!*

Inhabits wet streamsides, river shores,
marshes, and wet floodplains. Ranges
from N.S. to AK south to FL and CA; Mex.

LATE MAY–AUG.

APIACEAE: CARROT FAMILY
Mock Bishop's-weed
Ptilimnium capillaceum (Michaux) Rafinesque

Glabrous annual to 2.5′ (80 cm) tall, usually much-branched. Leaves twice pinnate, the main divisions opposite, all divisions threadlike. Flowers grow in flattish-topped umbels at ends of stalks 1.2–3.2″ (3–8 cm) long. Each umbel has finely dissected, leaf-like bracts at the base, from which arise 5–20 secondary stalks 0.25–0.8″ (6–21 mm) long. Each secondary stalk has about 5 short stalklets that terminate in a flower. The 5 petals are white, about 1 mm long and wide.

"Mock" here means "false"; the true Bishop's-weed is a Eurasian relative (*Aegopodium podagraria*) used medicinally and horticulturally. The genus name *Ptilimnium* means "wetland feather," in reference to the finely divided leaves and the plant's habitat.

Inhabits marshy borders of rivers, beaver ponds, and impoundments. Ranges from MA to MO south to FL and TX.

LATE MAY–EARLY AUG.

ADOXACEAE:
VIBURNUM & ELDERBERRY FAMILY
Black Elderberry;
Common Elderberry
Sambucus canadensis L.

Perennial, widely branching shrub, usually colonial, dying back to ground each winter. Leaves are opposite, once or twice pinnately compound. There are 5–11 leaflets in once-compound leaves, each one lanceolate, 2–6″ (5–15 cm) long and 0.8–2.4″ (2–6 cm) wide, tip acuminate, base roundish and almost sessile, margins serrate. Flowers grow terminally and from forks of branches in flat-topped clusters up to 8″ (20 cm) broad. Corollas are white, 5-lobed, 0.25″ (5–7 mm) across. The abundant fruits are juicy berries, deep violet-purple or blackish, 0.2″ (4–6 mm) long.

Elderberries have been used for pies, jams, and wine for centuries by European settlers and as food by Native Americans for thousands of years before that. The stems and foliage have a disagreeable odor that is imparted to the berries; drying the fruit and adding sugar helps immensely. *Unripe berries and other parts of the plant are toxic.* Indians used it to treat cuts and swollen limbs, also as a purgative and laxative.

Inhabits wet soil of riverbanks, marshes, blackwater river floodplains, and roadside ditches. Ranges from N.S. to Man. south to FL and TX; Mex.; West Indies.

LATE APR.–JULY

ADOXACEAE: VIBURNUM & ELDERBERRY FAMILY
Smooth Viburnum; Arrow-wood
Viburnum dentatum L. var. *lucidum* Aiton

Perennial woody shrub, 4–10′ (1.2–3 m) tall, much-branched. Leaves are opposite, with prominent veins, broadly to narrowly ovate, mostly 2–4″ (5–10 cm) long and 1.6–3.2″ (4–8 cm) wide, larger on sprout shoots. The leaf tip is acute, the base more or less heart-shaped, leafstalk 0.4–1.2″ (1–3 cm) long, margins sharply toothed, surfaces glabrate (underside has straight whitish hairs when young, some of these persisting on veins). Flowers grow densely in flat-topped umbels up to 4″ (10 cm) across, the 5 white petals forming a cup-shaped corolla with spreading lobes, 0.2–0.3″ (5–8 mm) across. Fruits are elliptical, about 0.3″ (8–9 mm) long, compressed lengthwise, blue-gray to blackish.

Although a widespread plant, populations in our region are small and easily overlooked. Shoots of young sprouts, and even some branches of adult plants, can be remarkably straight, hence the name Arrow-wood.

Inhabits wet soils of floodplain forests and streambanks. Ranges from N.B. to s Ont. and n OH south to ec GA (Burke County).

LATE MAR.–APR.

PLANTAGINACEAE : PLANTAIN FAMILY
Swamp Hedge-hyssop
Gratiola virginiana L.

Annual or short-lived perennial, stems spreading or sprawling, 4–16″ (10–40 cm) tall, rather succulent, glabrous. Leaves stalkless, oblanceolate to elliptic, 0.8–2″ (2–5 cm) long and 0.3–1″ (7–25 mm) wide, margins smooth or irregularly toothed. Flowers grow singly at leaf bases, on stalks less than 0.25″ (6 mm) long, each flower with 2 leafy bracts at base. Corolla tubular with 5 spreading lobes, 0.4–0.6″ (9–14 mm) long, white, lined with lavender.

Mud Hedge-hyssop (*Gratiola neglecta*) is similar, but flowers are on stalks 0.4″ (10 mm) or more long and are smaller (8–10 mm) and yellow inside; it occurs on shores of rivers and creeks, mostly in brownwater systems.

Inhabits wet depressions in river floodplains (primarily blackwater in our area), cypress-gum swamps, beaver ponds, and wet ditches. Ranges from NJ to IA south to FL and TX.

LATE MAR.–MAY

OLEACEAE: OLIVE FAMILY
Chinese Privet

Ligustrum sinense Loureiro

Perennial woody shrub up to 13′ (4 m), potentially a small tree to 30′ (9 m), twigs densely pubescent. Leaves are opposite, semievergreen, elliptical, up to 2.4″ (6 cm) long and 1″ (2.5 cm) wide, glabrous above, pubescent beneath, blunt-tipped. Leafstalks are up to 0.25″ (1–6 mm) long and pubescent. Flowers grow in terminal, many-branched clusters; the corolla is white, short-tubular, about 0.2″ (1.5–3 mm) long with 4 spreading lobes about same length. Fruits are dull blue-black, elliptical, 0.25″ (6–7 mm) long.

Chinese Privet is one of the worst invasive weeds in the Sandhills and lower Piedmont (others include Japanese Honeysuckle [*Lonicera japonica*] and Japanese Stiltgrass [*Microstegium vimineum*]). It tends to grow in dense thickets that shut out light to the herb layer over large expanses of river and stream floodplains. Birds eagerly consume the fruits and spread seeds widely.

Inhabits streamsides and river floodplains, moist roadsides, yards, disturbed woodlands, and urban and suburban thickets. Ranges from MD to MO south to FL and e TX.

MAY–EARLY JUNE

AMARYLLIDACEAE: AMARYLLIS FAMILY
Atamasco Lily

Zephyranthes atamasca (L.) Herbert

Glabrous perennial from a bulb, stem single or several together, 5–10″ (12–25 cm) tall. Leaves are numerous, ascending, or more or less prostrate, lustrous, linear, 8–16″ (20–40 cm) long and 0.2–0.3″ (3–8 mm) wide, tip acuminate or acute. The single funnel-shaped flower grows atop the stem, pointed upward. The 3 petals and 3 sepals are white (reddish in bud), lanceolate to narrowly elliptic, 2.8–4″ (7–10 cm) long. The 6 stamens are yellow, overtopped by the 3-parted style.

Atamasco Lily is one of our showiest spring flowers, locally carpeting the forest floor white. The generic name means "windflower"; the species name is a Native American word for "west" or "westerly," referring to the spring blooming period when westerly winds predominate. The shiny slender leaves form distinct flattish mats.

Inhabits bottomland hardwoods along brownwater rivers and adjacent clearings, less often along blackwater rivers and streambanks. Ranges from se VA to n FL and s MS.

MID-MAR.–APR.

OLEACEAE: OLIVE FAMILY
Fringetree
Chionanthus virginicus L.

Perennial woody tall shrub or small tree to 20′ (6 m) tall. Leaves are opposite, elliptic or obovate, to 8″ (20 cm) long and 4.8″ (12 cm) wide, acute or blunt-tipped, base tapered to a short stalk, smooth above, smooth to densely pubescent beneath, margins not toothed. Flowers bloom as leaves begin to develop, in small groups from leaf axils of previous year's twigs. The 4 petals are widely spreading or drooping, white, linear, 0.6–1.2″ (1.5–3 cm) long.

Fringetree is one of our most striking plants and puts on a remarkable floral show every spring. No wonder it is widely cultivated as a yard ornamental. Although the petals are slender, the plant makes up for that with an abundance of flowers. Formerly, doctors prescribed tinctures to treat disorders of various internal organs. A second species of *Chionanthus* occurs in eastern Asia.

Inhabits moist riverside slopes (hardwood and hardwood-pine) and oak-hickory forests. Ranges from NJ to WV and S MO south to C FL and E TX.

APR.–MAY

AQUIFOLIACEAE: HOLLY FAMILY
Possum Haw
Ilex decidua Walter

Perennial woody shrub or even a small tree, mostly 5–12′ (1.5–4 m) tall, but known to reach 30′ (9 m), stems often leaning, branches widely spreading. Leaves deciduous, oblanceolate to narrowly obovate, 1–2.8″ (2.5–7 cm) long and 0.3–1.2″ (8–30 mm) wide, glabrous and dull above, densely to sparsely pubescent on midrib beneath, margins crenate. Plants are either male or female (dioecious); female flowers grow from leaf axils, solitary on stalks up to 0.5″ (12 mm), male flowers 1 to several on much shorter stalks. Petals 5, white, mildly fragrant, resembling those of other hollies. Fruit red, lustrous, rounded, about 0.3″ (6–8 mm).

To see Possum Haw best, go canoeing or take a walk along a river trail; it is commonly found along streams. The berries provide food for catbirds, cardinals, waxwings, and other birds. Note that *Viburnum nudum* is also called Possum Haw.

Inhabits stream and river margins and is found well up onto adjacent forested slopes. Ranges from MD to S IN and S MO south to N FL and C TX.

MID-APR.–MID-MAY

AQUIFOLIACEAE: HOLLY FAMILY
Sarvis Holly

Ilex amelanchier M. A. Curtis ex Chapman

Perennial shrub from rhizomes, forming colonies. Stems 5–16′ (1.5–5 m) tall, twigs finely pubescent. Leaves deciduous, broadly elliptical, 1.6–3.5″ (4–9 cm) long and 0.6–1.7″ (1.5–4.5 cm) wide, dull above, downy beneath, margins smooth or finely toothed. Plants are either male or female (dioecious), flowers grow on stalks 0.5″ or more, solitary (3–5 or more if male) from leaf axils. There are 4 petals, white, waxy-textured, 0.25–0.4″ (6–8 mm) across. Fruit pinkish red, rounded, about 0.4″ (8–9 mm).

Sarvis Holly gets it name from the resemblance of its leaves to Sarvis Tree (*Amelanchier arborea*). The flowers are very like those of Large Gallberry (*I. coriacea*); but Sarvis Holly has only 4 petals, and fruits turn a bright cerise color in autumn.

Inhabits margins and sandbars of blackwater rivers, depressions and old stream channels in blackwater floodplains, and seasonally wet Carolina bays. Ranges on the Coastal Plain from se FL to nw FL and w LA.

LATE APR.–MID-MAY

COMMELINACEAE: DAYFLOWER FAMILY
Swamp Dewflower

Murdannia keisak (Hasskarl) Handel-Mazzetti
[*Aneilema keisak* Hasskarl]

Prostrate, colonial, annual aquatic, the stems creeping and rooting at lower nodes, the terminal portions ascending. Leaves are linear to elliptical, 0.8–2.4″ (2–6 cm) long and 0.2–0.5″ (4–12 mm) wide, base sessile, tip acute to short acuminate. Flowers grow singly (sometimes 2–4) from leaf axils, short-stalked, the 3 sepals greenish, the 3 petals pinkish white to purplish white, ovate, about 0.3″ (8 mm) long.

This is an import from Asia that has become an aggressive weed that displaces native plants with dense mats of vegetation. In particularly noxious infestations, it may cover the entire surface of a beaver pond. It should be eradicated wherever possible.

Inhabits river swamp forests in backwaters and side channels; also found in river shores, beaver ponds, and impoundments. Ranges from MD to KY and AR south to FL and LA.

LATE AUG.–OCT.

POLYGONACEAE:
SMARTWEED & BUCKWHEAT FAMILY
Arrowleaf Tearthumb

Persicaria sagittata (L.) Gross ex Nakai
[*Polygonum sagittatum* L.]

Sprawling, widely branched annual, stems
to 6′ (2 m) or longer, 4-angled, beset with
backward-pointing prickles. Each stem
node has a thin-textured collar split down
one side. Leaves are well-spaced, lanceolate to narrowly ovate, 1.2–3.2″ (3–8 cm)
long and 0.4–1.2″ (1–3 cm) wide, glabrous,
the tip acute, the base sagittate (with
2 backward-pointing lobes), leafstalks
0.25–1.2″ (5–30 mm) long. Flowers grow
3–12 in dense hemispherical clusters at
branch tips and on long stalks from leaf
axils. The 5-parted calyx is white to pinkish, 2.5 mm long; petals absent.

Well-named, Arrowleaf Tearthumb
clambers over other vegetation to form
tangles of wickedly prickly branches; don't
go there in short pants! However, like
all members of the genus *Persicaria*, it
produces abundant seeds that are eagerly
eaten by wood ducks and other water
birds.

Inhabits river marshes, beaver ponds,
margins of impoundments, and wet roadside ditches. Ranges from Newf. to Man.
south to FL and TX; also eastern Asia.

LATE MAY–OCT.

POLYGONACEAE:
SMARTWEED & BUCKWHEAT FAMILY
Swamp Smartweed

Persicaria setacea (Baldwin) Small
[*Polygonum setaceum* Baldwin]

Perennial, stems 2.2–5′ (0.7–1.5 m) tall,
slightly swollen at each node, the lowermost portion often trailing and rooting at
nodes. Each leaf node has a thin-textured
collar (in this family termed an ocrea)
with coarse, upward-pointing bristles.
Leaves are lanceolate, 2.4–6″ (6–15 cm)
long and 0.6–1.5″ (1.5–4 cm) wide, smooth
or with spreading hairs, tip acuminate,
base tapered to a very short stalk. Flowers
grow in dense, cylindrical, erect spikes
about 0.8–2.4″ (2–6 cm) long and 0.25″
(5–6 mm) wide. The 5-parted calyx is
white, about 0.2″ (3 mm) long; petals
absent.

This is a fairly robust smartweed, and
its white flower spikes are quite showy.
Slender Water-pepper (*P. opelousana*) is
shorter (1.5–2′), its leaves are less than 0.4″
(1 cm) wide, its lower spikes are shorter
and narrower, and its flowers are off-
white. Look for distinct resin dots on the
calyx.

Inhabits floodplain forests, beaver
wetlands, and margins of impoundments.
Ranges from se MA to s MI south to s FL
and e TX.

LATE JULY–OCT.

ASTERACEAE: ASTER FAMILY
Little Beggar-ticks; Swamp Beggar-ticks

Bidens discoidea (Torrey & Gray) Britton

Annual, stem to 3′ (1 m) tall (occasionally taller), glabrate, widely branched. Leaves are pinnately divided into 3 or 5 lance-shaped segments 0.8–3.6″ (2–9 cm) long, each tapering to a point, margins toothed. Flower heads grow at ends of stem and branches, on short to long stalks. The outer bracts are green, 0.4–1.2″ (1–3 cm) long, narrowly lance-shaped, the inner bracts a third as long. Ray flowers usually are absent; the disc is about 0.25″ (4–7 mm) wide, flowers mostly 15–20, deep yellow. Seeds are flattened, about 0.25″ (4–6.5 mm) long and 1–1.5 mm wide, tipped with 2 awns.

This common but overlooked plant has an ingenious method of living in wetlands with fluctuating water levels: seeds float about and then germinate when they make contact with an emergent log or a stem of a wetland shrub or tree, or when stranded ashore. The fibrous, stringy roots quickly develop and cling to the stem or log, some of them elongating and reaching soil far below.

Inhabits floodplain pools and oxbows, sluggish rivers, and beaver ponds. Ranges from N.S. to MN south to n FL and TX.

SEPT.–NOV.

ASTERACEAE: ASTER FAMILY
Butterweed; Smooth Ragwort

Packera glabella (Poiret) C. Jeffrey
[*Senecio glabellus* Poiret]

Glabrous annual with hollow stems 1–3′ (0.3–1 m) tall, branched in the inflorescence. Leaves are elliptic to oblanceolate, 2–8″ (5–20 cm) long and 0.8–2.8″ (2–7 cm) wide, deeply lobed, the lobes nearly opposite, irregular in shape, and toothed. Lower leaves are the largest and stalked; upper leaves are smaller and sessile. Flower heads grow in terminal branched clusters and from upper leaf axils, the green bracts tipped black. Discs are about 0.2″ (4 mm) broad, the flowers dull yellow; ray flowers are 0.4–0.5″ (10–13 mm) long, yellow. Fruits are dark brown nutlets about 1.5 mm long, with white hairs that soon drop off.

The butter yellow flowers are showy, even in the dark shade of its native swamps. In the Sandhills region, Butterweed is confined to SC and GA.

Inhabits wet spots and back channels of blackwater river bottomlands and cypress-gum swamps; also found in very wet streamheads. Ranges on the Coastal Plain from se NC to s FL and e TX, north in the interior to OH, MO, and SD.

MAR.–EARLY JUNE

ASTERACEAE: ASTER FAMILY
Tall Goldenrod
Solidago altissima L.

Perennial, stems 3–8' (1–2.5 m) tall,
densely downy. Leaves are abundant,
lanceolate, 2.4–6" (6–15 cm) long and
0.4–1.2" (1–3 cm) wide, tip acuminate,
base short-tapered and nearly sessile, margins serrate, roughish pubescent above,
and with 3 prominent veins. Flowers grow
in a large terminal inflorescence up to 1'
(30 cm) long, narrowly to broadly pyramidal, composed of many branches with
leafy bracts basally and a row of flower
heads terminally. Ray flowers are 0.2"
(2–4 m) long, yellow; disc flowers yellow.

With its great height, Tall Goldenrod
is an imposing plant. It is one of the last
plants to bloom in autumn. Late Goldenrod (*S. gigantea*) is very similar, except the
stem is hairless and glaucescent; it occurs
in the same habitats.

Inhabits river marshes, openings in
floodplain forests, margins of beaver
ponds and impoundments, wet meadows,
and roadsides. Ranges from N.S. to Sask.
south to FL and TX; Mex.

SEPT.–OCT.

HYPERICACEAE: ST. JOHN'S-WORT FAMILY
Needle-leaved St. John's-wort
Hypericum nitidum Lamarck

Perennial woody shrub mostly 3–6'
(1–2 m) tall, with many wide-spreading
branches forming a bushy crown, bark
not shreddy. Leaves opposite and sessile,
linear, like a spruce needle, 0.6–1" (15–25
mm) long and less than 2 mm wide, acute.
Some leaves also have a few small leaves
in axils. Flowers are numerous, growing in
clusters at 3–7 nodes at ends of branches,
petals 5, yellow, about 0.25" (5–7 mm)
long, stamens very numerous. Capsules
brown, dry, ovate with acuminate tip
(formed by the persistent styles).

Peelbark St. John's-wort (*H. fasciculatum*) is extremely similar, but flower clusters grow at only 1–3 nodes, leaves have
many more axillary leaves, older stem
bark peels away to reveal cinnamon inner
bark, and it grows in static (not moving)
water.

Inhabits shores, banks, and swamps of
blackwater rivers and streams. Ranges on
the Coastal Plain from n SC to c FL and
s AL. Known in our area from Darlington,
Kershaw, Lexington, and Richland Counties, SC; Macon County, GA.

JUNE–AUG.

HYPERICACEAE: ST. JOHN'S-WORT FAMILY
Streamside St. John's-wort
Hypericum nudiflorum Michaux ex Willdenow

Perennial semiwoody shrub with relatively few, spreading branches, 1.5–5′
(0.5–1.5 m) tall, stems and branches with
narrow wings. Leaves are opposite and
sessile, elliptic or broadly lanceolate,
0.8–3.2″ (2–8 cm) long and 0.2–1.2″ (0.5–3
cm) wide, blunt-tipped, base rounded to
short-tapered. Flowers grow in terminal
branched clusters, petals 5, yellow, 0.3″
(6–8 mm) long, stamens numerous. Capsule dry, ovoid, 0.25″ (4.5–6 mm) long and
a bit narrower.

Go canoeing to see this plant at its best,
as it is most often seen on riverbanks and
streambanks. The species name means
"naked flower," in reference to the very
small leaves in the inflorescences, unlike
most other St. John's-worts.

Inhabits riverbanks and streambanks
and cypress-gum swamps. Ranges in the
Piedmont and Coastal Plain from se VA
to nw FL, e TX, and AR; also Cumberland
Plateau of KY and TN.

JUNE–JULY

LINACEAE: FLAX FAMILY
Wetland Flax
Linum striatum Walter

Slender, glabrous perennial, stems single
or several together, 1–3′ (30–90 cm) tall,
with lengthwise striations or low ridges.
Leaves are numerous, opposite up to
midstem and alternate above, narrowly
elliptic, 0.4–1.2″ (10–30 mm) long and
0.2–0.4″ (3–10 mm) wide, tip blunt. Flowers grow along ascending to spreading
branches, one or more in bloom at a time
per branch, flower stalks 2–3 mm long.
The 5 petals are pale yellow, obovate, 0.2″
(3–5 mm) long. Fruit is a capsule, oval
in outline, 3 mm long, green with a very
short-pointed tip.

Wetland Flax differs from our other
flaxes in its habitat preference, its mostly
opposite leaves, and the larger size of the
leaves. Flaxes have interesting fruits: if you
slice one open, you'll notice the seeds are
shaped just like the sections of an orange.

Inhabits stream and river shores,
riverside marshes, beaver ponds and
impoundments, and wet roadside ditches.
Ranges from MA to s MI and se MO south
to nw FL and e TX.

MID-JUNE–EARLY OCT.

RANUNCULACEAE: BUTTERCUP FAMILY
Low Spearwort
Ranunculus pusillus Poiret

Annual, glabrous or glabrate. The stem grows up to 1.5′ (44 cm) long, the lower portion sometimes reclining, the upper portion ascending and with few to several branches. Leaves are lanceolate to oval, short-tapered to both ends, long-stalked, margins entire, wavy, or irregularly toothed; upper leaves are narrower and sessile. Flowers grow singly on long stalks from leaf axils, sepals 5, petals 1–3 (occasionally 5), pale yellow, less than 0.2″ (1–2 mm) long.

The tiny flowers help to make this plant inconspicuous, but as if to compensate, it can grow in large colonies. Plants often get coated by muddy deposits during flood events.

Inhabits shores, marshy borders, and backup channels of rivers and cypress-gum swamps. Ranges from s NY to MO south to FL and TX.

LATE APR.–MID-JUNE

RANUNCULACEAE: BUTTERCUP FAMILY
Hooked Buttercup
Ranunculus recurvatus Poiret

Perennial from a slightly swollen base, the stems short pilose, up to 2′ (60 cm) tall, branched only in upper portion. Leaves are ovate to rounded in outline, long-stalked, deeply 3-lobed; the lateral lobes also are usually cut or cleft, margins toothed, blades and stalks pilose. Flowers grow singly on short stalks from leaf axils, sepals 5, bent backward and longer than petals. The 5 petals are pale yellow, 0.2″ (2–4 mm) long, their stalks elongating in fruit.

Maybe it is the locations where this plant grows—moist hardwood forests, usually near creeks and associated with spring wildflowers—but I have pleasant memories of it. The small flowers are usually numerous enough to make this plant conspicuous. Other species of buttercups occur in our area but normally grow in nutrient-rich soil of brownwater rivers or are alien weeds.

Inhabits moist soil of streamsides, riverside slopes, and seeps. Ranges from s Que. to MN south to s GA and OK.

APR.–EARLY JUNE

XYRIDACEAE: YELLOW-EYED-GRASS FAMILY
Flatstem Yellow-eyed-grass
Xyris difformis Chapman

Perennial, stem single or a few together, mostly 12–20″ (30–50 cm) tall, flattened upward, narrowly winged. Leaves are all basal, 2-ranked and often fanlike, linear, flattened, 8–18″ (20–45 cm) long and 0.2–0.6″ (4–14 mm) wide, surfaces smooth, margins smooth to papillate (minutely bumpy). Flowers grow 1–2 at a time from an elliptical or ovoid, conelike head at tip of stem, the head about 0.4–0.6″ (10–15 mm) long and composed of overlapping brown scales. The 3 petals are yellow, obovate or obtriangular, about 0.2″ (4 mm) long, opening in midmorning.

Despite its broad habitat tolerance elsewhere, Flatstem Yellow-eyed-grass in the Sandhills region prefers blackwater stream and river shores and so usually does not occur with other *Xyris*. It was named by Alvan W. Chapman (1809–99), prolific botanist and explorer and author of three editions of *Flora of the Southern United States.*

Inhabits sandy or peaty shores of blackwater streams and rivers; sometimes found in gravel pits and wet roadsides. Ranges from N.S. to s Ont. and wi south to FL and TX.

AUG.–EARLY OCT.

COLCHICACEAE:
MEADOW-SAFFRON & BELLWORT FAMILY
Wild Oats; Straw Lily
Uvularia sessilifolia L.

Glabrous perennial, forming colonies via long stolons just beneath the soil surface, stems 4–18″ (10–45 cm) tall, usually with 1 branch. Leaves are pale green or glaucescent green, elliptic or ovate, mostly 1.6–2.8″ (4–7 cm) long and 0.8–1.25″ (2–3 cm) wide, tip acute, base sessile, margins smooth, surfaces dull. The solitary flower grows from an upper leaf axil, drooping; the 3 sepals and 3 petals are alike, straw-yellow, lanceolate, 0.7–1″ (1.7–2.5 cm) long, acute.

The drooping, straw-colored flowers have a fanciful resemblance to oats, which is a grass and totally unrelated. Early New England colonists ate young shoots like asparagus and also ate the roots. Native Americans made root tea to treat diarrhea and to heal broken bones.

Inhabits moist upper portions of river and stream floodplains. Ranges from N.S. to ND south to nw FL and n LA.

LATE MAR.–APR.

APOCYNACEAE:
DOGBANE & MILKWEED FAMILY
Climbing Dogbane
Trachelospermum difforme (Walter) Gray

Perennial, glabrous, slender twining vine, potentially to 20′ (6 m) or longer. Stems are purplish, the basal portion woody, the rest supple. Leaves are opposite or subopposite, more or less sessile, variable in shape from narrowly lanceolate to broadly obovate, 1.6–3.6″ (4–9 cm) long and 0.4–2.4″ (1–6 cm) wide, tip short-acuminate, margins entire. Flowers grow in branched clusters on a stalk from the leaf axils. The 5 petals are 0.3–0.4″ (7–11 mm) long, forming a tube with spreading lobes, straw-yellow to greenish yellow. The fruit is a slender pod 4–8″ (10–20 cm) long and 2 mm wide, twisting as it dries and releasing seeds that have silky hairs like a "parachute."

Unlike most members of this family, Climbing Dogbane lacks milky white juice. Young plants can be quite common in moist forests and present an identification challenge; they are erect and have 1 to several pairs of leaves. If the plants you see show a wide variation in leaf width and shape, then almost certainly you have Climbing Dogbane. There are 19 other species of this genus in Asia; this is the only one in North America.

Inhabits moist soil of floodplain forests, cypress-gum swamps, streamside slopes, and open marshes. Ranges from DE to IN and MO south to n FL and e TX.

MAY–JULY

SMILACACEAE: GREENBRIER FAMILY
Greenbrier; Horsebrier
Smilax rotundifolia L.

Perennial, tough-stemmed vine from long, tough, whitish underground runners, often forming dense colonies, climbing or scrambling via curly tendrils. Stems are green throughout, moderately prickly with broad-based prickles to 0.3″ (8 mm) long, the prickles green tipped with brown or black. Leaves are tardily deciduous, round to ovate, thickish-textured, tip acute, margins smooth (rarely minutely prickly), short-stalked. Flowers grow in small umbels from a few leaf axils, the 3 sepals and 3 petals alike, 0.25″ (5–6 mm) long, yellowish green. Fruits are berries, black, glaucescent, 0.2–0.3″ (5–8 mm) in diameter.

The propensity of Greenbrier to form impenetrable thickets or "brier patches" is immortalized in the Uncle Remus tale of Br'er Rabbit. Catbrier (*S. bona-nox*) has similar leaves but always has some that are narrower and with 2 roundish lobes at base (hastate shape); its leaf margins are prickly, and its stems have a granular or grainy surface.

Inhabits moist soil of river floodplains, vernal pools, shrubby streamheads, riverside slopes, seepage slopes, streamhead margins, pine flatwoods, and oak-hickory woods. Ranges from N.S. to s Ont. south to s FL and e TX.

LATE APR.–MAY

SMILACACEAE: GREENBRIER FAMILY
Jackson-brier
Smilax smallii Morong

Perennial, robust, high-climbing or scrambling vine from large rhizomes, climbing via curly tendrils. Lower parts of stem are brownish, up to 0.8″ (2 cm) thick, with scattered prickles to 0.4″ (1 cm) long, the upper parts greenish, with sparse prickles 0.2″ (3–4 mm) long, widely branched. Leaves are numerous, evergreen, narrowly to broadly elliptical, relatively thin-textured, tip acute, margins smooth, short-stalked. Flowers grow in small umbels from leaf axils, the 3 sepals and 3 petals alike, 0.25″ (5–6 mm) long, pale green or yellowish. Fruits are rather hard berries, brownish red, blackish red, or black, 0.25″ (5–7 mm) in diameter.

Jackson-brier is widely planted in the South as a yard or porch ornament. Its wide-spreading branches and dense foliage provide a measure of welcome shade. I have not been able to learn how it got its common name—which Jackson does it commemorate?

Inhabits wet soil of floodplain forests; commonly planted and adventive to roadside thickets, backyards, and urban lots. Ranges on the Coastal Plain from se VA to c FL, e TX, se OK, and s AR.

JUNE–JULY

VITACEAE: GRAPE FAMILY
Virginia Creeper
Parthenocissus quinquefolia (L.) Planchon

Perennial climbing or sprawling vine from a semiwoody rootstock, clinging via adhesive discs on tendrils. Leaves are palmately compound (handlike) on long stalks, with 5 (–7) oblanceolate or elliptic leaflets to 6″ (15 cm) long and 2.4″ (6 cm) wide. The leaflets are glabrate, pale beneath, margins toothed, tip acuminate, the base tapering to a very short stalk. Flowers grow in branched clusters opposite the leaves, the 5 petals about 0.2″ (2–3 mm) long, yellow-green.

Not only does Virginia Creeper have wonderful form, but this twining vine can transform an old tree snag or porch post into an art object. Moreover, its foliage turns brilliant red in the fall. However, be advised that *some people get dermatitis from the foliage, and the berries are reputed to be toxic.*

Inhabits mixed hardwood-pine slopes along streams and rivers, and oak-hickory woodlands; also found in roadside thickets and backyards. Ranges from ME to IA south to FL and TX.

MAY–JULY

ANACARDIACEAE:
CASHEW & SUMAC FAMILY
Poison Ivy

Toxicodendron radicans (L.) Kuntze
 var. *radicans*
[*Rhus radicans* L.]

Perennial high-climbing vine, climbing via slender rootlets. Stems grow to 65′ (20 m) long (often half that), the lower portion shaggy with reddish brown rootlets. The numerous leaves are divided into 3 leaflets. Each leaflet is ovate, mostly 2–6″ (5–15 cm) long, shiny and glabrous above, pubescent on veins beneath, tip acute to acuminate, margins with 1 to several (rarely 0) large teeth. Flowers grow in slender, elongate, spreading clusters from leaf axils, the 4–5 sepals and petals greenish yellow.

Poisonous! This plant causes dermatitis in most people, and people can also get a rash from pet fur that has been in contact with plant juices, as well as smoke from burning vines. Poison Ivy is a common plant, so people need to learn to identify it. Avoid grasping a tree trunk without first looking for a Poison Ivy vine. Leaves turn bright red or orange in fall; birds eat the fruits.

Inhabits moist to wet soils of floodplain forests, cypress-gum swamps, and wooded slopes; also found in moist soils of suburban woodlots and yards. Ranges on the Coastal Plain and Piedmont from N.S. to s FL and e TX; inland to PA, KY, AR.

LATE APR.–MAY

CARYOPHYLLACEAE:
PINK & SANDWORT FAMILY
Fringed Campion

Silene catesbaei Walter

Perennial, forming mats by rooting at nodes of runners, stems erect, to 10″ (25 cm) tall, with long soft hairs. Basal leaves form evergreen rosettes. Stem leaves are opposite, spatulate, 1–4″ (2.5–10 cm) long, tip blunt to acute, tapered to a short stalk or sessile, the margins pubescent. Flowers grow in terminal clusters, the 5 petals about 1″ (2.5 cm) long, pink, tip broader than base and deeply fringed.

Fringed Campion is a federally endangered species found primarily in our region. The intricately fringed petals are a unique feature in eastern U.S. *Silene* and render this plant unmistakable. Endangered in GA; threats include invasive Japanese Honeysuckle (*Lonicera japonica*) and overgrazing by deer.

Inhabits lower parts of hardwood slopes and moist stream terraces. Occurs in a 7-county area of c and wc GA (Twiggs to Talbot Counties); also in sw GA–nw FL.

MID-MAR.–MAY

ASTERACEAE: ASTER FAMILY
Three-nerved Joe-Pye-weed
Eutrochium dubium (Willdenow ex Poiret)
   E. E. Lamont
[*Eupatorium dubium* Willdenow ex Poiret]

Perennial, 1.5–5′ (0.45–1.8 m) tall (occasionally taller), stems purple-spotted, glabrate, solid. Leaves grow in whorls of 3–4, ovate to broadly lanceolate, 3–7″ (5–17 cm) long and 1.25–3.5″ (3–8.5 cm) wide, tip pointed, margins serrate. Note the distinctly 3-veined leaves, the numerous resin dots beneath, and the rugose leaf texture in sunny locations (much less rugose in shade). The inflorescence is convex, 3–12″ (7.5–30 cm) wide, disc flowers dull rosy pink, rays absent.

Joe Pye was a Native American medicine man in southeastern Massachusetts who used this plant to cure many ailments. Hollow Joe-Pye-weed (*E. fistulosum* (Barratt) E. E. Lamont) is much taller (to 10′), its leaves are much longer and occur in whorls of 4–7, the inflorescence is much larger, and the stems are hollow; it grows along streams and in swamps and wet ditches. Both species attract many butterflies.

Inhabits marshes, beaver ponds, cypress-gum swamp openings, and roadside ditches. Ranges mostly on the Coastal Plain from s N.S. to e GA.

JULY–MID-OCT.

ASTERACEAE: ASTER FAMILY
Leafy Elephant's-foot; Riverside Elephant's-foot
Elephantopus carolinianus Raeuschel

Perennial, stem 1 or sometimes 2–3, 8–27″ (20–70 cm) tall, branched above, with short to long hairs. Basal leaves usually absent; stem leaves elliptic to ovate, 4–10″ (10–25 cm) long and 1.6–4″ (4–10 cm) wide, tip acute, base tapered. Flowers grow in heads about 0.5″ (12 mm) across, each head with 3 leafy bracts at base, disc flowers pink to pale purple, rays absent.

All elephant's-foots are recognized by the set of 3 prominent leafy bracts beneath the flower heads. This species is notable among elephant's-foots for its lack of basal leaves.

Inhabits river floodplain forests and river shores and islands and is found along tributaries. Ranges from NJ to KS south to FL and TX.

AUG.–OCT.

LAMIACEAE: MINT FAMILY
Carolina Birds-in-a-Nest; Carolina Bogmint

Macbridea caroliniana (Walter) Blake

Perennial, usually colonial from the elongate rhizomes. Stems are 4-angled, normally 20–28″ (50–70 cm) tall, branched or not, erect or reclining (in which case it roots at stem nodes). Leaves are opposite, 2.4–5″ (6–13 cm) long and 0.6–1.2″ (1.5–3 cm) wide, margins bluntly toothed or smooth, surfaces with resin dots. The lower leaves are short-stalked; the upper, sessile. Flowers grow in terminal clusters of thick-textured bracts, generally one flower opening at a time from each subcluster. The corolla is 2-lipped, 1.2–1.6″ (3–4 cm) long, ranging from dark to pale pink with white stripes, the upper lip forming a hood over the stamens and style.

This beautiful but seldom seen plant gets its common name from the aspect of the flowers—like bird chicks peering out of a nest. To see it you must brave the hottest days of summer in swampy forests. The genus was named for Dr. James Macbride, late eighteenth- to early nineteenth-century doctor and naturalist of Charleston, SC. It is rare in NC, SC, and GA.

Inhabits blackwater swamps, especially their margins and where not frequently flooded; also found in roadsides and openings in wetlands. Ranges from SE NC to WC GA and S GA.

MID-JULY–MID-AUG.

POLYGONACEAE: SMARTWEED & BUCKWHEAT FAMILY
Longbristle Smartweed

Persicaria longiseta (de Bruijn) Kitagawa
[*Polygonum cespitosum* Blume var. *longisetum* (de Bruijn) Stewart]

Sprawling to erect annual, the stems widely branched, up to 2′ (0.7 m) long but often much shorter, slightly swollen at each node, glabrous. Each leaf node has a thin-textured collar with upward-pointing bristles 0.25–0.4″ (5–10 mm) long. Leaves are lanceolate to narrowly ovate, 0.8–2.8″ (2–7 cm) long and 0.4–1.2″ (1–3 cm) wide, glabrate, tapering to a blunt tip, the base tapered to a very short stalk. Flowers grow in dense, slender spikes about 0.4–1.2″ (1–3 cm) long, the calyx 5-parted, reddish pink, 2 mm long; petals absent.

Introduced from Asia during the twentieth century, Longbristle Smartweed has spread widely in the eastern United States and is becoming an invasive weed. Lady's Thumb (*P. maculosa*) is similar but larger in all dimensions; its stems range up to 2.5′ (80 cm), bristles on the node collars are only 2 mm long, and it avoids floodplain forests. Pennsylvania Smartweed or Pinkweed (*P. pensylvanica*) is usually 2–6′ (0.7–2 m) tall, with thick, dense spikes of pink flowers, and lacks bristles on the leaf node collars.

Inhabits floodplain forests, blackwater river shores, cypress-gum swamps, and wet roadside ditches. Ranges from NB to MN south to FL and TX.

LATE MAY–OCT.

BIGNONIACEAE: BIGNONIA FAMILY

Crossvine

Bignonia capreolata L.

Perennial woody vine, climbing to 80′ (25 m) or more. Leaves are opposite, composed of 2 pairs of ovate to elliptical leaflets with a terminal, 3-parted tendril. Leaf blades are 2.4–6″ (6–15 cm) long and 0.8–2.8″ (2–7 cm) wide, often persisting through winter. Two to 5 flowers grow from each leaf axil, broadly tubular with spreading lobes, 1.6–2″ (4–5 cm) long, dull red or maroon outside, yellow or dull red inside. The fruit is a dry capsule, flattened, to 6″ (15 cm) long and 1″ (2.5 cm) wide.

No other plant is quite like Crossvine (it is the sole member of its genus), with its paired leaflets marching up tree trunks via clinging tendrils. Cut a stem and you will see a cross-shaped pattern. Ruby-throated Hummingbirds eagerly sip nectar from Crossvine after their migration from Central American wintering areas.

Inhabits blackwater river floodplain forests, cypress-gum swamps; also found in drier soils of forests on riverside slopes. Ranges from MD to s OH and s MO south to c FL and e TX.

APR.–MAY

BIGNONIACEAE: BIGNONIA FAMILY

Trumpet-creeper; Trumpet-vine

Campsis radicans (L.) Seemann ex Bureau

Perennial woody vine, climbing to 80′ (25 m) or more via aerial roots, bark straw-colored and shreddy. Leaves are opposite, pinnate, divided into 7–15 leaflets. Each leaflet is ovate, 1.2–2.8″ (3–7 cm) long and 0.4–1.4″ (1–3.5 cm) wide, coarsely toothed. Flowers grow in terminal clusters with flowers radiating outward, long-tubular with spreading lobes, 2.5–3.25″ (6–8 cm) long, red or red-orange. Fruit a dry tubular pod, 4–7″ (10–18 cm) long and about 1″ (2–3 cm) wide.

Ruby-throated Hummingbirds switch to Trumpet-vine as Crossvine finishes blooming. Our species is popular in cultivation and has become established far removed from its original range. A second species occurs in east Asia.

Inhabits river floodplain forests, cypress-gum swamps, and drier soils on riverside slopes; garden escapes occur on roadsides. Ranges from NJ to IA south to c FL and e TX, spreading from cultivation elsewhere.

JUNE–JULY

SAPINDACEAE:
BUCKEYE & MAPLE FAMILY

Red Buckeye

Aesculus pavia L. var. *pavia*

Woody shrub or occasionally a small tree, 3–13′ (1–4 m) tall, usually with a single stem. Leaves are opposite, long-stalked, palmately divided (spread like a hand) into 5–7 leaflets. Each leaflet is 3–7.5″ (7.5–17 cm) long and 1.2–2.4″ (3–6 cm) wide, wider toward tip. Flowers grow in terminal clusters longer than wide. The tubular calyx is scarlet, 0.6–0.7″ (14–18 mm) long, petals scarlet, projecting beyond the calyx and somewhat spreading. The stamens conspicuously protrude beyond the petals.

Red Buckeye is a beautiful plant in flower and in autumn when leaves turn yellow-orange. It is an important nectar plant for Ruby-throated Hummingbirds. Painted Buckeye (*A. sylvatica* Bartram), a sister species of the Piedmont, may be found in rich woods along brownwater rivers; it differs in its greenish yellow to dull red calyx and petals, its shorter calyx 0.4–0.5″ (10–13 mm), and stamens that are shorter (to barely longer) than the petals.

Inhabits swamp forests of blackwater rivers, openings, and roadsides, especially in calcareous or marly soil. Ranges from se NC to n FL and west to e TX, up the Mississippi Embayment to se MO and s IL. It does not occur in the Sandhills of NC.

LATE MAR.–MID-MAY

CAMPANULACEAE:
BELLFLOWER & LOBELIA FAMILY

Cardinal Flower

Lobelia cardinalis L.

Perennial, stem erect, usually unbranched, pubescent or glabrate, mostly 1.5–6′ (0.5–2 m) tall. Leaves are elliptical to lanceolate, 2–8″ (5–20 cm) long and 0.8–2″ (2–5 cm) wide, tapered to base, the tip acute, margins toothed or crenate, leafstalks to 1.2″ (3 cm) long. Flowers grow in a dense raceme of several to many flowers, each flower on a bristly stalk 0.25–0.5″ (5–10 mm) long. The corolla is an intense crimson or deep red, 1.2–1.7″ (3–4.5 cm) long, short-tubular with 2 long flaring lobes above and 3 below forming a lip. The anthers are united into an erect tube about as long as upper flower lobes and curved at tip.

Cardinal Flower is one of North America's most spectacular wildflowers; several color variations have been developed horticulturally. To enjoy it in our area, go canoeing or check roadside river crossings. Ruby-throated Hummingbirds are the main pollinators, sipping the sugar-rich nectar as they migrate south. Indians used root and leaf teas to treat stomachaches, syphilis, and fevers.

Inhabits shores and banks of rivers, river floodplains, and cypress-gum swamps. Ranges from N.B. to MN south to n FL and e TX.

LATE JULY–LATE SEPT.

FABACEAE: PEA & BEAN FAMILY
Groundnut; Indian Potato
Apios americana Medikus

Perennial, twining, herbaceous vine to 10′ (3 m) long, dying back to ground in winter. Leaves are produced at intervals, pinnately divided into 5–7 ovate to narrowly ovate, short-stalked leaflets, each 1.2–2.7″ (3–7 cm) long. Flowers grow in stalked clusters from leaf axils, each cluster 2–6″ (5–15 cm) long, ranging from a few to many flowers. Each flower is 0.5″ (13 mm) across, the banner dull pinkish externally, pale purple-brown internally and on the keel. The wing petals are maroon.

Groundnut is named for its small but numerous and nutritious fleshy tubers, which were gathered by Native Americans and early settlers. Eaten raw or roasted, Groundnut has 3 times the protein of potatoes.

Inhabits margins of streams and rivers (especially at treefalls and openings), marshes, and beaver ponds. Ranges from N.S. to MN and SD south to FL and TX.

JUNE–AUG.

RANUNCULACEAE: BUTTERCUP FAMILY
Leatherflower; Marsh Clematis
Clematis crispa L.

Perennial herbaceous climbing vine, sometimes merely clambering over adjacent herbs, stems many-angled, glabrous. Leaves are pinnately compound, on stalks 0.4–2.5″ (1–6 cm) long, divided into 3–5 leaflets. Each leaflet is stalked, variable in shape and size but normally ovate, 1.25–3.6″ (3–9 cm) long and 0.4–1.6″ (1–4 cm) wide, margins toothless. Flowers are terminal, single, nodding, the showy sepals lavender or bluish, 1–2″ (2.5–5 cm) long, spreading to more or less recurved, long-pointed, margins crinkled; petals absent.

The flower is exquisite in its form and color. Typical of most clematis species, the fruits have long, silky-feathery styles that aid in dispersal by catching onto mammal fur or floating down a stream.

Inhabits streamside and riverside forests and shrubby thickets, river terraces, and edges of marshes and beaver ponds. Ranges from se VA to n FL and e TX, north to s IL; mostly on the Coastal Plain but scattered inland.

LATE APR.–JULY

FABACEAE: PEA & BEAN FAMILY
American Wisteria
Wisteria frutescens (L.) Poiret

Low- to high-climbing woody vine up to 48′ (15 m) long, but usually less than half that, the bark pale gray, young branches pubescent. Leaves are 4–12″ (10–30 cm) long, divided into 9–15 opposite leaflets. Each leaflet is 0.8–2.4″ (2–6 cm) long, glabrate above, has appressed hairs beneath, is broadly lanceolate to elliptic, tip acuminate, base contracted to a short stalk. Flowers grow in dense clusters 1.6–5″ (4–12 cm) long, each flower on a stalk 0.25″ (4–6 mm) long. Flowers are pea-shaped, the petals blue-violet to lavender, 0.6–0.8″ (1.5–2 cm) long, the standard erect. The pod is 2–4″ (5–10 cm) long and about 0.5″ (12 mm) wide, tan, glabrous.

Many people are unaware that we have a native (and beautiful!) wisteria; look for it when you go canoeing in late spring. Chinese Wisteria (*W. sinensis*) is larger in all respects and has densely pubescent pods; it is an aggressive and destructive weed—its weight and constricting stems can topple adult trees. It has been widely planted in urban and suburban areas.

Inhabits margins of blackwater rivers and streams and is often found at bridge crossings and other openings, as well as upslope into streamheads. Ranges on the Coastal Plain from se VA to n FL and LA.

APR.–MAY

APOCYNACEAE:
DOGBANE & MILKWEED FAMILY
Eastern Bluestar
Amsonia tabernaemontana Walter

Perennial from a thick rootstock, plant with milky sap. Stems single or several together, 1–2′ (30–70 cm) tall, glabrous, weakly branched or unbranched. Leaves are alternate, lance-shaped to ovate, up to 4.5″ (11 cm) long and 2″ (5 cm) wide. Flowers grow in a terminal cluster, pale blue, each forming a slender tube with 5 spreading lobes. Flowers are about 0.8″ (2 cm) across and star-shaped. Fruits are paired slender pods 2–4″ (5–10 cm) long.

The genus is named for Charles Amson, eighteenth-century Virginia physician. The specific epithet refers to Jacob Bergzabern, sixteenth-century German physician and herbalist, who Latinized his name to Jacobus Tabernaemontanus.

Inhabits moist riverbanks and adjacent mesic slopes, in our area only in higher-nutrient soils. Ranges from s VA to s IL and e KS south to nw FL and e TX.

APR.–EARLY MAY

ASTERACEAE: ASTER FAMILY
Mistflower; Ageratum

Conoclinium coelestinum (L.) DC.
[*Eupatorium coelestinum* L.]

Hairy perennial, colonial via slender rhizomes, stems 1–3′ (0.3–1 m) tall. Leaves are opposite, petioles up to 1″ (2.5 cm) long. Leaf blades are ovate to narrowly ovate, 1.75–3.5″ (4.5–9 cm) long and 0.8–2.3″ (2–6 cm) wide, margins with blunt teeth, lower surface with yellow resin dots. Numerous flowers occur in a terminal, dome-shaped cluster, disc flowers pale blue or lavender-blue, rays absent.

Mistflower is a plant whose original habitat is not known with certainty but was probably associated with river floodplains; today we find it almost always in disturbed places. It has long been in the horticultural trade.

Inhabits wet roadsides and margins of bottomlands and swamps; found at stream crossings and in wet meadows. Ranges mostly on the Coastal Plain and lower Piedmont from NJ to FL and TX; inland records may be from escaped garden plants.

LATE JULY–MID-OCT.

CAMPANULACEAE:
BELLFLOWER & LOBELIA FAMILY
Streamside Lobelia

Lobelia elongata Small

Perennial, stem erect, unbranched, smooth or somewhat pubescent basally, mostly 1.5–4′ (50–120 cm) tall. Leaves are well-spaced, elliptical to lanceolate, 1.2–6″ (3–15 cm) long and mostly 0.4–1.2″ (1–3 cm) wide, tapered to the base, tip acute, margins smooth or with tiny knoblike teeth, upper leaves smallest. Flowers grow in a one-sided, dense raceme of up to 40 flowers (seldom fewer than 10), each flower on a stalk 0.25″ (3–6 mm) long. The stalks and the calyx tube are hairless, subtended by a slender leaflike bract with knoblike teeth on the margins. The corolla is blue, 0.8–1″ (2–2.5 cm) long, tubular with 2 flaring lobes above and 3 below forming a lip, base of lip without hairs.

With its long wand of blue flowers, Streamside Lobelia is a striking and showy plant. From Savanna Lobelia (*L. glandulosa*) and Sandhills Lobelia (undescribed), it can be distinguished by the denser raceme, the much wider leaves, the longer calyx lobes, and its habitat.

Inhabits shores of streams and small rivers and wet roadside ditches at stream crossings. Ranges on the Coastal Plain from s DE to se GA, inland in NC and SC to the lower Piedmont.

LATE AUG.–EARLY OCT.

PHRYMACEAE: LOPSEED FAMILY
Winged Monkey-flower
Mimulus alatus Aiton

Glabrous perennial, stem 2–3.5′ (0.7–
1.2 m), rather succulent, narrowly winged
lengthwise on all 4 angles. Leaves are
opposite, lanceolate to narrowly elliptic,
2.4–5″ (6–13 cm) long and 1.2–2″ (3–5
cm) wide, tip acuminate, base tapered to
a short stalk. Flowers grow singly from
axils of upper leaves on stalks less than
0.75″ (15 mm) long. The 5 petals form an
upper and a lower lip, lavender-blue with
a yellow throat.

 Winged Monkey-flower belongs to a
large genus, several dozen of which occur
in western North America; only a few
occur east of the Mississippi. *Mimulus* is
the diminutive of "mime" or "mimic," in
reference to the facelike patterns on some
of the western species. Several of the more
striking species are in cultivation.

 Inhabits river shores, marshes, and
beaver wetlands, in relatively nutrient-rich
soils. Ranges from c MA to s IA south to
nw FL and e TX.

JULY–OCT.

IRIDACEAE: IRIS FAMILY
Stout Blue-eyed-grass
Sisyrinchium angustifolium P. Miller

Glabrous perennial, stems several to
many in a clump, 8–20″ (20–50 cm) tall,
0.2–0.25″ (2.5–5.5 mm) wide, broadly
winged, branched 1–2 times, bases with
few or no fibrous remains of previous
years' leaves. Leaves are basal only, erect,
grasslike, about as long and wide as the
stems, acuminate. One or a few flowers
grow terminally in a single cluster that
is partly enclosed by 2 spathelike bracts
0.7–1.5″ (1.8–3.8 cm) long. The 3 sepals
and 3 petals are alike, blue with a yellow
base, 0.3–0.5″ (8–12 mm) long, each with
a tiny point at the tip.

 Blue-eyed-grasses (genus *Sisyrinchium*)
are not grasses but members of the iris
family; unlike irises (genus *Iris*), the sepals
and petals are alike. Most plants of Stout
Blue-eyed-grass are multistemmed and are
showy when in bloom. Atlantic Blue-eyed-
grass (*S. atlanticum*) differs in its narrower
leaves and stems (2 mm or less wide) and
drier habitat.

 Inhabits streambanks and river shores,
river floodplains, open streamhead margins, and wet roadsides. Ranges from N.S.
to s Ont. south to n FL and s TX.

LATE MAR.–LATE MAY

CELASTRACEAE:
BITTERSWEET & EUONYMUS FAMILY

Heart's-a-Bustin';
Strawberry-bush

Euonymus americanus L.

Perennial shrub 2–6′ (0.6–2 m) tall, with few (often just one) stems, stems green. Leaves lance-shaped to ovate, 1.2–3.6″ (3–9 cm) long and 0.4–1.2″ (1–3 cm) wide, short-stalked, tapered to tip, margins crenate. Flowers 1–3, terminal or from axils of upper leaves, about 0.5″ (10–12 mm) wide, petals 5, yellowish green, ovate. Fruit is a capsule covered with dull, reddish pink bumps; it splits open to reveal the deep orange or scarlet seeds.

Heart's-a-Bustin' is known far more for its showy fruits and seeds than for its rather dull flowers. Its slender green stems will identify it at any season. Indians used the plant to ease stomachaches and painful urination; doctors formerly prescribed it as a diuretic, laxative, and general tonic.

Inhabits streamsides, riversides, and adjacent hardwood slopes; also found in cypress-gum swamps. Ranges from se NY to se MO south to n FL and e TX.

MAY–JUNE

VISCACEAE: MISTLETOE FAMILY

American Mistletoe

Phoradendron serotinum (Rafinesque)
M. C. Johnston ssp. *serotinum*

Perennial, diffusely branched shrub, parasitic on branches and trunks of trees. Leaves are opposite, thick and leathery, broadly elliptic to oblanceolate, 1.2–5″ (3–13 cm) long and 0.4–1.6″ (1–4 cm) wide, persistent beyond one growing season. Several to many flowers grow on leafless spikes 0.2–2″ (0.5–5 cm) long; the calyx is 3- to 5-parted and green, the corolla absent. Fruit is a berry, 0.25″ (4–6 mm) diameter, whitish, with sticky pulp and seeds.

Many families hang mistletoe from doorways at Christmastime, a tradition brought here by European ancestors (who used a distantly related species). American Mistletoe is a true parasite and obtains its nutrients from the host tree; however, while eventually weakening or killing certain branches, it rarely kills the tree outright. Birds consume the fruits, after which undigested seeds adhere to limbs and germinate. *The berries are poisonous to humans!*

Inhabits hardwood trees of various kinds, in our region mostly Swamp Black Gum (*Nyssa biflora*). Ranges from NJ to s OH and s MO south to s FL and s TX.

OCT.–NOV.

RANUNCULACEAE: BUTTERCUP FAMILY
Yellowroot

Xanthorhiza simplicissima Marshall

Perennial, colonial small shrub, stem single, 1–2.5′ (30–75 cm) tall, wood bright yellow. Leaves grow at the top of the stem, pinnately divided into 3–5 leaflets. Each leaflet is nearly sessile, ovate, irregularly divided, up to 3.2″ (8 cm) long and 4″ (10 cm) wide, tip acute, margins toothed, surfaces pubescent. The terminal leaflet is widest and 3-lobed. Flowers grow on long branching sprays from just below the leaves, the 5 sepals ovate with a pointed tip, less than 0.2″ (2–5 mm) long, maroon or brownish maroon, glossy; petals absent.

Yellowroot is the sole species in its genus. Once learned, it is instantly distinguishable from any other plant, with its stem-top leaves and arching sprays of maroon-brown flowers. The brilliant yellow wood of stems and roots was once used as a dye. Contains berberine, useful as an astringent, as an anti-inflammatory, as an antimicrobial, and to lower blood pressure.

Inhabits shaded streambanks, slopes along streams and rivers, and seepy streamheads. Ranges mostly in the Mountains and Piedmont from w NY to KY south to nw FL and e TX.

APR.–MAY

POACEAE: GRASS FAMILY
Japanese Stiltgrass; Microstegium

Microstegium vimineum (Trinius) A. Camus

Annual colonial grass. Stems are erect, ascending, or reclining (rooting at lower stem nodes), to 3′ (1 m) long, usually much-branched (these also rooting when reclining), leafy throughout. Leaves are lanceolate to linear-lanceolate, 0.8–3.2″ (2–8 cm) long and up to 0.6″ (15 mm) wide, tip acute, margins finely toothed. Numerous flowers grow in a terminal spikelike raceme 0.8–2.8″ (2–7 cm) long, often with 1–3 lateral racemes barely out of the upper leaf sheath. The flowers are paired, pale green, 0.25″ (4.5–5 mm) long, usually with a slender awn.

Japanese Stiltgrass was imported to the United States in the mid-1900s and quickly naturalized in the mid-South. Today it is one of the worst invasive weeds in the eastern United States, crowding out native plants by the acre in moist soils and on river floodplains. It is fire-intolerant and so will not invade longleaf pine communities that are fire-managed.

Inhabits nutrient-rich soils of river floodplains, especially where disturbed by prior logging; also roadsides at stream crossings, moist roadbeds, forest trails, and urban and suburban woodlots. Ranges from c MA to OH and MO south to n FL and e TX.

SEPT.–OCT.

JUNCACEAE: RUSH FAMILY
Creeping Rush; Water Rush
Juncus repens Michaux

Annual aquatic or semiaquatic, pale
green. When submersed, the stems creep
and root at the nodes, forming clonal
patches and sending up sterile, leafy
stems; when emersed, plants form tufts
of fertile stems. Erect stems grow up to
8″ (20 cm) long, leaves are mostly basal,
subopposite, linear, grasslike, soft. Five to
15 flowers grow in a cluster at stem tips,
green; sepals 0.2–0.3″ (4–7 mm) long,
petals nearly twice as long, longer than the
mature capsule.

Creeping Rush is hard to mistake for
any other plant, especially when submersed and forming mats of plants whose
stems wave in flowing water.

Inhabits blackwater rivers and streams,
beaver ponds, and impoundments. Ranges
on the Coastal Plain from s DE to s FL,
e TX, and AR; c TN; nw GA; Cuba.

JUNE–OCT.

BEAVER PONDS AND IMPOUNDMENTS

This community occurs where streams are dammed by beavers or humans. The importance of this community to aquatic flora and fauna is very high, since there are no natural lakes within the Sandhills region, only a scattering of small depression ponds and vernal pools. Humans began impounding streams and rivers within the past 12,000 years or so. Indians constructed weirs to concentrate fish, and colonists wanted to harness waterpower. In our area, several pre-Revolutionary impoundments still exist. During the past three centuries, beavers were nearly trapped to extinction for their valuable fur, and many populations of plants and animals declined severely. Today, however, beavers are once again common and are hard at work reshaping our streamhead communities and transforming them into ponds where aquatic flora and fauna find refuge.

TOP Beavers greatly modify the appearance and structure of streams and small rivers, in the process creating open, sunny habitats required by many plants and animals. BOTTOM Human-created impoundments mimic the characteristics of beaver ponds, but often on a larger scale. Here, Pond Cypress are dominant.

Typically the downstream sector of an impoundment is open water (perhaps with standing dead trees), while the upper sector grades into swamp forest. White Water-lily (*Nymphaea odorata*), Yellow Pondlily (*Nuphar advena*), Water-shield (*Brasenia schreberi*), and bladderworts (*Utricularia* spp.) occur in open water, while shallows and coves support emergent spikesedges (*Eleocharis* spp.), Southern Blue Flag (*Iris virginica*), Golden Club (*Orontium aquaticum*), Pickerelweed (*Pontederia cordata*), beaksedges (*Rhynchospora* spp.), Arrowheads (*Sagittaria* spp.), bulrushes (*Schoenoplectus* spp.), and Woolsedge (*Scirpus cyperinus*). Wet shores are dominated by a zone of sphagnum mosses, wetland shrubs, and coarse grasses; herbs such as Yellow Pitcher-plant (*Sarracenia flava*), Hard Pipewort (*Eriocaulon decangulare*), meadow-beauties (*Rhexia* spp.), and yellow-eyed-grasses (*Xyris* spp.) are conspicuous. Many of these herbs and shrubs also occur as epiphytes on stumps and on trunks of living trees.

Fauna associated with beaver ponds and impoundments are no less diverse and include otter, mink, herons and egrets, ducks, kingfishers, turtles, snakes, frogs and toads, fishes, dragonflies and damselflies, and many aquatic insects.

Beaver occupation typically is cyclical: The animals enter an uninhabited stream and build a dam, which floods the swamp forest. Trees become stressed or die, and beavers feed on the inner bark of these and smaller trees ashore. When the food supply runs out, the animals build another dam upstream. Eventually, the beavers have to migrate to another stream. During the years or decades of this cycle, plant and animal numbers fluctuate as the water level and nutrients vary.

Species List

The color after a name indicates the primary natural community or habitat. T = mentioned in text of another species; not pictured.

Agalinis fasciculata T ✳
  Fascicled Gerardia
Agalinis purpurea ✳
  Purple Gerardia
Alnus serrulata
  Tag Alder
Andropogon glomeratus ✳
  Bog Broomsedge
Aronia arbutifolia ✳
  Red Chokeberry

Bacopa caroliniana
  Blue Water-hyssop
Bidens discoidea ✳
  Little Beggar-ticks
Brasenia schreberi
  Water-shield
Carex glaucescens
  Glaucescent Sedge
Cephalanthus occidentalis
  Buttonbush

Clethra alnifolia var. *alnifolia* ❋
Sweet Pepperbush
Clethra alnifolia var. *pubescens* T ❋
Southern Sweet Pepperbush
Cuscuta compacta ❋
Compact Dodder
Cyrilla racemiflora ❋
Ti-ti
Decodon verticillatus
Water Willow;
Water Oleander;
Water Loosestrife
Diodia virginiana ❋
Virginia Buttonweed
Drosera capillaris ❋
Bog Sundew
Drosera intermedia
Spoonleaf Sundew
Dulichium arundinaceum
Three-way Sedge
Eriocaulon compressum ❋
Soft Pipewort
Eriocaulon decangulare ❋
Hard Pipewort
Eubotrys racemosa ❋
Swamp Sweetbells
Eupatorium mohrii T ❋
Mohr's Eupatorium
Eupatorium resinosum ❋
Resinous Boneset
Eutrochium dubium ❋
Three-nerved Joe-Pye-weed
Eutrochium fistulosum T ❋
Hollow Joe-Pye-weed
Gratiola viscidula T ❋
Sticky Hedge-hyssop
Habenaria repens
Water-spider Orchid;
Floating Orchid
Helianthus angustifolius ❋
Narrowleaf Sunflower
Hibiscus moscheutos ❋
Eastern Rose-mallow
Hydrocotyle umbellata
Water Pennywort
Hydrolea quadrivalvis
Waterpod
Hypericum fasciculatum T
Peelbark St. John's-wort
Hypericum galioides
Slender-leaved St. John's-wort

Hypericum mutilum
Dwarf St. John's-wort
Iris virginica
Southern Blue Flag;
Virginia Iris
Itea virginica ❋
Sweetspire
Juncus canadensis T ❋
Canada Rush
Juncus effusus
Soft Rush
Juncus repens ❋
Creeping Rush
Lindernia dubia
False Pimpernel
Linum striatum ❋
Wetland Flax
Ludwigia alternifolia
Tall Seedbox
Ludwigia decurrens T
Winged Primrose-willow
Ludwigia leptocarpa
Longpod Primrose-willow;
Water Willow
Ludwigia linearis ❋
Slender Seedbox
Ludwigia pilosa
Hairy Seedbox
Ludwigia sphaerocarpa T
Roundfruit Seedbox
Lycopus cokeri
Sandhills Bugleweed
Lyonia lucida
Shining Fetterbush
Mayaca fluviatilis
Bogmoss
Mikania scandens ❋
Climbing Hempweed
Murdannia keisak ❋
Swamp Dewflower
Nuphar advena
Yellow Pondlily; Cowlily;
Spadderdock
Nuphar sagittifolia T
Arrowleaf Pondlily
Nymphaea odorata
White Water-lily
Nymphoides cordata
Little Floating-hearts
Orontium aquaticum
Golden Club

Peltandra virginica
   Arrow Arum; Tuckahoe
Persicaria opelousana T ✺
   Slender Water-pepper
Persicaria pensylvanica T ✺
   Pinkweed
Persicaria sagittata ✺
   Arrowleaf Tearthumb
Persicaria setacea ✺
   Swamp Smartweed
Phoradendrum serotinum ✺
   American Mistletoe
Pluchea foetida
   Pallid Marsh-fleabane
Pontederia cordata
   Pickerelweed
Ptilmnium capillaceum ✺
   Mock Bishop's-weed
Rhexia virginica
   Virginia Meadow-beauty
Rubus argutus
   Southern Blackberry
Saccharum giganteum
   Giant Plumegrass
Sagittaria engelmanniana
   Engelmann's Arrowhead
Sagittaria latifolia T
   Broadleaf Arrowhead
Sagittaria macrocarpa
   Sandhills Arrowhead
Sambucus canadensis ✺
   Black Elderberry
Sarracenia flava ✺
   Yellow Pitcher-plant
Scutellaria integrifolia ✺
   Narrow-leaved Skullcap
Scutellaria lateriflora T ✺
   Mad-dog Skullcap
Smilax rotundifolia ✺
   Greenbrier; Horsebrier
Smilax walteri
   Coral Brier; Swamp Brier

Solidago altissima ✺
   Tall Goldenrod
Solidago gigantea T ✺
   Late Goldenrod
Solidago rugosa var. *celtidifolia* ✺
   Hackberry-leaved Goldenrod
Sophronanthe pilosa ✺
   Pilose Hedge-hyssop
Sparganium americanum
   American Bur-reed
Spiranthes cernua
   Nodding Ladies'-tresses
Styrax americanus ✺
   American Snowbell
Symphyotrichum dumosum ✺
   Rice-button Aster
Symphyotrichum novi-belgii
   New York Aster
Triadenum virginicum
   Pale St. John's-wort;
   Marsh St. John's-wort
Triadenum walteri T
   Walter's St. John's-wort
Utricularia biflora T
   Long-spurred Bladderwort
Utricularia inflata
   Big Floating Bladderwort
Utricularia olivacea
   Midget Bladderwort;
   Dwarf Bladderwort
Utricularia purpurea
   Purple Bladderwort
Utricularia radiata T
   Little Floating Bladderwort
Utricularia striata
   Fibrous Bladderwort
Vernonia noveboracensis
   New York Ironweed
Xyris fimbriata
   Fringed Yellow-eyed-grass
Zenobia pulverulenta ✺
   Honeycups

ASTERACEAE: ASTER FAMILY
Pallid Marsh-fleabane
Pluchea foetida (L.) A. DC.

Perennial, densely pubescent, the stem normally unbranched, 1.3–3′ (0.4–1 m) tall. Leaves are numerous, dark green, elliptic, 1.2–3.6″ (3–9 cm) long and 0.4–1.5″ (1–3.5 cm) wide, tip acute, base clasping the stem, margins finely toothed. Flower heads grow in dense clusters terminally and from upper leaf axils, each head essentially stalkless, about 0.3″ (8 mm) across. Disc flowers are creamy white, ray flowers absent.

As its Latin name denotes, the foliage of this plant has an unpleasant odor, but it is not fetid like spoiled meat. A close relative, Pink Marsh-fleabane (*P. baccharis*), is very similar, differing in its pink flowers and dusty gray-green foliage; it occurs in Carolina bays. Camphorweed (*P. camphorata*) also smells strongly, but it is taller, much-branched, and has ovate leaves on long stalks. It usually occurs in disturbed wet places, wet roadsides, and openings in swamp forests.

Inhabits wet soil of beaver ponds, impoundments, river shores, and Carolina bays. Ranges on the Coastal Plain from s NJ to s FL, e TX, and e AR.

LATE JULY–OCT.

NYMPHAEACEAE: WATER-LILY FAMILY
White Water-lily
Nymphaea odorata W. T. Aiton

Perennial aquatic from a very thick, long rhizome. Leaves float at water surface, from elongate, thick, fleshy stems. Leaves are round or nearly so, deeply notched at base, to 12″ (30 cm) across, purplish beneath, margins smooth or irregularly indented. Flowers float at the surface, each from a fleshy stalk, fragrant. Petals are numerous, lanceolate, mostly 1.6–4″ (4–10 cm) long, white, in some plants pink, stamens and styles numerous, yellow.

Familiar to just about everyone, White Water-lily is enjoyed in nature as well as in the water garden. Most parts of the plant, especially the starchy roots, were eaten by Native Americans, and the plant had medicinal uses as well. Aside from some magnolia trees, White Water-lily has the largest flowers in North America.

Inhabits impoundments, beaver ponds, roadside borrow ponds, and slow-moving rivers. Ranges from Newf. to Man. south to FL and TX.

MAY–SEPT.

MENYANTHACEAE:
BUCKBEAN & FLOATING-HEART FAMILY
Little Floating-hearts
Nymphoides cordata (Elliott) Fernald

Perennial aquatic from a thick rhizome.
Leaves grow on very long, slender stalks
and float at water surface, ovate and
cordate, up to 2.5″ (6 cm) long and wide,
variegated above with dull purple-brown,
the underside smooth. Flower clusters
grow from the stem shortly below the leaf;
flowers bloom singly or a few at a time at
water surface. The 5 petals are white; each
flower is about 0.5″ (12 mm) across.

The long blooming season, mottled
leaves, and delicate appearance make
Little Floating-hearts desirable in a water
garden. Locally abundant, the flowers
resemble floating confetti strewn on the
water. Big Floating-hearts (*N. aquatica*)
occasionally occurs in our region; its
leaves are larger (up to 7″ [18 cm]), leaf
undersides have a pebbly surface, and
flowers are about 0.75″ (19 mm) across.

Inhabits natural depression ponds, beaver ponds, and impoundments. Frequent
in the Carolinas, rare in GA (Richmond
and Macon Counties). Ranges from Newf.
to FL and LA, mostly on the Coastal Plain.

MAY–AUG.

ARALIACEAE: GINSENG FAMILY
Water Pennywort
Hydrocotyle umbellata L.

Perennial, aquatic or semiaquatic, stems
creeping and rooting at nodes. Leaves
grow singly from stem nodes, the stalks
hollow and 1.6–6″ (4–15 cm) or longer.
Leaf blades are peltate, circular, 0.4–1.6″
(1–4 cm) wide, margins crenate. Flowers
(15–50) grow in a globular umbel 0.4–0.8″
(1–2 cm) wide, atop a stalk as long or
longer than the leafstalks, petals 5, tiny,
greenish or whitish.

Creeping stems of Water Pennywort
often form large colonies whose leaves
stand up above the water surface or, most
often, are left stranded ashore as water
recedes. Whorled Pennywort (*H. verticillata*) is very similar in all dimensions, but
its flowers grow in 3–7 whorls of 2–7 flowers each; it prefers shores of blackwater
rivers.

Inhabits impoundments, beaver ponds,
and marshes. Ranges from N.S. to S MI
south to FL and TX; Mex.

LATE APR.–SEPT.

LENTIBULARIACEAE: BLADDERWORT FAMILY

Midget Bladderwort;
Dwarf Bladderwort

Utricularia olivacea Wright ex Grisebach

Perennial, aquatic, the stems submersed just below the surface, little-branched, each branch usually only once forked (several mm long) and bearing a single, insect-trapping bladder. Flowers grow at the water surface from stalks less than 0.3″ (2–8 mm) long. One flower is produced per stalk, 2 mm long, white, 2-lipped (upper largest), the spur swollen, about 0.5 mm long.

It is hard to imagine how small this plant is until you actually see it; the numerous flowers look like white specks on the water surface or on exposed mud. Like most bladderworts, it is sensitive to water levels and does not bloom every year. Midget Bladderwort is rare in NC, SC, and GA.

Inhabits shallow water or exposed mud of beaver ponds, impoundments, and natural depression ponds. Ranges on the Coastal Plain from S NJ to S FL and S MS; West Indies; Central America; South America.

AUG.–OCT.

ALISMATACEAE: ARROWHEAD FAMILY

Engelmann's Arrowhead

Sagittaria engelmanniana J. G. Smith

Perennial, fleshy, glabrous aquatic, emersed from shallow water or stranded ashore. Leaves are all basal, long-stalked, typically narrowly sagittate, the blade up to 8″ (20 cm) long and 2″ (5 cm) wide (but may be up to 4″ [10 cm] wide), the lobes less than 1″ (2.5 cm) wide. The flowering stem is 1–1.5′ (30–50 cm) tall, with flowers in 2–4 whorls, female below, male above. Each flower stalk is subtended by a bract up to 1.4″ (3.5 cm) long, pointed. Flowers are 0.75–1″ (18–25 mm) across, the 3 petals white, broadly obovate to rotund. Fruiting heads are round, each seed with an erect beak.

Named for the prominent nineteenth-century botanist George Engelmann, founder of the St. Louis Botanical Garden (now the world-famous Missouri Botanical Garden). Broadleaf Arrowhead (*S. latifolia*) has much broader leaves (to 9″ [23 cm] wide), glabrous or pubescent; the bracts are shorter (less than 0.75″ [19 mm]) and blunt, and each seed's beak projects sideways. It inhabits nutrient-rich marshes, river shores, and lakes.

Inhabits blackwater streamheads, beaver ponds, and impoundments. Ranges on the Coastal Plain from MA to FL and MS.

JUNE–SEPT.

ALISMATACEAE: ARROWHEAD FAMILY
Sandhills Arrowhead
Sagittaria macrocarpa J. G. Smith

Perennial (or annual?), glabrous aquatic from slender roots, emersed from very shallow water or stranded ashore. Leaves are all basal, long-stalked, the blades very slender, to 4″ (10 cm) long and 2 mm wide, not sagittate (no backward-pointing lobes). The flowering stem is 5–12″ (12–30 cm) tall, the flowers in 1–3 whorls, female below, male above. Each flower stalk is subtended by a bract to 2 mm long, pointed or blunt. Flowers are about 0.5″ (12 mm) across, the 3 petals white, obovate. Fruiting heads are round, each seed with a beak projecting sideways.

Sandhills Arrowhead was rediscovered in the 1990s after having been lost for a century. It is a rare species in NC and SC, although local populations may be large. It blooms best when stranded just out of water. Grassleaf Arrowhead (*S. gramineus*) grows from a thick rhizome and has broader leaves (up to 0.6″ [1.5 cm]), up to 7 flower whorls, and smaller seeds. It inhabits more-nutrient-rich streams, marshes, and lakes.

Inhabits blackwater streamheads, beaver ponds, and impoundments. Endemic to the Sandhills region from Moore County, NC, to Aiken County, SC; it should be sought in the Augusta, GA, area.

MAY–SEPT.

ORCHIDACEAE: ORCHID FAMILY
Nodding Ladies'-tresses
Spiranthes cernua (L.) Richard

Perennial, fleshy-textured, stems mostly 5–16″ (12–40 cm) tall, glabrous below, minutely downy above. Leaves are linear to narrowly lanceolate, erect, 2–10″ (5–25 cm) long and 0.25–0.8″ (6–20 mm) wide, glabrous, reduced in size upward. Flowers grow in a dense twisted spiral up to 6.5″ (17 cm) long and 1.2″ (3 cm) wide, in 2–4 ranks. The 3 sepals and 3 petals are 0.25–0.4″ (6–11 mm) long (the lip longest and widest), each more or less curved outward at the tip, white, pubescent on the outside. The lip petal is elliptical, 0.25″ (4–6 mm) wide, strongly curved downward and with a frilled margin.

Get to know this fairly common orchid so you can compare it with uncommon and rare species of *Spiranthes*. The flowers grow in twisted "braids" and are faintly fragrant. Fragrant Ladies'-tresses (*S. odorata*) has flowers that smell of vanilla or jasmine, its flower lip is ovate and more pointed at the tip, and it grows in wooded swamps, often in shallow water.

Inhabits margins of beaver ponds, impoundments, streamheads, and creeks; also in wet roadside scrapes and rights-of-way. Ranges from N.S. to s Ont. and MN south to n FL and se TX.

MOSTLY MID-SEPT.–MID-NOV.

DROSERACEAE: SUNDEW FAMILY
Spoonleaf Sundew
Drosera intermedia Hayne

Perennial, leaves sometimes grow in a simple basal rosette but more often in pseudo-whorls along a stem up to 4″ (10 cm) long, the spread of the leaves 3–6″ (7.5–15 cm) across. Leaf blades narrowly elliptical, 0.3–0.8″ (8–20 mm) long, much shorter than the long stalks, strongly red-tinged, covered with gland-tipped hairs. Flowering stems several, leafless, without gland-tipped hairs, 3.5–8″ (9–20 cm) tall, maroon or dark green; flowers bloom one at a time as the upper stem uncoils, petals 5, white, 0.25–0.35″ (5–8 mm) long.

Spoonleaf Sundew loves to grow in the wettest mucky or peaty soils. Because it is a much larger plant with more leaves than our other sundews, Spoonleaf Sundew often catches larger prey such as dragonflies, butterflies, beetles, and even small frogs.

Inhabits boggy streamheads as well as shores, stumps, and logs of beaver ponds and impoundments; usually associated with sphagnum moss. Ranges from Newf. to MN south to n FL and e TX; Cuba; Hispaniola; Venezuela; Guyana; se Brazil.

JULY–SEPT.

ROSACEAE: ROSE FAMILY
Southern Blackberry
Rubus argutus Link

Perennial, stems few to many, up to 6.5′ (2.2 m, rarely to 3 m) long, erect to leaning or arching, distinctly angled, glabrate. Prickles are broad-based and curved; they occur on stems, leafstalks, principal leaf veins, and inflorescence branches. Leaves are divided into 3 leaflets on flowering branches, 5 leaflets on nonflowering branches. Leaflets are elliptic, 1.2–4.7″ (3–12 cm) long and 0.4–2.4″ (1–6 cm) wide, glabrate above, densely pubescent beneath, tip acute, base rounded, margins toothed or double-toothed. Flowers grow in leafy, several-flowered clusters; the 5 petals are white, obovate, 0.8–1″ (2–2.5 cm) long. The fruit is an aggregate berry, black, 0.4–1″ (1–2.5 cm) long and 0.4–0.6″ (1–1.5 cm) wide, juicy.

Blackberries (genus *Rubus*) are among our most sought-after native fruits, in part due to their taste and variety of uses (pies, tarts, cobblers, ice cream, on cereal), but also due to their relative abundance and ease of gathering—but watch those prickles! A word to the wise: bears also love the berries.

Inhabits moist to wet soils of beaver ponds, impoundments, riverside slopes, floodplain forests, cypress-gum swamps, streamheads, rights-of-way, and roadsides. Ranges from MA to MO south to FL and TX.

MID-APR.–MID-MAY

RUBIACEAE: MADDER FAMILY
Buttonbush
Cephalanthus occidentalis L.

Perennial woody shrub, emergent from shallow water, widely branched. Leaves are opposite, ovate to elliptic, 2.4–6″ (6–15 cm) long and 1.2–4″ (3–10 cm) wide, acute or with a driptip. Flowers grow in dense globes at branch tips and from leaf axils, the globes 0.8–1.4″ (2–3.5 cm) across. Petals are white, slender, tubular with short flaring lobes, 0.25–0.5″ (7–12 mm) long; the styles extend well beyond petals.

Buttonbush is a plant that is like no other and is instantly recognizable by its ball-like heads of flowers, opposite leaves, and aquatic habitat. It has been used in the past medicinally for toothache and eye inflammation and to stop bleeding.

Inhabits beaver ponds and impoundments, as well as shores of sluggish rivers and oxbows. Ranges from N.S. to s Ont. and CA south to FL and TX; Mex.; Central America.

JUNE–AUG.

NYMPHAEACEAE: WATER-LILY FAMILY
Yellow Pondlily; Cowlily; Spadderdock
Nuphar advena (Aiton) R. Brown ex Aiton f.

Perennial aquatic from a very thick, long rhizome. Leaves are of two types, floating or submersed, from thick fleshy stems. Floating leaves are ovate to roundish, deeply notched or cordate at base, to 15″ (37 cm) long and 11″ (27 cm) wide, thick-textured. Submersed leaves (often not present) are pale green, ovate to elliptical, the surfaces undulate or wavy, thin-textured. Flowers float at or just above water surface, each from a thick fleshy stalk; petals are numerous, rounded, yellow, curving over the stamens and styles.

Yellow Pondlily has been used for a variety of skin and internal maladies. In the NC Sandhills, some plants have longer and narrower floating leaves and abundant, elongate submersed leaves. Such plants are Arrowleaf Pondlily (*N. sagittifolia*), a species of the middle and outer Coastal Plain of se VA to ne SC, but the intermediate leaf shape of Sandhills plants suggests past hybridization.

Inhabits impoundments, beaver ponds, and slow-moving rivers. Ranges from ME to WI south to FL and TX; n Mex.; Cuba.

LATE APR.–MID-OCT.

ARACEAE: ARUM FAMILY
Golden Club

Orontium aquaticum L.

Perennial aquatic from a stout rhizome, the plant essentially stemless. Leaves are all basal, elliptic, 6–8″ (15–20 cm) long and 2–4″ (5–10) cm wide, dark green above, pale gray and shiny beneath, acute- to blunt-tipped, short-tapered to thick stalks 4–12″ (10–30 cm) long. Leaf orientation varies from erect to floating horizontally. Flowers grow in a dense, terminal, golden-yellow tapered cylinder 1.6–4″ (4–10 cm) long (the spadix), atop a white, succulent, thick stalk 12–20″ (30–50 cm) long, surrounded basally by a green sheath 4–12″ (10–30 cm) long (the spathe). Fruits are dull blue-green berries; when ripe they become submerged by the curving stalks.

Golden Club brings a brilliant touch of yellow to swamps and beaver wetlands in spring. The leaves are noted for their ability to completely shed water, never getting soaked or wet on the upper surface—try it!

Inhabits beaver wetlands, impoundments, pools and backwaters in swamp forests, and shores of sluggish streams. Ranges mostly on the Coastal Plain from MA to FL and LA; scattered inland to C NY, WV, KY, and TN.

MAR.–APR.

HYPERICACEAE: ST. JOHN'S-WORT FAMILY
Dwarf St. John's-wort

Hypericum mutilum L.

Perennial, stems solitary to numerous, 6–28″ (15–70 cm) tall, usually with short ascending branches. Leaves are opposite, sessile, ovate to triangular, 0.5–1.2″ (12–30 mm) long and 0.25–0.7″ (5–15 mm) wide, 3–5 nerved, tip acute. The lower leaves larger than the upper. Flowers grow terminally in small groups, petals 5, yellow, 0.2″ (2–3 mm) long.

Dwarf St. John's-wort is named for its small flowers, not the size of the plant, although small and unbranched plants do occur. Canada St. John's-wort (*H. canadense*) is similar but has slender leaves (1–3 mm wide) and occurs in streamhead margins and depression ponds. The genus *Hypericum* is well-developed in our region and challenging to professional botanists and amateurs alike; however, seeking them out will bring you into some wonderful habitats.

Inhabits beaver ponds, blackwater stream margins, depression ponds, and roadside ditches. Ranges from Newf. to Man. south to S FL and C TX.

JUNE–SEPT.

HYPERICACEAE: ST. JOHN'S-WORT FAMILY
Slender-leaved St. John's-wort
Hypericum galioides Lamarck

Perennial woody shrub mostly 2.5–5′ (0.8–1.5 m) tall, with many wide-spreading branches, bark not shreddy. Leaves opposite and sessile, narrowly oblanceolate to broadly linear, 0.8–1.2″ (2–3 cm) long and up to 0.25″ (5 mm, rarely to 7) wide, blunt-tipped, base tapered. Some leaves also have a few small leaves in axils. Flowers are numerous, growing in clusters at 3–7 nodes at ends of branches, corollas about 0.6″ (1.5 cm) across, petals 5, yellow, stamens very numerous. Capsules brown, dry, oval with acuminate tip (formed by the persistent styles).

Mostly a plant of the lower Coastal Plain, Slender-leaved St. John's-wort appears to be spreading inland to impoundments and beaver ponds. From Needle-leaved (*H. nitidum*) and Peelbark (*H. fasciculatum*) St. John's-worts it can be distinguished by its broader leaves that are wider toward the tip and always show some of the leaf surface beneath.

Inhabits margins of impoundments and beaver ponds; also found in blackwater river shores and swamps. Ranges on the Coastal Plain from e NC to n FL and e TX.

JUNE–AUG.

ONAGRACEAE: EVENING-PRIMROSE FAMILY
Tall Seedbox
Ludwigia alternifolia L.

Short-lived, usually glabrate perennial, stems erect, up to 4′ (1.2 m) tall, slightly winged lengthwise, with ascending branches. Leaves are well-spaced, lance-shaped to narrowly elliptic, tapered to both ends, 2–4″ (5–10 cm) long and 0.4–0.6″ (1–1.5 cm) wide, essentially sessile. Flowers grow singly in axils of the branch leaves, petals 4, yellow, broadly obovate, about 0.25″ (6 mm) long and wide. The fruit is a dry capsule, 4-angled, brown.

Get to know this common plant as the basis from which to compare other seedboxes. The more or less cubical capsule, prominent in fall and winter, gives this and most other seedboxes their common name.

Inhabits margins of impoundments, beaver ponds and depression ponds; also found in streamside marshes and wet roadside ditches. Ranges from MA to s Ont. and IA south to n FL and e TX.

MID-JUNE–SEPT.

ONAGRACEAE: EVENING-PRIMROSE FAMILY
Longpod Primrose-willow; Water Willow

Ludwigia leptocarpa (Nuttall) Hara

Densely pubescent annual, stems erect, up to 3′ (1 m) tall, with many spreading or ascending branches. Leaves are lance-shaped to narrowly elliptic, up to 4.7″ (12 cm) long and 1.2″ (3 cm) wide, tapered to both ends, tip acuminate, stalk mostly less than 0.4″ (1 cm) long. Flowers grow singly in leaf axils at the tip of a long floral tube 1.2–1.6″ (3–4 cm) long. The 5–7 petals are yellow, broadly obovate, 0.25–0.4″ (6–10 mm) long and wide. Fruits are cylindrical, curved upward, with 5–7 sharp, spreading lobes at the tip, 1.2–2″ (3–5 cm) long.

The distinctive, long floral tubes (later to become the seedpods) should clinch identification of this common wetland plant. Do not confuse this "Water Willow" with another plant of the same name that has rosy pink flowers (*Decodon verticillatus*). Winged Primrose-willow (*L. decurrens*) is similar to Longpod Primrose-willow but has 4 petals; the capsule is half as long and not curved, and the stem is winged lengthwise.

Inhabits impoundments and beaver ponds, often growing from stumps or on floating peat and mud mats. Ranges from s VA to se MO south to c FL and e TX; tropical America.

MID-JUNE–SEPT.

ONAGRACEAE: EVENING-PRIMROSE FAMILY
Hairy Seedbox

Ludwigia pilosa Walter

Densely hairy perennial, stems erect, up to 3′ (1 m) tall, with many spreading or ascending branches, the stem and leaves often blotched with maroon. Stem bases become spongy-thickened when submersed, and plants produce horizontal leafy shoots (stolons) at ground level in late summer/fall. Leaves are alternate, lanceolate to elliptic, tapered to both ends, 1.6–2.8″ (4–7 cm) long and about 0.4″ (1 cm) wide, sessile. Flowers grow singly in leaf axils, sessile, petals none or minute. The 4 sepals are cream-colored or pale yellowish green, broadly ovate with a long tip, about 0.2″ (4 mm) long. The capsule is oval-shaped, 0.2″ (3–4 mm) long.

The dense hairs and lack of yellow petals distinguish this common wetland plant from other *Ludwigia* in our region. Roundfruit Seedbox (*L. sphaerocarpa*) is similar but often grows taller (to 4′ [1.2 m]) and has distinctly rounded capsules, and the stem and leaf hairs are relatively sparse and much shorter; it occurs in similar habitats.

Inhabits impoundments and beaver ponds; also found in riverine marshes. Ranges from s VA to n FL and s TX. Apparently rare in the GA Sandhills, documented from Richmond County.

MID-JUNE–MID-OCT.

LENTIBULARIACEAE: BLADDERWORT FAMILY
Big Floating Bladderwort
Utricularia inflata Walter

Perennial aquatic. The nonflowering stems are submersed, much-branched and -forked, bearing abundant insect-trapping bladders on filiform segments. The flowering portion of the stem can be up to 10″ (25 cm) tall, erect, and floats on the surface, supported by a whorl of 4–9 inflated leaves, each leaf more than 2.4″ (6 cm) long, wider toward tip and with many short branchlets at tip. Three to 15 flowers are produced, 0.8–1″ (20–25 mm) long, yellow, 2-lipped and spurred, the spur shorter than lower lip and blunt.

Big Floating Bladderwort may look like a plant designed by a committee, but it gets the job done and has mastered its environment. Little Floating Bladderwort (*U. radiata*) is similar but smaller in all respects; its floating leaves are shorter and taper to both ends (not definitely wider toward tip), and it has a shorter flowering stem (up to 5″ [12 cm]) and smaller flowers (0.6–0.8″ [about 15–20 mm]). It occurs in the same habitats plus Carolina bays.

Inhabits shallow water of beaver ponds, impoundments, and slow-moving streams. Ranges on the Coastal Plain from se MA to s FL, e TX, and se OK.

LATE APR.–EARLY JULY, OCCASIONALLY LATER

LENTIBULARIACEAE: BLADDERWORT FAMILY
Fibrous Bladderwort
Utricularia striata Le Conte ex Torrey
[*Utricularia fibrosa* Walter]

Perennial aquatic, the stem stranded ashore when flowering. Leaves are of 2 types: those with bladders or those without; all are forked 3–4 times with filiform segments. The flowering stem grows up to 1′ (30 cm) tall, with 2–6 flowers. Flowers are 0.6–1″ (14–25 mm) long, yellow, 2-lipped and spurred, the spur shorter than to slightly longer than the lower lip, and blunt.

The numerous bladders trap tiny aquatic invertebrates that augment the plant's nutrients and minerals, thus making it (and our other bladderworts) a carnivore. Two-flowered or Long-spurred Bladderwort (*U. biflora*) is similar but lacks the bladderless leaves; it flowers later (late June–Sept.) and has smaller flowers (0.4–0.6″ [about 12 mm]), and the spur conspicuously exceeds the lip and is pointed.

Inhabits shallow water and shores of beaver ponds, impoundments, borrow ponds, and wet ditches. Ranges on the Coastal Plain from se MA to c FL and e TX.

LATE APR.–EARLY JULY

XYRIDACEAE: YELLOW-EYED-GRASS FAMILY
Fringed Yellow-eyed-grass

Xyris fimbriata Elliott

Perennial, stem single or several together, mostly 2–5′ (0.6–1.5 m) tall, base not or hardly swollen. Leaves are all basal, 2-ranked, linear, flattened, 16–28″ (40–70 cm) long and 0.4–0.8″ (10–20 mm) wide, surfaces smooth, margins minutely bumpy (papillose), bases straw-colored to pinkish. Flowers grow 1–3 at a time from an elliptical, conelike head atop the stem, the head 0.4–1″ (10–25 mm) long and composed of overlapping brown scales. Brown, deeply fringed sepals project from the scales. The 3 petals are yellow, obovate, 0.2–0.3″ (5–8 mm) long, opening in midmorning.

This is the largest *Xyris* in North America and is identified by its great size, deeply fringed sepals, and habit of growing in water. Small's Yellow-eyed-grass (*X. smalliana*) differs in its lustrous leaves that are pink basally and its sepals that have minute cuts rather than long fringes; its flowers open in the afternoon. Named for John K. Small (1869–1938), author of three editions of *Manual of the Southeastern Flora*.

Inhabits bottoms and exposed margins of depression ponds, beaver ponds, and impoundments. Ranges on the Coastal Plain from se VA to c FL and e TX; s NJ; nw GA; c TN.

LATE AUG.–EARLY OCT.

SMILACACEAE: GREENBRIER FAMILY
Coral Brier; Swamp Brier

Smilax walteri Pursh

Perennial vine from rhizomes, forming dense colonies, high climbing or scrambling via curly tendrils. Stem brownish green throughout, sparsely prickly or without prickles. Leaves are deciduous, narrowly to broadly ovate, thinnish-textured, tip acute, margins smooth, short-stalked. Flowers grow in umbels from several leaf axils, the 3 sepals and 3 petals 3 alike, 0.2–0.3″ (5–8 mm) long, yellowish. Fruits are berries, bright red, 0.3–0.4″ (8–10 mm) in diameter.

In late fall and winter, Coral Brier is one of our most striking plants, with its numerous clusters of brilliant red berries. Some people place sprays of them on mailboxes and lampposts as Christmas decorations.

Inhabits perennially wet soil of beaver ponds, impoundments, wet streamheads, and cypress-gum swamps. Ranges on the Coastal Plain from s NJ to c FL, e TX, and w TN.

LATE APR.–MAY

BETULACEAE: BIRCH & ALDER FAMILY
Tag Alder
Alnus serrulata (Aiton) Willdenow

Perennial woody shrub with multiple
stems 4.8–13′ (1.5–4 m) tall. Leaves are
ovate to broadly ovate, 0.8–4.8″ (2–12
cm) long and 0.4–3.2″ (1–8 cm) wide,
sharply toothed, with short hairs on veins
beneath, the veins more or less parallel.
Male flowers grow densely on drooping
catkins 1.6–3.2″ (4–8 cm) long and 0.25″
(5–6 mm) wide, dull yellow, lacking petals.
Female flowers are less conspicuous, on
short erect catkins to 0.4″ (1 cm) long,
brown. The fruiting catkin is broadly
ovate, 0.8″ (2 cm) long, woody and conelike, each "scale" a winged fruit.

Tag Alder is among our first flowering
plants of spring, the yellow male catkins
never failing to attract our attention as
a sign of warmer weather to come. Native Americans made a bark tea to treat
childbirth pain, toothache, and diarrhea;
they also used it as a blood purifier and
an emetic.

Inhabits a wide variety of wetlands,
including streambanks and riverbanks,
marshes, beaver ponds and impoundments, streamhead thickets, and floodplains. Ranges from N.S. to n IN and MO
south to FL and TX.

MID-FEB.–MAR.

ERICACEAE: BLUEBERRY & AZALEA FAMILY
Shining Fetterbush
Lyonia lucida (Lamarck) K. Koch

Perennial shrub to 7′ (2.2 m) high,
branches usually broadly spreading.
Leaves are evergreen, elliptic to ovate,
thick and leathery, glabrous, lustrous,
to 3.5″ (9 cm) long and 2.75″ (7 cm)
wide. Flowers grow in rows of axillary
clusters toward branch tips; they resemble
Southern Highbush Blueberry (*Vaccinium
formosum*) flowers but are pink-tinged or
red-tinged and narrower.

Shining Fetterbush is a handsome
and easily recognized plant year-round.
It is abundant in the Carolina Sandhills
but apparently uncommon to rare in the
GA portion. The genus commemorates
John Lyon (1765–1814), Scottish-born
botanist and explorer of the southern
Appalachians.

Inhabits streamheads, beaver ponds
and impoundments, blackwater river
floodplain forests, cypress-gum swamps,
and other wetland situations. Ranges from
se VA to s FL and e TX; nw GA; w Cuba.

APRIL–MAY

HYPERICACEAE: ST. JOHN'S-WORT FAMILY
Pale St. John's-wort; Marsh St. John's-wort

Triadenum virginicum (L.) Rafinesque
[*Hypericum virginicum* L.]

Glabrous perennial, stems 8″–2′ (20–60 cm) tall. Leaves are opposite, dark green, sessile with bases clasping stem, elliptical, 0.8–2.4″ (2–6 cm) long and 0.3–1″ (8–25 mm) wide, tip rounded, dotted on underside with pale glands. Flowers grow in small clusters terminally and in leaf axils, the 5 petals dull whitish suffused with pink or purple, elliptical, 0.3–0.4″ (7–10 mm) long.

Pale St. John's-wort is a common plant of many wetland situations. The flowers are an unusual and hard-to-describe color (some folks prefer "salmon colored"). Walter's St. John's-wort (*T. walteri*) is similar, but all leaves are tapered to stalks; it occupies similar habitats but prefers areas with seepage.

Inhabits beaver ponds, river marshes, cypress-gum swamps, and boggy places, and it is often found on mossy logs. Ranges from N.S. to s Ont. south to FL and MS, most abundant on the Coastal Plain.

JULY–SEPT.

LYTHRACEAE: LOOSESTRIFE FAMILY
Water Willow; Water Oleander; Water Loosestrife

Decodon verticillatus (L.) Elliott

Perennial shrub with many narrow, arching stems 3–6′ (1–2 m) long, rooting at tips, stems spongy-thickened below water line. Leaves whorled or opposite, narrowly to broadly lance-shaped, to 8″ (20 cm) long and 2″ (5 cm) wide, tip acuminate, base tapered to a stalk up to 0.75″ (15 mm) long. Flowers grow in axils, 0.4–0.5″ (9–12 mm) long, petals 5, pink to rosy, margins crinkled.

Although the plant looks unkempt with stems oriented every which way, Water Willow has very showy flowers. It often forms a dense zone around the edge of open water, adding abundant decaying material and slowly building up soil from unstable mud. The flowers may remind you of Crêpe Myrtle, which is in the same plant family.

Inhabits margins of beaver ponds, old impoundments, boggy depressions, and marshes. Ranges from N.S. to Ont. south to C FL and e TX.

JULY–SEPT.

MAYACACEAE: BOGMOSS FAMILY

Bogmoss

Mayaca fluviatilis Aublet

Perennial(?) aquatic, emersed or submersed, creeping on mud or floating in
shallow water, stems elongate, lax. Leaves
are pale green, 0.25–0.35″ (5–8 mm)
long, about 0.5 mm wide, very dense
and oriented 90 degrees from the stem.
Single pink flowers grow from slender
erect stalks, the 3 petals pink to whitish,
0.3–0.5″ (7–12 mm) across.

The very leafy creeping stems resemble
a moss or a clubmoss, hence the name.
Often overlooked, this diminutive plant is
a beautiful wildflower when seen up close.
In our 3 states, Bogmoss is much more
common in the Sandhills region than
elsewhere.

Bogmoss inhabits boggy or sphagnous
margins of beaver ponds, impoundments,
wet streamheads, and cypress-gum
swamps. Ranges from NC to FL and TX;
West Indies, Mex.; Central America;
South America.

MAY–JULY

LENTIBULARIACEAE: BLADDERWORT FAMILY

Purple Bladderwort

Utricularia purpurea Walter

Perennial aquatic, the nonflowering stems
submersed, much-branched. The branches
are opposite or whorled, forked several to
many times, bearing abundant bladders
on filiform segments. The flowering portion of the stem is 2–3.5″ (5–9 cm) tall,
erect, and extends above the surface. One
to 3 flowers grow atop the stem, 0.3–0.5″
(9–12 mm) long, purple-pink with a yellow or white "eye," 2-lipped and spurred,
the spur 0.25″ (3–5 mm) long and blunt.

Purple Bladderwort is a rare plant in
our region, but when it blooms, the numerous flowers can color the water surface
purple. The action of the traplike bladders
of this genus—rapidly opening, bringing
in water and prey, and closing—has been
measured in milliseconds. It is the fastest
movement known in the biological world.

Inhabits beaver ponds, impoundments,
and slow-moving streams. Ranges on the
Coastal Plain from N.S. to S FL and SE TX;
also in Great Lakes states; West Indies;
Mex.; Central America; South America.

MAY–SEPT.

MELASTOMATACEAE:
MELASTOME & MEADOW-BEAUTY FAMILY
Virginia Meadow-beauty

Rhexia virginica L.

Perennial, to 3′ (1 m) tall, usually branched, stem and leaves more or less hairy. Leaves are opposite, sessile, usually ascending, broadly lanceolate to ovate, to 2.8″ (7 cm) long and 1″ (2.5 cm) wide, prominently 3-nerved, tip acute to acuminate, margins finely toothed. Flowers grow in a branched inflorescence from upper leaf axils. The 4 petals are rosy, obovate to broadly elliptical, 0.6–0.8″ (15–20 mm) long, each petal oblique (lengthwise, one half is larger than other) and with gland-tipped hairs on the backside. The 8 stamens and anthers are bright yellow and curved. The fruit is a capsule shaped like an old cream pitcher, narrowed beyond the middle to a short neck, then flared to the 4 glabrous sepals.

Virginia Meadow-beauty varies tremendously in size over its vast range, but in the Sandhills region it usually stands 1.5–2.5′ (45–80 cm) tall. Its flowers are small for the size of the plant and have a deeper hue than those of other *Rhexias*.

Inhabits beaver ponds, impoundments, riverine marshes, and seepage slopes. Ranges from s N.S. to WI south to n FL and e TX.

LATE JUNE–SEPT.

ASTERACEAE: ASTER FAMILY
New York Ironweed

Vernonia noveboracensis (L.) Michaux

Perennial, lacking basal leaves, stems single to several, 5–10′ (1.5–3 m) tall, branched from uppermost portion. Leaves are numerous, lanceolate, 4–10″ (10–25 cm) long and 0.6–1.6″ (1.5–4 cm) wide, tip acuminate, short-tapered basally, margins finely toothed, underside sometimes pubescent. Flowers grow at ends of branches in a large flat-topped cluster, the heads about 0.5–0.6″ (12–15 mm) across, disc flowers purple, ray flowers absent.

This tall and imposing plant makes striking patches of color in wet streamside marshes and meadows. It is sparsely distributed in our region. Formerly, New York Ironweed was used medicinally to treat irregular menses.

Inhabits wet soils of riverside marshes, beaver ponds, impoundments, and meadows. Ranges from MA to PA south to nw FL and s AL.

LATE JULY–SEPT.

CABOMBACEAE: WATER-SHIELD FAMILY
Water-shield
Brasenia schreberi J. F. Gmelin

Perennial aquatic from a creeping root-stock, stem long and flexible; stem and leafstalks thickly covered with clear, viscous jelly. Leaves are alternate, floating from long flexible stalks, peltate, elliptic, 1.6–4.4″ (4–11 cm) long and 0.8–2.4″ (2–6 cm) wide. Flowers grow singly from leaf axils, slightly raised above water surface, purple or maroon, the 5 petals 0.5–0.8″ (12–20 mm) long, recurved to reveal erect stamens.

Water-shield's flowers are quite hand-some, but it is the underwater parts of the plant that steal the show—who can forget the feel of the stem and leafstalks, with their jellylike coating? It makes any field trip a success! However, the function of this coating is not known.

Inhabits beaver ponds, impoundments, and river oxbows. Ranges across much of the globe; in North America from N.S. to MN south to FL and TX; also B.C. to CA.

JUNE.–OCT.

IRIDACEAE: IRIS FAMILY
Southern Blue Flag; Virginia Iris
Iris virginica L. var. *virginica*

Perennial from a thick rhizome 0.4–0.8″ (1–2 cm) diameter, stems 1.5–3′ (0.5–1 m) tall, usually with 1–2 branches. Leaves are swordlike, 1.25–3′ (0.4–1 m) long and (1–3 cm) wide, erect, equitant. Flowers grow at tips of stem and branches from long sheathing bracts (spathes), the corolla tube 0.4–0.8″ (1–2 cm) long. There are 3 sepals, blue to violet-blue, splotched with yellow centrally, 2.4–3.2″ (6–8 cm) long and 0.8–1.4″ (2–3.5 cm) wide, curved outward; 3 petals, smaller than sepals and erect.

Iris was the rainbow goddess of Greek mythology, and the flowers of this world-wide genus encompass all colors of the rainbow and then some. In France an iris is the national emblem, the fleur-de-lys. Native Americans used the somewhat toxic rhizomes of Southern Blue Flag as a purgative.

Inhabits beaver ponds, impoundments, marshes, and river shores. Ranges on the Coastal Plain and lower Piedmont from se VA to c FL and e TX.

LATE APR.–MAY

ASTERACEAE: ASTER FAMILY
New York Aster

Symphyotrichum novi-belgii (L.) Nesom
   var. *elodes* (T. & G.) Nesom
[*Aster novi-belgii* L. var. *elodes* (T. & G.) Gray]

Glabrous or glabrate perennial, stems single or several, leaning to erect, mostly 2–5′ (0.6–1.5 m) tall, unbranched to weakly branched. Leaves are linear to lanceolate, 2–6″ (5–15 cm) long and up to 0.8″ (2 cm) wide. Lower leaves are long-tapered to their bases; upper leaves are sessile and more or less clasping the stem, tip acuminate, margins smooth. Flower heads grow at ends of branches, the bracts of the heads with somewhat recurved tips. Rays are 0.4–0.8″ (1–2 cm) long, blue to pale violet; disc flowers yellow.

New York Aster is most abundant in near-coastal situations from Lab. to SC, but it is found locally inland to the Sandhills of NC and SC. It does well in garden situations. Our plant is the narrow-leaved extreme, var. *elodes*, which is less branched than plants of the more northern var. *novi-belgii*.

Inhabits moist to wet soils of beaver ponds, impoundments, river shores, and marshes. Ranges on the Coastal Plain from N.B. to nc SC.

LATE SEPT.–MID-NOV.

PLANTAGINACEAE: PLANTAIN FAMILY
Blue Water-hyssop

Bacopa caroliniana (Walter) B. L. Robinson

Succulent perennial from creeping rhizomes, usually forming colonies, stems thick, pubescent, ascending or erect, 4–12″ (10–30 cm) tall. Leaves are opposite, ovate to widely elliptic, 0.5–1.2″ (12–28 mm) long and 0.3–0.7″ (7–15 mm) wide. Flowers grow from leaf axils on stalks shorter than the leaf blades, the 5 petals bright blue, each 0.4″ (9–11 mm) long.

The bright blue flowers, long flowering period, and low-growing, matlike aspect of this plant might make it a choice member of wet-soil gardens.

Inhabits pond margins, marshes, river shores, and wet roadsides. Uncommon in our area. Ranges on the Coastal Plain from se VA to s FL and e TX.

MAY–SEPT.

HYDROLEACEAE: HYDROLEA FAMILY

Waterpod

Hydrolea quadrivalvis Walter

Perennial, aquatic or semiaquatic, stems succulent (fleshy-textured), crooked, lower portion creeping and rooting at nodes, upper portion erect, pilose. Leaves alternate, short-stalked, lanceolate or oblanceolate, to 4.8″ (12 cm) long and 1″ (2.5 cm) wide, tapering basally, margins entire or wavy. Some leaves have short spines in axils. Flowers grow in small clusters from leaf axils in upper half of stem, the corolla is about 0.3″ (7–9 mm) long, tubular with 5 lobes, blue.

Although small, the flowers of Waterpod are a handsome rich blue. The capsules, or pods, are capable of floating long distances and are excellent dispersal agents.

Inhabits marshes, beaver ponds, impoundments, and sluggish river shores. Ranges on the Coastal Plain from se VA to c FL and se LA; inland to ne MS, n AL, and c TN.

JUNE–SEPT.

LINDERNIACEAE: FALSE-PIMPERNEL FAMILY

False Pimpernel

Lindernia dubia (L.) Pennell var. *dubia*

Glabrous annual, stems widely branched from near base, up to 8″ (20 cm) tall but often half that, four-angled. Leaves are opposite, 0.4–1″ (10–25 mm) long and 0.2–0.3 (5–9 mm) wide, minutely toothed, short-stalked. Flowers grow singly on slender stalks from leaf bases; stalks are shorter than leaves. The corolla is pale lavender-blue, about 0.3″ (7–10 mm) long, composed of a tube that spreads into a 2-lobed upper lip and a 3-lobed lower lip.

The tiny flowers resemble some orchids and are well worth examining with a hand lens. A second variety (*L. dubia* var. *anagallidea*) is closely similar, but its flowers grow on stalks that are 1–3 times as long as the leaves; it occupies the same habitats.

Inhabits vernal pools, wet borrow pits, and exposed margins of depression ponds, impoundments, and beaver ponds. Overall, this species ranges through se Canada and most of the U.S.; Mex., Central America; South America.

JUNE–SEPT.

PONTEDERIACEAE: PICKERELWEED FAMILY
Pickerelweed
Pontederia cordata L.

Stout perennial aquatic from a thick rhizome, plants emersed from water or stranded ashore, 1.3–3′ (0.4–1 m) tall. Leaves are all basal, erect, ovate to lance-shaped, 2.8–7″ (7–18 cm) long and 0.8–4.5″ (2–11 cm) wide, the base heart-shaped (not in lance-shaped leaves), leaf-stalks up to 1′ (30 cm) long. Flowers grow terminally on a stalk a bit longer than the leaves, the stalk with 1 bract and 1 sheath just below the flowers. The flowering spike is 3–6″ (7–15 cm) long and 1–2″ (2.5–5 cm) wide, short-tapered to tip. Each flower is funnel-shaped, 6-parted, 0.5–0.8″ (12–19 mm) long including spreading lobes, blue or lavender-blue, one upper lobe with a yellow blotch.

Pickerelweed's leaves vary greatly in width and shape, giving rise to 2 named varieties; our plants are the wide-leaved var. *cordata*. The genus is strictly New World, with 5 species ranging from Canada to Argentina.

Inhabits beaver ponds, impoundments, and river marshes. Ranges from N.S. to MN south to FL and TX; Central America; South America.

MAY–OCT.

ORCHIDACEAE: ORCHID FAMILY
Water-spider Orchid; Floating Orchid
Habenaria repens Nuttall

Perennial, semiaquatic, 4–32″ (10–80 cm) tall. Leaves are strongly ascending, narrowly lance-shaped, 2–9.5″ (5–24 cm) long and 0.2–0.8″ (4–20 mm) wide, tip acuminate, base clasping and sheathing the stem. Flowers grow in a dense terminal raceme, pale green or whitish green. Side sepals are lance-shaped, about 0.25″ (3–7 mm) long, upper petals are threadlike, the lip linear, about 0.25″ (4–7 mm) long with threadlike divisions.

As its name implies, this orchid grows closely associated with water, among rank herbs along shores or on floating sphagnum/mud mats. It is probably increasing in number, due to widespread building of impoundments, backyard ponds, and reservoirs.

Inhabits beaver ponds and impoundments and is sometimes found in ponded roadside ditches. Ranges on the Coastal Plain from e NC to s FL and e TX; West Indies, Mex., Central America, South America.

MAY–OCT.

ARACEAE: ARUM FAMILY
Arrow Arum; Tuckahoe
Peltandra virginica (L.) Schott

Perennial, glabrous aquatic from short thick rootstock, emergent in shallow water or stranded ashore. Leaf blades are 6–18″ (15–45 cm) long and 3.2–10″ (8–25 cm) wide, with hastate bases (2 lobes angling outward), tip acute to acuminate, pale green or glaucescent beneath, leafstalks 8–24″ (20–60 cm) long. Flowers grow densely on a yellowish cylindrical stalk (spadix) atop a leafless stem 4–10″ (10–25 cm) long; the spadix is enclosed within a green sheathlike envelope (spathe) 5–7″ (12–18 cm) long with a narrow opening along one side. Flowers are tiny and lack sepals and petals. Fruits are fleshy berries, green to blackish; when mature the stem bends down to water or soil.

Captain John Smith of the Virginia Colony reported that the Indians gathered large quantities of Tuckahoe, roasted them in pit fires for 24 hours, and then ate them; Smith said that they tasted like potatoes.

Inhabits beaver wetlands, river marshes, floodplain pools, and cypress-gum swamps. Ranges from Que. to MI south to FL and TX.

MAY–JUNE

TYPHACEAE: CAT-TAIL FAMILY
American Bur-reed
Sparganium americanum Nuttall

Perennial glabrous aquatic, emergent from shallow water. Stems are 1–2.5′ (0.3–0.7 m) tall, fleshy-textured, angled in a zigzag fashion in the inflorescence. Leaves are basal and also grow partway up the stem, 2-ranked, linear, up to 3′ (1 m) long, 0.25–0.75″ (6–18 mm) wide, flattened but fleshy in texture, tip blunt. Flowers grow in round heads of many sessile flowers. The 1–4 female heads grow in axils of leaflike bracts, about 0.5–1″ (13–25 mm) across, pale green. The 1–6 male heads are smaller and higher on the stem, whitish, their bracts much smaller. Fruits form a hard, compact, green sphere up to 1.4″ (3.5 cm) across with projecting persistent styles.

With its irislike leaves and ball-shaped flowering and fruiting heads, American Bur-reed is unique in our flora and is a characteristic plant of blackwater stream systems. It was named by Thomas Nuttall (1786–1859), English-born botanical and ornithological explorer who was the first curator of the Harvard Botanic Garden.

Inhabits slow-moving blackwater creeks and rivers, beaver ponds, and impoundments. Ranges from Newf. to MN south to c FL and c TX.

MAY–SEPT.

CYPERACEAE: SEDGE FAMILY
Glaucescent Sedge
Carex glaucescens Elliott

Densely tufted perennial from short rhizomes, plant more or less glaucescent, especially leaf undersides and stem. Leaves are very long and grasslike, 2–3′ (0.6–1 m) long and to 0.3″ (8 mm) wide, pleated lengthwise (forms "m" in cross section), with a long, tapering point. The flower-bearing stem grows up to 3′ (1 m) long, terminated by a straw-colored male spike and 3–5 green female spikes below. Female spikes are cylindrical, 1–1.7″ (2.5–4.5 cm) long, on curving or drooping stalks. Spikes are composed of rows of many simplified flowers without petals, soon developing into hardened seeds with a granular coat (perigynium), each flower with a basal scale that has a long, sharp point.

Get to know this sedge, for it is a common plant and may be a gateway to the large and interesting family of sedges. Sedges are highly useful to animals as food, nesting material, and basic habitat (much of a marsh or swamp is composed of sedges). "Glaucescent" means somewhat whitened, and this is an attractive feature of this plant.

Inhabits beaver ponds, impoundments, seepage slopes, river marshes, cypress-gum swamps, and wet roadsides. Ranges on the Coastal Plain from e MD to c FL, e TX and s AR; rarely inland to nw GA and c TN.

EARLY JULY–EARLY SEPT.

CYPERACEAE: SEDGE FAMILY
Three-way Sedge
Dulichium arundinaceum (L.) Britton

Perennial from horizontal rhizomes, usually forming colonies. Stems up to 23″ (60 cm) tall (rarely more), bluntly 3-angled, ribbed. Leaves in 3 ranks, to 3″ (7.5 cm) long and 0.3″ (7 mm) wide, margins rough, base clasping, tip pointed. Flowers grow within scales, parts reduced (no petals or sepals), numerous on twice-branched clusters from upper leaf axils, 3–7 flowers per branchlet, green at first then turning brownish.

Three-way Sedge gets its name from the strictly 3-ranked leaf arrangement, best seen from directly above.

Inhabits cypress-gum swamps, beaver ponds, marshes, and wet roadside ditches. Ranges from Newf. to MN south to FL and TX; also MT to B.C. and CA.

JULY–SEPT.

JUNCACEAE: RUSH FAMILY
Soft Rush
Juncus effusus L. ssp. *solutus* (Fernald & Wiegand)
   Hamet-Ahti

Perennial, usually forming dense tufts
of sharp-tipped stems 18–45″ (0.5–1.2 m)
tall, stems green, photosynthetic. Leaves
rudimentary or absent. Flowers grow in
a loose cluster from the upper portion of
stem, not terminal; the number of flowers
varies greatly. Each flower is composed of
3 sepals and 3 petals that look alike, 0.2″
(2.5–3 mm) long, light brown. Capsule
brown, about same length as flowers, the
tip rounded or flattish.

   Rushes (*Juncus*) are a worldwide group
of about 300 species, many of which are
important components of wetland habitats
as habitat structure, food, cover, and nesting material. Rushes generally have round
stems in cross section, as opposed to
triangular in the sedge family (Cyperaceae). From sedges and grasses, rushes can
be distinguished by their 6-parted flower
(3 sepals, 3 petals). Up close with a hand
lens, rush flowers are handsome.

   Inhabits beaver ponds, impoundments,
wet ditches, river shores, marshes, and
borrow pits. Ranges from Newf. to MN
south to FL and TX; Mex.

JUNE–SEPT.

POACEAE: GRASS FAMILY
Giant Plumegrass
Saccharum giganteum (Walter) Persoon
[*Erianthus giganteus* (Walter) C. E. Hubbard]

Perennial coarse grass, stems 6–13′
(2–4 m) tall, stem nodes bearded. Leaves
grow to 19″ (50 cm) long and 1″ (2.5 cm)
wide, long-acuminate, leaf sheaths with
short to long hairs. The inflorescence is
terminal, mostly 8–16″ (20–40 cm) long
and 3.2–6″ (8–15 cm) wide, silvery and
often lightly purple-tinged, all branchlets
strongly upward-pointing. Individual
flowers are very hairy, with straight awns
0.4–1.2″ (10–30 mm) long.

   Plumegrasses are the tallest of our
native grasses. When flowering, the inflorescence is narrow, but as seeds ripen,
it spreads out to form a showy plume.
The long hairs of the flowers give the
plume its silvery look. Foxtail Plumegrass (*S. alopecuroides*) and Bent-awn
Plumegrass (*S. brevibarbe* var. *contortum*)
are similar but not so tall; their stems are
glabrate, their inflorescences are narrower
(strongly reddish in the latter), and both
species have twisted awns. They prefer
oak-hickory woodlands, forest openings,
and roadsides.

   Inhabits wet soil of beaver ponds,
impoundments, marshes, and depression
ponds. Ranges on the Coastal Plain from
se NY to s FL, e TX, and se OK; scattered
inland to c KY, c TN, w NC, n AL.

SEPT.–OCT.

DEPRESSION PONDS AND VERNAL POOLS

These communities occur in shallow depressions that hold water seasonally (rarely permanently); the depressions are usually ponded during winter and remain wet to dry in summer. Rainfall is the sole source of water. The margin burns frequently from fires in adjacent pinelands; the deeper central portion burns irregularly or not at all. The main difference between depression ponds and vernal pools is hydroperiod—that is, the cycle of water filling and evaporating. Vernal pools dry out every summer, but depression ponds remain partly ponded except during extreme droughts. Dominant plants in depression ponds are grasses and sedges, along with Soft Pipewort (*Eriocaulon compressum*), False Pennywort (*Centella erecta*), Redroot (*Lachnanthes caroliniana*), Mohr's Eupatorium (*Eupatorium mohrii*), Quill-leaved Arrowhead (*Sagittaria isoetiformis*), Shrubby Seedbox (*Ludwigia suffruticosa*), Fibrous Bladderwort (*Utricularia striata*), and Lance-leaved Violet (*Viola lanceolata* var. *vittata*). This habitat is essential to breeding Gopher Frogs (*Rana capito*).

Naturally rare in the Sandhills region, isolated depressions are entirely dependent on rainfall for water input. Here, Redroot and White Meadow-beauty grow during a low-water period.

Vernal pools differ from depression ponds in their shallower basins, shorter hydroperiods, and shorter fire-return intervals. They may be ponded in winter but invariably dry out in summer and therefore are burned along with surrounding uplands. Shrubs that can tolerate seasonally dry soils occur here: Dangleberry (*Gaylussacia frondosa* and *G. tomentosa*), Gallberry (*Ilex glabra*), and Staggerbush (*Lyonia mariana*). Sawbrier (*Smilax glauca*) and/or Greenbrier (*S. rotundifolia*) may form a marginal zone. Grasses and sedges dominate, along with Maryland Meadow-beauty (*Rhexia mariana* var. *mariana*), White Meadow-beauty (*Rhexia mariana* var. *exalbida*), and Rice-button Aster (*Symphyotrichum dumosum*).

Species List

The color after a name indicates the primary natural community or habitat.

T = mentioned in text of another species; not pictured.

Agalinis purpurea
Purple Gerardia
Burmannia biflora
Blue Burmannia
Centella erecta ❀
False Pennywort
Chamaecrista nictitans ❀
Sensitive Partridge-pea
Eriocaulon compressum
Soft Pipewort; Hatpins
Eupatorium mohrii T ❀
Mohr's Eupatorium
Hypericum canadense ❀
Canada St. John's-wort
Lachnanthes caroliniana
Redroot
Ludwigia linearis
Slender Seedbox;
Narrowleaf Seedbox
Ludwigia suffruticosa
Shrubby Seedbox
Mitreola sessilifolia ❀
Small-leaved Miterwort
Nuphar advena ❀
Yellow Pondlily; Cowlily
Nymphaea odorata ❀
White Water-lily

Nymphoides cordata ❀
Little Floating-hearts
Panicum virgatum var. *cubense* ❀
Savanna Panic-grass
Pluchea foetida ❀
Pallid Marsh-fleabane
Rhexia mariana var. *exalbida*
White Meadow-beauty
Rhexia mariana var. *mariana*
Maryland Meadow-beauty
Rotala ramosior
Toothcup
Sagittaria isoetiformis
Quill-leaved Arrowhead
Sclerolepis uniflora
Pink Bog-button
Stachys hyssopifolia
Hyssop Hedge-nettle
Utricularia radiata T ❀
Little Floating Bladderwort
Viola lanceolata
Lance-leaved Violet
Xyris jupicai
Richard's Yellow-eyed-grass
Xyris smalliana T ❀
Small's Yellow-eyed-grass

MELASTOMATACEAE:
MELASTOME & MEADOW-BEAUTY FAMILY
White Meadow-beauty

Rhexia mariana L. var. *exalbida* Michaux

Perennial, colonial, to 14″ (35 cm) tall,
usually unbranched. Leaves are opposite,
short-stalked, narrowly lanceolate to
linear, 0.8–1.5″ (2–3.5 cm), tapered to both
ends, with sparse hairs. Flowers grow in
a branched inflorescence from upper leaf
axils. The 4 petals are white to pinkish,
obovate to broadly elliptical, 0.4–0.8″
(10–18 mm) long, each petal oblique
(lengthwise, one half is larger than other);
the 8 stamens and anthers are yellow and
curved. The fruit is a capsule shaped like
an old cream pitcher, narrowed beyond
the middle to a neck, then flared to the
4 glabrate sepals.

White Meadow-beauty is often seen
on roadsides, where its colonial growth
may cover sizeable patches. Intermediates
are known between it and *R. mariana*
var. *mariana*, so don't expect to identify
all plants. In general var. *exalbida* has
smaller flowers that are white or pinkish
(vs. pink), and the plants are shorter
and usually unbranched (vs. taller and
much-branched).

Inhabits moist to dryish roadside
ditches and banks, depression ponds,
and vernal pools. Ranges on the Coastal
Plain from se NC to s FL and e TX.

LATE MAY–SEPT.

ALISMATACEAE: ARROWHEAD FAMILY
Quill-leaved Arrowhead

Sagittaria isoetiformis J. G. Smith

Perennial, glabrous aquatic, emersed from
shallow water or stranded ashore, but
blooming best when emersed. Leaves are
all basal, semi-terete (half-circular in cross
section), bladeless (or rarely with a small,
linear, terminal blade), up to 12″ (30 cm)
long, tapering to tip, not sagittate (no
backward-pointing lobes). The flowering
stem is about as long as the leaves, with
flowers in 2–4 whorls, female below, male
above. Each flower stalk is subtended by
a bract to 2 mm long, blunt. Flowers are
about 0.75″ (19 mm) across, the 3 petals
white, obovate. Fruiting heads are round,
each seed with a beak projecting up or
angling outward.

Quill-leaved Arrowhead is a rare plant
in our region, being more numerous on
the flatter portions of the Coastal Plain.
From Sandhills Arrowhead it may be distinguished by its much longer leaves that
look like knitting needles or like leaves of
Soft Rush (*Juncus effusus*).

Inhabits nonflowing water of depression
ponds, clay soil Carolina bays, cypress-
gum ponds, and wet roadside ditches.
Ranges on the Coastal Plain from e NC
to s FL and se MS.

JUNE–SEPT.

VIOLACEAE: VIOLET FAMILY
Lance-leaved Violet
Viola lanceolata L.

Perennial, glabrate, often colonial via runners at the soil surface. Leaves are erect or ascending, narrowly to broadly lanceolate, the blades mostly 2–5″ (5–12 cm) long, tip acute, base tapered to long slender stalk, margins crenate, leafstalk about as long as blade. Flowers grow on slender stalks independent of leaves, 0.4–0.6″ (1–1.5 cm) across. The 5 petals are white, the lowest petal (the lip) slightly larger and with purple lines. The lip also has a backward-pointing, blunt spur.

Lance-leaved Violet occurs in two varieties: var. *vittata*, whose leaves are erect and with relatively long and slender leaves, and var. *lanceolata*, whose leaves are relatively shorter and wider, variously oriented. Not all plants can be confidently assigned to variety.

Inhabits wet or moist soil of depression ponds, beaver ponds, and Carolina bays (var. *vittata*); streamhead margins, seepage slopes, and beaver ponds (var. *lanceolata*). Overall, the species ranges from s N.S. to e MN south to s FL and e TX; var. *vittata* ranges on the Coastal Plain from e NC to nw FL and e TX.

MID-MAR.–EARLY MAY

ERIOCAULACEAE: PIPEWORT FAMILY
Soft Pipewort; Hatpins
Eriocaulon compressum Lamarck

Perennial aquatic, normally submerged with flowering stems extending above water, but whole plant may be stranded during drought. Leaves all basal, thin-textured, mostly 1.2–8″ (3–20 cm) long and up to 0.25″ (6 mm) wide, acuminate. Stems single or several, 8–18″ (20–45 cm) tall, ribbed lengthwise, each topped by a flattish or somewhat domed head. Heads white, 0.4–0.75″ (10–18 mm) wide, easily compressed, composed of tiny flowers.

When abundant, Soft Pipewort can look like confetti around the edges of a lake or throughout a shallow pond. It blooms earlier than Hard Pipewort (*E. decangulare*) and has shorter and thinner-textured leaves that lie flat on the ground.

Inhabits depression ponds, beaver ponds, and impoundment lakes. Ranges on the Coastal Plain from s NJ to s FL and e TX; scattered records inland.

LATE MAY–JULY

HAEMODORACEAE: BLOODWORT FAMILY
Redroot

Lachnanthes caroliniana (Lamarck) Dandy

Perennial, from red-orange rhizomes and roots. Stems 12–28″ (30–70 cm) tall, occasionally taller, densely short white woolly in upper third. Leaves are mostly basal, sword-shaped (like an iris), flattened, the bases equitant, the longer ones 12–19″ (30–50 cm) long and up to 0.6″ (1.5 cm) wide, the few stem leaves progressively smaller. Flowers grow in a single row on each of 5–10 branches atop the stem, forming a convex to flattish corymb. The 3 sepals and 3 petals look like they are covered in white wool on the outside; the petals are about 0.3″ (7–9 mm) long, yellow and glabrous inside, spreading somewhat in age, stamens 3, longer than petals.

The roots and rhizomes of Redroot are filled with an intense red-orange sap that will stain skin and clothing; an older name is *Lachnanthes tinctoria*. The term "equitant" means arranged in 2 ranks (one rank on each side of stem), with the bases overlapping. Irises and many yellow-eyed-grasses (*Xyris* spp.) also have equitant leaves.

Inhabits depression ponds and impoundments with fluctuating water levels; also found in wet savannas and seepage slopes. Ranges on the Coastal Plain from se MA to s FL and se LA; sw N.S.; nw VA; c TN; w Cuba.

JUNE–EARLY SEPT.

ONAGRACEAE: EVENING-PRIMROSE FAMILY
Shrubby Seedbox

Ludwigia suffruticosa Walter

Glabrous perennial, often colonial via leafy runners. Stems are unbranched (occasionally with a few branches), mostly 1–2.5′ (30–80 cm) tall. Leaves are alternate, sessile, erect, linear to broadly linear, 0.4–1.6″ (1–4 cm) long and 0.2–0.4″ (3–10 mm) wide, tip acuminate. Flowers grow in a dense, elliptical, headlike spike about 1″ (25 mm) long. The 4 sepals are broadly ovate, yellow or greenish yellow, about 0.2″ (2.5–3 mm) long; petals are absent or minute.

Despite having no petals, Shrubby Seedbox is plenty conspicuous because of its dense heads of flowers; the sepals are a bright yellowish green. The common name is a misnomer, as the erect stems are solitary and not at all shrubby in aspect.

Inhabits seasonally inundated depression ponds and clay-based Carolina bays; rarely found on wet roadsides. Ranges on the Coastal Plain from se NC to s FL and se AL.

MID-JUNE–SEPT.

ONAGRACEAE: EVENING-PRIMROSE FAMILY
Slender Seedbox; Narrowleaf Seedbox

Ludwigia linearis Walter

Glabrate, slender perennial from basal horizontal shoots; stems up to 2.5′ (80 cm) tall, with strongly ascending branches. Stem bases become spongy-thickened when submersed. Stem leaves are alternate, linear to narrowly lanceolate, 1.2–2.8″ (3–7 cm) long and up to 0.2″ (5 mm) wide, essentially sessile; leaves of basal shoots are shorter and wider. Flowers grow singly in leaf axils at the tip of a floral tube 0.25″ (5–7 mm) long. The 4 petals are yellow, obovate, about 0.2″ (3–4 mm) long and wide. The fruit is a capsule, 0.3″ (6–8 mm) long.

Even when flowering, this plant often goes unnoticed because of its small flowers and rather "ordinary" aspect. But as a biological entity, it has mastered how to survive in its world, and that alone is worth our admiration.

Inhabits shores and exposed bottoms of impoundments, beaver ponds, vernal pools, and depression ponds. Ranges on the Coastal Plain from s NJ to n FL, e TX, se OK, and AR; also n AL to c TN and n GA.

MID-JUNE–SEPT.

XYRIDACEAE: YELLOW-EYED-GRASS FAMILY
Richard's Yellow-eyed-grass

Xyris jupicai L. C. Richard

Annual or short-lived perennial, stem usually solitary, mostly 6–27″ (15–70 cm) tall, flattened above but not winged. Leaves are all basal, 2-ranked, linear, flattened, mostly 4–18″ (10–45 cm) long and 0.1–0.4″ (2–10 mm) wide, surfaces smooth, margins smooth to papillate (minutely bumpy). Flowers grow 1–2 at a time from an elliptical or ovoid, cone-like head atop the stem, the head about 0.4–0.6″ (10–15 mm) long and composed of overlapping brown scales. The 3 petals are yellow, obtriangular (widest at summit), about 0.2″ (3–4 mm) long, opening in morning.

Richard's Yellow-eyed-grass is relatively "weedy" and likely to turn up in disturbed habitats. It resembles Flatstem Yellow-eyed-grass (*X. difformis*), but the scapes lack wings. Louis C. M. Richard (1754–1821) was a French botanist and professor of medicine.

Inhabits sandy or peaty soils of depression ponds, Carolina bays, wet roadsides, scrapes, and gravel pits. Ranges from NJ to s FL and se TX; throughout much of tropical America.

LATE JULY–SEPT.

MELASTOMATACEAE:
MELASTOME & MEADOW-BEAUTY FAMILY
Maryland Meadow-beauty

Rhexia mariana L. var. *mariana*

Perennial, often colonial, to 28″ (70 cm) tall, much-branched. Leaves are opposite, short-stalked, elliptic to lanceolate, to 2.6″ (6.5 cm), tapered to both ends, with sparse hairs. Flowers grow in a branched inflorescence from upper leaf axils. The 4 petals are pink to pale pink, obovate to broadly elliptical, 0.6–1″ (15–25 mm) long, each petal oblique (lengthwise, one half is larger than other); the 8 stamens and anthers are yellow and curved. The fruit is a capsule shaped like an old cream pitcher, narrowed beyond the middle to a neck, then flared to the 4 sepals. The sepals have gland-tipped hairs.

This meadow-beauty was named by Linnaeus for the Maryland colony (*mariana* in Latin). Intermediates are known between it and *R. mariana* var. *exalbida*; see that variety for differences. Nash's Meadow-beauty (*R. nashii*) is similar, but note the latter's brighter, rosy-pink petals and gland-tipped hairs on the backside of the petals (vs. ordinary pink and hairless).

Inhabits depression ponds, vernal pools, beaver ponds, and moist to wet roadside ditches. Ranges from se MA to s IL south to s FL and e TX.

LATE MAY–SEPT.

OROBANCHACEAE: BROOMRAPE FAMILY
Purple Gerardia

Agalinis purpurea (L.) Pennell

Much-branched annual, 1.3–3′ (0.4–1 m) tall, stems smooth and more or less 4-angled. Principal leaves are opposite, linear, to 1.5″ (4 cm) long and 0.1″ (2 mm) wide. Flowers grow at and near ends of branches, the flower stalks less than 0.25″ (1–4 mm) long. The corolla is horn-shaped (petals form a short tube with 5 flaring lobes), 0.8–1.4″ (2–3.5 cm) long, pale purple or pink, speckled inside with dark purple and with 2 pale yellow lines.

All members of this genus are parasitic while young on other plants' roots but later sever all connections. Fascicled Gerardia (*A. fasciculata*) is very similar but taller, coarser, and with more or less rough stems; it grows in moist to dry roadsides and disturbed sites.

Inhabits a wide variety of wet places, including pond and lake margins, beaver ponds, seepage bogs, swamp openings, marshes, wet flatwoods, and roadside ditches. Ranges from N.S. to MN south to FL and e TX.

MID-AUG.–LATE OCT.

ASTERACEAE: ASTER FAMILY
Pink Bog-button
Sclerolepis uniflora (Walter) B.S.P.

Glabrous perennial, spreading via slender whitish rhizomes to form colonies. Flowering stems are produced in very shallow water or when stranded, erect, 4–16″ (10–40 cm) tall, usually unbranched. Leaves are numerous, in whorls of 3–6, sessile, linear or needlelike, 0.3–0.8″ (8–20 mm) long and less than 2 mm wide, acute. The flowering head is solitary, terminal, 0.4–0.6″ (10–15 mm) across, disc flowers pink or purplish; rays absent.

This attractive plant does not even have a common name, so I have coined one here. Pink Bog-button is very sensitive to water levels and may not flower at a site for a number of years, even though vegetative plants can be found. It is the sole species in its genus, *Sclerolepis* being one of 50 genera endemic to the Coastal Plain. Rare in NC.

Inhabits peaty-muddy soil of natural depression ponds, Carolina bays, and cypress-gum ponds; found occasionally on shores of small blackwater rivers. Ranges on the Coastal Plain from SC NH to N RI; S NJ to SE MD; E NC to EC GA (Jefferson and Jenkins Counties) to N FL and SE LA.

JUNE–AUG.

LAMIACEAE: MINT FAMILY
Hyssop Hedge-nettle
Stachys hyssopifolia Michaux var. *hyssopifolia*

Perennial from long rhizomes, usually forming colonies, stems 8–20″ (20–50 cm) tall (rarely taller), 4-angled, glabrous to pubescent on the angles. Leaves are opposite, linear to narrowly lanceolate, 1.2–3.2″ (3–8 cm) long and 0.2–0.4″ (3–9 mm) wide, margins crenate, leafstalks short, up to 0.2″ (4 mm) long. Flowers grow in terminal spikelike inflorescences composed of opposite clusters separated by a length of stem. Each cluster is composed of 1 or a few flowers, subtended by a leaflike bract. Corollas are 0.3–0.5″ (8–12 mm) long, tubular with 2 flaring lobes, the upper lobe forming a hood, the lower a 3-part lip, pink to purple-pink.

Hyssop Hedge-nettle was named for the narrow leaves, which are reminiscent of the Eurasian garden hyssop (*Hyssopus officinalis* L.). It is rare in our region; a record from Baldwin County, GA, needs confirmation.

Inhabits natural depression ponds, vernal pools, and Carolina bays. Ranges on the Coastal Plain from SE MA to SW GA; also in scattered places inland and at the head of Lake Michigan.

JUNE–AUG.

BURMANNIACEAE: BURMANNIA FAMILY
Blue Burmannia
Burmannia biflora L.

Annual, stem very slender and thread-like, 1.25–8″ (3–20 cm) tall. Leaves are alternate, tiny and scalelike, 1–2 mm long. Flowers number 1–10 (rarely up to 17), 1 flower terminal, the rest in erect lateral spikes. The corolla is blue with a whitish tip, 0.25″ (3–6 mm) long and wide, 3-winged.

Blue Burmannia is a truly exquisite wildflower, but it is a "belly plant"—you must get down to its level to appreciate its beauty. Our burmannias apparently are mycotrophic; that is, they derive nutrients from decaying material via associations with soil fungi. Despite their short stature, burmannias have solved the problem of seed dispersal by producing dustlike seeds easily carried by wind.

Inhabits seasonally ponded depressions, seepage slopes, and wet streamhead margins, usually in full sun. Ranges on the Coastal Plain from se VA to s FL and e TX.

JULY–OCT.

LYTHRACEAE: LOOSESTRIFE FAMILY
Toothcup
Rotala ramosior (L.) Koehne

Glabrous annual, branched or not, 4–18″ (10–45 cm) tall, green suffused with red. Leaves are opposite, linear to narrowly lanceolate, 0.4–2.2″ (1–5.5 cm) long and up to 0.4″ (10 mm) wide, short-tapered to both ends, sessile. Flowers grow singly in axils of many leaves, the calyx roundish or ellipsoid, 0.2″ (3–4.5 mm) long, greenish tan, petals absent or, if present, purplish white and soon dropped.

Most plants are strongly tinged red, and some plants are entirely so, making this otherwise inconspicuous little plant very distinct. It was discovered by André Michaux in the 1790s in Cross Creek (now Fayetteville), NC.

Inhabits receding shorelines of vernal pools, depression ponds, and impoundments. Ranges from c MA to s MN south to s FL and c TX; Pacific states; tropical America.

JUNE–MID-OCT.

ROADSIDES AND DISTURBED GROUND

Roadsides can often be productive places to find native plants. We often think of roadsides as dominated by nonnative grasses and forbs; in many instances that is the case, but in fact many native plants can compete with the aliens. This is especially true where roads pass through natural communities (vs. highly modified communities such as pine plantations and cropfields), due to the greater number of native plants available for colonization of the roadside. In addition to roadsides, other kinds of disturbed ground include utility company rights-of-way, borrow pits and scrapes, abandoned fields, clearcut areas, industrial sites, and suburban developments.

Whether mown, timbered, scraped, or burned, roadsides and disturbed ground provide early successional habitats favored by many wildflowers. Here, Showy Jointweed is dominant.

Plants that occur on roadsides and other disturbed ground are those that tolerate or even require high levels of sunlight. In the natural scheme of things, these plants are quick to colonize places where the soil has been disturbed, such as treefalls that create a gap in the forest canopy, hurricane blowdowns, burned areas, and areas of slumping soil on steep slopes. These days, following decades of fire suppression, a number of native plant species that are part of the longleaf pine ecosystem and oak-hickory woodlands are more numerous on roadsides and in rights-of-way than they are within their native habitats. The reason? In the absence of fire, hardwood trees have grown unnaturally tall and dense, blocking sunlight from reaching the ground; seeds are unable to germinate in such shady conditions.

Once plants are established on roadsides, frequent mowing and/or spraying will ensure that woody shrubs and trees do not displace them. In the past several decades, many roadsides have been seeded with alien grasses that form dense colonies and thatchlike growth, making it difficult for other species to compete. Thus, roadside plants have to be tough—and resourceful—to withstand these pressures. Note that many roadside plants produce seeds with parachutelike plumes that carry them effortlessly in the breeze, while others produce tough root systems that last for years; still others produce hundreds of seeds per fertilized flower. There are many ways to survive in disturbed soil habitats.

Species List

The color after a name indicates the primary natural community or habitat. T = mentioned in text of another species; not pictured.

Agalinis fasciculata T ✳
  Fascicled Gerardia
Andropogon virginicus T ✳
  Oldfield Bluestem
Apocynum cannabinum
  Indian Hemp;
  Hemp Dogbane
Baccharis halimifolia
  Groundsel-tree
Bidens bipinnata
  Spanish Needles
Bidens polylepis
  Tickseed Sunflower;
  Ditch Daisy
Callicarpa americana ✳
  Beauty-berry
Centrosema virginianum ✳
  Spurred Butterfly-pea
Chamaecrista fasciculata
  Common Partridge-pea
Chrysopsis gossypina var. *gossypina* ✳
  Gossamer Golden-aster
Chrysopsis mariana ✳
  Maryland Golden-aster
Cirsium horridulum
  Yellow Thistle
Clitoria mariana ✳
  Butterfly-pea
Conoclinium coelestinum ✳
  Mistflower
Crocanthemum canadense ✳
  Canada Frostweed
Crocanthemum rosmarinifolium
  Rosemary Frostweed;
  Rosemary Sunrose
Croptilon divaricatum
  Slender Scratch-daisy
Crotalaria spectabilis
  Showy Rattlebox

Croton glandulosus var. *septentrionalis*
  Doveweed; Toothed Croton
Diodia teres
  Poor Joe; Buttonweed
Diodia virginiana
  Virginia Buttonweed
Eragrostis curvula
  Weeping Lovegrass
Eragrostis spectabilis
  Purple Lovegrass
Erechtites hieraciifolius
  Fireweed; Pilewort
Erigeron strigosus ✳
  Slender Daisy-fleabane
Eupatorium capillifolium T
  Slender Dog-fennel
Eupatorium compositifolium
  Coastal Plain Dog-fennel
Froelichia floridana
  Tall Cottonweed
Froelichia gracilis T
  Slender Cottonweed
Geranium carolinianum
  Carolina Crane's-bill
Helenium amarum
  Bitterweed
Helianthus angustifolius
  Narrowleaf Sunflower
Houstonia caerulea
  Bluets; Quaker Ladies;
  Innocence
Houstonia pusilla
  Early Bluet; Star-violet
Hypericum gentianoides
  Pineweed; Orange-grass
Hypericum lloydii ✳
  Piedmont St. John's-wort
Hypochaeris radicata
  Hairy Cat's-ear

Ipomoea lacunosa ✳
  Small White Morning-glory
Ipomoea pandurata
  Wild Sweet Potato; Manroot
Krigia cespitosa T
  Opposite-leaved Dwarf-dandelion
Krigia virginica
  Virginia Dwarf-dandelion
Lactuca canadensis
  Yellow Wild Lettuce
Lespedeza bicolor
  Bicolor Bush-clover
Lespedeza cuneata
  Sericea; Chinese Bush-clover
Linum medium T ✳
  Spreading Flax
Lonicera japonica
  Japanese Honeysuckle
Ludwigia alternifolia ✳
  Tall Seedbox
Marshallia obovata var. *scaposa* ✳
  Savanna Barbara's-buttons
Monarda punctata ✳
  Spotted beebalm
Morella cerifera T ✳
  Common Wax-myrtle
Nuttallanthus canadensis
  Common Toadflax
Nuttallanthus texensis T
  Texas Toadflax
Oenothera laciniata
  Cutleaf Evening-primrose
Opuntia humifusa ✳
  Prickly Pear
Oxalis stricta
  Common Yellow Wood-sorrel
Packera anonyma
  Small's ragwort
Passiflora incarnata
  Maypops; Passion Flower
Phytolacca americana
  Pokeweed
Pityopsis pinifolia
  Sandhills Golden-aster
Pluchea camphorata T ✳
  Camphorweed
Polygala curtissii
  Curtiss's Milkwort;
  Appalachian Milkwort
Polygala polygama
  Bitter Milkwort

Polygonella americana ✳
  Showy Jointweed
Polygonella gracilis T ✳
  Slender Jointweed
Polypremum procumbens
  Rustweed; Juniper-leaf
Portulaca pilosa
  Hairy Purslane; Kiss-me-quick
Potentilla canadensis
  Dwarf Cinquefoil;
  Running Cinquefoil
Potentilla recta
  Sulphur Cinquefoil
Prunus angustifolia
  Chickasaw Plum
Pueraria montana var. *lobata*
  Kudzu
Pyrrhopappus carolinianus
  False Dandelion
Rhexia mariana var. *exalbida* ✳
  White Meadow-beauty
Rhexia mariana var. *mariana* ✳
  Maryland Meadow-beauty
Rhus michauxii ✳
  Michaux's Sumac
Rhynchospora inexpansa
  Nodding Beaksedge
Richardia brasiliensis T
  Brazilian Clover
Richardia scabra
  Mexican Clover
Robinia hispida var. *hispida* T ✳
  Common Bristly-locust
Rosa carolina
  Carolina Rose
Rosa multiflora
  Multiflora Rose
Rubus cuneifolius
  Sand Blackberry
Rubus flagellaris
  Northern Dewberry
Rumex acetosella T
  Sheep Sorrel
Rumex hastatulus
  Heartwing Sorrel
Sabatia angularis T ✳
  Bitterbloom
Salvia lyrata
  Lyre-leaved Sage
Sida rhombifolia
  Diamondleaf Fanpetal

Smilax smallii ❀
Jackson-brier
Solanum carolinense
Carolina Horse-nettle
Stylisma pickeringii ❀
Pickering's Morning-glory
Symphyotrichum grandiflorum ❀
Rough Aster
Teesdalia nudicaulis
Shepherd's Cress
Trichostema dichotomum
Common Blue-curls
Trichostema setaceum T
Slender Blue-curls
Tridens flavus
Redtop; Purpletop

Triodanus biflora T
Venus's Looking-glass
Triodanus perfoliata
Venus's Looking-glass
Verbena brasiliensis
Brazilian Vervain
Vicia villosa var. *varia*
Winter Vetch
Viola bicolor
Wild Pansy
Wahlenbergia marginata
Asian Rockbell
Wisteria sinensis
Chinese Wisteria

ASTERACEAE: ASTER FAMILY
Coastal Plain Dog-fennel

Eupatorium compositifolium Walter

Annual or short-lived perennial, stems single or several together, 2–7′ (0.7–2.2 m) tall. Branches crowded, ascending to spreading, leaves alternate or a few opposite, 1–2.5″ (2.5–6 cm) long, dissected into linear segments about 2 mm wide. Inflorescence terminal, large and much-branched, the tiny heads with 3–5 white disc flowers, sweetly fragrant, rays absent.

A closely similar species is Slender Dog-fennel (*E. capillifolium* [Lamarck] Small), differing in its filiform leaf segments (less than 1 mm), flowers creamy white and less fragrant; it occurs on the Coastal Plain and Piedmont and inland to TN. Despite their unsavory reputation as weeds (a widely used alternate name is Yankee-weed), both dog-fennels have subtly but pleasantly fragrant flowers.

Inhabits a wide range of dry to mesic situations in pinelands and oak-hickory forests, especially where the soil has been disturbed; also roadsides, rights-of-way, and old fields. Ranges on the Coastal Plain from se VA to s FL, e TX, se OK, and s AR.

MID-SEPT–MID-NOV.

ASTERACEAE: ASTER FAMILY
Groundsel-tree

Baccharis halimifolia L.

Perennial woody shrub 3–14′ (1–4 m) tall with ascending branches. Leaves are obovate to elliptic, tapered to a short stalk, 1.2–2.8″ (3–7 cm) long and 0.4–1.6″ (1–4 cm) wide, coarsely toothed in the outer half. Flowers grow in numerous small heads on branch tips, 3–5 heads in a cluster, dioecious (sexes on separate plants). Disc flowers are creamy white, rays absent. The seeds have long wispy white plumes attached to one end.

Groundsel-tree originated in maritime habitats but has spread far inland due to its ability to disperse seed via wind and to germinate in disturbed soils. Now it is commonly seen on roadsides and is a nuisance in our region, as it invades seminatural habitats. It is among our latest-flowering plants.

Inhabits roadsides and disturbed moist to dry soils, including openings within natural communities. Ranges on the Coastal Plain and lower Piedmont from MA to FL, TX, and OK; expanding inland; West Indies.

LATE SEPT.–MID-NOV.

ASTERACEAE: ASTER FAMILY
Fireweed; Pilewort

Erechtites hieraciifolius (L.) Raf. ex DC.
  var. *hieraciifolius*

Annual, stem erect, unbranched, hairless
and rather fleshy-textured, mostly 2–5′
(0.6–1.5 m) tall, but may be less than
1′ (0.3 m) or reach 10′ (3 m). Leaves
lance-shaped to elliptic, 2–10″ (5–20 cm)
long and 0.2–2.6″ (0.5–6.5 cm) wide,
irregularly toothed and/or lobed, tip
acute, base tapered, upper leaves sessile.
Flower heads grow in branched clusters
(panicles) atop stem; the bracts form a
cylinder 0.4–0.8″ (10–20 mm) long with
a dilated base. Disc flowers are cream-
colored or pinkish-tinged, rays absent.
Fruiting heads are moplike, white, each
seed with a white "parachute."

Fireweed seems to be everywhere due
to the seeds' ability to disperse on the
slightest breeze. It springs up almost magi-
cally in the middle of dense forests following a treefall, fire, or other disturbance.

Inhabits all sorts of communities, from
open fields to deep forests, wherever soil
has been disturbed or turned. Ranges
from Newf. to Sask. south to FL and TX;
tropical America.

JULY–NOV.

FABACEAE: PEA & BEAN FAMILY
Sericea; Chinese Bush-clover

Lespedeza cuneata (Dumont-Cours.) G. Don

Perennial from a short-lived woody
crown, stems slender, 2–5′ (0.6–1.5 m)
tall, with dense, upwardly appressed hairs.
Leaves are abundant, short-stalked, oriented upward. The 3 leaflets are narrowly
obelliptic or oblinear, 0.4–1″ (1–2.5 cm)
long and up to 0.25″ (2–5 mm) wide, surfaces with dense, short, appressed, white
hairs, tip blunt with a tiny point. Flowers
are solitary or 2–4 from axils of upper
and midstem leaves, on stalks about 1 mm
long. Petals are creamy white, 0.3″ (6.5–9
mm) long, the banner with purple or
violet veins.

Sericea is an eastern Asian plant
brought to this country to control erosion and for wildlife food plots (quail,
doves, etc.). It has spread dramatically
along roadsides, rights-of-way, and
clearings, and it is a nuisance in natural
longleaf pine and other communities. It
should be eradicated wherever possible.

Inhabits roadsides, rights-of-way,
clearings, and wildlife food plots and
has moved into dry longleaf pinelands.
Ranges from MA to s Ont., WI and NE
south to FL and TX.

JULY–SEPT.

ROSACEAE: ROSE FAMILY
Chickasaw Plum
Prunus angustifolia Marshall

Perennial woody shrub, usually forming dense colonies, plants mostly 3–6.5′
(1–2 m) high, branches abundant,
glabrous. Leaves are broadly lanceolate to
elliptic, 1.6–2.8″ (4–7 cm) long and 0.4–1″
(1–2.5 cm) wide, glabrate, tip acute to acuminate, base blunt, margins finely toothed
or crenate, leafstalk less than 0.4″ (1 cm)
long, reddish. Flowers appear just before
leaves, covering outer parts of branches
and twigs, 0.4–0.6″ (10–15 mm) across,
the 5 petals white. The fruit is a juicy
drupe, red or yellow, 0.8–1″ (2–2.5 cm)
across.

A sure sign of spring, Chickasaw Plum
forms clouds of white along roadsides and
in abandoned fields, soon to be forgotten
after the flowers drop. But return again
later! The fruits are large and brilliantly
colored and make tasty preserves. The
Chickasaws are a tribe of Native Americans originally from Mississippi.

Inhabits dry sandy roadsides, clearings,
abandoned fields, and woodland borders.
Ranges from NJ to MO and CO south to
n FL, TX, and NM.

MID-MAR.–EARLY APR.

ROSACEAE: ROSE FAMILY
Multiflora Rose
Rosa multiflora Thunberg

Perennial woody shrub with long, arching, spreading branches, the plant often
forming dense thickets. Plants grow to
6.5′ (2 m) tall, most branches are similar
in length, glabrous, with curved prickles.
Leaves are pinnate, the leafstalks with 2
narrow, fringed stipules appressed to the
base. The 7–9 leaflets are elliptic, mostly
0.4–2″ (1–5 cm) long, nearly sessile, margins toothed, glabrous above, pubescent
below. Flowers grow several to many in
clusters at ends of branches, the corolla
0.8–1.6″ (2–4 cm) across, its 5 petals white
(occasionally pale pink), stamens numerous and yellow.

A prolific fruiter, Multiflora Rose was
introduced and planted for wildlife as well
as for the horticultural trade. Birds and
mammals have spread it widely, so today
it is a major invasive weed over much of
eastern North America and costs millions
of dollars to control.

Inhabits dry roadsides, rights-of-way,
and openings in a variety of woodlands;
not fire-tolerant. Ranges from N.S. to
s Ont. south to FL and TX. Native to
e Asia.

MID-MAY–JUNE

ROSACEAE: ROSE FAMILY
Sand Blackberry
Rubus cuneifolius Pursh

Perennial, stems few to many, up to 5′
(1.5 m) long but usually less than 3′ (1 m),
erect, distinctly angled, densely downy.
Prickles are broad-based and curved; they
occur on stems, leafstalks, leaf veins, and
inflorescence branches. Leaves are divided
into 3 leaflets on flowering branches, 5
leaflets on nonflowering branches. Leaflets
are obovate to oblanceolate, 0.8–2″ (2–5
cm) long, glabrate, and dull green or grayish green above, densely downy beneath
with pale tan or whitish hairs, tip blunt
to acute, base short-tapered, margins
toothed or double-toothed. Flowers grow
in leafy clusters of 3–9 flowers; the 5 petals
are white, obovate, 0.4–0.6″ (1–1.5 cm)
long. The fruit is an aggregate berry, black,
to 1″ (2.5 cm) long and 0.6″ (1.5 cm) wide,
juicy.

Sand Blackberry's leaves are often a
distinctive grayish green color above,
and the twigs and leaf undersides are a
pale tan to dusty whitish color—easy to
recognize once learned.

Inhabits dry soil of roadsides, rights-
of-way, clearings in oak-hickory woods,
turkey oak scrub, and longleaf pinelands.
Ranges from CT to FL and MS, mostly on
the Coastal Plain.

LATE APR.–LATE MAY

ROSACEAE: ROSE FAMILY
Northern Dewberry
Rubus flagellaris Willdenow

Perennial, stems few to many, up to 6′
(2 m) long, trailing or weakly arching,
not angled, glabrate, often red- or purple-
tinged. Prickles are broad-based and
curved; they occur on stems, leafstalks,
and inflorescence branches. Leaves
are divided into 3 leaflets on flowering
branches, 5 leaflets on nonflowering
branches. Leaflets are ovate to narrowly
elliptic, 0.8–2.8″ (2–7 cm) long and 0.4–2″
(1–5 cm) wide, glabrous above, glabrous
to finely pubescent beneath, tip acute to
acuminate, base short-tapered to rounded,
margins toothed or double-toothed. Flowers grow singly or in small clusters, the 5
petals white, obovate, 0.6–1″ (1.5–2.5 cm)
long. The fruit is an aggregate berry, black,
to 1″ (2.5 cm) long and wide, juicy.

This trailing blackberry may cut your
ankles and shins but will reward you with
some of the best-tasting berries around.

Inhabits dry to moist soil of roadsides,
rights-of-way, fallow fields, clearings in
oak-hickory woods, and longleaf pinelands. Ranges from s QUE. to MN south
to sw GA and AR.

LATE APR.–LATE MAY

SOLANACEAE: TOMATO & POTATO FAMILY
Carolina Horse-nettle
Solanum carolinense L. var. *carolinense*

Perennial, stem 8–24″ (20–60 cm) tall
(occasionally taller), prickly, stellate-
pubescent, branches few. Leaves are ovate
to elliptic, 2.8–5″ (7–12.5 cm) long and
1.2–3.2″ (3–8 cm) wide, irregularly lobed,
the lobes with sharp tips, the surfaces
stellate-pubescent, major veins with scattered prickles. Flowers grow in terminal, few-flowered clusters. Corollas are
0.9–1.2″ (2.3–3 cm) across; the 5 petals are
fused, the outer halves spreading to form
a star shape. Petals are lavender to white,
the stamens yellow and pressed together
to form a cone. The fruit is a yellow berry,
0.4–0.6″ (1–1.5 cm) in diameter.

Although native, this familiar plant has
adapted to human-disturbed places and
has become weedy. The yellow prickles
are potently sharp! Carolina Horse-nettle
is mildly toxic to adults, but could be
poisonous to children. Despite this, Indians
used it as a painkiller and diuretic. Many
members of this plant family contain
potent alkaloids, including nicotine.

Inhabits roadsides, pastures, fallow
fields, farmyards, waste places, and floodplain forests. Ranges throughout eastern
North America, scattered in the West.

MAY–JULY

CONVOLVULACEAE: MORNING-GLORY FAMILY
Wild Sweet Potato; Manroot
Ipomoea pandurata (L.) G. F. W. Meyer

Perennial trailing or low-climbing vine
from a massive root, glabrous or sparsely
pubescent. Leaves are alternate, broadly
ovate, the margin entire or with a narrowed central portion, 1.6–3.2″ (4–8 cm)
long and 1.2–3.2″ (3–8 cm) wide, base
cordate (with notch or sinus), tip acute,
often pubescent beneath. Flowers grow
1–5 from leaf axils, the corolla bell-shaped
and widely flaring, 2.4–3.2″ (6–8 cm) long,
white with maroon center.

The two common names used here refer
to this plant's large root, reminiscent of
the cultivated Sweet Potato (*I. batatas*) but
not as tasty. Many other common names
have been given to this widespread and
distinctive plant. The species name *pandurata* means fiddle-shaped, a rather fanciful
reference to the leaf shape. Roots may extend 2 feet or longer and weigh 15 pounds;
they were sought by Native Americans for
use as a diuretic and laxative.

Inhabits roadsides, rights-of-way, and
disturbed soils; found less often in longleaf pinelands and oak-hickory woods.
Ranges from CT to s Ont. and KS south
to c FL and e TX.

MID-MAY–EARLY AUG.

CAPRIFOLIACEAE: HONEYSUCKLE FAMILY
Japanese Honeysuckle
Lonicera japonica Thunberg

Perennial trailing or high-climbing vine, the climbing portion woody and tightly constricting the host trunk. Leaves opposite, more or less evergreen, pubescent to glabrous, elliptical, 1.2–3″ (3–7.5 cm) long and 0.6–1.6″ (1.5–4 cm) wide, tip blunt to acute, margins toothless. Note that leaves of new shoots usually produce several narrow lobes. Flowers grow in pairs from leaf axils, very fragrant, white fading to dull yellow. Corollas are 1.2–2″ (3–5 cm) long, tubular with 2 flaring lips, the upper with 3–4 short lobes, the lower unlobed, stamens and style prominent. Berries lustrous black, *poisonous*.

Though lovely, Japanese Honeysuckle is one of the worst invasive weeds in the southeastern United States (others include Chinese Privet [*Ligustrum sinense*] and Japanese Stiltgrass [*Microstegium vimineum*]), where it covers acres of forest floor, smothering herbs and shrubs and strangling small trees. Worse, it is hard to eradicate. Fire keeps it out of longleaf pine communities. Japanese Honeysuckle has been used medicinally for centuries in east Asia; it has antiviral and antibacterial properties, and it lowers cholesterol.

Inhabits roadside thickets, urban and suburban yards, and other disturbed places, as well as bottomland forests, riverside slopes and terraces, and unburned oak-hickory woodlands. Ranges from MA to KS south to FL and TX.

LATE APR.–MID-JUNE

APOCYNACEAE:
DOGBANE & MILKWEED FAMILY
Indian Hemp; Hemp Dogbane
Apocynum cannabinum L.

Perennial herb with a few wide branches, up to 4.6′ (1.5 m) tall; stem and branches turn brittle and die back to ground in winter. Leaves are opposite, short-stalked, elliptic to broadly lance-shaped, 1.6–5.5″ (4–14 cm) long and 0.6–2.4″ (1.5–6 cm) wide, smooth to hairy beneath. Flowers grow in clusters from upper leaf axils, each flower white to greenish white, 0.2″ (3–5 mm) long, cup-shaped with 5 pointed lobes. Fruits are long, drooping pods that eventually split open to release seeds that blow away on long silken "parachutes."

Nothing else in our area looks quite like Indian Hemp. Older stems have strong but pliable fibers in them that were used by Native Americans for string and rope. The plant contains glycosides, which may be toxic to the heart, hence the name "dogbane"—harmful to dogs.

Inhabits dry to moist rights-of-way, roadsides, openings in woods, and loamy soil areas in pinelands. Ranges from Que. to WA south to FL, TX, and CA.

LATE MAY–MID-JULY

ROADSIDES AND DISTURBED GROUND **317**

RUBIACEAE: MADDER FAMILY
Virginia Buttonweed
Diodia virginiana L.

Perennial from a semiwoody root crown, stems widely spreading to erect, 5–24″ (10–60 cm) long, branched. Leaves opposite, sessile, broadly lance-shaped, 0.8–2.8″ (2–7 cm) long and 0.2–0.5″ (4–12 mm) wide, acute-tipped, sparsely to moderately hairy on margins and veins, often yellow-green. Flowers grow singly from leaf axils, sessile; the 4 petals form a tube 0.3–0.4″ (7–9 mm) long, with spreading lobes about 0.2″ (3–4 mm) long. Sepals usually 2, persisting on top of the mature fruit.

Unlike Poor Joe (*D. teres*), this grows in moist to wet soil, but like Poor Joe, it often grows in weedy situations.

Inhabits moist to wet or occasionally inundated soils of roadside ditches, borrow pits, pond shores, streamsides, and beaver marshes. Ranges from s CT to KS south to FL and TX.

JUNE–NOV.

RUBIACEAE: MADDER FAMILY
Mexican Clover
Richardia scabra L.

Annual, stem spreading to ascending, up to 28″ (70 cm) long where not mown but usually much shorter, much-branched, pilose. Leaves are opposite, elliptic, 1–2.8″ (2.5–7 cm) long and 0.4–0.8″ (1–2 cm) wide, tip acute, very short-stalked, glabrous except hairy midrib and margins. Flowers grow in dense, roundish, terminal clusters from leaflike bracts. Corollas are white, funnel-shaped, 3–10 mm long, with 4–6 pointed, flaring lobes.

Despite its name, Mexican Clover is not a clover at all, as you can tell from the flowers, which are not pealike flowers, and from the lack of bean pods. This is one of our most common weeds. Brazilian Clover (*R. brasiliensis*) is very similar, but corollas are only 3–7 mm long and leaves are hairy above and below; it is perennial from a thick rootstock.

Inhabits dry roadsides, fallow fields, pastures, yards, and other disturbed areas. Ranges mostly on the Coastal Plain from s NJ to s FL, c TX and AR; Mex.; Central America; South America. Original range unclear; U.S. occurrences may be all alien or perhaps native in southernmost regions.

JUNE–OCT.

TETRACHONDRACEAE:
TETRACHONDRA FAMILY
Rustweed; Juniper-leaf
Polypremum procumbens L.

Glabrous perennial from a root crown, the numerous "stems" (actually branches) radiating outward, prostrate to ascending, freely branched, mostly green but some are rust-colored or orange. Leaves are opposite, linear, 0.4–1″ (1–2.5 cm) long and 0.5–2 mm wide, tip acute to acuminate. Flowers grow singly from leaf axils, more or less sessile, the 4 petals white, each with an obovate lobe about 2 mm long.

Probably everyone who uses this guide has seen this plant before, for it is a common weed of poor soils. It is another of our plants "without a home" (its natural habitat is uncertain). In taxonomic circles Rustweed also seems to be without a home, as it has been placed in at least 4 different families.

Inhabits sandy roadsides, rights-of-way, and disturbed soil situations in pinelands and pine-oak-hickory woods. Ranges from se NY to MO south to FL and TX.

JUNE–SEPT.

BRASSICACEAE
Shepherd's Cress
Teesdalia nudicaulis R. Brown

Glabrous winter annual (basal rosette of leaves grows in late fall and lasts through winter), 1–8 stems grow up to 10″ (25 cm) tall. Basal leaves form a rosette, each leaf prostrate to ascending, 0.4–1.6″ (1–4 cm) long and up to 0.3″ (8 mm) wide, pinnately lobed, tapered to the stalk. The few stem leaves are much smaller, linear, sessile, ascending. Flowers grow in a dense terminal cluster that eventually elongates into a cylinder of flowers and fruits, the flower/fruit stalks eventually 0.2–0.3″ (4–8 mm) long. The 4 petals are white, elliptic, 1–2 mm long. The fruit is a flattened, rotund capsule, about 0.2″ (3 mm) long, notched at the tip.

Shepherd's Cress is originally from Europe, now rapidly spreading in the northern portions of our region. Plants begin to bloom when only a few inches tall, yet they occur in such numbers as to render them attractive.

Inhabits dry to very dry sandy soil of roadsides, cemeteries, sandpits, and disturbed ground. Ranges from MA to SC; also scattered locations in the Midwest and Pacific states.

LATE FEB.–MID-APR.

**EUPHORBIACEAE:
EUPHORBIA & SPURGE FAMILY**
Doveweed; Toothed Croton

Croton glandulosus L.
  var. *septentrionalis* Mueller-Aargau

Annual from a spicy fragrant taproot,
widely branched, to 2′ (0.7 m) or so tall,
densely stellate pubescent. Leaves relatively sparse, often in whorls or pseudo-
whorls, stalks 0.2–1.6″ (0.5–4 cm) long.
Leaf blades lance-shaped or narrow elliptical, 1.2–3.6″ (3–9 cm) long and 0.2–1.6″
(0.5–4 cm) wide, crenate, gray-green color.
Flowers grow on terminal leafy stalks,
female flowers small and inconspicuous, dull green-brown, male flowers
with 4 white petals.

Doveweed is a widespread, probably nonnative plant that is here to stay.
Despite its weedy tendencies, it is quite
striking and easy to recognize.

Inhabits cropfields, fallow fields,
wildlife food plots, roadsides, and other
disturbed sites. Widespread in eastern United States; originally from the
neotropics.

MID-MAY–OCT.

AMARANTHACEAE: AMARANTH FAMILY
Tall Cottonweed

Froelichia floridana (Nuttall) Moq.

Annual, stem normally single, 3–6′
(1–2 m) tall, branches paired or solitary
from upper leaf bases. Most of the plant
is covered with short, white or pale gray,
matted hairs with the texture of cotton.
Leaves opposite, well-spaced, lance-
shaped or narrowly elliptic, the larger
ones 2–4.8″ (5–12 cm) long and 0.25–1″
(5–25 mm) wide, blunt, short-stalked.
Flowers grow at tips of branches in dense
spikes 1.2–2.4″ (3–6 cm) long, densely cottony white, petals absent.

Well-named, Tall Cottonweed stands
above most other herbaceous vegetation,
and its flower spikes look like pointy tufts
of cotton. Slender Cottonweed (*F. gracilis*
[Hooker] Moq.) has similar but much
smaller spikes and has several stems that
spread low to the ground with branches
reaching upward 1–2′ (up to 70 cm).
Slender Cottonweed is spreading in the
Sandhills region along railroads and in
vacant lots and waste places.

Inhabits disturbed soil of roadsides,
fallow fields, wildlife food plots, railroads,
and clearings in pinelands. Ranges from
NC to FL, LA, and W TN; also MD and DE.

JUNE–OCT.

POLYGONACEAE:
SMARTWEED & BUCKWHEAT FAMILY
Heartwing Sorrel
Rumex hastatulus Baldwin

Glabrous annual, stems single or several, up to 2′ (60 cm) tall, branched in upper two-thirds, usually reddish-tinged. Leaves are lanceolate to oblanceolate, the blades 0.8–2.4″ (2–6 cm) long, with 2 widely spreading, pointed lobes at the base, the tip blunt. Leafstalks are half as long as blades or longer. Flowers grow loosely to densely in whorls of 3–6 along branches, each flower from a slender stalk 1.5–2.5 mm long. The 6 sepals are roundish with a cordate base, 0.2″ (2.5–3.2 mm) long and wide, dull white to pinkish; petals absent.

This weedy native makes large splashes of reddish color in fields in the spring, often contrasting with the pale blue of toadflaxes (*Nuttallanthus*). Named by William Baldwin (1779–1819), Georgia physician and prolific botanical collector. Sheep Sorrel (*R. acetosella*), a Eurasian weed, is similar but usually shorter, the flowers only 1.2–1.7 mm long, and is perennial from slender horizontal rhizomes.

Inhabits sandy soils of fallow fields, roadsides, pastures, and waste places. Ranges from se NY to KS south to S FL and NM.

MAR.–EARLY MAY

PHYTOLACCACEAE: POKEWEED FAMILY
Pokeweed
Phytolacca americana L.

Robust glabrous perennial to 10′ (3 m) tall, one or more thick, succulent stems grow from a root crown, the stems bright purple or magenta. Leaf blades are elliptic to broadly lanceolate, 3.2–12″ (8–30 cm) long and 1.2–5″ (3–12 cm) wide, tip acute, tapered to base, margins smooth, leafstalks 0.4–2″ (1–5 cm) long. Flowers grow on racemes of mostly 10–30 flowers, racemes arching to nodding, 2–8″ (5–20 cm) long; blooming proceeds from the base outward. The 5 sepals are dull white or greenish, about 0.2″ (2–3 mm) long, petals absent. The fruit is a juicy berry, 0.3–0.4″ (7–10 mm) wide, deep purple or blackish.

Familiar to just about everyone, Pokeweed has long been used as a salad green and was made famous in Tony Joe White's 1969 song "Poke Salad Annie." *Warning!* Use only very young leaves for salads, *older leaves and berries are poisonous!* The name "poke" is a corruption of the Algonquian word *pakon*, meaning bloody, in reference to the lurid color of the stem.

Inhabits disturbed soils in all sorts of habitats, including at treefalls in the middle of dense forests. Ranges from Que. to Ont. south to FL and TX.

MAY–OCT.

ASTERACEAE: ASTER FAMILY
Small's Ragwort
Packera anonyma (A. Wood) W. A. Weber & A. Löve
[*Senecio smallii* Britton]

Perennial, 12–28″ (30–70 cm) tall, usually unbranched, with white hairs becoming denser toward base. Leaves are mostly basal, erect to ascending, narrowly elliptical or lanceolate, 2–6″ (5–15 cm) long and 0.4–1.5″ (1–3.5 cm) wide, short-toothed. The middle and upper leaves are much smaller and tend to be deeply lobed or cut. Flower heads are numerous in terminal branched clusters and from upper leaf axils. The disc is about 0.25″ (5–8 mm) broad, with deep yellow flowers, the ray flowers 0.4–0.6″ (10–15 mm) long and yellow. Fruits are dark brown nutlets about 1.6 mm long, with white hairs that sail in the breeze.

This is a native plant that seems not to have a home; that is, it is not tied to any particular natural habitat but occurs in disturbed soils and open areas of many kinds.

Inhabits roadsides, rights-of-way, woodland clearings, pastures, and disturbed soils. Ranges from s PA to KY south to FL and MS.

MAY–EARLY JUNE

ASTERACEAE: ASTER FAMILY
Tickseed Sunflower; Ditch Daisy
Bidens polylepis S. F. Blake

Annual from a taproot, stem to 6′ (2 m) tall, glabrate, widely branched. Leaves are pinnate, divided into 5–7 lance-shaped segments 1.2–4″ (3–10 cm) long; each segment may be divided or lobed. Flower heads grow at ends of stem and branches, on short to long stalks; the 12–21 outer bracts are green, linear, 0.3–0.6″ (8–15 mm) long, with bristly hairs. Ray flowers are yellow, large and showy, 1–1.6″ (2.5–4 cm) long; the disc is about 0.4–0.6″ (10–15 mm) wide, deep yellow. Seeds are flattened, about 0.25″ (5–7 mm) long and 0.2″ (2.5–3.5 mm) wide, awns 0–2.

This primarily midwestern plant has spread in the past 50 years to the southeastern and Atlantic states, creating showy patches. Tickseed Sunflower is often confused with members of the genus *Coreopsis*, but it differs in the numerous outer bracts with bristly hairs, and wingless seed (vs. wing broad and toothed). Very similar is *Bidens aristosa* (same common names); it differs primarily in its fewer flower head bracts (8–12) that are only 0.25–0.3″ (5–8 mm) long and lack spinelike hairs, and it occupies the same habitats.

Inhabits moist to wet roadside ditches, marshes, and meadows. Ranges from NJ to CO south to GA and NM.

AUG.–OCT.

ASTERACEAE: ASTER FAMILY
Bitterweed

Helenium amarum (Rafinesque) H. Rock

Annual, stem 4–20″ (10–50 cm) tall
(occasionally taller), usually widely
branched to form a bushy aspect. Leaves
are abundant, linear, 0.8–2.8″ (2–7 cm)
long and less than 0.2″ (4 mm) wide,
punctate (tiny rounded depressions on
surfaces), slightly fragrant. Flower heads
grow terminally, 0.6–1″ (1.5–2.5 cm)
broad, rays yellow, disc dull yellow.

In 1817 Constantine Rafinesque, the
original describer, said, "The whole plant
is odoriferous and intensely bitter, it gives
an abominable taste to the milk of the
cows that feed on it in summer." Originally a southern species, it has aggressively expanded northward.

Inhabits open roadsides, rights-of-
way, fallow cropfields, pastures, and waste
places. Ranges from MA to MI south to FL
and TX; Mex.

MAY–NOV.

ASTERACEAE: ASTER FAMILY
Narrowleaf Sunflower

Helianthus angustifolius L.

Perennial, stem single or multiple, 3–6′
(1–2 m) tall, hispid (with rough hairs),
sometimes reclining on other vegetation. Lower leaves opposite, upper leaves
alternate, linear, 2.4–8″ (6–20 cm) long
and 0.2–0.6″ (4–14 mm) wide, margins usually rolled under, blades nearly
sessile. The upper surface is very rough
(scabrous); lower surface is densely
pubescent. Flowering heads are terminal,
disc flowers dark purplish brown, about
0.6″ (15 mm) across, ray flowers bright
yellow, 0.8–1.6″ (2–4 cm) long.

Narrowleaf Sunflower is one of our
showiest plants. Although widespread,
it is absent from many seemingly suitable
places.

Inhabits moist to wet roadside ditches,
pinelands, flatwoods, and margins of
beaver ponds. Ranges mostly on the
Coastal Plain from se NY to c FL and e TX,
scattered inland to OH and MO.

LATE AUG.–OCT.

ASTERACEAE: ASTER FAMILY
Sandhills Golden-aster

Pityopsis pinifolia (Elliott) Nuttall
[*Heterotheca pinifolia* (Elliott) Ahles]

Perennial, up to 1.5′ (0.5 m) tall but often much shorter. Stems are slender, with crowded linear leaves 3–4″ (7–10 cm) long and 0.2″ (3 mm) wide, leaf tips pointed. Flower heads grow in a flat-topped inflorescence, each head 1–1.5″ (2.5–3.5 cm) wide, long-stalked. Ray and disc flowers are yellow. Shorter and broader basal leaves are produced in late fall; these overwinter but usually disappear by blooming time.

Although generally considered to be a very uncommon plant in natural, fire-maintained communities, Sandhills Golden-aster may be abundant where the topsoil has been scraped away, as well as on roadsides. One local name is Taylor County Golden-aster, in reference to its occurrence in western GA.

Found in very dry to dry sandy soils of longleaf pinelands, turkey oak scrub, roadsides, and disturbed areas. Endemic to the Sandhills region, documented only from 10 counties in NC, 2 in SC, 6 in GA, and 1 in AL.

LATE JUNE–SEPT.

ASTERACEAE: ASTER FAMILY
Slender Scratch-daisy

Croptilon divaricatum (Nuttall) Rafinesque
[*Haplopappus divaricatus* (Nuttall) Gray]

Winter annual (basal leaves are produced in autumn, overwinter, usually wither by flowering time) from a taproot, the slender stem 16″–4.5′ (0.4–1.4 m) tall, branched above, with simple and gland-tipped hairs. Stem leaves oblanceolate, 1–4″ (2.5–10 cm) long and 0.2–0.5″ (3–12 mm) wide, sharp-tipped, margins few-toothed, tapered to sessile base, with rough hairs above. Flower heads grow at ends of slender branches, bracts of the head form a short cylinder or tube, with prominent gland-tipped hairs. Ray flowers yellow, spreading 0.7–1″ across, disc flowers dull yellow.

Although quite weedy in nature, Slender Scratch-daisy has pretty, butter-yellow flowers; a large group of plants is a handsome sight.

Occurs in poor sandy soil in a variety of disturbed habitats, including roadsides, fallow fields, rights-of-way, and openings in dry oak-hickory woodlands and pinelands. Ranges on the Coastal Plain from se VA to c FL, e TX, and s AR.

AUG.–OCT.

ASTERACEAE: ASTER FAMILY
Hairy Cat's-ear
Hypochaeris radicata L.

Perennial from a thick rootstalk and a flat rosette of basal leaves, stems solitary to many, leafless, glabrous or pubescent, 12–24″ (30–60 cm) tall. Leaves all basal, 2–6″ (5–15 cm) long, oblanceolate, irregularly or pinnately dissected or lobed, densely pubescent with hispid hairs. Flower heads grow singly at tip of stem and from ends of branches, 0.8–1.2″ (2–3 cm) across, rays abundant, yellow; disc flowers absent. Seeds are about 0.25″ (5 mm) long, with long feathery hairs.

Hairy Cat's-ear is an aggressive alien weed that produces prolific amounts of seeds that float on the wind via the plumose seeds, just like "parachutes" of dandelions. It presently is not a serious problem in natural habitats, but chemical manufacturers make millions of dollars by selling weed-killers to rid lawns of Hairy Cat's-ear and other unwanted plants.

Inhabits roadsides, fallow fields, lawns, urban parks, and many other disturbed places. Ranges in North America from ME to B.C. south to FL and TX; originally from Eurasia.

APR.–JULY

ASTERACEAE: ASTER FAMILY
False Dandelion
Pyrrhopappus carolinianus (Walter) DC.

Biennial, rarely perennial, stem green, sparsely branched in upper third, 1–3′ (0.3–1 m) tall, pubescent in upper half. Leaves are basal or near-basal, sometimes to midstem or higher, oblanceolate, 3.2–10″ (8–25 cm) long, irregularly lobed or dissected, or merely toothed, tip acute. The basal leaves are stalked; the stem leaves, sessile. Flower heads terminate the stem and branches, ray flowers abundant, pale yellow, about 1″ (2–2.5 cm) long; disc flowers are absent. Seeds are cylindrical, tapered to both ends, 0.2″ (4–4.5 mm) long, with a long beak leading to a "parachute" of feathery hairs.

Common Dandelion (*Taraxacum officinale*) looks similar only at a distance; its stems are hollow and tan-colored and lack stem leaves, and its flowers are deeper yellow. The original habitat of False Dandelion is unknown; today it only occurs in disturbed places.

Inhabits roadsides, fallow fields, disturbed soils, and forest clearings. Ranges from se PA to MO south to c FL and e TX.

APR.–JUNE

ASTERACEAE: ASTER FAMILY
Virginia Dwarf-dandelion
Krigia virginica (L.) Willdenow

Annual with numerous, essentially leaf-less stems up to 1′ (30 cm) tall, but mostly half as tall. Leaves are nearly all basal, spreading flat or ascending, oblanceolate, up to 4″ (10 cm) long and 1″ (2.5 cm) wide. Stems are terminated by a single, flat-topped head of abundant yellow ray flowers, the rays 0.25–0.4″ (6–10 mm) long, disc flowers absent. Seeds develop a "parachute" of straw-colored bristles at one end, forming a round ball atop each stem.

The fruiting head is a miniature version of Common Dandelion (*Taraxacum officinale*), and the feathery bristles serve the same purpose: to act as a parachute to disperse seeds. Opposite-leaved Dwarf-dandelion (*K. caespitosa*) is similar but taller (up to 50 cm), the stems are branched, and it has opposite leaves on the stems.

Inhabits roadsides, rights-of-way, abandoned fields, yards, and other disturbed areas, generally in poor soil. Ranges from ME to MN south to c FL and c TX.

LATE MAR.–EARLY JUNE

ASTERACEAE: ASTER FAMILY
Yellow Wild Lettuce
Lactuca canadensis L.

Biennial, 3–10′ (1–3 m) tall, glabrous, sap milky. Leaves are lanceolate or oblanceo-late, 4–10″ (10–25 cm) long, 1–4″ (2.5–10 cm) wide, acute, irregularly dissected or merely toothed (sometimes entire). Leaf bases are tapered to the stem and some-what clasping. The upper part of stem is widely branched (sometimes narrowly), each branch terminated by a flower head. Heads about 0.4″ (10 mm) across, ray flowers numerous, yellow to deep yellow, disc flowers absent. Seeds disperse via a "parachute" of white hairs.

This is one of two native species of yellow-flowered wild lettuces in our region; two others are nonnatives. The commercial or garden lettuce is *L. sativa*, in cultivation for millennia and a staple of our diet. Yellow Wild Lettuce has not been grown as a food plant, but the dried sap was once thought (erroneously) to have narcotic qualities, since it looks and smells like opium.

Inhabits roadsides, fallow fields, disturbed ground, and openings in oak-hickory woods. Ranges from N.S. to B.C. south to FL and CA.

LATE MAY–OCT.

FABACEAE: PEA & BEAN FAMILY
Showy Rattlebox

Crotalaria spectabilis Roth

Annual from a woody taproot, to 39″ (1 m) tall (sometimes taller), stem sparsely hairy, glaucescent, often purple-tinged. Leaves unlobed, obovate, 2–8″ (5–20 cm) long; stipules ovate, 0.25–0.4″ (5–8 mm) long. Lots of flowers grow on 1 to many stalks up to 19″ (0.5 m) long, petals rich yellow, about 0.7–1″ (15–25 mm) long. Pod 1.2–2″ (3–5 cm) long and 0.6″ (1.4 cm) thick.

Showy Rattlebox has a well-deserved name, and there are few in the bean family that can trump it. However, it is an invasive alien, and it has an unsavory reputation, particularly among farmers, but seldom causes problems in natural communities.

Inhabits cropfields, fallow fields, wildlife food plots, roadsides, and other disturbed sites. Widespread in eastern United States, originally from south Asia.

JULY–SEPT.

FABACEAE: PEA & BEAN FAMILY
Common Partridge-pea

Chamaecrista fasciculata (Michaux) Greene
    var. *fasciculata*
[*Cassia fasciculata* Michaux]

Coarse annual herb to 28″ (0.7 m) tall, with widely spreading branches. Leaves are finely divided into 12–36 linear to elliptic leaflets. Each leaflet is 0.4–1″ (1–2.5 cm) long and up to 0.25″ (2–6 mm) wide, mildly sensitive (folds up after contact). Flowers grow in small clusters in leaf axils, the 5 yellow petals more or less equal, 0.4–0.8″ (1–2 cm) long, stamens 10. Pods are 1.25–2.75″ (3–7 cm) long and 0.2–0.3″ (5–7 mm) wide.

Common Partridge-pea is a native with weedy habits, so it may be found in many disturbed areas. It generally avoids fire-maintained communities. Other geographical varieties have been described, but they do not occur in our region. Cherokee Indians used a root tea to relieve fatigue. The flattish, spreading petals of *Chamaecrista*, *Senna*, *Cassia*, and their nearest relatives do not look like typical pea flowers (the pods reveal that they are true legumes); they are placed in a distinct subfamily (Caesalpinioideae).

Inhabits woodland trails and openings, roadsides, rights-of-way, cropfields, pastures, yards, and logging roads. Ranges from MA to MN south to FL and TX; Mex.

MID-JUNE–SEPT.

ROSACEAE: ROSE FAMILY
Dwarf Cinquefoil; Running Cinquefoil

Potentilla canadensis L.

Perennial, the runnerlike stems creeping along the ground and rooting at nodes, up to 2′ (60 cm) or so long but only a few inches in depauperate plants, stems with long, silky hairs. Leaves grow at most nodes; they are palmately 5-lobed, the lobes oblanceolate to obovate, 0.4–1.6″ (1–4 cm) long and 0.3–0.8″ (8–20 mm) wide, toothed in the outer third, the lower surface and leafstalks with long, appressed, silky hairs. Flowers grow singly from leaf axils on stalks 0.8–2.4″ (2–6 cm) long; the 5 petals are yellow, obovate, or obdeltate, 0.3–0.4″ (7–10 mm) long.

The word "cinquefoil" is French for "five leaves," in reference to the leaf shape. Five-fingers (*P. simplex*) is very similar, but it has much longer leaflets and in our area inhabits moist floodplain forests and their margins. To make a positive identification, be sure the first flower on a given stem of *P. canadensis* grows from the first fully developed leaf; the first flower grows from the second fully developed leaf in *P. simplex*.

Inhabits roadsides, rights-of-way, yards, and other disturbed soil; also found in oak-hickory woodlands. Ranges from N.S. to s Ont. south to c GA (Bibb, Harris, and Johnson Counties) and MO.

LATE MAR.–EARLY JUNE

ROSACEAE: ROSE FAMILY
Sulphur Cinquefoil

Potentilla recta L.

Perennial, stems solitary or several, erect, mostly 8–24″ (20–60 cm) tall, densely hairy. Leaves are palmately 5–7 lobed, the lobes oblanceolate, 0.8–4″ (2–10 cm) long and 0.3–1.2″ (8–30 mm) wide, margins coarsely toothed, surfaces and leafstalks densely hairy, leafstalks longer than the blade. Flowers grow in terminal, branched, nearly flat-topped inflorescences, the 5 petals pale yellow, obovate or obdeltate, 0.4–0.6″ (9–15 mm) long.

Sulphur Cinquefoil occurs mostly north of our range, where it is a common sight in old fields and meadows. It is one of the more beautiful—and welcome—Eurasian weeds.

Inhabits dry to moist roadsides, rights-of-way, and other disturbed soil sites. Ranges from Newf. to MN south to wc GA (Harris County) and TX.

APR.–EARLY JUNE

CISTACEAE: ROCKROSE FAMILY
Rosemary Frostweed; Rosemary Sunrose

Crocanthemum rosmarinifolium (Pursh) Barnhart
[*Helianthemum rosmarinifolium* Pursh]

Perennial, 8–19″ (20–50 cm) tall, plant densely pubescent with very short, stellate hairs that impart a pale gray-green cast. Leaves 10–30, ascending to erect, lance-shaped to broadly linear, 0.6–1.6″ (1.5–4 cm) long and up to 0.3″ (2–7 mm) wide, on short stalks up to 0.2″ (3 mm) long. Flowers grow from short branches on stalks up to 0.5″ (12 mm) long, the 5 pale yellow petals 0.4–0.6″ (8–12 mm) long.

Rosemary Frostweed is an unusual native plant, in that it seems not to have a natural habitat—all known populations occur in disturbed places. Its flowers are smaller and paler than those of Canada Frostweed (*C. canadense*), but many plants produce only flowers without petals ("cleistogamous," meaning "hidden flower"), and these are not noticed because they are hidden within the unopened sepals.

Inhabits dry to very dry roadbanks, rights-of-way, airfields, and other disturbed areas, generally within the longleaf pine ecosystem. Ranges on the Coastal Plain from se NC to nw FL, c TX, and se OK.

MID-MAY–MID-JUNE

HYPERICACEAE: ST. JOHN'S-WORT FAMILY
Pineweed; Orange-grass

Hypericum gentianoides (L.) B.S.P.

Annual, 4–20″ (10–50 cm) tall; the slender branches are strongly ascending to erect, most plants forming bushy tufts. Leaves opposite, sessile, linear or scalelike, up to 0.25″ (2–5 mm) long and 0.5 mm wide, acute. Flowers grow alternately on terminal branches, petals 5, yellow, 0.2″ (2–4 mm) long.

Although annual, the base of the plant gets tough and semiwoody by the end of the growing season and remains through winter. One of our most familiar roadside "weeds" but entirely native. The species name *gentianoides* means "gentian-like," referring to small, slender, European gentians known to Linnaeus.

Inhabits roadsides, lawns, pastures, fallow cropfields, rock outcrops, and other disturbed situations. Ranges from ME to Ont. and MN south to FL and TX.

JULY–OCT.

ONAGRACEAE: EVENING-PRIMROSE FAMILY
Cutleaf Evening-primrose
Oenothera laciniata Hill

Biennial, pubescent, the lower stems prostrate to ascending, the upper stems ascending to erect, branched, the whole plant up to 30″ (75 cm) long, but often much shorter. Leaves are broadly lanceolate to elliptic, 1–4″ (2.5–10 cm) long, acute to blunt-tipped, short-tapered to base. Leaf margins are irregularly pinnate or toothed, rarely entire, the lowest leaves on stalks up to 1.2″ (3 cm) long, upper leaves sessile. Flowers grow terminally and from upper leaf axils. The sepals form a narrow tube 0.8–1″ (20–25 mm) long with 4 lobes 0.25–0.5″ (6–12 mm) long and swept back (reflexed); the 4 petals are pale yellow, 0.4–0.8″ (10–20 mm) long and wide, each with a shallow notch at the tip.

Cutleaf Evening-primrose, like some other roadside species, has been "trained" to spread its stems sideways so as to avoid being cut by mowers. It is another native species that appears to lack a natural habitat, being found only in highly disturbed sites. Despite the fact that this plant opens its flowers throughout the day, the name "evening-primrose" has stuck.

Inhabits open roadsides, fallow fields, wildlife food plots, and other disturbed soil sites. Ranges from s ME to ND south to FL and TX.

MAR.–JULY

OXALIDACEAE: WOOD-SORREL FAMILY
Common Yellow Wood-sorrel
Oxalis stricta L.

Annual or short-lived perennial, stem single, much-branched, 6–24″ (15–60 cm) tall, sparsely hairy or smooth (but may be densely pubescent out of our range). Leaves grow on long stalks, the 3 leaflets 0.4–0.8″ (10–20 mm) long, obovate, deeply notched. Flowers grow in groups of 5–7 (sometimes fewer) on stalks 1.2–3.6″ (3–9 cm) long from leaf axils. The 5 petals are yellow, 0.3–0.4″ (8–11 mm) long and curved outward. The fruiting capsule is about 0.4″ (1 cm) long, pale green, cylindrical, tapered to a pointed tip.

This is one of the commonest plants in eastern North America, in part due to its ability to colonize a wide variety of natural and disturbed habitats, from deep forests to lawns.

In our area it inhabits roadsides, clearings, yards, rights-of-way, and oak-hickory woods; it avoids fire-managed habitats. Ranges from Newf. to Sask. south to FL and LA.

MID-APR.–OCT.

MALVACEAE: MALLOW FAMILY

Diamondleaf Fanpetal

Sida rhombifolia L.

Annual, up to 30″ (80 cm) tall, usually with sparse, ascending branches, plant stellate-hairy (hairs with several branches radiating from one point). Leaves relatively sparse, rhombic (diamond-shaped or spindle-shaped), mostly 1.2–3.2″ (3–8 cm) long, grayish green, tapered to both ends, nearly sessile, margins smooth or crenate. Flowers grow singly from leaf axils, their stalks up to 1.2″ (3 cm) long, the 5 petals 0.3–0.4″ (8–10 mm) long, creamy yellow or straw-yellow, each petal bent obliquely.

The words "Diamondleaf Fanpetal" give a pretty good description of the main features of this plant. It is a weedy alien and may show up almost anywhere, as it seems not to have a habitat preference.

Inhabits roadsides, fallow fields, pastures, gardens, disturbed soil, and waste ground. Ranges throughout much of the tropics and subtropics, in the U.S. north to VA and AR.

JUNE–OCT.

ROSACEAE: ROSE FAMILY

Carolina Rose

Rosa carolina L.

Perennial woody shrub, potentially to 3′ (1 m) tall, but our plants are normally 8–18″ (20–45 cm), widely branched, with slender, straight thorns. Leaves are pinnate, the leafstalks with 2 narrow stipules appressed to the base. The 5–7 (up to 9) leaflets are elliptic, 0.6–1.6″ (1.5–4 cm) long, nearly sessile, margins toothed. Flowers grow singly at ends of branches, 1.4–2.2″ (3.5–5.5 cm) across, the 5 petals pale pink to deep pink, stamens numerous, yellow.

Its low stature and relatively short blooming period probably keep Carolina Rose from being a popular garden subject, but it could work well in a dry, natural garden setting. It is one of only two native roses in our region; the other roses are garden escapes, adventive from the horticultural trade, or planted for wildlife.

Inhabits dry roadsides, rights-of-way, openings in oak-hickory woods, and rocky slopes. Ranges from s N.B. to s Ont. south to FL and TX.

MID-MAY–JUNE

GERANIACEAE: GERANIUM FAMILY
Carolina Crane's-bill

Geranium carolinianum L. var. *carolinianum*

Annual from overwintering basal leaves.
Stems erect to spreading, 4–24″ (10–60
cm) tall, widely branched, with dense,
downward-pointing hairs. Leaves are
pubescent, 0.6–1.2″ (1.5–3 cm) long and
1.2–2″ (3–5 cm) wide, palmately dissected
into 5–7 deep lobes, these again divided
into linear segments. Basal and lower
leaves are long-stalked; upper ones are
short-stalked to sessile. Flowers grow
in pairs from upper branches, forming
clusters of 4–12 flowers. Petals 5, pale pink,
about 0.25″ (5 mm) long. Fruit is a dry
capsule, tapered to a beaklike tip, the
whole 0.4–0.6″ (10–14 mm) long.

The name "crane's-bill" comes from
the long beak of the fruit. Although a very
weedy species, Carolina Crane's-bill is a
native member of our flora and should not
be confused with alien (nonnative) plants,
which can spread to the detriment of native vegetation.

Inhabits dry to moist clearings, roadsides, pastures, cropfields, town parks, and
forest openings. Ranges from MA to B.C.
south to FL and S CA.

LATE MAR.–JUNE OR LATER

FABACEAE: PEA & BEAN FAMILY
Bicolor Bush-clover

Lespedeza bicolor Turczaninow

Perennial shrub with thick stems and
widely spreading branches, 3–10′ (1–3 m)
tall, with or without short, appressed
hairs. Leaves are alternate, the stalks
0.8–2.4″ (2–6 cm) long. The 3 leaflets are
elliptic to ovate, 0.8–2″ (2–5 cm) long
and 0.4–1.2″ (1–3 cm) wide, surfaces with
sparse, appressed hairs, tip blunt with a
tiny point. The numerous flowers grow
in branched clusters (panicles) from the
outer branches of the plant and/or in loose
racemes from axils of upper stem leaves.
Petals are rosy or purple, 0.4–0.5″ (10–12
mm) long. The pod is broadly elliptic
0.25–0.3″ (6–8 mm) long, with a long
point (persistent style).

Bicolor Bush-clover is a native of Japan,
brought to the United States to control
erosion and for wildlife food plots (quail,
doves, etc.). It has spread dramatically in
many parts of the Coastal Plain, where it
often is a noxious weed in longleaf pine
communities. It should be eradicated
wherever possible.

Inhabits roadsides, rights-of-way, wildlife food plots, dry longleaf pinelands, and
oak-hickory woodlands. Ranges from MA
to S Ont. and IA south to FL and TX.

MID-JUNE–SEPT.

RUBIACEAE: MADDER FAMILY
Poor Joe; Buttonweed
Diodia teres Walter

Annual, stems 6–24″ (15–60 cm) tall,
branched or not, pale green. Leaves opposite, sessile, narrowly to broadly lance-
shaped, 0.8–1.6″ (2–4 cm) long and 0.2″
(2–4 mm) wide, sharp-tipped, with sparse,
appressed hairs. Flowers grow singly
from leaf axils, sessile, petals 4, white or
lavender-pink, tube about 0.25″ (4–5 mm)
long, 4 spreading lobes 1–2 mm long. The
4 sepals persist on top of the mature fruit.

Poor Joe is named not for any attribute
of the plant but for the poor sandy soil
that it thrives in—often where few other
plants will grow. One of our weediest of
native species.

Inhabits dry, nutrient-poor sandy
soil in all sorts of disturbed situations:
roadsides, trails, scrapes, rights-of-way,
landfills, building sites, and cropfields.
Ranges from MA to WI south to FL and
TX; Mex.; Central America.

JUNE–NOV.

POLYGALACEAE: MILKWORT FAMILY
Curtiss's Milkwort;
Appalachian Milkwort
Polygala curtissii Gray

Glabrous annual, branched or not, 5–15″
(12–35 cm) tall. Leaves are linear to narrowly lanceolate, 0.5–1.3″ (12–30 mm) long
and up to 0.2″ (4 mm) wide, tip acute.
Flowers grow in a terminal head; the
stem below the flowers elongates greatly
as fruits are produced. The flowering
portion of the stem is about 0.5″ (12 mm)
long and wide. Flowers are bright pink
to rose-purple, the spread wings about
0.4″ (10 mm) across, the slender, pointed
flower bracts persistent.

Maryland Milkwort (*P. mariana*) is very
similar but has paler pink flowers, and the
bracts drop promptly after flowering; it
is a Coastal Plain endemic. Both species
occur in the Sandhills region, but neither
is common here.

Inhabits fields, roadsides, rights-of-
way, and openings in oak-hickory woods.
A Piedmont/Mountain species, ranging
from se PA to OH south to sc GA and
ne MS.

JUNE–AUG. (OR LATER)

POLYGALACEAE: MILKWORT FAMILY
Bitter Milkwort
Polygala polygama Walter

Glabrous biennial or short-lived perennial, 8–18″ (20–45 cm) tall, several unbranched stems arise from one point. Leaves are broadly linear to oblanceolate, 0.7–1.5″ (1.7–3.7 cm) long, tip sharply pointed. Flowers grow loosely in narrow terminal clusters up to 3″ (7.5 cm) long (much longer in fruit), pink to rosy, the spread wings about 0.5″ (12 mm) across.

In the Sandhills region, Bitter Milkwort is much more likely to be found in GA and SC than in NC. Late in the season it produces fertile but petal-less flowers, called cleistogamous ("hidden") flowers, at or near ground level.

Inhabits fields, roadsides, rights-of-way, and openings in oak-hickory woods. A wide-ranging species, from N.S. to MN south to FL and TX.

MAY–JUNE

PORTULACACEAE: PURSLANE FAMILY
Hairy Purslane; Kiss-me-quick
Portulaca pilosa L.

Annual, with succulent, prostrate, spreading stems and branches. Leaves are oblanceolate, to 1.2″ (3 cm) long and 0.3″ (8 mm) wide, succulent-textured, tip blunt or rounded, with coarse hairs in leaf axils. Flowers grow singly in leaf axils, sessile, the petals usually 5, magenta to maroon, the stamens 8 or more, yellow.

Each flower lasts only a few hours, giving rise to one of the common names. "Purslane" is an English corruption of *porcelaine*, an old French word for plants of this genus.

Inhabits roadsides, sidewalks, waste ground, yards, and other disturbed situations. Ranges from NC to AR and NM south to S FL and S TX; Mex.; Central America.

JUNE–EARLY OCT.

ASTERACEAE: ASTER FAMILY
Yellow Thistle

Cirsium horridulum Michaux var. *horridulum*

Biennial, forming a large basal rosette the first year, then a very thick stem the second; stem 2–3′ (0.7–1 m) tall, with dense cobwebby hairs (entangled). Leaves spread widely, up to 1′ (30 cm) long and 4″ (10 cm) wide, the blades covered with cobwebby hairs, irregularly lobed and dissected, each division prickle-tipped. One to 5 (or more) heads grow at top of stem on thick stalks, the outer bracts loose, erect, leaflike, with long prickles. Heads are about 2″ (5 cm) across, the disc flowers all alike, dull yellow or maroon; rays absent. Seeds are black with white plumes forming a "parachute."

The Latin name is well-chosen, for Yellow Thistle is a formidable plant with its imposing size and abundant painful prickles. Most plants in the Sandhills region produce maroon flowers. The white, flosslike plumes of fruiting thistles are eagerly sought by goldfinches to line their nests. Botanists are unclear about its original habitat, as it does not now occur in any natural communities in our area.

Inhabits dry to moist roadsides, abandoned fields, rights-of-way, and other disturbed sites. Ranges on the Coastal Plain and lower Piedmont from s ME to c FL and e TX; c TN.

EARLY APR.–MID-JUNE

FABACEAE: PEA & BEAN FAMILY
Winter Vetch

Vicia villosa Roth ssp. *varia* (Host) Corbier

Annual, biennial, or short-lived perennial, stems trailing or low-climbing, 1.5–3′ (0.5–1 m) long, glabrate. Leaves are divided into 14–20 leaflets plus a branched, curling tendril at the tip used for climbing. The leaflets are narrowly elliptic, 0.6–1.2″ (1.5–3 cm) long, more or less pubescent on surfaces. Ten to 20 flowers grow in 1-sided, spikelike racemes, the flower stalks 1–2 mm long, the petals purple to violet-purple, the standard 0.5–0.7″ (1.2–1.7 cm) long. Pods are green, turning brown, 0.8–1.6″ (2–4 cm) long and 0.3–0.4″ (7–10 mm) wide, compressed lengthwise.

Vetches of various species were introduced to North America as fodder for livestock; others hitched rides in hay bales or in packing material. To learn them, you need to consult a technical reference. Winter Vetch produces many showy flower clusters and so is hard to miss.

Inhabits roadsides, fallow fields, and agricultural areas. Ranges from ME to MT south to GA and CA. Originally from Europe.

MAY–JUNE, OCCASIONALLY LATER

FABACEAE: PEA & BEAN FAMILY
Kudzu

Pueraria montana (Loureiro) Merritt

Perennial, trailing, scrambling, or high-climbing vine up to 100′ (30 m) long from a thick rootstalk, the stems with dense brownish hairs. Leaves are divided into 3 leaflets, each leaflet broadly ovate or rotund, the margin entire or irregularly 2–3 lobed, 2–8″ (5–20 cm) long and broad, densely pubescent beneath. Leafstalk usually longer than leaf, brownish hairy. Flowers grow in dense, fragrant, spikelike racemes from leaf axils, the 5 petals purple or violet-purple, the standard (the erect petal) obovate, 0.6–1″ (1.5–2.5 cm) long and with a yellow blotch.

Kudzu is here to stay, so we might as well deal with it. We can admire the flowers' sweet fragrance and the "monster" shapes that smothering vines create. Kudzu was brought to the Southeast from eastern Asia in the 1920s and 1930s as a soil stabilizer; it did the job but now is tough to control. "Goat patrols" have proven successful locally. Despite popular fears, Kudzu does not invade undisturbed forest habitats; because it requires high light levels, it remains on the outside. Fortunately, kudzu is cold-sensitive, so its prolific growth disappears over winter.

Inhabits roadside thickets, forest and woodland edges, abandoned fields, vacant lots, and other disturbed soil sites. Ranges from N.S. to NY and NE south to FL and TX.

MID-JULY–SEPT.

RUBIACEAE: MADDER FAMILY
Early Bluet; Star-violet

Houstonia pusilla Schoepf

Slender annual, 0.8–4″ (2–10 cm) tall. Basal leaves are produced in autumn but usually wither by flowering time, opposite and conspicuously stalked, the blades ovate or elliptical, about 0.25″ (3–5 mm) long. Stem leaves are lanceolate and smaller. Flowers grow singly at stem tip or also on 1–2 long stalks from stem leaf axils. Petals 4, violet with a red throat, corolla tube 0.2–0.25″ (3–5 mm) long, lobes about the same and spreading horizontally.

Early Bluet is very well-named, as it is one of our earliest spring plants, often forming violet patches on roadsides in the company of the pale blue flowers of Wild Pansy (*Viola bicolor*).

Inhabits roadsides, old fields, lawns, and other disturbed sites. Ranges from MD to NE south to nw FL and e TX.

MAR.–MID-APR.

PASSIFLORACEAE: PASSION-FLOWER FAMILY
Maypops; Passion Flower
Passiflora incarnata L.

Perennial glabrate vine, climbing or
sprawling via tendrils to 13′ (4 m) long.
Leaves are palmately 3-lobed, 2.4–6″ (6–15
cm) long and wide, the lobes finely serrate,
acute to acuminate, stalks 0.4–1.6″ (1–4
cm) long. Flowers grow singly from leaf
axils, the 5 sepals 1–1.4″ (2.5–3.5 cm) long,
green below and white above, the 5 petals
bluish to whitish, 1.2–1.6″ (3–4 cm) long.
Each flower has a "corona" (crownlike
structure) of dozens of threadlike segments up to 1.2″ (3 cm) long, banded with
violet-purple and whitish. At the center of
the corona are 5 protruding stamens and 3
diverging styles. The fruit is a large berry,
pale green, broadly elliptical, 1.6–2.8″
(4–7 cm) long.

"Maypop" is a corruption of the
Powhatan Indian word *mahcawq*. Indians
used it as a sedative and muscle relaxant.
The story of the Passion is reflected in the
flower: the 5 sepals and 5 petals corre-
spond to the ten apostles; the corona, the
crown of thorns; the 5 anthers, 5 wounds;
the conjoined bases of the styles, the pillar
of the cross; the 3 stigmas (tips of the
styles), 3 nails.

The natural habitat is not known with
certainty; now a weed of fallow fields,
clearings, fencerows, roadside thickets,
and rights-of-way. Ranges from s PA to
e OK south to FL and TX.

MAY–AUG.

VERBENACEAE: VERBENA FAMILY
Brazilian Vervain
Verbena brasiliensis Vellozo

Perennial, stems solitary or several
together, 3–8′ (1–2.5 m) tall, sharply
4-angled, upwardly scabrous on angles.
Leaves are relatively few, opposite, nearly
sessile, elliptic, 1.6–4″ (4–10 cm) long and
0.4–1″ (1–2.5 cm) wide, tip acute, tapered
to base, margins toothed. Flowers grow
in spikes up to 1.6″ (4 cm) long from
branches at top of stem. Each flower
emerges from overlapping scales, the 4
petals 0.2″ (3–4 mm) long, short-tubular
with flaring lobes, pale violet to bluish
purple, pubescent.

This common alien commands attention with its height and flower color, especially when growing in a massed group.

Inhabits dry to moist soils of roadsides,
clearings, pastures, field margins, and
openings on floodplains. Ranges from VA
to MO south to FL and TX; CA–OR. It is
native to South America.

MID-MAY–EARLY OCT.

FABACEAE: PEA & BEAN FAMILY
Chinese Wisteria

Wisteria sinensis (Sims) DC.

High-climbing woody vine up to 100′ (30 m) long, the bark pale gray, young branches pubescent. Leaves are 6–16″ (15–40 cm) long, divided into 9–13 opposite leaflets. Each leaflet is lanceolate to elliptic, 2.4–3.2″ (6–8 cm) long, glabrate to pubescent, tip acuminate, base contracted to a short stalk. Flowers grow in dense clusters 6–12″ (15–30 cm) long, petals blue-violet to lavender, about 1″ (2.3–2.6 cm) long, the standard erect, fragrant. The pod is 4–6″ (10–15 cm) long and about 1.2″ (3 cm) wide, tan, with velvety, appressed hairs.

Chinese Wisteria has been widely planted in urban and suburban areas for its large, showy, and fragrant flower clusters. However, it is an aggressive and destructive weed—its weight and constricting stems can topple adult trees. Underground rootstocks are massive and hard to kill without the aid of chemicals.

Inhabits yards, roadsides, and empty lots, invading woodlands of all sorts. Ranges from s VT to MI and MO south to FL and TX.

APR.–MAY

PLANTAGINACEAE: PLANTAIN FAMILY
Common Toadflax

Nuttallanthus canadensis (L.) D. A. Sutton
[*Linaria canadensis* (L.) Dumont]

Biennial or winter annual, stem slender, glabrous, 8–28″ (20–70 cm) tall from a basal rosette of prostrate, leafy stemlets about 4″ (10 cm) long. Stem leaves are alternate, linear, more or less erect, 0.25–0.8″ (5–20 mm) long, occurring mostly below midstem. Flowers grow singly from very short stalks along the upper half of stem. Corollas are tubular and 2-lipped, upper lip pale blue or whitish, lower lip blue or lavender-blue with a white bump near base, with a curved spur descending from the base of the flower.

Although native, Common Toadflax is very weedy and has successfully colonized all sorts of human-modified land; it is especially numerous in fallow fields where it and Heartwing Sorrel (*Rumex hastatulus*) form bright patches of color in spring. Texas Toadflax (*N. texanus*) is expanding in our area from the Southwest; it has larger flowers (up to twice as large) that are much paler (pale lavender-blue all over).

Inhabits dry soil of fallow fields, roadsides, yards, suburban parks, and other disturbed soil situations. Ranges from N.S. to MN and SD south to FL and TX.

MID-MAR.–EARLY MAY

LAMIACEAE: MINT FAMILY
Lyre-leaved Sage
Salvia lyrata L.

Perennial from a basal rosette of leaves, the stem solitary or a few together, 4-angled, 1–2′ (30–70 cm) tall, unbranched or with 1–2 pairs of branches. Five to 15 basal leaves lie on the ground, each elliptic to obovate, 2–7.5″ (5–17 cm) long, pinnately lobed or dissected, margins with small teeth, bases abruptly narrowed to leafstalks 0.8–3.2″ (2–8 cm) long. The central portion of the upper leaf surface is often marked with purplish. Stem leaves, if present, are 0.8–3.2″ (2–8 cm) long, unlobed to shallowly pinnately lobed. Flowers grow in pairs along the upper stem and branches, pale to medium blue, about 0.6–1.2″ (1.5–3 cm) long, tubular with 2 flaring lobes, the lower lobe forming a lip.

Lyre-leaved Sage occurs mostly on moist roadsides, leaving us to wonder what its natural habitat is—possibly bottomland forests on river floodplains. Native Americans used the root as a salve and vegetative parts for coughs and as a laxative.

Inhabits moist roadsides and lawns; found less often on riverside terraces and streambanks. Ranges from sw CT to MO south to FL and e TX.

APR.–MAY

LAMIACEAE: MINT FAMILY
Common Blue-curls
Trichostema dichotomum L.

Annual or short-lived perennial, stems 6″–2′ (15–60 cm) tall, much-branched (opposite), obscurely 4-angled, pubescent, usually also with gland-tipped hairs. Leaves are opposite, elliptic to broadly lanceolate, 0.8–2.8″ (2–7 cm) long and 0.25–0.8″ (5–20 mm) wide, tip blunt, base tapered to a short stalk, margins entire or crenate. Flowers grow on short stalks from axils of the branch leaves. There are 5 petals, the upper 4 lanceolate and erect, 0.2″ (2–4 mm) long, the lower petal forming a lip 0.25–0.4″ (5–10 mm) long, pale bluish white with dark blue spots. The long stamens are blue, at first erect but then curved forward and downward.

Common Blue-curls has lots of charm; the flowers are small yet orchidlike and with beautiful architecture. After fruits have dropped, the sepals remain, looking like tiny, pointed sugar scoops. Slender Blue-curls (*T. setaceum*) is half as tall and has narrow leaves less than 0.25″ (5 mm) wide; it is scarce in loamy sand soils in longleaf pinelands.

Inhabits dry disturbed soil of roadsides, rights-of-way, fallow fields, and suburban yards; also found in openings in oak-hickory woodlands. Ranges from s ME to MI south to FL and MO.

AUG.–OCT.

RUBIACEAE: MADDER FAMILY
Bluets; Quaker Ladies; Innocence

Houstonia caerulea L.

Perennial, stem slender and delicate, 2–7″ (5–17 cm) tall, unbranched. Basal leaves ovate to obovate, 0.2–0.3″ (3–8 mm) long and up to 0.25″ (2–5 mm) wide, leafstalks about as long as blades. Stem leaves few, opposite, much reduced in size. Flowers grow singly at stem tips or also on 1–2 long stalks from stem leaf axils, petals 4, pale blue or whitish, throat yellow. The corolla tube is 0.2–0.3″ (4–7 mm) long, the 4 lobes spread horizontally, 0.25–0.3″ (5–8) mm long.

Bluets are familiar to almost everyone, since they often grace our backyards, schoolyards, roadsides, and cemeteries. To many they are a symbol of spring and of life's annual renewal. And although a delicate-looking plant, Bluets can withstand everything from mowing to flooding to fire.

Inhabits roadsides, lawns, clearings, and other disturbed soil sites, in our area originally on creekbanks and in oak-hickory woodlands. Ranges from N.S. to s Ont. south to sc GA, c AL, and n LA.

LATE MAR.–MAY

CAMPANULACEAE:
BELLFLOWER & LOBELIA FAMILY
Venus's Looking-glass

Triodanis perfoliata (L.) Nieuwland

Winter annual (basal leaves develop in fall and overwinter), the stems erect, up to 2′ (60 cm) tall, occasionally taller, often branched from the base but not from the upper part of the stem. Lower to midstem leaves are ovate, 0.4–1.2″ (1–3 cm) long, sessile and clasping stem, margins crenate. Basal leaves are larger and with a short stalk, forming a rosette. Flowers are single (occasionally more) in axils of mid- to upper stem leaves, sessile. The 5 petals are blue to reddish violet, short-tubular with 5 flaring, pointed lobes, the whole flower 0.4–0.6″ (1–1.5 cm) across.

Venus's Looking-glass is named for its resemblance to a closely related European plant whose seeds appear to have a polished, mirrorlike coating. A second species (*T. biflora*) differs in having non- or barely clasping leaves, and its flowers grow only in the uppermost portion of the stem.

Inhabits roadsides, suburban lawns and gardens, fallow fields, and other disturbed situations. Ranges from ME to B.C. south to FL and TX; Mex.; West Indies.

APR.–JUNE

VIOLACEAE: VIOLET FAMILY
Wild Pansy
Viola bicolor Pursh
[*Viola rafinesquii* Greene]

Winter annual (basal leaves are produced in the fall and overwinter), stems slender, up to 1′ (30 cm) tall but often half that, glabrous, few- to many-branched. Leaves are mostly 0.4–1.2″ (1–3 cm) long, the blade broadly elliptical, margins irregularly toothed, leafstalk longer than blade. A deeply cut stipule (leaflike structure) clasps the stem at the base of the leaf. Flowers grow on slender stalks from leaf axils, the 5 petals white to pale blue, the 3 lower petals with dark blue lines. The lowest petal is largest and forms a lip and also a blunt spur that points backward.

Wild Pansy is a native plant, but it does best in open mowed roadsides, where it is among our earliest species to bloom, along with Early Bluet (*Houstonia pusilla*) and Shepherd's Cress (*Teesdalia nudicaulis*). Its natural habitat is not known with certainty.

Inhabits dry soil of open roadsides, lawns, suburban lots, fallow fields, and pastures. Ranges from MA to CO south to FL and AZ.

EARLY MAR.–APR.

CAMPANULACEAE:
BELLFLOWER & LOBELIA FAMILY
Asian Rockbell
Wahlenbergia marginata (Thunberg) DC.

Slender, glabrate perennial, stems solitary or several together, mostly 5–23″ (12–60 cm) tall, with ascending to erect branches. Leaves grow mostly on lower half of stem, linear to lanceolate, 0.4–1.6″ (1–4 cm) long, tip acute, margins entire to toothed. Flowers grow terminally on naked stalks 0.4–2″ (1–5 cm) long, the 5 petals pale blue, 0.2–0.3″ (5–8 mm) long, forming a tube and somewhat spreading, acute lobes.

This recent introduction (earliest specimen 1937 in FL) has rapidly colonized the southeastern United States, especially in poor sandy soils. It is native to southeastern Asia, Australia, and New Zealand. The genus commemorates Goran Wahlenberg (1780–1851), Swedish doctor of medicine and botany.

Inhabits dry sandy roadsides, fallow fields, rights-of-way, and gravel pits. Ranges on the Coastal Plain and lower Piedmont from se NC to s FL, e TX, and s AR.

LATE MAR.–OCT.

ASTERACEAE: ASTER FAMILY
Spanish Needles
Bidens bipinnata L.

Annual with a taproot, stem to 5′ (1.5 m) tall, glabrate, widely branched. Leaves are 2 to 3 times pinnate, dissected into lance-shaped or ovate segments 0.2–1.6″ (0.5–4 cm) long. Flower heads grow at ends of stem and branches on short to long stalks, the outer bracts green and slender. Ray flowers are absent or, when present, numbering 3–5, yellow, to 0.4″ (10 mm) long. The disc is 0.2–0.4″ (4–10 mm) wide, composed of 10–20 (or more) flowers, yellowish. The slender seeds are 0.3–0.5″ (7–12 mm) long, flattish to 4-sided, tipped with 3–4 barbed awns.

Spanish Needles should be familiar to most people as one of those plants whose pesky seeds cling to clothing and animal fur. Thanks to minutely barbed awns, the seeds hold on tenaciously—a very ingenious adaptation when you think about how plants solve the problem of dispersing their seeds.

Inhabits all sorts of disturbed places: roadsides, fallow fields, pastures, orchards, and gardens. Ranges from MA to Ont. south to FL and Mex.

LATE JULY–OCT.

POACEAE: GRASS FAMILY
Weeping Lovegrass
Eragrostis curvula (Schrader) Nees

Perennial grass, forming large tussocks. Fresh leaves and stems are bright green but age to dull straw color. Leaves grow upward initially then spread outward and down to ground, up to 3′ (1 m) long and less than 0.2″ (1.5–3 mm) wide, tips extremely long-tapering, margins somewhat rough. Flowering stems several, up to 3′ (1 m) tall, with open panicles in upper third, branches spreading 2–4″ (5–10 cm), flowers dark gray-green.

Weeping Lovegrass was imported from southern Africa as a soil stabilizer, especially for soft sands such as those we have in the Sandhills. It does its job well but aggressively spreads to other disturbed areas. When sterile it closely resembles Wiregrass (*Aristida stricta*), especially from late summer to winter, when its leaves become inrolled; but basal portions are flat or flattish (vs. always rounded), and leaf tips are much longer-tapered.

Inhabits roadsides, trails, construction sites, railroad banks, rights-of-way, and sand and gravel pits. Ranges through much of the southern half of the United States.

MAY–JUNE

POACEAE: GRASS FAMILY
Purple Lovegrass
Eragrostis spectabilis (Pursh) Steudel

Perennial, forming domelike tufts. Leaves spreading, up to 16″ (0.4 m) long and up to 0.3″ (2–8 mm) wide, pilose on both surfaces and on sheaths, margins somewhat rough. Flowering stems many, widely spreading to form very open inflorescences, bright red to purple, ½–¾ height of whole plant. Flowers tiny, bright purple-red.

Purple Lovegrass is a delightful plant that brightens old fields and roadsides in the fall. Here the color purple refers to the artist's purple, which is decidedly red-toned and not violet, as we have mistakenly used the word.

Inhabits old fields, abandoned sandy pastures, roadsides, railroad banks, rights-of-way, and openings in pinelands. Ranges from ME to ND south to FL and TX.

AUG.–OCT.

POACEAE: GRASS FAMILY
Redtop; Purpletop
Tridens flavus (L.) A. S. Hitchcock

Perennial grass from a short rhizome, stems 2.5–5′ (0.8–1.5 m) tall, glabrous. Leaves grow at the base and lower half of stem, linear, up to 2′ (60 cm) long and mostly 0.2–0.5″ (4–12 mm) wide; the underside is pubescent, margins roughish. Flowers grow toward tips of horizontal or arching branches, forming an open or "airy" inflorescence up to 16″ (35 cm) long and pyramid-shaped. The spikelets are dull reddish or purple, 5–8 flowered, 0.25–0.3″ (6–8 mm) long.

Redtop is a common roadside plant in our three states, sometimes coloring roadbanks purple but avoiding very dry sandy soils.

Inhabits roadsides, rights-of-way, fallow fields, and other disturbed soil situations; also found in open oak-hickory-pine woodlands. Ranges from NH to s WI and e NE south to FL and TX; ne Mex.

LATE JULY–OCT.

CYPERACEAE: SEDGE FAMILY
Nodding Beaksedge
Rhynchospora inexpansa (Michaux) Vahl

Glabrous perennial with grasslike leaves, the stems several from a leafy base, 16″–3′ (0.4–1 m) tall, ascending and arching. Leaves are mostly basal, but several occur up stem, up to 1′ (30 cm) long and to 0.2″ (4 mm) wide, long-acuminate. Flowers grow from slender stalks in arching or drooping clusters from upper leaf axils and at stem tip; each flower is covered by overlapping brown scales 0.2″ (4–5 mm) long, sepals and petals absent. The fruit is a hard nutlet (called an achene in this family) 2–2.5 mm long and 1 mm wide, flattened, the surfaces with many transverse ridges, capped by a triangular beak about 1 mm long, with 6 barbed bristles attached to the base.

Rhynchospora is the largest genus of plants in the southeastern United States (66 species) and a critical component of the longleaf pine ecosystem. The genus is too technical to go into in this guide, but I offer one species that is easy to recognize and that is often found in disturbed places.

Inhabits moist pine savannas, flatwoods, roadsides, logging roads, woodland openings, and rights-of-way. Ranges on the Coastal Plain from s DE to n FL, e TX, and s AR; nw GA; ne AL.

JULY–SEPT.

Places to Visit

North Carolina

IN THE SANDHILLS

Calloway Preserve NC 211 in Hoke County. Owned by The Nature Conservancy, Southern Pines. (910) 246-0300. Features excellent longleaf pine and streamhead communities. Fire management is also restoring former pine plantations to natural longleaf.

Carver's Creek State Park Johnson Farm Rd., Fayetteville, Cumberland County. N.C. Department of Environment and Natural Resources. High-quality longleaf pine uplands, streamheads, a cypress-gum swamp, beaver ponds, and a millpond dotted with cypress are features of this new park. Sandhills Pyxie-moss occurs here.

Eastwood Preserve North of Pinehurst. Administered by N.C. Plant Conservation Program in Raleigh. (919) 733-6930. This is an assemblage of conservation parcels, one with public access, the rest private. Features high-quality longleaf pine uplands and boggy streamheads. Public access is only via Beulah Hill Church Rd. at NC 73.

Fort Bragg Military Reservation U.S. Army. Stretching between Southern Pines and Fayetteville, this is the largest remaining block of Longleaf Pine in the Sandhills region. It is a de facto preserve for the federally endangered Red-cockaded Woodpeckers and dozens of other rare animals and plants. You may drive across parts of it on paved roads but NOT ON DIRT ROADS. A system of walking trails is being developed along the base's perimeter, which traverses several different longleaf pine and wetland habitats. Specific questions may be addressed to the Endangered Species Branch, (910) 396-2544.

Pinehurst Greenway Trails 395 Magnolia Rd., Pinehurst, Moore County. Administered by the town of Pinehurst. (910) 295-2817. Five miles of easy trails wind through longleaf pine country, but fire suppression has limited the numbers of native wildflowers.

Sandhills Game Land Off US 1 in Richmond, Scotland, and Moore Counties. N.C. Wildlife Resources Commission, Hoffman. (910) 281-3917. Sandhills Game Land is the second-largest remaining block of longleaf pine in the Sandhills region (65,000 acres) and features a wide variety of excellent fire-managed pine communities, streamheads, seepages, beaver ponds, impoundments, and blackwater river floodplain forests. Open to the public via an extensive network of sand roads.

Sandhills Horticultural Gardens Sandhills Community College, 3395 Airport Rd., Pinehurst, Moore County. (910) 695-3882. Primarily a horticulture and sculpture garden, the Gardens also maintains a nature trail and boardwalk through longleaf pine woodland and a streamhead.

Southern Pines Greenway Trails Town of Southern Pines, 482 East Connecticut Ave., Southern Pines, Moore County. (910) 692-2463. More than twelve miles of trails in several properties meander through longleaf pine, pine-oak-hickory, and streamhead habitats and around two impoundments. Controlled burns are conducted in a few areas. Resinous Boneset (*Eupatorium resinosum*) can be seen along Reservoir Park Trail.

Weymouth Woods State Nature Preserve 1024 Fort Bragg Rd., Southern Pines, Moore County. (910) 692-2167. weymouth.woods@ncmail. net. Owned by N.C. Department of Environment and Natural Resources. Excellent longleaf pine and streamhead communities are managed by prescribed fire specifically to promote Sandhills plants and animals. Includes an area of old-growth pines (460 years!) and a ridge with Sandhills Pyxie-moss.

OTHER NEARBY PLACES

Cape Fear Botanical Gardens 536 North Eastern Blvd., Fayetteville, Cumberland County. (910) 486-0221. This area features horticultural plantings, theme gardens, and a visitors/education center. Nature trails lead to rich hardwood forests along the Cape Fear River with spring flora characteristic of the lower Piedmont.

Clark Park Nature Center 631 Sherman Dr., Fayetteville, Cumberland County. (910) 433-1579. Operated by the city's Parks Department. This is one of Fayetteville's natural highlights due to its impressive displays of spring wildflowers in rich hardwoods along the Cape Fear River, characteristic of the lower Piedmont.

Jones Lake State Park/Bladen Lakes State Forest NC 242 North, Elizabethtown, Bladen County. (910) 588-4550. Large Carolina bay pocosins, bay lakes, and pine flatwoods dominate this area southeast of the Sandhills.

Lumber River State Park Princess Ann Rd., Orrum, Robeson County. (910) 628-4564. lumber.river@ncmail.net. Noted for its excellent canoeing, the Lumber River supports broad cypress-gum swamps, hardwood slopes, and small areas of longleaf pine habitat.

North Carolina Botanical Garden Off US 15-501, University of North Carolina, Chapel Hill, Orange County. (919) 962-0522. ncbg@unc.edu. The NCBG features native plantings representing natural regions of the state, including the Sandhills. It also has natural woodlands, horticultural plantings, an education/visitors center, and rare species propagation.

Pee Dee National Wildlife Refuge U.S. Fish and Wildlife Service, US 52 North, Wadesboro, Anson County. (704) 694-4424. PDNWR lies in the lower Piedmont and features excellent floodplain forests along Brown Creek and beaver marshes that occupy old river channels. A rare Piedmont longleaf pine forest harbors Coastal Plain species.

Uwharrie National Forest U.S. Forest Service, NC 24/27 East, Troy, Montgomery County. (910) 576-6391. In the ancient Uwharrie Mountains in the lower Piedmont, Uwharrie National Forest has varied hardwood and hardwood-pine forests. There are small areas of Piedmont longleaf pine forest and streamhead seepages, both with Coastal Plain plants.

South Carolina

IN THE SANDHILLS

Carolina Sandhills National Wildlife Refuge US 1 north of McBee, Chesterfield County. U.S. Fish and Wildlife Service. (843) 335-8401. Many longleaf pine communities occur here, running the gamut from turkey oak scrub to wet streamheads and beaver ponds. Fire management provides conditions favorable to rare plants and Red-cockaded Woodpeckers.

Cheraw State Park US 1 north of Patrick, Chesterfield County. S.C. Department of Parks, Recreation, and Tourism. Contains limited longleaf pine uplands, grading down to oak-hickory forest and maple-gum swamp forest. Hudsonia Flat features dry to moist pine flatwoods dominated by many species of shrubs, including Sand Myrtle and Dwarf Witch-alder. This site has the only occurrence of Golden Heather (*Hudsonia ericoides*) in the southeastern United States.

Fort Jackson Military Reservation U.S. Army. SC 12, east side of Columbia, Richland County. Limited access; restrictions apply. Features longleaf pine uplands, streamheads, and seepage slopes.

Goodale State Park Off US 1 northeast of Camden, Kershaw County. SC Department of Parks, Recreation, and Tourism. Park phone (803) 432-2772. Features hiking trails, an impoundment with cypress trees, and a canoe trail.

Peachtree Rock Nature Preserve Off SC 6 south of Edmund, Lexington County. The Nature Conservancy. (803) 254-9049. This site features remarkable sandstone outcrops, various longleaf pine communities, and populations of Rosemary and Sandhill Wild-buckwheat.

Sand Hills State Forest US 1, Patrick, Chesterfield County. Adjacent to Carolina Sandhills National Wildlife Refuge, it provides a similarly large area of fire-managed longleaf and mixed pine-oak communities. Sugarloaf Mountain is a 160-foot hill capped with ironstone and with an interesting mix of Mountain Laurel, Creeping Blueberry, and Sandhills Pyxie-moss.

OTHER NEARBY PLACES

Congaree National Park Off SC 48 south of Hopkins, Richland County. National Park Service. (803) 776-4396. Contains the largest expanse of old-growth floodplain forest in the United States, with many national and state champion trees. Features an excellent 2.4-mile boardwalk.

Little Pee Dee State Park Along SR 22, off SC 57, southeast of Dillon, Dillon County. S.C. Department of Parks, Recreation, and Tourism. Interesting ridge-and-swale topography supports dry sandhills, pine-hardwood forests, marshes, and swamp forests.

Longleaf Pine Heritage Preserve Off SR 101, southwest of Lynchburg, Lee County. This site features moist longleaf pine flatwoods and savannas. Rare species include Chaffseed and Red-cockaded Woodpecker.

Savage Bay Heritage Preserve US 1 to SR 385, northeast of Camden, Kershaw County. Large Carolina bay with Pond Cypress, Red Bay, Ti-ti, and Honeycups; dry sand rim with longleaf pine–turkey oak scrub.

Sumter National Forest US 221 and SC 28 and 23 west of Edgefield, Edgefield and McCormick Counties. U.S. Forest Service. Long Cane Ranger District. (803) 637-5396. Features various forest communities typical of the lower piedmont.

Georgia

IN THE SANDHILLS

Baldwin State Forest US 441 south of Milledgeville, Baldwin County. Georgia Forestry Commission. Includes Bartram Educational Forest. Primarily devoted to timber management and a seed orchard, it also has a longleaf pine–mixed oak community on relic sand dunes, plus several streamheads.

Black Creek Natural Area Taylor County. Features streamheads with Atlantic White Cedar (*Chamaecyparis thyoides*).

Fall Line Sandhills Natural Area North of GA 96, west of Butler, Taylor County. Georgia Department of Natural Resources. Harbors a nice array of Sandhills region animals and plants, a number of them rare. The habitats include excellent depression ponds and former pine plantations; the latter are being restored to original longleaf pine.

Fort Benning Military Reservation U.S. Army. Southeast of Columbus in Chattahoochee and Muscogee Counties. Limited access; restrictions apply. Features extensive longleaf pine, oak-hickory, and streamhead communities. For specific questions, contact the Conservation Branch at (706) 544-6206 or 544-7319.

Fort Gordon Military Reservation U.S. Army. Southwest of Augusta in Richmond, McDuffie, Columbia, and Jefferson Counties. Limited access; restrictions apply. Features excellent longleaf pine communities, turkey oak barrens, and streamheads with Atlantic White Cedar.

OTHER NEARBY PLACES

Beaverdam Wildlife Management Area North of Dublin on Old Toomsboro Rd. Georgia Department of Natural Resources. Features extensive mature bottomland hardwoods, cypress-gum forests, and small oxbow lake, all in the Oconee River floodplain, with a mix of Piedmont and Coastal Plain plants.

Bibliography

Barry, J. M. 1980. *Natural Vegetation of South Carolina*. Columbia: University of South Carolina Press.

Brown, L. 1979. *Grasses: An Identification Guide*. Boston: Houghton Mifflin.

Chafin, L. G. 2007. *Field Guide to the Rare Plants of Georgia*. Athens: State Botanical Garden of Georgia.

Christensen, N. L. 2000. "Vegetation of the Southeastern Coastal Plain." In *North American Terrestrial Vegetation*, 2nd ed., edited by M. G. Barbour and W. D. Billings, 397–448. Cambridge: Cambridge University Press.

Coffey, T. 1993. *The History and Folklore of American Wildflowers*. Boston: Houghton Mifflin.

Duncan, W. H., and M. B. Duncan. 1987. *The Smithsonian Guide to Seaside Plants of the Gulf and Atlantic Coasts*. Washington, D.C.: Smithsonian Institute Press.

Earley, Lawrence S. 2004. *Looking for Longleaf: The Fall and Rise of an American Forest*. Chapel Hill: University of North Carolina Press.

Flora of North America Editorial Committee. 1993– . *Flora of North America North of Mexico*. New York: Oxford University Press. As of 2010, sixteen of the projected thirty volumes have been published. This is a technical work with drawings of at least one species in all genera; 22,000 species will be covered.

Foote, L. E., and S. B. Jones Jr. 1989. *Native Shrubs and Woody Vines of the Southeast*. Portland, Ore.: Timber Press.

Foster, S., and J. A. Duke. 1990. *A Field Guide to Medicinal Plants: Eastern and Central North America*. Boston: Houghton Mifflin.

Frost, C. 1998. "Presettlement Fire Frequency Regimes of the United States: A First Approximation." *Proceedings of the Tall Timbers Fire Ecology Conference* 20:70–81. Tallahassee, Florida.

Georgia Plant Atlas. www.plantbio.uga.edu/herbarium/Georgia Atlas/. Update of Jones and Coile 1988.

Godfrey, R. K. 1988. *Trees, Shrubs, and Woody Vines of Northern Florida and Adjacent Georgia and Alabama*. Athens: University of Georgia Press.

Godfrey, R. K., and J. W. Wooten. 1979–81. *Aquatic and Wetland Plants of Southeastern United States*. 2 vols. Athens: University of Georgia Press.

Harrington, H. D. 1977. *How to Identify Grasses and Grasslike Plants*. Chicago: Swallow Press.

Harris, J. G., and M. W. Harris. 2000. *Plant Identification Terminology: An Illustrated Glossary*. 2nd ed. Spring Lake, Utah: Spring Lake Publishing.

Jones, S. B., Jr., and N. C. Coile. 1988. *The Distribution of the Vascular Flora of Georgia*. Athens: Department of Botany, University of Georgia.

Justice, W. S., C. R. Bell, and A. H. Lindsey. 2005. *Wild Flowers of North Carolina*. 2nd ed. Chapel Hill: University of North Carolina Press, Chapel Hill.

Kirkman, L. K., C. L. Brown, and D. J. Leopold. 2007. *Native Trees of the Southeast*. Portland, Ore.: Timber Press.

Kricher, J. C., and G. Morrison. 1988. *A Field Guide to Eastern Forests of North America*. Boston: Houghton Mifflin.

Lance, R. 2004. *Woody Plants of the Southeastern United States: A Winter Guide*. Athens: University of Georgia Press.

Nelson, G. 2005. *East Gulf Coastal Plain Wildflowers*. Guilford, Conn.: Falcon Press.

———. 2006. *Atlantic Coastal Plain Wildflowers*. Guilford, Conn.: Falcon Press.

Peterson, L. A. 1977. *A Field Guide to Edible Wild Plants of Eastern and Central North America*. Boston: Houghton Mifflin.

Platt, W. J. 1999. "Southeastern Pine Savannas." In *Savannas, Barrens, and Rock Outcrop Plant Communities of North America*, edited by R. C. Anderson, J. S. Fralish, and J. M. Baskin, 23–51. Cambridge: Cambridge University Press.

Porcher, R. D., and D. A. Rayner. 2001. *A Guide to the Wildflowers of South Carolina*. Columbia: University of South Carolina Press.

Radford, A. E., H. E. Ahles, and C. R. Bell. 1968. *Manual of the Vascular Flora of the Carolinas*. Chapel Hill: University of North Carolina Press.

Smith, R. M. 1998. *Wildflowers of the Southern Mountains*. Knoxville: University of Tennessee Press.

Snyder, L. H., Jr., and J. G. Bruce. 1986. *Field Guide to the Ferns and Other Pteridophytes of Georgia*. Athens: University of Georgia Press.

Sorrie, B. A., and A. S. Weakley. 2001. "Coastal Plain Vascular Plant Endemics: Phytogeographic Patterns." *Castanea* 66:50–82.

Southeastern U.S. Flora Atlas. In progress; available at University of North Carolina at Chapel Hill herbarium website: www.herbarium.unc.edu/.

Walker, H. J., and J. M. Coleman. 1987. "Atlantic and Gulf Coastal Province." In *Geomorphic Systems of North America*, Centennial Special, vol. 2., edited by W. L. Graf, 51–110. Boulder, Colo.: Geological Society of America.

Weakley, A. S. 2010. "Flora of the Southern and Mid-Atlantic States." Working draft. Consists of keys, synonyms, and brief synopses of all vascular species. Available at University of North Carolina at Chapel Hill herbarium website: www.herbarium.unc.edu/.

Weber, N. S., and A. H. Smith. 1985. *A Field Guide to Southern Mushrooms*. Ann Arbor: University of Michigan Press.

Wharton, C. H. 1978. *The Natural Environments of Georgia*. Bulletin 114, Department of Natural Resources, Georgia Geologic Survey, Atlanta.

Photo Credits

All photos are by the author except as noted below.

Brady Beck *Chimaphila maculata, Clitoria mariana, Drosera capillaris* (flower), *Habenaria repens, Hexastylis* new species, *Hypericum gentianoides, Lespedeza capitata, Lilium catesbaei, Oenothera fruticosa, Packera glabella, Persicaria sagittata, Polypremum procumbens, Rhexia virginica, Rhododendron viscosum, Stylodon carneus, Vernonia angustifolia, Wisteria sinensis.*

Breath O'Spring, Inc. (Jim Drake) *Isotria verticillata.*

Richard LeBlond *Calpogon tuberosus, Morella pumila* (flower), *Pinguicula caerulea* (flower).

Gil Nelson *Burmannia capitata, Clematis crispa, Croomia pauciflora, Crotalaria purshii, Hylodesmum nudiflorum, Liatris tenuifolia, Lobelia glandulosa, Malaxis unifolia, Pluchea foetida, Solidago fistulosa.*

North Carolina Botanical Garden—Justice Collection *Lobelia puberula, Viburnum prunifolium.*

Hugh and Carol Nourse *Berlandiera pumila, Clinopodium georgianum, Crataegus uniflora, Crotalaria spectabilis, Elliottia racemosa, Euonymus americanus, Goodyera pubescens* (flower), *Houstonia purpurea, Iris virginica, Listera australis, Medeola virginiana, Mitchella repens, Murdannia keisak, Nolina georgiana* (flower), *Polygonatum biflorum, Rosa carolina, Salvia lyrata, Sericocarpus tortifolius* (side view), *Sida rhombifolia, Silene catesbaei, Thaspium trifoliatum, Trichostema dichotomum, Uvularia puberula.*

Jeffrey Pippen *Aureolaria virginica, Cirsium virginianum, Elephantopus carolinianus* (flower), *Phoradendron serotinum.*

Richard Porcher *Aletris aurea, Baccharis halimifolia, Baptisia perfoliata, Chamaecrista fasciculata, Cicuta maculata, Gentiana catesbaei, Hibiscus moscheutos, Hydrolea quadrivalvis, Ilex decidua, Lithospermum caroliniense, Lysimachia quadrifolia, Mimulus alatus, Peltandra virginica, Portulaca pilosa, Sabatia brachiata, Smilax glauca, Uvularia sessilifolia.*

Index

When more than one page number is given, the number in **bold** indicates the primary entry for a species.

About the Author

Wayne Irvin

Bruce Sorrie started his career as a photographer in the U.S. Navy and then held various positions as an ornithologist before it became clear that his deepening interest in plants was pointing toward a career in botany. Now 30 years into his botany career, Bruce is recognized as one of the foremost authorities on the flora of the Coastal Plain, which extends from Massachusetts to Texas. He works as an inventory biologist with the North Carolina Natural Heritage Program, where he performs county-by-county surveys of natural areas, habitats, and rare species in the Sandhills region and lower Piedmont. Bruce is author of over 50 published papers, a regional reviewer for the Flora of North America series, a research associate at the University of North Carolina herbarium, and a photographer. Birding remains his most enthusiastic hobby, which he pursues throughout the Americas, with Brazil and Jamaica being his most recent trips. Bruce lives in Whispering Pines, N.C.